ANIMALS AND THE LIMITS
OF POSTMODERNISM

D1615840

CRITICAL PERSPECTIVES ON ANIMALS: THEORY, CULTURE, SCIENCE, AND LAW

CRITICAL PERSPECTIVES ON ANIMALS: THEORY, CULTURE, SCIENCE, AND LAW
SERIES EDITORS: GARY L. FRANCIONE AND GARY STEINER

The emerging interdisciplinary field of animal studies seeks to shed light on the nature of animal experience and the moral status of animals in ways that overcome the limitations of traditional approaches to animals. Recent work on animals has been characterized by an increasing recognition of the importance of crossing disciplinary boundaries and exploring the affinities as well as the differences among the approaches of fields such as philosophy, law, sociology, political theory, ethology, and literary studies to questions pertaining to animals. This recognition has brought with it an openness to a rethinking of the very terms of critical inquiry and of traditional assumptions about human being and its relationship to the animal world. The books published in this series seek to contribute to contemporary reflections on the basic terms and methods of critical inquiry, to do so by focusing on fundamental questions arising out of the relationships and confrontations between humans and nonhuman animals, and ultimately to enrich our appreciation of the nature and ethical significance of nonhuman animals by providing a forum for the interdisciplinary exploration of questions and problems that have traditionally been confined within narrowly circumscribed disciplinary boundaries.

The Animal Rights Debate: Abolition or Regulation? Gary L. Francione and Robert Garner

Animal Rights Without Liberation: Applied Ethics and Human Obligations, Alasdair Cochrane

Animalia Americana: Animal Representations and Biopolitical Subjectivity, Colleen Glenney Boggs

Experiencing Animal Minds: An Anthology of Animal-Human Encounters,
edited by Julie A. Smith and Robert W. Mitchell

Being Animal: Beasts and Boundaries in Nature Ethics, Anna L. Peterson

ANIMALS AND THE LIMITS
OF POSTMODERNISM

Gary Steiner

COLUMBIA UNIVERSITY PRESS   NEW YORK

COLUMBIA UNIVERSITY PRESS

Publishers Since 1893

NEW YORK   CHICHESTER, WEST SUSSEX

cup.columbia.edu

Copyright © 2013 Gary Steiner

Library of Congress Cataloging-in-Publication Data

Steiner, Gary, 1956–
  Animals and the limits of postmodernism / Gary Steiner.
    p. cm.—(Critical perspectives on animals)
    Includes bibliographical references (p.   ) and index.
    ISBN 978-0-231-15342-3 (cloth : alk. paper)—ISBN 978-0-231-15343-0 (pbk. : alk. papter)—
    ISBN 987-0-231-52729-3 (e-book)
    I. Animals (Philosophy)   2. Animal rights.   3. Animal wefare—Moral ethical aspects
4. Postmodernism.   I. title
  BI05.A55S74 2013
  179´.3—dc23

                                                                          2012029892

Columbia University Press books are printed on permanent and durable acid-free paper.
This book is printed on paper with recycled content.
Printed in the United States of America

c 10 9 8 7 6 5 4 3 2 1
p 10 9 8 7 6 5 4 3 2 1

COVER ILLUSTRATION: Michael Sowa, *Tigerhase*

References to Internet Web sites (URLs) were accurate at the time of writing.
Neither the author nor Columbia University Press is responsible for URLs
that may have expired or changed since the manuscript was prepared.

In loving memory of my father
James Steinberg Steiner (1925–2012)
He lived his life deliberately

CONTENTS

CHAPTER 6
Cosmopolitanism and Veganism
195

ACKNOWLEDGMENTS

A couple of years ago, Gary Francione and I were having a talk about the state of contemporary animal studies, particularly in literature and philosophy departments in North America. We were both well aware of the increasing interest of postmodern thinkers in questions bearing upon the moral status of animals, and we were both convinced that the prevailing postmodern approaches are a dead end, if a well-intentioned one. I wondered aloud why someone didn't write a book that analyzed the fundamental limitations of postmodernism in ethics generally and regarding the moral status of animals in particular. Gary's response was that I ought to write such a book. And so this book was born. I am profoundly indebted to Gary Francione, not only for his encouragement on this project but also for his friendship and his ongoing engagement with my work.

While working on the book I received unexpected inspiration from Philippe Dubois, who has generously permitted me to audit his French courses at Bucknell University. Twice while working on the book I audited Philippe's seminar on the French tradition of gastronomic thought. At first it did not occur to me how relevant the writings of thinkers such as Rabelais, Montaigne, Brillat-Savarin, Grimod, and Barthes would be to my endeavor to develop a vegan imperative. But Philippe's extraordinary pedagogy, as well has his very serious personal engagement with questions bearing on the ethics of diet, provided an important stimulus to my thinking, particularly when I was working on the final chapter.

As with my work on previous books, I benefited greatly from a number of detailed discussions with Marc Lucht about the book's central themes. I thank him for taking the time to read a good deal of the manuscript, for directing me to texts that proved to be of vital importance for the development of my arguments, and for helping me to bring to concrete expression some very complex ideas bearing upon the nature and limits of postmodern thought.

I had the opportunity to develop and experiment with my ideas for this book in a variety of far-flung venues, including Virginia Tech, Hamilton College, Yale, the University of Edinburgh, Macquarie University in Sydney, the University of Heidelberg, and the University of Vienna. Erwin Lengauer has been a most gracious host on several occasions at the University of Vienna and has introduced me to a number of interesting people who are deeply committed to the cause of animal rights. On one of these occasions I also gave a talk at the University of Heidelberg, and Erwin went to the trouble to chauffeur my spouse and me on an enjoyable two-day drive from the one venue to the other that took us through Tübingen, Munich, and Salzburg. Matt Chrulew and Deborah Bird Rose hosted a terrific workshop on continental philosophy and ethology in Sydney at which I made the acquaintance of a number of extremely sharp and interesting people doing work on animal minds and animal ethics, including Jeffrey Bussolini, Dominique Lestel, Hollis Taylor, and Brett Buchanan.

While working on this book I have benefited from conversations and collaborative work with many other people as well. The following merit special mention: Esther Bauer, Rob Boddice, Anna Charlton, Antonio Di Fenza, Nathalie Dupont, Joe Fell, Alex Lyras, Saundra Morris, Steve Newmyer, and Harold Schweizer. I am indebted to the Interlibrary Loan department at Bucknell University and particularly to Dan Heuer, who was unrelenting in tracking down a large number of often obscure texts for me. Dan's commitment to providing me with support mirrors the enthusiastic support that I have received from the Bucknell administration, which has generously funded my research and travel and has provided me with much-appreciated additional support under the auspices of the Harris Chair. I would also like to extend my sincere appreciation to Wendy Lochner at Columbia University Press, who has been an energetic advocate of my work and of this book in particular. Wendy is also a most enthusiastic sponsor of the Critical Perspectives on Animals series at Columbia that I coedit with Gary Francione. It is to a great extent to Wendy's credit that Columbia has published such a rich array of texts on animals in recent years. I also extend sincere thanks to Anne McCoy and Anita O'Brien for their efforts to ensure that my vision for this book would be realized.

Chapter 5 of this book is adapted from "Toward a Non-Anthropocentric Cosmopolitanism," originally published in *Anthropocentrism: Humans, Animals, Environments*, ed. Rob Boddice, Brill Publishers, 2011. I thank Brill for their kind permission to use this material.

My most heartfelt word of thanks goes to Paula Davis, the love of my life, who has provided me with unremitting understanding and support, and who manages to bear me and my weirdness as if I were, as she sometimes says, "light as a feather."

ANIMALS AND THE LIMITS
OF POSTMODERNISM

INTRODUCTION

> When someone says that by extending justice as far as animals we destroy
> justice, he does not realise that he himself is not preserving justice, but in-
> creasing pleasure, which is the enemy of justice.
>
> —Porphyry, *On Abstinence from Killing Animals*

In recent years there has been a great profusion of scholarly writing about
the mental capacities and the moral status of nonhuman animals. While
much of this writing has come from ethologists, historians, and philosophers writing under the influence of traditional humanistic thought, an
increasingly large proportion of it has come from postmodern thinkers
who see in humanism a fundamental obstacle to the prospect of doing
justice to the experiential capacities and the moral worth of animals.[1] A
key prejudice of traditional humanistic thought is that there is an essential divide between human beings and nonhuman animals: only human
beings possess reason or language; hence only human beings can perform
a variety of cognitive functions traditionally considered to be essential
for possessing full moral status. These functions include the ability to
form intentions, contemplate the consequences of different possible
courses of action, establish abstract principles, and articulate and respect
rights and responsibilities. The Western philosophical tradition has assumed that because animals lack these capacities, they either possess no
inherent moral worth or possess moral worth fundamentally inferior to
that of human beings. A number of postmodern thinkers challenge the
human exceptionalism that lies at the core of humanism, thereby opening up the prospect of acknowledging that animals are cognitively and
experientially much more like human beings than the tradition had been
willing to admit.

This acknowledgment would appear to hold the promise of according
to animals a more adequate sense of their inherent moral worth, and of

motivating humanity to take considerably more seriously our moral obligations toward our animal kin. And yet this is precisely what one does *not* find in postmodern writings on animals. Instead one encounters a panoply of vague gestures toward some indeterminate sense of continuity between human and animal life, and a general sense that we ought to have more compassion for animals. An examination of the terms of postmodernism makes it clear why its proponents never get to the point of making definitive claims about the moral status of animals: fundamental to postmodernism is the endeavor to challenge the pretensions of traditional philosophy to objective truth and determinate principles. From an epistemological standpoint, this endeavor is born of the belief that all experience is essentially obscure and indeterminate, and that any characterization of experience in perspicuous terms is an idealized distortion of the irreducible complexity of experiential phenomena. From a political standpoint, the endeavor is born of a conviction that abstract principles are simply tools for the suppression of difference; the appeal to abstract principles, we are told, simply reproduces established regimes of dominance and submission. Principles thus become reduced to nothing more than weapons in polemical struggles in which those in power seek to preserve their position of dominance and thwart the endeavor of the powerless to attain recognition and empowerment.

The notion of principles is part of a larger ensemble of notions such as selfhood, agency, right, norms, responsibility, and rational argumentation, notions that are absolutely essential to the humanism that is a prime target of much contemporary postmodern thought. In seeking to dismantle humanism, postmodernism poses a radical challenge to all these notions. Thus one may recognize that animals have rich subjective lives that are in fundamental respects very much like the lives of human beings; but one, we are urged, should not attempt to advance any definitive principles on the basis of this recognition. On the last page of my previous book, *Animals and the Moral Community*, I assert that "what is absolutely clear is that cosmic justice demands universal veganism, the refusal to consume animal products of any kind."[2] A great many humanist thinkers, even those who make a place for animals as members of the moral community, refuse to embrace veganism as a strict ethical duty. Humanists who reject veganism do so because they consider animals to be morally inferior to human beings. Postmodernists, on the other hand, refuse to embrace anything like ethical veganism because of their epistemological and political opposition to principles.

The embrace of postmodernism leaves animals in an extraordinarily precarious position. It is fair to say that life is essentially precarious and that no appeal to principles can change this fact. But it is quite another thing to dispense with principles altogether. Even if they have no ultimate metaphysical basis and their application is not reducible to an a priori recursive procedure, principles have the potential to remind us of our moral connectedness and obligations to other sentient beings. One of the aims of this book is to show that the postmodern critique of principles is born of a basic misunderstanding of what principles are, how they are formed, and how they can regulate our conduct. A related aim is to argue that the postmodern rejection of principles is itself an unwitting evasion of responsibility. Postmodern work on animals shares with a good deal of humanist thought an implicit commitment to what I call "feel-good ethics," ethical commitments and sensibilities that permit us to express general abhorrence at the treatment of oppressed groups such as animals but do not push us out of our comfort zones by requiring us to take concrete steps to ameliorate the oppression we so abhor. As regards the plight of animals, Derrida once stated that he was "a vegetarian in [his] soul" but scrupulously refused to articulate any principled commitment to vegetarianism, let alone to veganism.[3] If such a position appeals to our desire to do justice to the irreducible complexity of reality, it equally appeals to a primordial desire in us not to have to rethink fundamentally our place and prerogatives in the moral scheme of things.

Thus while postmodernism may outwardly appear to hold the promise of dispossessing us of idealized distortions and of providing us with a more adequate grasp of reality, its real function is to leave reality and our relationship to it essentially unchanged—which is to say that it can offer us no prospect of progress in the endeavor to reduce the violence that we encounter in the world every day. My focus in this book, as in the two books that preceded it, is the moral status of animals and the need to articulate and live in accordance with moral principles that do justice to animals.[4] Postmodernism takes its bearings from Nietzsche's perspectivism and a pointedly polemical conception of discourse. I argue in the first two chapters that this leaves postmodernism ill-equipped to make coherent sense of the proposition that peace is to be preferred to violence. This essential limitation of postmodernism has tragic implications for human interrelationships as well as for our relationships with animals.

But it would be a mistake to conclude, as Hilary Putnam does, that postmodernism is "lacking in intellectual substance."[5] It is this misunderstanding of postmodernism that has led so many people to reject it without attempting to examine its basic commitments. Postmodernism is many things, but the various viewpoints that express the postmodern ethos share a commitment to the fundamental indeterminacy of meaning. This ethos is "amorphous, protean, and shifting," which is to say that it resists simple reduction to a straightforward definition.[6] Some postmodern thinkers, such as Heidegger and Lacan, retain conspicuous humanist commitments. Others, particularly poststructuralists such as Derrida, offer thoroughgoing criticisms of humanism. When I explore the commitments and the limits of postmodernism in this book, I am referring primarily to poststructuralism. Nonetheless, an examination of other postmodern thinkers (such as Heidegger, whom I discuss at length) makes it clear that they are in no better position than the poststructuralists to articulate clear principles that can govern ethical and political decision making.[7] Like Nietzsche before them, contemporary postmodern thinkers seek to debunk the Cartesian understanding of reality by returning us to the very realm of obscurity and confusion that Descartes considered to be the enemy of truth. But unlike Nietzsche, contemporary postmodern thinkers seek to wed this view of reality to a political program for the liberation of oppressed segments of humanity—even though Foucault himself acknowledges at the end of volume 1 of *The History of Sexuality* that the terms of postmodern thought render the prospect of liberation as illusory as the ideal of absolute knowledge that the proponents of postmodern thought wish to dispel.[8]

The fatal limitation of postmodernism is not that it lacks intellectual substance, but rather that it embraces two notions that are fundamentally incompatible with one another: a commitment to the indeterminacy of meaning and a sense of justice that presupposes the very access to a sense of determinacy that postmodern epistemology dismisses as illusory. Postmodern appeals to justice are fundamentally incoherent in the absence of humanistic notions such as agency and responsibility. The goal of contemporary reflections on the problem of oppression should not be to move toward some ill-conceived "posthumanist" future but instead to revise traditional humanist conceptions so that they better reflect the lives and needs of sentient beings. Contemporary postmodern thought expresses an awareness that the traditional distinction between human beings as agents and animals as biological reaction devices is woefully reductive, and that our culture has employed this reductive characterization to justify the subjection of animals for the gratification of human desires. But too many postmodern thinkers fail to recognize something of crucial importance: that human beings are different from animals in being capable of articulating and living in accordance with ethical principles. The humanistic tradition has erred in supposing that the possession of this capacity makes human beings morally superior to animals. We can correct this error not, as many postmodern thinkers suppose, by dispensing with humanism altogether but instead by divesting humanism of its anthropocentric prejudice. Human beings can and ought to strive to live in accordance with principles. To the extent that many animals have rich subjective lives that in essential respects are like those of human beings, one of these principles is that we ought to strive as far as possible to avoid doing violence to humans and animals alike.

The tragedy of postmodernism as regards animals is that it comes so close to embracing a notion of human-animal continuity and kinship but fails to advance so much as one clear principle regarding our treatment of animals. In this book I take the prospect of committing ourselves to veganism as a candidate for a principled way of seeking to do justice to the moral status of animals. Along the way I discuss a number of postmodern thinkers, but my main focus is Derrida, both because the anthropocentric prejudices of so many other postmodern thinkers have been amply exposed and because Derrida does by far the best job of any postmodern thinker of showing the limitations of traditional thought and of gesturing toward the prospect of affirming a fundamental kinship between human beings and animals. But even Derrida fails to articulate any clear moral principles bearing on our relationship to animals. I take this failure as an index of the best we can hope for from postmodern thought regarding the moral status of animals. It is against this background that I argue for the need to remain humanists just a little bit longer, and to seek to develop and live in accordance with principles such as the vegan imperative, which in my judgment holds unparalleled promise as a basis for reorganizing our lives in a way that truly extends the scope of justice so as to include animals as its beneficiaries.

CHAPTER ONE

The Use and Disadvantages of Nietzsche for Life

THE AMBIVALENCE OF POSTMODERNISM

The possibility of declaring veganism a fundamental moral principle depends, like the possibility of declaring any principle whatsoever, on the identification of a stable and enduring foundation upon which the principle can be justified. If veganism is to be considered a moral obligation, then it must be possible to derive it from a set of guiding convictions about the way things are and ought to be. This in turn, as trivial as it might seem, depends on there being something like "the way things are and ought to be." But are we any longer entitled to speak of things like reality and the ought, of enduring foundations and moral imperatives? Or is it instead the case, as so many postmodern thinkers declare today, that what we call principles are in fact fictions, mere inventions that serve ulterior motives of power and specifically the endeavor to proclaim the dominance of a particular perspective over all others? Even the briefest survey of contemporary postmodern work being done on animals shows that it has become enormously popular to dismiss all talk of enduring truth and authoritative principles, and to focus instead on the irreducible multiplicity of worldly phenomena and the supposed impossibility of transcending particular perspectives. Typical of this shift from the sobriety of principled judgment to the celebration of irreducible *différance* is Cary Wolfe's suggestion that any attempt to ground ethical judgment in reasoned principles "reduces ethics to the very antithesis of ethics by reducing the aporia of judgment in which the possibility of justice resides to the mechanical unfolding of a positivist calculation."[1] For Wolfe, following Derrida, the possibility of justice "resides in the aporia of judgment" in the sense that true justice depends on a case-by-case examination of life situations. To seek to subsume a variety of life situations, regardless of how similar or comparable they may seem, under unitary principles is fundamentally to do violence to the irreducibility of the individual situation; it is to "reduce" or deny the complexity and uniqueness of the individual situation by forcing it into a one-size-fits-all abstraction that bears no necessary relationship to any of the particular situations that it has been invoked to govern.

To follow this line of reasoning is to succumb to a temptation with dire consequences for ethics. For in entering this poppy field, we abandon the ideal of truth, and we render obscure if not entirely incoherent the idea of a basis for making ethical determinations that can be discussed and defended. As regards truth, Alain Boyer reminds us of "the mephitic swamps that abandoning the idea of historical ('factual') truth leads to: the gulag, or the gas chambers, never existed, etc."[2] To embrace a "philosophy of interpretation," according to which discourses simply express perspectives rather than identifiable states of affairs, is to abandon altogether the very idea of facts: "No facts, nothing but interpretations. There is no sense or spirit to the institutions, but as many meanings as there are forces confronting one another in a struggle to take ahold of the system and give it a *dominant* signification."[3] If discourses are no longer considered to have identifiable and critically discussable relationships to historical objects of discourse, if (as Descombes observes) discourses are simply expressions of attempts to achieve dominance, then it becomes impossible to speak in any straightforward way of the "fact" of Auschwitz or the "fact" of the Soviet gulag. For if there is "an ontological abyss between the words we use," on the one hand, and "truth and meaning," on the other, then either language is no longer about reality or "reality" is simply the content of some of our discourses rather than the measure of the truth of those discourses.

This descent into what Bacon would have called a "Tarturus of confusion and turmoil" also brings with it a crisis in ethics.[4] If "every reading is interpretative and consequently 'violent'" (in the sense that utterances or "readings" simply express different perspectives, each of which seeks to establish dominance over the others), then it becomes impossible to justify one reading over all others inasmuch as what we call "justification" is in reality nothing more than the forceful assertion of one point of view over all others.⁵ Thus it becomes impossible to speak coherently of the inherent wrongness of rape, child murder, or the exploitation of animals, each of these assertions being putatively nothing more than the assertion of a perspective and a forceful attempt to subsume an array of particulars under a generalization. "Nothing remains then but the subjective evaluation (without a subject, of course!) of the *creator of value*."⁶

And yet many of the postmodern thinkers writing on animals today express a sincere concern for the fortunes of animals and other oppressed beings, and a sense of revulsion at the ways in which human beings have systematically subjected and exploited animals. The problem is not that being postmodern entails a lack of concern for ethical questions or an insensitivity to suffering. The problem is rather that the philosophical tenets of postmodernism, the ideas so vaunted today (primarily in literature departments in North America) as products of "theory," make it impossible to speak coherently and consistently about states of affairs in the world and how we ought to address them. There is, as Richard Wolin puts the point, "a lethal self-contradiction at the heart of the deconstructionist enterprise." A key tenet of much contemporary postmodern thought, and certainly of Derrida's thought, is Saussure's claim that linguistic signifiers get their meaning not from their relationship to a reality outside of language but instead from their relationship to the larger context of signifiers and signification. The relationship of the signifier to meaning thus becomes arbitrary. "Hence, if 'difference' is prior to 'presence' and our signifiers are totally arbitrary, then the primordial goal of Western metaphysics—a systematic account of truth—becomes a linguistic and epistemological impossibility." And yet when Derrida and his adherents lodge a critique of the traditional philosophical picture of the relationship between language and reality, they are "implicitly staking claims about the relationship between cognition and the external world" and are arguing "even if only implicitly" that their "account is more verisimilar vis-à-vis the way things really are than the leading competing accounts."⁷ The postmodern denial of truth is itself a truth claim.

What we are left with is an "endemic mistrust of positive truth claims" and the inability "to articulate a constructive critical standpoint," on the one hand, and a sincere concern for problems of exploitation and suffering, on the other. It is worth considering carefully Wolin's claim that "Derrida's virtuoso dismantlings of logocentric philosophical prejudices have left interpretation frozen in an originary impotence in the stead of originary 'presence.'"[8] For if Wolin is right—and I believe he is—then the kind of concern that contemporary postmodern thinkers express for animals cannot be grounded in postmodern convictions but instead must be grounded in traditional philosophical commitments and principles— commitments and principles whose death has been triumphantly proclaimed by postmodern thinkers, only to be marshaled implicitly by those same thinkers in the service of an ideal of liberation.[9]

Thus the postmodern project suffers from a fundamental instability. It seeks to debunk traditional notions such as truth, principle, and autonomy, but it is equally committed to making truth claims and ethical pronouncements that depend on the very notions that it treats in such dismissive terms. How can a philosophy—and postmodernism is indeed that—that is beset with such a fundamentally contradictory nature have captured the imagination of so many careful and well-intentioned thinkers? The answer, I think, is that the guiding tenets of postmodernism outwardly appear to hold the promise of undermining an entire tradition of thinking about reality and human existence that has come to be recognized as suffering from some serious deficiencies. The development and articulation of these guiding tenets have been influenced more by the work of Friedrich Nietzsche than by the work of any other single figure or school of thought, so much so that one cannot adequately appreciate the nature and motivations of postmodern thought without proceeding from a reflection on Nietzsche.

NIETZSCHE'S CRITIQUE OF METAPHYSICS

The critique of "the metaphysics of presence" so endlessly written about in postmodern thought has its historical precursor in Nietzsche. The notion of an enduring reality outside the system of signification; the idea of an autonomous "subject"; the proposition that there are truths about the self and reality that can be known from something like an objective, transpersonal, and transhistorical standpoint; and the vision of time as an eschatological unfolding from an *arche* to a *telos*—all these ideas are objects of postmodern derision, and all find their most insistent and thoroughgoing critique in the writings of Nietzsche.

Nietzsche is an uncommonly seductive thinker. "To understand him beyond the charm of his way of thinking, one must be wary of falling in love with him. Given the hardness of Nietzsche's proposals, a hardness often forgotten or forgiven through the seductiveness of his style, empathy is the worst method."[10] Nietzsche appeals to the destructive part of our nature, to that part of us that would gladly part company with origins, reasons, and the demands of any authority other than those of our own will. To borrow a popular postmodern formulation, Nietzsche appeals to that part of us that seeks to escape "the law of the father." But is every law and every authority other than the sheer will to will *worth* evading? To those individuals whom Jacques Bouveresse masterfully characterizes as "the new Dionysians," the answer is a resounding yes.[11] But anyone enticed into answering in the affirmative must reckon with the pernicious implications of Nietzsche's thought and must ultimately confront the following sorts of questions: "Is it life that we should take as a model? . . . Why say *yes* to nature rather than to culture? What is a human being, in fact, if not this living creature in revolt against life itself, who refuses to follow life's pitiless logic to the end?"[12] The Nietzschean critique of metaphysics, reason, and humanism entails a rejection of the *nomos-physis* distinction and an embrace of the sheer play of violent natural forces. Indeed, Nietzsche's entire critique of liberal political ideals is designed to return us to exactly that violent state of nature that the embrace of *díke* or justice in classical Greece was supposed to overcome.

In antiquity Hesiod and Ovid relate stories of a mythic golden age in which human beings lived in harmony with one another and their natural surroundings, only to fall from this state of grace and into a condition of violence.[13] Hesiod states that this fall made it necessary for Zeus to confer the law of *díke* (justice) on human beings, a law that imposed mutual obligations of nonharm. Hesiod also states that this law obligates human beings but not nonhuman animals, inasmuch as the latter are non-linguistic (which is to say, nonrational) beings and hence cannot "listen to justice." Animals are hopelessly enmired in a violent state of nature, whereas human beings can employ reason to transcend this state toward a context of peaceful interrelationships. Almost every Western thinker from Epicurus to John Rawls embraces this conception of justice and the fundamental distinction between humans and animals that it presupposes. Since Hesiod, the dominant line of thinking has been that the rational ability to comprehend and respect the law enables human beings to depart from natural violence, and that the inability of animals to grasp the law leaves them fundamentally without protection and without any share in justice.

Hesiod's vision of justice is one according to which *nomos*, or law, can take precedence over *physis*, or wild nature. Nietzsche derides this very aspiration, which is founded on the notion that reality has a rational, knowable structure. Nietzsche, in effect, rejects the proposition advanced by Hegel that the real is rational, and he denounces attempts to subject *physis* to rational ordering as life-denying efforts to insulate us from the violent forces of nature. Nietzsche finds inspiration in Schopenhauer for his rejection of an identity between the real and the rational and for his consequent rejection of the idea that history traces out a teleological progression. For Schopenhauer, the real is essentially nonrational and forever lies beyond the grasp of rational contemplation. Rationality is a capacity possessed by those beings with a sufficiently high degree of consciousness that they can reflect in abstract terms on the eternal cycles of generation and destruction in nature. Reflection discloses to rational subjects certain eternal facts about the world, such as that the individual will is merely a momentary manifestation of one "universal will-to-live," that there is no ultimate purpose to willing, that willing is inseparable from destruction and suffering, and that the will is therefore "eternally unsatisfied."[14] Schopenhauer concludes that "life has no *genuine intrinsic worth*," and "that human existence must be a kind of error" whose significance Schopenhauer considers to be comparable to that of "a drop of water, seen through a microscope and teeming with *infusoria*, or that of an otherwise visible little heap of cheese-mites whose strenuous activity and strife make us laugh."[15] All life and all striving are essentially meaningless. This holds even for the life of human beings, who enjoy the distinction of possessing rationality.

> This world of humanity is the kingdom of chance and error. These rule in it without mercy in great things as in small; and along with them folly and wickedness also wield the scourge. Hence arises the fact that everything better struggles through only with difficulty; what is noble and wise very rarely makes its appearance, becomes effective, or meets with a hearing, but the absurd and per-

verse in the realm of thought, the dull and tasteless in the sphere of art, and the wicked and fraudulent in the sphere of action, really assert a supremacy that is disturbed only by brief interruptions. . . . The essential purport of the world-famous monologue in Hamlet is, in condensed form, that our state is so wretched that complete non-existence would be decidedly preferable to it.[16]

Thus optimism is "not merely an absurd, but also a really wicked, way of thinking, a bitter mockery of the unspeakable sufferings of mankind," not to mention of the sufferings of animals.[17]

And yet for all that, Schopenhauer does not opt for a rejection of the *nomos-physis* distinction and an embrace of the violence that characterizes the inner nature of the world-will. Schopenhauer sees an inner compatibility between the meaninglessness of existence, the ineluctable character of suffering, and the proposition that suffering merits our concern and even a sense of moral responsibility. Optimism is a mockery of suffering in the sense that it presupposes the possibility of an end to suffering; that is, it fails to recognize the inner nature of things and subscribes to an ideal that is utterly at odds with the *factum brutum* of existence. One target of Schopenhauer's remarks in this connection is the Enlightenment philosophies of history, with their confidence in the power of reason to bring about continual progress toward an ideal culmination modeled on Christian eschatology.[18] The Christian ideal seeks liberation from this world altogether, whereas the Enlightenment ideal of progress seeks liberation from suffering within the context of worldly existence. Schopenhauer rejects both these aspirations as illusory: there is no world beyond that of the universal will to live, and willing is ineluctably bound up with suffering. Moreover, attempts to escape suffering, for example by taking recourse to suicide, reflect a misunderstanding of the terms of existence. To the extent that the individual will is merely a momentary manifestation of the world-will, extinguishing an individual will does nothing to alter the inner nature of things, which consists in endless cycles of generation, corruption, and suffering. "The earth rolls on from day into night; the individual dies; but the sun itself burns without intermission, an eternal noon. Life is certain to the will to live; the form of life is the endless present; it matters not how individuals, the phenomena of the Idea, arise and pass away in time, like fleeting dreams. Therefore suicide already appears to be a vain and therefore foolish action."[19] Schopenhauer argues that there are only two appropriate responses to the interminable reality of suffering, and he openly acknowledges that neither of them can alter what the young Nietzsche would later call "the terror and horror of existence."[20]

The first is to gain knowledge, and the second is to seek to ameliorate suffering in the world. When we gain knowledge of the inner nature of things, we do nothing to alter that inner nature, but we nonetheless, on Schopenhauer's view, gain momentary release from suffering.[21] It is particularly through art in its various forms that we contemplate the Platonic Idea (i.e., gain insight into the eternal nature of things) and put ourselves in a position to affirm and deny the will—to affirm it in the sense that we acknowledge its ineluctable character, and deny it in the sense that we suspend our own acts of willing in those moments when we are engaged in detached contemplation. Like Hegel before him, Schopenhauer sketches a hierarchy of the various artistic forms, from architecture and sculpture at the bottom to poetry and music at the top. But whereas Hegel, who believed that the real is the rational, gave pride of place to poetry among the arts, Schopenhauer inverts the top of Hegel's hierarchy and places music above poetry on the grounds that only music directly conveys the inner nature of things rather than providing the mediation of a Platonic Idea. Music, on Schopenhauer's view, gives us the most immediate possible contact with the inner nature of existence, which cannot be grasped conceptually.[22]

But art grasps only the "purely knowable side of this world." There remains for Schopenhauer, if only paradoxically, the imperative to act in ways that seek to reduce suffering in the world. Schopenhauer is one of the few figures in the Western philosophical tradition to argue that duties of justice are not merely the product of reciprocal agreements of nonharm among rational beings but are instead ordained by the nature of the cosmos itself. Schopenhauer argues against Hobbes that "the concepts of right and wrong, even for the state of nature, are indeed valid and by no means conventional."[23] Locke had already at least implicitly made this argument against Hobbes in the *Second Treatise of Government*; but he had done so on the basis of divine warrant, presupposing a divine creator, an intelligible *logos* of existence, and the fundamental superiority of human beings over all other forms of earthly life. Schopenhauer, on the other hand, advances a conception of "eternal" as opposed to merely "temporal" justice that extends not only to human beings but to all sentient life.[24] In spite of the fact that there is no inner meaning or ultimate purpose to existence, those beings capable of recognizing the reality of suffering (namely, human beings) have obligations to ameliorate it, regardless of whether the beings whose suffering we seek to reduce are capable of acting comparably toward us. Eternal justice does not involve the reciprocity demanded by the temporal justice that characterizes human relations.

Schopenhauer's call for eternal or "heavenly" justice is a modification of Hesiod's call for a departure from violent nature. Hesiod considers justice to be a relationship that prevails exclusively between human beings, who as rational beings are capable of "listening to justice." This means, as the Stoics would later argue, that animals lie entirely outside the sphere of justice, and that nothing we do to animals can be considered an injustice. In effect, we may continue to practice violence toward animals even though we must observe mutual obligations of respect and nonharm in the human sphere. Schopenhauer's critique of the *principium individuationis*, his recognition of the ephemeral character of all particular manifestations of the world-will including human individuals, leads him to recognize the anthropocentric character of the traditional conception of justice. It leads him to articulate a conception of justice according to which we have duties of nonharm in regard to all sentient life, in spite of the fact that "the terror and horror of existence" cannot ultimately be overcome, and in spite of the fact that nonrational sentient life cannot take on obligations toward us.

These commitments regarding the inner nature of existence and the place of the human individual in the cosmic scheme of things deeply inform Nietzsche's critique of Western metaphysics, although Nietzsche parts company with Schopenhauer in his assessment of the proper response to the problem of suffering. Schopenhauer acknowledges the violent and chaotic inner nature of things but adheres to the classical formula according to which human beings can transcend the state of nature. His departure from the tradition consists in his recognition that this transcendence is provisional and temporary at best, and in his appeal to eternal justice. Schopenhauer adheres to the traditional formula of human striving according to which our highest aspiration ought to be to ameliorate suffering, and he illuminates the paradox involved in taking this aspiration seriously when we recognize that it is ultimately futile.

Nietzsche, for his own part, rejects the very terms of the traditional model: he acknowledges Schopenhauer's insight into the horrible inner nature of things, but from this recognition he derives the conclusion that *suffering must be affirmed* rather than ameliorated. One tragic error of contemporary postmodern thought is the supposition that one can accept Nietzsche's critique of metaphysics but reject his affirmation of violence and suffering. For in fact the two are inseparable.

Nietzsche writes in *Daybreak* that "we have thought the matter over and finally decided that there is nothing good, nothing beautiful, nothing sublime, nothing evil in itself, but that there are states of soul in which we impose such words upon things external to and within us. We have again *taken back* the predicates of things, or at least remembered that it was we who *lent* them to them."[25] All value-predicates are human inventions. Kant had proposed that Plato's error had been to suppose that "ideas are archetypes of the things themselves," whereas for Kant these archetypes are "to be found only in our minds."[26] But if for Kant the thing-in-itself is essentially unknowable, the good can nonetheless be articulated (if only abstractly) in postulates of pure practical reason. Nietzsche radicalizes Kant's critique of traditional claims to know the thing-in-itself, rejecting altogether Kant's claims to apodeictic knowledge and deriding Kant's ethics as "moral Tartuffery."[27] Truth and the good are products not of rational contemplation but rather of our creative will: reality is not what we find but what we say it is. To adhere to the traditional prejudices that there is an independent reality, that it is knowable beyond particular perspectives, that it assigns to human beings a proper place in the cosmos that brings with it a set of obligations to act in ways that benefit or at least avoid harming others, is not simply a mistake; it is downright disingenuous.

The young Nietzsche offers an analysis of the relationship between language and the world that overturns the traditional idea of language as a mirror of reality. Philosophers from Aristotle to Descartes had articulated a classical formula according to which certain forms of language are capable of capturing the structure of an external reality that itself is independent of language, Aristotle offering a model according to which the predicative structure of assertions can correspond to the predicative structure of reality, and Descartes offering a vision of an ideal language that could order our thinking about reality with the same degree of precision as that seen in mathematics.[28] Nietzsche rejects this vision of language altogether.

> The significance of language for the evolution of culture lies in this, that mankind set up in language a separate world beside the other world, a place it took to be so firmly set that, standing upon it, it could lift the rest of the world off its hinges and make itself master of it. To the extent that man has for long ages believed in the concepts and names of things as in *aeternae veritates* he has appropriated to himself that pride by which he raised himself above the animal: he really thought that in language he possessed knowledge of the world.

This vision of language is bound up with "the *belief that the truth has been found.* . . . A great deal later—only now—it dawns on men that in their belief in language they have propagated a tremendous error. . . . *Logic* too depends on presuppositions with which nothing in the real world corresponds."[29] No longer a means for securing access to the real, language as Nietzsche sees it has an arbitrary relationship to reality. Language, like logic, is a tool of creation rather than of discovery. Thus the young Nietzsche could proclaim that "our salvation [*Heil*] lies not in *knowing*, but in *creating*! Our greatness lies in the highest illusions, in the noblest emotions. If the universe is of no concern to us, then we ought to have the right to despise it."[30]

Is Nietzsche's rejection of Schopenhauerian compassion for all suffering a consequence of his untethering of language from reality, or is his view of language itself a consequence of what Zarathustra calls "the will's ill will against time"?[31] Either way, the connection between the two is inseparable in Nietzsche; one cannot accept the one without accepting the other. Schopenhauer was able to avoid this predicament by seeing in aesthetic contemplation the prospect of disclosing Platonic Ideas that convey to us essential truths about the world, one of which is that suffering is a universal and interminable condition that merits our compassion. Compassion links us at a fundamental level to other forms of life and elicits a sense of cosmic justice. Nietzsche, by denying anything more than an arbitrary connection between language and reality, places us in an adversarial relationship to the world: "*If the universe is of no concern to us, then we ought to have the right to despise it.*" This sounds an awful lot like the spirit of revenge against time that is the object of Zarathustra's opprobrium.

In one of his early writings, Nietzsche advances a conception of sense perception that fundamentally informs his view of language. He characterizes the experience of a perceptual object and its subsequent description in language in the following manner: "To begin with, a nerve stimulus is transferred into an image: first metaphor. This image, in turn, is imitated in a sound: second metaphor. And each time there is a complete overleaping of one sphere, right into the middle of an entirely new and different one." Even sense perception itself has a linguistic character, being the formation of a metaphor. But if metaphors have an irreducibly arbitrary dimension in their relationships to their referents, then neither language nor even experience can have anything like the transparent connection to reality that the tradition sought. "We believe that we know something about the things themselves when we speak of trees, colors, snow, and flowers; and yet we possess nothing but metaphors for things—metaphors which correspond in no way to the original entities." Not even concepts have any correspondence to nature, being formed only "by overlooking what is individual and actual."[32]

This analysis of the relationship among perception, language, and reality leads Nietzsche to the conclusion that "our experiences . . . [are] much *more* that which we put into them than that which they already contain! Or must we go so far as to say: in themselves they contain nothing? To experience is to invent?"[33] The traditional model of language found in Aristotle and Descartes is one according to which reality is not an invention but instead is something we can discover when we employ reason in the right manner. Certain forms of language, namely, certain kinds of assertions, capture the *logos*, or structure, of reality by establishing a correspondence with it. This presupposes an independent reality that is capable of being found but for the most part remains concealed. In *Twilight of the Idols*, Nietzsche dismisses once and for all this ideal of a "true world":

> The true world—unattainable, indemonstrable, unpromisable; but the very thought of it—a consolation, an obligation, an imperative. . . . The true world—unattainable? At any rate, unattained. And being unattained, also *unknown*. Consequently, not consoling, redeeming, or obligating; how could something unknown obligate us? . . . The

'true' world—an idea which is no longer good for anything, not even obligating—an idea which has become useless and superfluous—*consequently*, a refuted idea: let us abolish it![34]

Metaphysics had depended on a fundamental distinction between appearance and reality and the need for "the sage, the pious, the virtuous man" to pierce the veil of Maya and disclose the inner nature of things and its attendant imperatives for human conduct. If, as Schopenhauer recognized, the inner nature of things is finally unknowable, why should we pay it any respect at all, why suppose that it has any binding force on us whatsoever? Why not respond instead with derision and mockery, or at least abandon the aspiration to master reality? The tradition has sought to master reality by knowing it and by finding means to ameliorate the suffering that it metes out. To follow Nietzsche is to abandon both these endeavors and to see in both an expression of the spirit of revenge against the destructive power of time.

In a passage in his notebooks from the 1880s, Nietzsche elaborates on the tradition's commitment to the existence of a "true" world.

> This world is apparent; consequently there is a true world . . . this world is a world of becoming; consequently there is a world of being;—all false conclusions. . . . It is suffering that inspires these conclusions: fundamentally they are *desires* that such a world should exist; in the same way, to imagine another, more valuable world is an expression of hatred for a world that makes one suffer: the *ressentiment* of metaphysicians against actuality is here creative.[35]

The world of endless becoming in which we find ourselves causes us confusion and pain; therefore we deny or devalue it by supposing that it is a merely "apparent" world beyond which lies an ideal world of perfect clarity and satisfaction. We then seek to articulate reasons for our suffering, such as that "suffering is a consequence of error" or "suffering is a consequence of guilt."[36] We do so because we cannot endure the prospect that suffering has no meaning, that we simply suffer unto death. The same spirit of *ressentiment* that leads humanity to embrace ascetic ideals leads the metaphysician to posit a fictitious higher world. The metaphysical impulse, like the turn to ascetic ideals, is "an expression of the basic fact of the human will, its *horror vacui: it needs a goal*—and it would rather will nothingness than *not* will."[37] The underlying intent is to provide relief from suffering. But

> the preoccupation with suffering on the part of metaphysicians—is quite naive. "Eternal bliss": psychological nonsense. Brave and creative men *never* consider pleasure and pain as ultimate values—they are epiphenomena: one must *desire* both if one is to achieve anything—. That they see the problem of pleasure and pain in the foreground reveals something weary and sick in metaphysicians and religious people. Even morality is so important to them only because they see in it an essential condition for the abolition of suffering.[38]

Nietzsche's critique of metaphysics is a dismissal of the aspiration to transcend the realm of becoming toward a realm of ideal permanence. The metaphysician principally seeks prophylaxis from suffering and death. Once we get past this "psychological nonsense," we will be in a position to confront reality on its own terms and live a life of affirmation rather than one of denial. Intimately bound up with the affirmation of life is a recognition of the inevitability of, indeed of the *need for*, suffering. "Today, when suffering is always brought forward as the principal argument *against* existence, as the worst question mark, one does well to recall the ages in which the opposite opinion prevailed because men were unwilling to refrain from *making* suffer and saw in it an enhancement of the first order, a genuine seduction to life."[39] In those ages, humanity embraced suffering, reveled in festivals of cruelty, and eschewed what would later come to be called morality.[40] In *The Birth of Tragedy*, Nietzsche offers an account of the rise of metaphysics and laments the loss of an appreciation for the virtues of suffering. The figure of Dionysus represents the early Greeks' appreciation of existence as a stream of becoming, fraught with danger and destruction. This appreciation was expressed in its purest form through music. "The Dionysian musician is, without any images, himself pure primordial pain and its primordial re-echoing." Apollinian "images" serve to mediate between us and the inner nature of things, thereby offering the prospect of "redemption through illusion." Apollo also symbolizes "the apotheosis of individuation," hence a moment of distance from the world and the prospect of self-knowledge. The task of life is to find an appropriate balance between the Apollinian and the

Dionysian; pure Dionysian reverie is unsustainable, whereas an excess of the Apollinian brings with it a divorce from reality (through a failure to recognize that the individual is not metaphysically primary) and the loss of the fundamental "truth" disclosed by the Dionysian festival.[41]

Those ages in which "men were unwilling to refrain from *making* suffer and saw in it an enhancement of the first order, a genuine seduction to life," were ages in which humanity embraced the Dionysian, with its affirmation of "a hidden substratum of suffering." These were ages in which "*excess* revealed itself as truth." The intoxication of the Dionysian festival facilitated the overcoming of individuality, that antagonist of true art, thereby liberating us from the illusion that we are the authors of art rather than merely its "images and artistic projections."[42] In those bold times when humanity could embrace the inevitability of suffering and permit art to create monuments to pain and destruction, it was possible to attain genuine self-knowledge, which was not about the individual or an ideal reality but rather about the tragic inner nature of things that had been Schopenhauer's concern. Nietzsche would never abandon his fealty to the image of Dionysus. As late as *Twilight of the Idols* he would continue to appeal to the image of Dionysus as the symbol of the primacy of the affects over the mediation of Apollinian images, a primacy that corresponds to the reality of becoming and constant self-transformation over any kind of permanence or stability. This is one of the clearest expressions of the distance that Nietzsche takes from Schopenhauer: Nietzsche dismisses Schopenhauer's affirmation *and denial* of the will as a sign of Schopenhauer's "nihilistic" repudiation of "the great cultural facts of humanity."[43]

Nietzsche sees in the turn from *mythos* to *logos* the beginnings of this repudiation of "great cultural facts." Where "true culture" would consist in a mythic embrace of the inner nature of things and a "conception of culture as a new and improved *physis*, without inner and outer, without dissumulation and convention, culture as a unanimity of life, thought, appearance and will," the Socratic turn to the ideal of an intelligible world signifies a "mendacious" denial of reality and a breakdown of the Dionysian awareness of our inner connection with nature.[44] Socrates is "an opponent of tragic art" in that he "conceives it to be his duty to correct existence" by pretending that reality can be known and suffering conquered.[45] This "Greek cheerfulness," this mendacious optimism of theoretical man, must itself ultimately have recourse to myth; but its manner of regarding existence remains forever deficient in privileging being over becoming, intelligibility over chaos, and harmony over discord. To invert these relationships is to return to a more adequate way of grasping our relationship to nature, a way whose possibility was shown to us by the tragic Greeks. It is to recognize that if existence is to be justified, it cannot be done through purporting to render existence comprehensible, nor by substituting beautiful images for the ugly core of reality. "For it is only as an *aesthetic phenomenon* that existence and the world are eternally *justified*"—which is to say that it is only through an open embrace of "appearance" and the abandonment of the ideal of a "true" world behind phenomena that we genuinely reconcile ourselves to the terms of existence.[46]

Ethical Implications of Nietzsche's Critique of Metaphysics

But what is the *meaning* of such a "reconciliation," and is it the kind of reconciliation to which we ought to aspire? Nietzsche's critique of modern ideals is founded on his early insight that "our whole modern world . . . proposes as its ideal the theoretical man equipped with the greatest forces of knowledge, and laboring in the service of science, whose archetype and progenitor is Socrates."[47] Our commitments to democracy, the rule of law, and the dignity of the individual all reflect the modern form of a perversion of life and an elevation of our lowliest tendencies whose roots are found in the Socratic turn. Nietzsche's debunking of traditional metaphysics sets the stage for his wholesale repudiation of modern ideals and his attempt at a revaluation of all values that would reestablish our archaic connection with the inner nature of things.

A key element of Nietzsche's critique of modern values is his evaluation of the modern conception of human subjectivity. Hume had lodged a critique of the notion of the self as an autonomous agency that brings about effects in the world. For Hume, the idea that the self causes its own actions is predicated on the same misunderstanding that leads us to suppose that events cause other events: we experience nothing but the constant conjunction of events that we *call* acts of will and events that we *call* the effects of those acts. The self is really "nothing but a bundle or collection of different perceptions, which succeed each other with an inconceivable rapidity, and are in a perpetual flux and movement."[48] Our attributions of personal identity to these bundles are attempts to confer a sense of sameness over time to what is really a flux of becoming. Properly understood, that is, divested of the illusions of a metaphysics of presence, personal identity is seen to be a "grammatical" rather than a "philosophical" matter.[49] Nietzsche declares that "Hume was right; habit (but not only that of the individual!) makes us expect that a certain often-observed occurrence will follow another: nothing more! That which gives us the extraordinary firmness to our belief in causality . . . is belief that every event is a deed, that every deed presupposes a doer, it is belief in the 'subject.' Is this belief in the concept of subject and attribute not a great stupidity?" We purport with our appeals to subjectivity to ground experience in the metaphysical notion of substance, whereas in reality the subject "is simply a formulation of our grammatical custom that adds a doer to every deed." Indeed, "the concept of substance is a consequence of the concept of subject: not the reverse! . . . 'The subject' is the fiction that many similar states in us are the effect of one substratum: but it is we who first created the 'similarity' of these states." To say that personal identity or agency is a "grammatical" matter is to say that it is a feature of certain interpretive activities, an invention or projection rather than a reality that we discover. "The 'subject' is only a fiction: the ego of which one speaks when one censures egoism does not exist at all."[50] The self is a trope.

This dismantling of the subject corresponds to the young Nietzsche's critique of language in "On Truth and Lie": just as there is no essential connection between language or concepts and the things and events we seek to describe, there is no unitary ground or principle that connects the disparate moments of our experience. To attribute underlying intentions to an agency with purposes is to "corrupt for ourselves the *innocence of becoming*."[51] An authentic embrace of becoming demands a rejection of "the soul atomism" of Christianity, which understands the self as essentially "something indestructible, eternal, indivisible, as a monad, as an atomon."[52] Here it is worth asking whether Nietzsche himself is not committing "a great stupidity": Must human subjectivity be understood in specifically metaphysical terms? If subjectivity is "simply a formulation of our grammatical custom," and if customs change, then what is to prevent us from revising and refining notions such as that of subjectivity through critical reflection? And if the answer to this question is that "critical reflection" is itself nothing more than "a formulation of our grammatical custom," is this answer not blatantly contradictory to the extent that it *marshals critical reflection* precisely in order to discredit the very idea of critical reflection?

Nietzsche evades these questions and develops a critique of the notion of subjectivity designed to discredit the notions of autonomy, equality, responsibility, and democracy. The primary object of Nietzsche's critique is the Cartesian notion of the self as *res cogitans*.

> When I analyze the process that is expressed in the sentence, "I think", I find a whole series of daring assertions that would be difficult, perhaps impossible, to prove; for example, that it is *I* who think, that there must necessarily be something that thinks, that thinking is an activity and operation on the part of a being who is thought of as a cause, that there is an "ego," and, finally, that it is already determined what is to be designated by thinking—that I *know* what thinking is.[53]

Descartes had appropriated the soul doctrine of Christianity, according to which the soul is an immutable substance that is not subject to earthly cycles of generation and corruption but is instead subject to supernatural (which is to say divine) creation and annihilation. Thus the soul or mind (which for Descartes are the same) transcends the body, is not bound to perish with the death of the body, and is superior to the body in virtue of possessing the faculties of reason and will. Reason and will are what make us most like our divine creator, and they confer on us prerogatives that no other earthly beings enjoy, in particular the prerogative to employ science to "render ourselves the masters and possessors of nature."[54] Nietzsche questions the very foundations of this entire conception of the nature and vocation of humanity: "From where do I get the concept of thinking? Why do I believe in cause and effect? What gives me the right to speak of an ego, and even of an ego as cause, and finally of an ego as the cause of thought?" If I develop my intuitions about the nature of thinking from a process of comparing my different mental states with one another, then I cannot rightfully claim any certainty regarding a supposedly common feature or ground of thinking.[55] I am forced to conclude with Hume that "every thing, that exists, is particular" and that "therefore it must be our several particular perceptions, that compose the mind."[56] I must further conclude that I do not really have any clear conception of what "thinking" *is*, inasmuch as every comparison I make between my mental states, and every assertion I make about these states, is a metaphor whose relationship to its many referents is merely arbitrary.

The consequence of this rejection of a centered self that underlies my various experiences is a loss of the autonomy of thought that Descartes and Kant had attributed to the subject. No longer are thoughts products of my deliberate mental activity. "With regard to the superstitions of logicians, I shall never tire of emphasizing a small terse fact, which these superstitious minds hate to concede—namely, that a thought comes when 'it' wishes, and not when 'I' wish, so that it is a falsification of the facts of the case [*eine Fälschung des Thatbestandes*] to say that the subject 'I' is the condition of the predicate 'think'."[57] *It is a falsification of the facts of the case*: on the one hand, facts are merely inventions or interpretations; on the other hand, when it suits Nietzsche, there are "facts of the case," and they can be falsified. In the case at hand, Nietzsche offers as a fact the illusory character of the soul as it was conceived by Descartes and the Christian tradition. In place of the idea of a unitary soul or rational self that transcends embodiment, Nietzsche asserts the primacy of embodied existence. This assertion is a corollary to Nietzsche's rejection of the "true," higher world of the tradition: where the tradition—this includes Plato, Christianity, and Descartes—had asserted a dualism according to which the ever-changing world of embodiment is a realm of mere appearance in comparison with the "true" world of pure spirit and permanence, Nietzsche follows Schopenhauer in asserting the reality of the one world of becoming. But instead of abandoning the notion of soul altogether, Nietzsche adapts it to his vitalist vision: "Our body is but a social structure composed of many souls."[58] What can this mean, if until now we have identified the notion of soul with permanence, immutability, and transcendence, all qualities that Nietzsche purports to have debunked as products of mendacity and evasion? Henceforth soul is to mean something different, something to be understood not as part of a realm of pure being but rather as part of a stream of sheer becoming. "The 'soul', the 'ego' posited as primeval fact, and introduced everywhere where there is any becoming."[59] Schopenhauer, too, had sought to debunk the soul-doctrine of Christianity, substituting in its place the doctrine of the world-will and the recognition that certain manifestations of willing qualify as individuals. Nietzsche radicalizes the *principium individuationis* by proposing that the self is nothing unified but is, like the nature of which it is essentially a part, a multiplicity of selves, egos, wills, or souls. Nietzsche's purpose in denying the "true" world of metaphysics is "to translate man back into nature . . . to see to it that man henceforth stands before man as even today, hardened in the discipline of science, he stands before the rest of nature . . . that may be a strange and insane task, but it is a *task*."[60] Schopenhauer had failed to complete this task in that he still clung to the ideas of rationality and responsibility and saw in them the prospect of a human transcendence of nature, even if that transcendence could only be temporary and incomplete. In his own way, Schopenhauer was too wedded to the soul-doctrine that he himself had subjected to critique.

For Nietzsche, translating humanity back into nature requires a very specific dilution of the notion of soul, so that it no longer bears any resemblance to the "mendacious" conception of soul adhered to by the tradition. *Soul now signifies affects or drives.* These are now what can be said to possess agency, if anything can. Where the tradition had opposed reason to passion or drives and had offered a view of virtue as the conquest or regulation of passion by reason, Nietzsche inverts the relationship in a way that recalls Hume's assertion that "reason is, and ought only to be the slave of the passions."[61] But where Hume believed that a coherent theory of human responsibility and civic order could be founded on the primacy of the passions, Nietzsche laments our culture's loss of faith in the proposition "that man has value and meaning only insofar as he is *a stone in a great edifice*; and to that end he must be *solid* first of all, a 'stone'— and above all not an actor!"[62] To recognize the primacy of the affects in human life is to *decenter* action so that it no longer makes sense to speak of actions as having been performed by traditional agents or subjects. It is to accept Zarathustra's belief that "body am I entirely, and nothing else; and soul is only a word for something about the body. The body is a great reason, a plurality with one sense," in comparison with which spirit in the traditional sense is a "little reason . . . a little instrument and toy of your great reason."[63] Once we dispense with the idea of consciousness as the center and agent of experience, we open ourselves to the fact that we can

> think, feel, will, and remember, and also . . . "act" in every sense of
> that word, and yet none of all this would have to "enter our con-
> sciousness" (as one says metaphorically). The whole of life would

be possible without, as it were, seeing itself in a mirror. Even now, for that matter, the greatest part of our life actually takes place without this mirror effect; and this is true even of our thinking, feeling, and willing life, however offensive this may sound to older philosophers. *For what purpose*, then, any consciousness at all when it is in the main *superfluous?*[64]

More than superfluous, in fact, the appeal to consciousness and reason is *opposed* to life. Every interpretation, even a life-denying one, serves a purpose. The interpretation of human existence that places conscious-ness and reason at the center is designed to serve "the instinct for the preservation of life," which "tries with all its force to make us forget that at bottom it is instinct, drive, folly, lack of reasons." What is needed in place of such an interpretation is one that recognizes that "the tragic, too, with all its sublime unreason, belongs among the means and necessities of the preservation of the species." What is needed is a full embrace of "this whole marvelous uncertainty and rich ambiguity of existence," rather than the endeavor to insulate and protect us from existence through the flight to reason and the ideal of a detached self that hovers above the realm of becoming. "One thing is needful," Nietzsche tells us. "To 'give style' to one's character—a great and rare art! . . . It will be the strong and domineering natures that enjoy their finest gaiety in such constraint and perfection under a law of their own." The law of reason is a law for the many, for "the weak characters without power over themselves" who must flee into fictions designed to conceal their lowly status.[65]

Here it finally becomes clear what purpose is served by the interpreta-tion of human existence in terms of soul or subjectivity: the purpose is *to level genuine distinctions* between different "types" of human being in order to neutralize the natural advantage enjoyed by what Nietzsche calls the "higher" type. The Christian notion of the immortal soul and the mod-ern conception of the subject serve an interest in democratizing the hu-man condition by representing all human beings as essentially the same as one another: all souls are equally subject to original sin and divine Provi-dence; all subjects possess innate ideas (Descartes), unite their experi-ences in terms of the transcendental unity of apperception (Kant), etc.; all citizens are equal before the law (Locke, Rousseau, Mill, Hayek, Rawls, Habermas, . . .). But this democratizing move is life-denying in that it suppresses the highest instances of human potential. Notwithstanding his suggestion that unreason can serve the preservation of the species, Nietzsche ultimately considers the Darwinian focus on the "struggle for *existence*" to reflect a deficient understanding of the human condition. For "where there is struggle, it is struggle for *power*. One should not mistake Malthus for nature."[66] Malthus had focused on the struggle for survival, focusing on what Nietzsche calls the weaker type and failing to appreciate what Nietzsche considered his own great realization: that "life is will to power," and that the affirmation of life demands not the survival of the species but the cultivation of the most superior members of the species.[67]

This is the upshot of Nietzsche's critique of reason, selfhood, and the traditional ideal of equality: that all these notions criminalize and confine the higher type of person, and that they do so in the service of rendering the weak among us (which for Nietzsche is most of us) dominant over the rare, superior type of human being. In reality "*there are altogether no moral facts.* . . . Morality is merely an interpretation of certain phenomena—more precisely, a misinterpretation."[68] An interpretation can be a misinterpretation only in relation to a given standard or measure of correctness. Nietzsche's standard is the extent to which an interpretation does justice to the *factum brutum* of wild *physis*. Tragic art is essentially a correct interpretation of things. Traditional morality is a misinterpretation to the extent that it denies the inherent differences between individuals, differences that are not matters of choice or initiative but rather are "inherited."[69]

But every interpretation, even and perhaps especially a misinterpretation, serves a specific purpose. Traditional morality is a manifestation of "the instinct of decadence; it is the exhausted and disinherited who in this way take their revenge and play the master." Even the morality of the weak, of the slave, serves the will to power; it is "the means the weak employ to keep themselves on top. . . . The declining instincts have become master over the ascending instincts—The will to nothingness has become master over the will to life!" The morality of the weak is mendacious in that it purports to be a product of dispassionate reason, when in fact "moral evaluation is an *exegesis*, a way of interpreting. The exegesis itself is a symptom of certain physiological conditions. . . . Who interprets?—Our affects." The body, again, is a multiplicity of souls, which is to say that it is an empire of drives or affects functioning in the service of the will to power. All interpretations are "symptoms of physiological conditions"; in the case of the lower type of human being, the condition is one of resistance, of *ressentiment* toward what anyone can plainly see is the "higher" type. The endeavor to counter and criminalize the higher type, which Nietzsche takes to be central to "Christian-European morality," shows that "our moral judgments are signs of decline, of disbelief in life, a preparation for pessimism."[70]

What, then, is this higher type of human being, and why is anything other than the endeavor to permit this rare type to flourish a denial of life? Why sacrifice the many for the few? Is this not precisely the kind of morality—and even Nietzsche calls it a form of morality—of which Socrates struggles so energetically to dispossess Thrasymachus early in the *Republic*, the morality according to which might makes right? In embracing a way of life that celebrates our Dionysian immersion in *physis*, is Nietzsche not recommending that we reject Hesiod's advice to depart from a state of violent nature, and that we embrace violence and mock traditional ideals of peace, love, and reciprocity as "great stupidity"?

Nietzsche's characterization of the higher type proceeds from his conviction that "life itself is essentially appropriation, injury, overpowering of what is alien and weaker; suppression, hardness, imposition of one's own forms, incorporation and at least, at its mildest, exploitation." The higher type of human being, the "aristocratic" type, "therefore accepts with a good conscience the sacrifice of untold human beings who, *for its sake*, must be reduced and lowered to incomplete human beings, to slaves, to instruments."[71] The higher type of person subscribes to a morality with an essentially different logic than that to which the lower type subscribes. "The noble type of man experiences *itself* as determining values" rather than seeing moral values as something to which the noble type is subject. Where the lower type would subject everyone, including the higher type, to a universally binding moral law, higher individuals see this aspiration as a will to nothingness and seek instead "to be the poets of [their] life."[72] The higher type says, "I have killed the law, the law anguishes me as a corpse does a living man: if I am not *more* than the law I am the vilest of all men."[73] The higher type revels in "self-glorification"; he "delights in being severe and hard with himself and respects all severity and hardness."[74] In being willing to abandon the notion of a higher, guiding law, the aristocratic type demonstrates a courageous willingness to set sail upon an "open sea" and "face any danger." The creed of the higher type of person is "live at war with your peers and yourselves! Be robbers and conquerors as long as you cannot be rulers and possessors, you seekers of knowledge! Soon the age will be past when you could be content to live hidden in forests like shy deer."[75]

The higher type of human being is therefore one who accepts an essential "order of rank" in the world, the primacy of violence over compassion and peace, the notion that values are invented rather than discovered, and the proposition that truly higher culture—whatever that ultimately is supposed to mean—depends fundamentally on conflict.[76] "Nothing has become more alien to us than that desideratum of former times, 'peace of soul', the *Christian* desideratum; there is nothing we envy less than the moralistic cow and the fat happiness of the good conscience. One has renounced the *great* life when one renounces war."[77] It is difficult to read a passage such as this and not think of Ernst Jünger's glorification of war or Walter Benjamin's critique of the Futurist notion that "war is beautiful."[78] If morality is understood as an aesthetic activity in the sense that it is an activity of free invention, and if the apotheosis of this activity is the waging of war, then one ought to take very seriously Benjamin's concern over the aestheticization of the political. For the view that Nietzsche articulates is one with dire consequences for the traditional ideals of compassion, respect, reciprocity, and justice, ideals that Nietzsche derides in their traditional form and seeks to "revalue" in accordance with his endeavor to "reestablish *order of rank*."

Nietzsche offers as historical exemplars of the aristocratic type figures such as Napoleon, "the most isolated and late-born man there has ever been . . . this synthesis of the *inhuman* and *superhuman*"; Caesar and Alcibiades, "those magical, incomprehensible, and unfathomable ones" who exhibited "a real mastery and subtlety in waging war" even against themselves; and Dostoevsky, in whom Nietzsche sees a great contemporary example of "the strong human being under unfavorable circumstances," specifically the circumstances of having been "ostracized by society" and hence having been "made sick."[79] Christian morality, "the morality of the herd," seeks to promote the interests of the lowly by articulating moral rules designed to insulate the weak from danger; it criminalizes the higher type as part of this effort. Traditional morality has a taming function; it seeks to neutralize the threat posed by "the most beautiful specimens of the 'blond beast.'" It does so in the name of "improving" humanity, but in reality "it *ruined* man, it weakened him."[80] Traditional values have so corrupted the higher type through this process of criminalization that Nietzsche found it necessary to open the preface to the *Genealogy* with the assertion that "we are unknown to ourselves, we men of knowledge." The "slave revolt in morality" that is the subject of the *Genealogy*, the overthrow of the aristocratic morality of the higher type of human in favor of a morality of *ressentiment* designed to promote the interests of the weak, has been so successful that "we are necessarily strangers to ourselves, we do not comprehend ourselves, we *have* to misunderstand ourselves."[81] The task of a revaluation of all values is thus first of all the task of acquiring self-knowledge.

But it is not a task for everyone; indeed, it is a task for very few. This is worth bearing in mind when we feel excitement welling up within us as we read Nietzsche. Is this ultimately an open sea upon which we should want to embark along with Nietzsche? Are we even being invited on the journey? Nietzsche is addressing only those rare geniuses among us who truly qualify as masters, those powerful and resourceful few who are capable of seeing through the mendacity of traditional morality and recognizing the true meaning of freedom. Christianity had characterized freedom in its ideal form as an *imitatio dei*. Kant had conceived it as the capacity to legislate and subject oneself to a moral law founded on the principle of respect for all rational beings. Nietzsche dismisses both these formulations as features of a decadent morality. In their place he offers a vision of morality in terms of "relations of supremacy" and an analysis of freedom of the will as "essentially the affect of superiority in relation to him who must obey."[82] Given the primacy of the affects in Nietzsche's account of human action, this is the only possible meaning of freedom: the lack of external constraint that Hobbes had seen to be the essence of free will. Free will in its traditional formulation is simply "the foulest of all theologians' artifices," a pretext for holding individuals responsible and justifying the imposition of punishment.[83] Stripped of this artifice, free will promises to become what it authentically is: the feeling of joy attendant upon conquest of another.

Accordingly, morality, if there is still such a thing, has nothing to do with mutual obligations but instead signifies "commanding and obeying, on the basis . . . of a social structure composed of many 'souls'."[84] Both the "master" and "slave" moralities detailed by Nietzsche in *On the Genealogy of Morals* conform to this formula, the essential difference being that the master morality does so in a life-affirming manner and the slave morality in a life-denying one. If one conceives of ethics along the lines proposed by Heidegger in the "Letter on 'Humanism,'" the specifically moral sense of the master and slave moralities becomes clear: Heidegger thinks of ethics in terms of dwelling (*ethos*), so that ethics is a matter of finding one's proper place in the cosmic scheme.[85] One's ethics is one's way of being at home in the world. For the Nietzschean slave, being at home in the world involves a "plebeian antagonism to everything privileged and aristocratic."[86] The slaves seek "to take their revenge and play the master" through a calculus of strength in numbers. This, too, is will to power, but in this case "the will to nothingness has become master over the will to life!"[87] Christianity, democracy, socialism—*any* style of moral evaluation that seeks to equalize people and mitigate violence is subject to this limitation. All such evaluations are "made from a definite perspective: that of the preservation of the individual, a community, a race, a state, a church, a faith, a culture." As such, they are "the expression of the diseased condition in man" and would ideally be superseded by "an *experimental morality*: to give oneself a goal."[88]

Justice as Decisionism

Experimental morality, indeed: one that is attainable by the very few, and at the cost of the many. And more than that, a morality according to which there are no principles or guidelines for setting a goal for oneself, inasmuch as the type of person who is entitled to legislate goals is not subject to any law or condition other than the legislator's own aesthetic vision. "In place of 'moral values', purely naturalistic values. Naturalization of morality," which brings with it "a theory of the forms of domination" and "a perspective theory of affects."[89] The departure from a state of nature recommended by Hesiod, Socrates, Rawls, and the rest presupposes the primacy of thought over affect and the superiority of a way of life governed by law (*nomos*) rather than by drives (*physis*). The "naturalization of morality" reverses these relationships. It celebrates "the rich ambiguity of existence," and in doing so it has won the praise of countless postmodern thinkers. But what these thinkers have failed to grasp is the tremendous price we pay for denying the priority of *nomos* over *physis*. For it returns us to precisely the state of nature that we sought to exit through our appeal to the notion of justice. It leaves Orestes to be pursued by the Eumenides, who in their blind rage are incapable of subjecting their affective responses to any kind of rational consideration. In the name of preserving putatively genuine distinctions between "types" of individual, Nietzsche refuses to acknowledge any principles or expectations that would be equally binding on everyone. He opts instead for a perspectivism that leaves room for as many conceptions of value as there are interpreters. But this perspectivism is no relativism. Perspectives correspond to types of human being: each has its proper place in an order of rank, and those perspectives that most actively (as opposed to "reactively") achieve dominance count in the Nietzschean calculus as the "most life-affirming" perspectives.

Nietzsche's perspectivism thus demands a rejection of the notion of justice in the abstract. "To speak of just or unjust *in itself* is quite senseless; *in itself*, of course, no injury, assault, exploitation, destruction can be 'unjust', since life operates *essentially*, that is in its basic functions, through injury, assault, exploitation, destruction and simply cannot be thought of at all without this character."[90] Thus not only is there no "in itself" of justice, but certain perspectives will more adequately express justice than others. Those perspectives that proclaim justice to consist in the promotion of democratic ideals are life-denying, whereas those that affirm the prerogative of the higher individual to enslave and subjugate others in the service of a self-posited goal are life-affirming. Vincent Descombes has very effectively drawn out the implications of Nietzsche's ideal of an "affirmation of life": "The philosophy that chooses to understand autonomy as irresponsibility ends up in an apology of tyranny."[91]

There is no accepting Nietzsche's critique of reason and his perspectivist celebration of "the rich ambiguity of existence" without accepting this consequence. As appealing and seemingly liberating as vague gestures toward ambiguity and multiplicity may be—and contemporary postmodern writing, particularly on ethics and politics, is rife with them—the fact remains that the ambiguity and multiplicity we are talking about here are characteristics of a world whose violent unpredictability must be reckoned and addressed through concrete action. The "constant deferrals" and "infinite postponements" of postmodern discourse seek to reveal the impossibility of reducing knowledge and action to determinate formulas. The postmodernist is thus faced with a dilemma: paralysis through the impossibility of ever making a binding judgment, or action through the assertion of a perspective that in some inexplicable sense affirms life—inexplicable in that it stands above the law and expresses a singular exception and therefore cannot be grounded in rational principles that transcend the specifics of the case at hand.

Postmodern thought has not yet come to terms with this dilemma. Thus it has not yet confronted the decisionistic implications of the model of action that it has inherited from Nietzsche. Nietzsche, in rejecting general principles for the legitimation of action and opting instead for aesthetic justifications to be offered by unique actors in unique circumstances, implicitly endorses what Carl Schmitt would later characterize as the politics of the exception. Schmitt developed this politics under the influence of Hobbes, Bonald, de Maistre, and Donoso Cortés, who proceeded from a conception of human beings as fundamentally violent and evil and argued for the need for sovereign rulers who could make sovereign decisions without having to subject their decisions to endless debate.[92] In matters of political sovereignty, the emergency situation must be treated as the normal situation, since sovereign states are in a constant state of war with one another (Hobbes: not necessarily actually warring, but always predisposed to war), and every subject in a political state is potentially an enemy of the state. The exigencies of action in an essentially hostile and threatening environment make "the exception . . . more important . . . than the rule . . . because the seriousness of an insight goes deeper than the clear generalizations inferred from what ordinarily repeats itself."[93] "The seriousness of an insight" here corresponds to the Nietzschean artist's insight that "one thing is needful": in both cases, the sovereign actor (the political sovereign for Schmitt, the aristocratic individual for Nietzsche) cannot be bound by rules or general principles since no such generalizations can adequately capture the exigency of the present, unique moment and the unique style with which the sovereign individual responds to that exigency.

Karl Löwith recognized that in appealing to the sovereign exception and the moment of decision, Schmitt "leaves human affairs in their corrupt condition" rather than seeking to transcend that state of corruption toward a peaceful human community characterized by solidarity rather than enmity.[94] Indeed, Schmitt categorically rejects the possibility of anything like a cosmopolitan human community since for him the political is defined essentially by the distinction between friend and enemy.[95] To eliminate enmity between human beings once and for all would be to dissolve the political. Such a possibility simply does not make sense to Schmitt because he adheres to the wisdom of Thrasymachus and Hobbes that hostility is the defining characteristic of political relations. In Schmitt, as in Nietzsche, there is an essential connection between the ineradicable nature of hostility and the politics of the exception: if our "natural" state, which is a state of violence and enmity, is absolutely insuperable, then there is no general standpoint that could serve as the basis for the *legitimation* of decisions and courses of action. There is simply the exigency of action in the present moment, an exigency that consists in the imperative to achieve dominance over our perceived enemy. The politics of the exception involves "the kind of decision that is not bound by anything beyond itself," and to this extent the politics of the exception exhibits "a nihilistic ground. . . . Schmitt's decision in favor of the political is not a decision in favor of a definite and authoritative subject area, as it is in religious, metaphysical, moral, or spiritual decisions generally; rather, it is nothing other than a *decision in favor of decisiveness*—regardless of what this is actually in favor of."[96]

This logic holds *mutatis mutandis* for the Nietzschean artist-aristocrat. This type is faced with the task of choosing in exigent circumstances; but, in virtue of standing above every law, the higher type's choice is not determined in advance by any "definite and authoritative subject area" or vision of the "right" kind of life. There is no essential content, no inherent meaning, no rationally articulable principles on the basis of which life is to be understood and choices made. The aristocrat simply chooses in accordance with a unique style that remains inexplicable precisely on account of its uniqueness. Here the link between decisionism and violence is as indissoluble as in Schmitt's concept of the political. When the Nietzschean aristocrat chooses, "the readiness for death and for killing, rather than any kind of ordering of social life as is proper to the primordial meaning of the *polis*, becomes the 'highest court of appeal.' "[97] It is in this sense that the Nietzschean perspective, like Schmitt's, is irretrievably nihilistic.

And violent. One can imagine Nietzsche and Schmitt reacting in equally dismissive terms to Kant's project of enlightenment and his ideal of perpetual peace. To reject reason as the highest court of appeal is at the same time to reject the possibility of progress through time toward a rationally intelligible goal. Divested of any sense of eschatology, time becomes an endless unfolding with no inner logic and no essential direction. Contingency reigns. Here a bridge to the postmodern ethos can be

seen in the work of Michel Foucault. In his exploration of the significance of contingency for the exercise of human freedom, Foucault follows Baudelaire in seeing modernity as "the ephemeral, the fleeting, the
contingent." Foucault notes that for Baudelaire "the modern moment . . .
consists in recapturing something eternal that is not beyond the present
instant, nor behind it, but within it."[98] Foucault appropriates key aspects
of Baudelaire's characterization of the artist and applies them to the task
of exercising freedom: here, as in Nietzsche, the actor is first of all an artist. The artist "transfigures the world. His transfiguration does not entail
an annulling of reality, but a difficult interplay between the truth of what
is real and the exercise of freedom. . . . Baudelairian modernity is an exercise in which extreme attention to what is real is confronted with the
practice of a liberty that simultaneously respects this reality and violates
it." The Baudelairian artist is a "dandy who makes of his body, his behavior, his feelings and passions, his very existence, a work of art. Modern
man, for Baudelaire, is not the man who goes off to discover himself, his
secrets and his hidden truth; he is the man who tries to invent himself."[99]

Free of any eschatological illusions, the modern individual faces no
ground other than that of sovereign decision. If the eternal is completely
subordinated to the present instant, then it is very difficult if not impossible to understand how what is being subordinated could qualify as
eternal. Thus the task of the artist threatens to become one of inventing
"eternity," and there can be as many different interpretations of eternal
truth as there are artists. In Foucault's analysis, this task and prerogative
of invention falls to all of us, not simply to the putatively higher type of
individual. Every free being faces the task of self-invention. This task,
however, does not proceed ex nihilo but instead follows from specific
historical antecedents. We "are historically determined, to a certain extent, by the Enlightenment"; indeed, it is from the Enlightenment that
we have inherited a conception of ourselves as beings capable of individual self-determination. But instead of understanding this capacity in
terms of Kantian autonomy and subjection to the moral law, our task
is to "transform the [Kantian] critique . . . into a practical critique that
takes the form of a possible transgression." Rather than "search for formal structures with universal value," we are to "treat the instances of discourse that articulate what we think, say, and do as so many historical
events," in an effort to "give new impetus, as far and wide as possible, to

the undefined work of freedom."[100] The work of freedom is essentially "transgressive" in the sense that it must always seek to resist and transcend anything posited as established principle or authority.

Kant had stated something close to this in his own essay on enlightenment when he wrote that no group of human beings should ever "be entitled to commit itself by oath to a certain inalterable set of doctrines." Any such commitment "would be a crime against human nature" inasmuch as it would preclude all further rational evaluation of the doctrines in question and would thereby prevent the process of enlightenment.[101] But Kant believed in the possibility of progress and subscribed to an ideal of perpetual peace. For him the *procursus* of reason had as its regulative ideal the vision of cosmopolitan peace that Kant develops in his political writings. Foucault opts instead for the Nietzschean vision of life, giving primacy to "forms of power relation" and asking, entirely rhetorically, how "the growth of capabilities [can] be disconnected from the intensification of power relations."[102]

Foucault's emphasis on the fundamentally transgressive character of freedom shows that he considers any such disconnection to be impossible in principle. He embraces Nietzsche's genealogical method, which seeks to uncover "the singularity of events outside of any monotonous finality."[103] The singularity of events signifies the irreducibility of individual moments, an irreducibility for which Nietzsche sought to account by arguing that comparisons between seemingly similar events give us nothing more than arbitrary metaphors that fail to capture the things themselves. If moments have a "singular" character, if every event is exceptional and every decision sovereign in Schmitt's sense, then the self must forever remain an "aesthetic illusion," and action can never be guided by "any monotonous finality" such as that seen in Christian eschatology or the Enlightenment ideal of inevitable progress.[104] Genealogical method, which is the "method" that led Nietzsche to his just-so story about the conquest of the higher type of human by the slave revolt in morality, "rejects the metahistorical deployment of ideal significations and indefinite teleologies." This debunking of metaphysical impulses opens the way to recognizing that "the history of reason . . . was born . . . from chance" and that "the concept of liberty is an 'invention of the ruling classes' and not fundamental to man's nature or at the root of his attachment to being and truth. What is found at the historical beginning of things is not the inviolable identity of their origin; it is the dissension of other things. It is disparity."[105] The difference between the bourgeois "concept of liberty" and freedom as Nietzsche and Foucault envision it is that liberty signifies the agency of a metaphysical subject whose actions are regulated by autonomous reason, while freedom signifies the dispersion of conduct into individual moments of resistance against opposing forces. These are moments that have no essential connection with one another, indeed no connection apart from the fact that certain groupings of affects and moments of resistance can be associated with certain bodies. But if we trace Nietzsche's and Foucault's commitments all the way to their logical conclusion—if anything like logical conclusions are permitted here—then even the body is not something metaphysically or even physically stable but instead is itself "a movable host of metaphors, metonymies, and anthropomorphisms."[106]

By focusing on disparity and multiplicity in this way, Foucault, like Nietzsche, gives primacy to error over truth, to what Descartes called obscurity and confusion over clarity and distinctness. In place of an approach that searches for coherent truths, Foucault sees in Nietzsche's genealogical method an approach that promises "to identify the accidents [and] minute deviations" at the core of things. The proper aim of a critical examination of history "is to discover that . . . the exteriority of accidents" rather than "truth or being [lies] at the root of what we know and what we are." And again, precisely as in Nietzsche and Schmitt, the core or origin of what we know and what we are is a violent one. The whole purpose of genealogy is "to reestablish the various systems of subjection" and "the hazardous play of dominations" at work in history. Where traditional philosophy seeks origins in the sense of *Ursprung*, a unified and gathering source of things, genealogy seeks origins in the sense of *Herkunft*, the "unstable assemblage of faults, fissures, and heterogeneous layers that threaten the fragile inheritor from within or underneath." Origin in the sense of *Herkunft* is fundamentally tied to the body, that "locus of a disassociated self . . . and a volume in perpetual disintegration." In focusing on the body rather than the mind or soul as the seat of human experience, genealogical method concerns itself with precisely those dangers, threats to well-being, and perpetual conflicts that lead Nietzsche and Schmitt to subscribe to a politics of the exception. But as a descriptive endeavor, genealogy as Foucault sees it seeks not to justify certain sorts of sovereign decisions but rather to examine the ways in which competing discourses or interpretations serve the power interests of respective parties to conflict. "If interpretation is the violent or surreptitious appropriation of a system of rules, which in itself has no essential meaning, in order to impose a direction, to bend it to a new will, to force its participation in a different game, and to subject it to secondary rules, then the development of humanity is a series of interpretations. The role of genealogy is to record its history: the history of morals, ideals, and metaphysical concepts, the history of the concept of liberty and the ascetic life."[107]

To accept this characterization of interpretation is to reduce *all* interpretive activity to polemics in the literal sense of the word. Discourse is nothing more or less than warfare. Interpretation is "violent or surreptitious appropriation," there is "no essential meaning," and the only purpose to interpretation that Foucault will acknowledge is that of subjection. But what about genealogy itself—is it, too, not a form of interpretation? Then how can it escape Foucault's verdict that discourse is violent appropriation? Foucault proceeds as if Nietzsche's distinction between *Ursprung* and *Herkunft* were a sort of get-out-of-jail-free card that exempted genealogical discourse from the charge of polemical appropriation, as if there were at least one form of discourse that can achieve something like objectivity in its observations about history and the human condition. Foucault, like Nietzsche, confronts neither the dilemma of postmodernism that I have sketched above nor the self-contradictory nature of a philosophical discourse that implicitly claims absolute truth in the exact moment that it reduces all truth to perspective. "The historical sense can evade metaphysics and become a privileged instrument of genealogy if it refuses the certainty of absolutes." Only by refusing such absolutes can genealogy be capable of "liberating divergence and marginal elements."[108] This desire to "liberate divergence" can be traced back to the critique of Hegel's totalizing vision of the dialectic. Vincent Descombes notes that Kojève gave great impetus to this critique by offering an interpretation of Hegel that emphasized the role of violence in historical progress and thereby gave rise to "a *terrorist conception of history*" according to which all action must be understood as "opposition to an adversary." Kojève conceived of human freedom in terms of the same Baudelairian dandyism to which Foucault would appeal a generation later.[109] Where freedom is understood in terms of pure negation or pure self-invention, the only consequence can be that interpretation is sovereign self-assertion, with "no essential meaning" other than to dominate the other by subsuming it into oneself.

Postmodern thinkers like Foucault, who follow Nietzsche in giving priority to the polemical particularity of *Herkunft* over the metaphysical totality of *Ursprung*, seek to avoid a key mistake made by the tradition, namely, the mistake of seeking to derive concrete reality from metaphysical absolutes that appear to have the status of fictions in comparison with the concrete realities that they are supposed to ground and explain. Kant's transcendental turn makes it impossible, or at least highly implausible, to suppose that we can establish knowledge of God, the soul, and human freedom. The critique of reason reduces all these to postulates of pure practical reason: concepts to which recourse is necessary in order to think through the human condition, but concepts only and not entities whose actuality could be known. But for all that, Kant does not find it necessary to abandon the notion of human subjectivity altogether. Instead he radicalizes the Cartesian notion of the *res cogitans* so that it becomes the form that coherent experience takes. No longer a metaphysically stable being that transcends and unifies individual moments of experience, the self (unity of apperception) is a transcendental condition for the possibility of coherent experience generally and for scientific knowledge in particular. Kant recognizes that we are able to subject our own experience to critique, even though we can no longer purport to know our own nature as minds or souls as Descartes had sought to do. This possibility of critical self-examination lies at the core of Kant's vision of ethical existence. And even if Kant erred by remaining too wedded to a Christian conception of existence according to which the mind transcends our embodied condition, we have much to learn from his conception of reason and its role in ethics. For even if reason can never become completely transparent to itself—and there are a variety of reasons for thinking that it cannot, some of them ideological and others psychoanalytic—thinkers from Aristotle to Freud have been right to propose that *nous* has something like an eternal character and can therefore function as the regulative standard for the progress of our attempts to clarify our thinking and justify our actions.[110]

A colossal and tragic error of postmodern thinkers is to suppose that because the *metaphysical* notion of the subject has no basis in reality, and because reason does not consist of a timeless network of transparent truths, reason and agency are therefore nothing more than aesthetic illusions—illusions that either deny life or function as instruments of domination (or both). In either case, the task of "theory" becomes to debunk the notions of agency and reason, with an eye toward liberating us from pernicious forms of illusion. But to what end? To the end of directing our attention toward life-affirming illusions? Toward some underlying truth, even though postmodernism has done its best to dismantle or at least cast serious suspicion on the very notion of truth? Again, in either case, the postmodern thinker stands in need of some regulative notion on the basis of which truth can be distinguished from error (even though the Nietzschean program purports to opt for error rather than truth!) or on the basis of which "life-affirming" illusions can be distinguished from "life-denying" ones. But postmodernism faces a dilemma that it cannot resolve: either quietistic staring at the movable host of metaphors, or choices that remain utterly decisionistic in virtue of their lack of anything like a ground for the comparison and evaluation of different events, situations, and possibilities.

Against this background, the increasing preoccupation of postmodern thinkers with the treatment of animals raises important and troubling questions: What motivates the current interest in animals on the part of postmodern thinkers? To what extent, and on what grounds, are these thinkers concerned with the problem of violence toward animals? Is this concern ultimately motivated by a concern for animals or by a concern for humans? Do postmodern thinkers make any specific moral claims on behalf of animals? Or on behalf of humans, for that matter? If they do, is the proclamation of such moral claims consistent with the terms of postmodernism? And if these thinkers do not advance any specific moral claims, does this omission on the part of postmodern thinkers tell us something crucial about the *limits* of postmodernism?

CHAPTER TWO

Postmodernism and Justice

JUSTICE AND THE POSTMODERN DILEMMA

If justice is about anything, it is about affirming a sense of responsibility to others. Hesiod saw this when he asserted that the law of justice requires us to practice nonharm toward others who are reciprocally required to practice nonharm toward us. Epicurus was committed to a similar conception of justice and added the characterization, embraced in our own time by John Rawls, that justice is at least implicitly a contractual arrangement between parties who can recognize both what they get and what they give when they enter into mutual agreements of nonharm. In its classical formulation, justice is a bond of noninterference whose parties are committed to principles of equality, reciprocity, and mutual respect. These principles give rise to an acknowledgment that we *owe* something to others who in key respects are like us. To a great extent, the function of the law is to enforce justice obligations when they fail to be respected by individuals or groups that are acting on the basis of selfish interests rather than a sense of responsibility to others. Even thinkers such as Schopenhauer, who seek to modify our understanding of justice so as to dispense with the classical equality and reciprocity requirements (thereby making it possible to acknowledge duties of "eternal justice" toward *all* sentient beings), see justice in terms of fairness and responsibility to others.

In the face of this traditional conception of justice as a sense of responsibility that can be articulated in terms of clear principles, postmodern thinkers argue that we must take "the aporia of judgment" as our point of departure in rethinking the notion of justice. Our failure to do so, we are warned, leads us to reduce ethical judgment to "the mechanical unfolding of a positivist calculation."[1] The logic driving this admonition is that genuine ethical judgment can occur only in active, concrete circumstances in which we feel the exigency of the particular situation and the claim that the concrete other exerts on us. To reduce ethics and justice to rules or principles is to transform the urgency of choice into the mechanical application of something like a recursive procedure, a procedure that could not possibly address and do justice to the minute particularities and singularity of each individual situation that the rule or procedure was designed to govern. Responsibility can never be reduced to "positivist" principles or procedures. It must be taken up anew with each concrete, irreducible situation that confronts us. "Responsibility, then, becomes a permanent capacity for reopening any and all of the complacencies into which we have fallen, every form of good conscience. It means a deeply self-subversive willingness . . . to lay ourselves open to the sufferings of others, to the pressures and exigencies of the world."[2]

Say the question is whether it is permissible to eat animal flesh. Do we have duties of justice toward animals not to kill and eat them? Thinkers on both sides of the divide between the tradition and postmodernism have addressed this question, and with different results—not different in that one group says "yes" and the other "no" (or vice versa), but different in the sense that adherents of the traditional conception of justice tend to be willing to arrive at a yes-or-no answer to the question, whereas postmodern thinkers maintain that the nature of responsibility precludes any such categorical answer. Traditionalists say that eating animals is permissible, that eating some animals but not others is permissible, that eating animals raised in certain circumstances but not others is permissible, or that eating animals is categorically impermissible. For example, Peter Singer, who is widely thought of in our popular consciousness as an advocate of vegetarianism, states that he "can respect conscientious people who take care to eat only meat that comes from" animals who are raised free-range and "have a pleasant existence in a social group suited to their behavioral needs, and are then killed quickly and without pain."[3] There is a set of principles at work here: sentient beings have interests; we are obliged to refrain from interfering with sentient beings in ways that prevent the realization of their interests, unless we can justify such interference; most nonhuman animals lack the cognitive sophistication to have a sense of the future, hence being deprived of the future cannot properly be considered a harm to those animals. From these principles, Singer concludes that we are not harming the animals we typically eat in our culture when we convert them into sources of food by killing them. The only constraint here is that we raise the animals in comfortable circumstances and kill them painlessly.

Here is another, more straightforward example of a traditional answer to the question—traditional not in the sense that the conclusion is typical of traditional thinkers, but rather in the sense that the manner of argumentation involves clear principles. Gary Francione states that treating animals as property is categorically impermissible because it is an infringement on the freedom and dignity of animals. If a being is sentient in the sense that "there is an 'I' who has subjective experiences," then we must consider that being's interests equally with the interests of all other sentient beings. Singer purports to do this but concludes that certain forms of meat eating are perfectly acceptable—that he "can respect" people who eat humanely raised animals. Francione radicalizes—or, more accurately, applies consistently—the principle of equal consideration of interests and concludes that we must forswear the consumption of meat on the grounds that killing animals, even if we do so painlessly, unjustifiably prevents animals from pursuing their interest in continued existence.[4] Francione acknowledges that morality is not like mathematics; it does not always give us clear, certain answers in all situations.[5] Thus, for example, if your house is on fire, your child and your dog are trapped inside the house, and you can save only one of them, you might well choose to save your child rather than your dog.[6] But this is very different than saying that your child is more deserving of being saved than your dog, that your child has more of a right to be saved. The reason for this is that if we acknowledge that all sentient beings have equal inherent worth, then we cannot morally privilege one sort of sentient being over another without violating the principle of equal consideration of interests. Even though he considers many animals to be "subjects-of-a-life" with inherent moral worth, Tom Regan ultimately privileges the moral status of human beings when he argues that it would be justifiable to sacrifice the lives of a million dogs to save one human life.[7] His reasoning is similar to Singer's: animals such as dogs lack the cognitive apparatus to enable them to contemplate the distant future, hence such animals have less to lose by dying than humans do. For Francione, on the other hand, to be sentient is *eo ipso* to have an interest in continued existence, quite apart from whether the being in question can conceptualize the future and contemplate it as such.[8]

Now consider the postmodern answer to the question concerning the permissibility of eating animal flesh. The short answer is that there is no one answer, for any such answer would reduce ethics to "the mechanical unfolding of a positivist calculation." Postmodernists argue that thinkers such as Singer, Regan, and Francione reduce ethics to this sort of calculation, thereby deactivating our face-to-face confrontation with the other, disburdening us of the concrete exigency of choice and responsibility, and permitting us to retreat into the self-congratulatory repose of "good conscience." To take on the burden of genuine responsibility is to renew actively in each particular set of circumstances our awareness of the suffering and vulnerability of the other, and to acknowledge the essential obscurity of the task of responsibility. To seek to reduce this task to a set of rules or principles would be to abdicate the task altogether. Therefore you find postmodern thinkers deploring human violence against animals in very general terms, but you will not find postmodern thinkers proclaiming categorically that, for example, we should forswear the consumption of meat—or, for that matter, that meat eating is categorically permissible, or that raising animals in so-called free-range circumstances makes killing them for human consumption permissible, and so on.[9]

Exemplary in this regard are two statements made by Derrida. The first consists of four fateful words that ultimately tell us everything about the nature and limitations of an approach to ethics that would dispense altogether with principles: "Later here signifies never."[10] Derrida's immediate concern in making this statement is to explain why he cannot at this point in his lecture offer a complete examination of Heidegger's discussion of animals, a discussion in which Heidegger offers the judgment that "the animal is world-poor" in comparison with human beings, who are "world-forming" beings.[11] Derrida is not simply saying that he may never find the time to return to a consideration of Heidegger's text; he is saying that, given the structure of "deferral" that characterizes all forms of signification, any consideration of this or any other text unavoidably has the structure of infinite postponement. There just is no such thing as determining the meaning of a text. The same holds for our attempts to arrive at clear principles for ethical conduct. Thus Derrida expresses a "desire to escape the [traditional] alternative of a projection that appropriates and an interruption that excludes."[12] To posit a rule or a principle, such as that eating meat is categorically wrong, not only constitutes an evasion of genuine responsibility, it does violence to forms of otherness that cannot really be subsumed under a rule without being forced to sacrifice their otherness. Ethical principles are "projections that appropriate" in the sense that they force what is different or "other" into a totalizing vision of sameness.

Increasingly, postmodern thinkers have focused attention on the endeavor to show how traditional representations of normality, while seemingly innocuous and well intended, actually do violence to those who do not fit into the representation; much work has been done to show the oppressive character of traditional representations of what constitutes "normal" (i.e., white, male, western European) humanity, "normal" (i.e., heterosexual) sexuality, "normal" (i.e., strictly male or strictly female) gender identity, and "normal" physical ability (for which there is an emerging discipline to which some refer as "crip studies"). In each case, the concern is to bring to light injustices that have been and are being done to those who have been branded in one way or another as "abnormal," injustices perpetrated through the endeavor to "normalize" the other and/or criminalize and oppress the other for *being* other. The attention that postmodern thinkers have increasingly been devoting to the problem of violence toward nonhuman animals constitutes an expansion of this concern for the oppressed other. And while this concern is sincere and laudable, it proceeds from a logic—the logic of the trace—that ultimately cannot make coherent sense of the idea of responsibility.

This brings me to the second of Derrida's statements. In an interview, he says that the killing of animals by humans is "monstrosity," but he goes on to say that he is "not recalling this in order to start a support group for vegetarianism, ecologism, or for the societies for the protection of animals."[13] This is the critical upshot of the principle that "later here signifies never"—that the infinite postponement of meaning brings with it the infinite postponement of *action*. Even some postmodern thinkers have recognized the inner tension between the imperative to acknowledge the other, infinite though the task of that acknowledgment may be, and the imperative to act. Stephen White offers an analysis of responsibility according to which we must recognize two dimensions, one of them "modern" and the other "postmodern." The modern dimension is the responsibility to act, and the postmodern dimension is the responsibility to otherness. The responsibility to otherness is infinite in the sense that it cannot be reduced to a closed set of rules or principles. The responsibility to act is oriented on knowledge, justification, and action and fails (so White claims) to acknowledge human finitude.[14] Presumably the responsibility to act fails to acknowledge finitude to the extent that it seeks to reduce questions of ethics to simple, timeless rules; we thereby render ourselves blind to the uniqueness of concrete others and our own inability to grasp the infinite multiplicity of concrete situations and exigencies.

But as much as he would like to affirm the importance of the responsibility to otherness, White concludes his exploration of postmodern responsibility with the acknowledgment that in ethical and political matters we must ultimately privilege the sense of responsibility to act.[15] The implicit reasoning behind this privileging of the traditional conception of responsibility is that, as Descartes stated when he proposed his provisional morality, action "permits no delay."[16] By their nature, ethical questions demand that we choose courses of action that we can justify; without this requirement of rational justification or legitimation, action becomes arbitrary and we are left with the polemical conception of action so cheerfully offered up to us by Nietzsche. To give priority to, or to confer exclusivity on, the sense of responsibility to otherness in ethical questions is to promote, if only against one's own intention, a model of responsibility that seems unable to achieve exactly what its proponents would like to achieve: an active taking of responsibility in the face of the other.

But perhaps one will say that this simply cannot be true, that postmodern thinkers show a persistent concern for concrete exigencies of action and are anything but quietistic in their reception of contemporary ethical and political problems. Richard Bernstein notes, for example, that a concern for ethics and politics underlies everything that Derrida wrote. It is not the case simply "that in addition to his reflections on speech, writing, metaphysics, logocentrism, etc., [Derrida] *also* 'has' an ethics and a politics. . . . Derrida's ethical-political horizon is 'a point of departure' for virtually everything he has written." Thus Bernstein considers "grotesque and even perverse" the suggestion that Derrida's thought has quietistic implications.[17] Bernstein shares with us an important insight:

that postmodern thinkers such as Derrida are far from indifferent in their personal attitudes about many of the concrete injustices that we witness every day. But the question is whether the philosophical terms of postmodernism, specifically the terms of deconstruction, can serve as the foundation for ethics in the sense of a program of action that we can explain and justify to others. My contention is that *the terms of deconstruction are so fundamentally at odds with any such conception of ethics that the expression* "postmodern ethics" is an oxymoron. Once we have examined the logic of the trace and drawn out its implications for grasping and responding to suffering and injustice, it will become clear that one cannot consistently adhere both to deconstructive commitments and to a coherent conception of ethics.

It is one thing to say that "the entire project of deconstruction . . . is driven by an ethical desire to enact the ethical relation," where the ethical relation is understood as "the aspiration to a nonviolent relation to the other."[18] But it is quite another to say that deconstruction can fulfill this aspiration. Derrida for his part believes that ethics imposes on us "an unconditional commandment, so to speak, not to wait" in the face of our responsibility to the other. He maintains that "if *différance* was simply infinite postponement, it would be nothing. . . . *Différance* . . . is not opposed to ethics and politics, but is their condition." In situating ethics and politics against the background of irreducible *différance*, Derrida equates the tasks of ethics with the predicament of Kierkegaard's Abraham. Ethics now becomes a situation in which "the general categories have to be overcome, when I am alone facing a decision. A decision is something terrible."[19]

By assimilating ethics *tout court* to the predicament of Kierkegaard's Abraham, Derrida tells us something fateful about his entire conception of the ethical. Kierkegaard saw Abraham's predicament as one that raised him momentarily *above* the ethical: Abraham's singular relation to God puts him in a position in which he must respond to a commandment (namely, to kill Isaac) that cannot be made intelligible to others; the very nature of the imperative in this singular instance is so uniquely reflective of Abraham's inward relation to God that it cannot be communicated in the realm of the universal, which is to say the ethical.[20] By characterizing ethics in terms that Kierkegaard reserved for the sphere of faith, Derrida transforms the very idea of ethics such that it now pertains to *nothing but* incommunicable singularities. To redefine ethics in this manner is to distort it, to do something every bit as "grotesque and even perverse" as the suggestion that Derrida the man was unconcerned with ethical problems. For while we are sometimes faced with singular exigencies in the face of which we may ultimately consider ourselves duty-bound to make choices that we cannot explain to others and that others may actually find criminal (from the standpoint of the ethical, Abraham is a murderer, not the father of faith), this is not the basic character of many, perhaps most of the ethical exigencies we face on a regular basis. To treat every ethical decision as if it were comparable to Abraham's burden is to deny the possibility of the kind of "engaged fallibilistic pluralism" that Bernstein advocates; it is, if only unwittingly (and rather ironically, given that its proponents seek to undermine the subject-based model of experience) to adhere to a model according to which each individual must decide for herself or himself, without the benefit of dialogue and the counsel of others.[21] If every ethical decision is understood on the model of Kierkegaard's Abraham, then there simply is no possibility of dialogue or counsel with another mortal being. There is simply what Locke refers to in the *Second Treatise of Government* as "the appeal to Heaven," that desperate, final court of appeal to which we must have recourse when reason is unable to avert a state of war with our fellow human beings.[22]

Once again we are led to a specifically polemical conception of choice and action. That the proponents of this view intend nothing of the kind is entirely beside the point. It may well be the case that a "philosophy of alterity" seeks to avert "violence toward otherness," but in the absence of anything like criteria for distinguishing and evaluating the various singularities that confront us, we are powerless to act in anything other than an arbitrary manner.[23] What makes this approach fundamentally polemical is the fact that its proponents take as their point of departure perceived acts of violence and oppression against "others" that demand our concern and our action; thus the problem is set up in advance as one of having to counter oppressive power dynamics. If, as Foucault argues, all forms of discourse are essentially polemical, then deconstruction, too, as a form of discourse has a polemical function. It is not simply neutral, it does not simply describe; it "intervenes."[24] But does not intervention presuppose a prior perceiving and grasping of situations, problems, and exigencies? Exactly what kind of perceiving and grasping are at work here?

THE (IL)LOGIC OF THE TRACE

Consider Lyotard's characterization of the shift from the modern to the postmodern: where the modern "produces a discourse of legitimation" that requires recourse "to some grand narrative," the postmodern is characterized by "incredulity toward metanarratives."[25] Any story that purports to secure a timeless truth about human existence, reality, and the relationship between the two counts as a metanarrative in this sense. Such stories presuppose that we can transcend our finitude toward some "transcendental signified," some anchor point in reality outside the temporally conditioned character of our experience, and that our ability to reach such an absolute, godlike vantage point can disclose for us essential, timeless truths and goals for our striving. Stories such as Plato's account of the forms, Anselm's or Aquinas's proofs of God's existence, Descartes's dream of clear and distinct insight and the prospect of using physics to render human beings "the masters and possessors of nature," and Hegel's vision of the realization of absolute spirit all qualify as metanarratives in the sense intended by Lyotard. All have become objects of "incredulity." A particular object of incredulity is Kant's program for perpetual peace, which Lyotard cites as exemplary of "the Enlightenment narrative" and which Derrida suggests is based on Kant's unfulfillable wish to eliminate or at least limit the phenomenon of "undecidability" that constitutes "the law of the text in general."[26]

But if undecidability constitutes "the law of the text in general," and if, as Derrida is famous for having proclaimed, "there is nothing outside the text," then is not the claim that undecidability constitutes a law just another "metanarrative"?[27] Derrida tried at one point to avoid this implication by suggesting that his statement "there is nothing outside the text" has been widely misunderstood, and by explaining that "when I say that there is nothing outside the text, I mean that there is nothing outside context, everything is determined."[28] But this does not show the question to be misguided or unfounded; in fact, it clarifies the stakes of the question by showing that Derrida's claim about a "law of the text" is really a claim that *all* "contexts and singularities" are characterized by essential "effects of confusion [*brouillage*], simulacrum, parasiticity [*parasitage*], equivocality, [and] undecidability."[29] This concern is not a matter of foolish consistency; I am not *simply* trying to show that Derrida has contradicted himself. I am trying to show that, if only against his own intention, Derrida develops his entire program of deconstruction, his notions of *différance*, the trace, the supplement, the mark, and play, implicitly on the basis of an ability to "see" an essential truth about reality, an ability that he denies to proponents of the tradition with whose conclusions he differs. There is a sense of seeing or grasping at work here: language functions in a strictly law-governed way, we can perceive this lawlike character, and that character is best expressed through terms such as "undecidability." And yet the very notion of undecidability, as Derrida develops it, is utterly incompatible with this characterization of seeing or grasping.

The notion of undecidability is central to Derrida's project of deconstruction, a project inspired by Heidegger's critique of the notion of presence and his endeavor to rethink our understanding of being in terms of temporality. A useful point of entry into the critique of the metaphysics of presence is Heidegger's rethinking of the notions of being and essence. Traditionally essences were thought of as stable, permanent, unchanging presences. In the medieval Christian thought that would guide Descartes, the essence of a thing is that one property that is so definitive of the thing that the property could not be removed from the thing without the thing ceasing to be the thing that it is. In the case of bodies, Descartes states that their essence is to be extended, which is to say that they have volume or take up space. All other properties of bodies, such as color or scent, are "accidents" in the sense that they can change without altering the essential nature of bodies. The only property of bodies that can never change or be removed from them is that they are "extended, flexible, and changeable."[30] By the same token, thinking is the essence of the mind; activities such as sensation and imagination are simply modes or forms of thinking.[31] This conception of essences is part of a traditional endeavor to understand the real in terms of substance, something permanent or "present" in which variable qualities inhere. Stability and permanence are given priority over alteration and obscurity. In antiquity this orientation on presence led to the notions of *hypokeimenon* and *substantia*, and in modernity it led to the Cartesian-Kantian duality of subject and object.

That all these conceptions of substance misunderstand being and thinghood is clear, Heidegger suggests, from the fact that they all conceive of being and essence in static, present terms rather than in active terms. The original and fundamental meaning of essence, Heidegger proposes, signifies the ways in which things "come to presence" from out of a mysterious, unperceived origin. Heidegger is able to make his point more simply in German than it can be expressed in English because the German term for essence (*Wesen*) can function either as a noun or as a verb. In the case of *wesen*, the verb has a linguistic priority over the noun inasmuch as the noun *Wesen* was formed from the verb.[32] Heidegger argues that our understanding of *Wesen* as a noun is the product of a reduction from an active sense of *wesen* as gathering, holding sway, developing, and decaying.[33] The active sense of *wesen* brings together everything that is involved in the primordial conflict and struggle out of which things *emerge into* presence and "separate into opposites." Heidegger presents a contrast between the traditional understanding of being, essence, and thinghood as presence (in Greek *parousia*; in German *Anwesenheit*) and what he considers to be an earlier, more primordial Greek understanding of being as emergence of things from out of hiddenness. Corresponding to this distinction is that between *idea* and *physis*, the distinction between the way things appear to perception or ideation and the way in which they actually come to appearance. In the traditional understanding of being as idea, "the essent [*das Wesende*] becomes an object, either to be beheld . . . or to be acted upon. . . . The original world-making power, *physis*, degenerates into a prototype to be copied and imitated." The understanding of being as *idea*, which long ago became "the sole and decisive interpretation of being," elides altogether the activity of *physis* as "emerging power."[34] What is truly "essential" to being is that it has the character not of sheer presence but rather of "bringing forth into unconcealment."[35]

This is not to say that things cannot appear as present or be construed in terms of their sheer presence. It is to say that this is not all that things are, and in particular that it is not "primordially" what things are. Heidegger's protracted reflections on modern technology and the question "What is a thing?" lead him to two interrelated conclusions: that the Western philosophical tradition's turn away from *physis* (emergence from out of concealedness) and toward the understanding of things in terms of presence is born of an interest in mastering reality, and that our orientation on presence has led to a fundamental distortion of the real and a tragic misunderstanding of human existence. Our traditional orientation on presence and the calculative-instrumental mode of thinking that drives it have put us at odds with nature. Our focus on present entities rather than on their original mode of unconcealment, the forgottenness or oblivion of being, has led to "the homelessness of contemporary human beings." To reestablish a sense of nearness to being, a sense of dwelling in its proximity, we must take a "step back that lets thinking enter into a questioning that experiences."[36] This step back into a thinking that questions is a step back from calculative rationality, which represents beings in terms of their knowability and manipulability. It is a step back into what Heidegger calls reflective or meditative thinking, a thinking attended by a sense of piety and openness to the fundamental mystery of *physis*. There is a certain modesty to this kind of thinking, in that it recognizes the essential limits of human understanding and willing and gives a fundamental priority to questioning. "For questioning is the piety of thinking."[37] The contemplative thinking that steps back from action and valuing and is capable of dwelling in essential questions is "more rigorous than conceptual thinking" to the extent that it is "recollection of being and nothing else."[38]

From the standpoint of calculation and concrete action, this thinking that purports to be more rigorous than conceptual thinking appears empty and ineffectual. But it is this outward appearance that Heidegger and Derrida after him are at pains to show to be a tragic misunderstanding. Calculative-instrumental thinking, which Heidegger believes has predominated in our culture at least since Plato, has done violence to the truth of being by representing the world, human existence, and the relationship between the two in reified and hence distorted terms. Indeed, on Heidegger's and Derrida's view, *all* representing is *mis*representing to the extent that it gives priority to *idea* or *eidos* over *physis*, to clarity and determinacy over obscurity and mystery. The "step back" urged by Heidegger in response to this reduction of being is a step back from metaphysics itself.

Derrida embraces this aspiration, radically calling into question precisely the sorts of "oppositions" that from the standpoint of the *idea* appear to be stable and self-grounding. In the *Introduction to Metaphysics*, Heidegger appeals to the Heraclitean notion of a primordial conflict at the core of being, which "first caused the realm of being to separate into opposites; it first gave rise to position and order and rank."[39] This notion implicitly plays a central role in Derrida's critique of metaphysics, in which "ethical-ontological distinctions . . . set up value-oppositions clustered around an ideal and undefinable limit, [and] moreover *subordinate* these values to each other (normal/abnormal, standard/parasite, fulfilled/void, serious/nonserious, literal/nonliteral, briefly: positive/negative and ideal/non-ideal)." Metaphysical thinking, thinking in terms of presence rather than in terms of *physis* (the ways in which things emerge of their own accord, beyond human knowing and willing), is "the enterprise of returning 'strategically', ideally, to an origin or to a 'priority' held to be simple, intact, normal, pure, standard, self-identical, in order *then* to think in terms of derivation, complication, deterioration, accident, etc."[40] Certain recurring pairs of conceptual oppositions, such as that between "normal" and "abnormal" or between "good" and "evil," are regarded by metaphysical thinking as "presences," as properties etched into the permanent structure of reality, rather than being oppositions that arise at the level of ideation, posterior to the violent interplay of forces that makes the appearance of anything like clarity and stability possible in the first place. As Nietzsche recognized, notions such as those of order and rank are not metaphysically fixed but instead are products of this violent interplay of forces. Once we recognize the primordial significance of the notion of "essence," we should see that there is nothing "essential" about good and evil, normal and abnormal; they are designations that appear to be fixed but in fact are continually in flux, subject to the vicissitudes of time and perspective.

Or, more precisely, on Derrida's view, subject to the play of *différance*. Every binary, hierarchical opposition "is an effect of *différance*, as is the effect of language that impels language to represent itself as expressive re-presentation, a translation on the outside of what was constituted inside." Binary oppositions are no more stable than the language we use to express them. From the standpoint of calculative rationality, we have a desire that language have a capacity for transparent representation, an ability to depict things exactly as they are outside of language. But if there is nothing outside the text, then there is no access to things the way they are, independent of language. "The representation of language as 'expression' is . . . what Kant would have called a transcendental illusion. . . . Doubtless Western metaphysics constitutes a powerful systematization of this illusion."[41] For Kant, one fateful form of transcendental illusion is Plato's mistaken supposition that "ideas are archetypes of the things themselves, and not, in the manner of the categories, merely keys to possible experience."[42] Another is Descartes's supposition that the "I think" confirmed the existence of a metaphysically real self or subject of experience rather than simply being the form that unified experience takes. For Kant, any metaphysical position that declares categories of thought to pertain to entities that are "transcendentally real" as opposed to merely "transcendentally ideal" succumbs to transcendental illusion.[43]

Derrida radicalizes Kant's insight into transcendental illusion by applying it to language itself. Kant recognized the transcendental conditions at the foundation of human experience, which is to say that he recognized the constitutive role played by human thought in the experience of the world as a *knowable* spatio-temporal *topos*; and he implicitly treated language as a medium in which we could attain the apodeictic certainty promised by the turn to transcendental idealism.[44] In stating that "the principles [of transcendental idealism] transcend the limits of experience," Kant was expressing the belief that the language of metaphysics, properly conceived, could provide a characterization of a truth that ultimately resides outside of language. Thus Kant subscribed to a conception of language that, on Derrida's account, is susceptible to precisely the kind of transcendental illusion with which Kant charged Plato and Descartes. Language cannot achieve the kind of expression that Plato, Descartes, or even Kant intended since "expression" in this sense would amount to something contradictory: employing language to capture a truth that resides outside of language and fundamentally beyond the grasp of human finitude.

> Expressivity is in fact always already surpassed, whether one wishes it or not, whether one knows it or not. In the extent to which what is called "meaning" (to be "expressed") is already, and thoroughly, constituted by a tissue of differences, in the extent to which there is already a text, a network of textual referrals to other texts . . . the presumed interiority of meaning is already worked upon by its own exteriority. It is always already carried outside itself. It always already differs (from itself) before any act of expression. . . . Only on this condition can it "signify."[45]

Where Kant believed in the transparent expressivity of the language of transcendental idealism, Derrida maintains that language by its very nature always involves a surplus or supplement and hence that acts of signification can never capture enduring, determinate truths.

Derrida's thesis—and it is a thesis—that acts of signification have this specific character follows from his critique of Saussure's thesis about the functioning of linguistic signs. Saussure had proposed a conception of the sign as a complex of a concept (the "signified") and a sound-image (the "signifier"), and he had argued that linguistic signs are arbitrary in the sense that the signifier has a conventional (as opposed to a "natural") relationship to the signified. Saussure had conceived of "structure" as "a system in the collective mind of the speakers," which is to say that he considered it possible that certain linguistic "differences" can become fixed into "oppositions."[46] Derrida calls this concept of structure into question by observing that it presupposes a "center," and by radically challenging the very idea of such a center. "The function of this center was not only to orient, balance, and organize the structure . . . but above all to make sure that the organizing principle of the structure would limit what we might call the *play* of the structure." In order for the system to possess systematicity, it must have an underlying organizing principle, one that relates the various "oppositions" to one another in a coherent, which is to say repeatable and recognizable, manner. But, Derrida suggests, this "center" has always been conceived as lying outside the structure that it governs. "It has always been thought that the center, which is by definition unique, constituted that very thing within a structure which while governing the structure, escapes structurality." Saussurean structure thus has a "contradictorily coherent" character in locating the center both within and outside the system of signs.[47] To this extent, Saussure succumbs to the transcendental illusion of traditional metaphysics; he implicitly subscribes to the doctrine of a "transcendental signified," a metaphysically stable presence outside the play of differences.[48]

Thus Saussure does not think the sign radically enough. To do so would be to acknowledge the fundamental role of "play" in signification, and to recognize that "the history of metaphysics" is the history of a variety of "metaphors and metonymies" for the concept of structure.[49] This assertion recalls Nietzsche's characterization of the body as "a moveable host of metaphors, metonymys, and anthropomorphisms."[50] Just as the body is not anything metaphysically stable but instead is a complex interrelationship of forces (it is "a social structure composed of many souls"), so the concept of structure is not anything stable but is instead, like *all* concepts, the representation of something fluid and dynamic as if it were fixed and knowable.[51] The moment we recognized the illusory character of metaphysical claims about a stable center, the moment we began "thinking that there was no center, that the center could not be thought in the form of a present-being . . . was the moment when language invaded the universal problematic, the moment when . . . everything became discourse." No longer are we to conceive of language as the representation of a reality outside of language. Signifiers do not refer to things in the world but instead refer to (which is to say that they get their meaning from) other signifiers within a system of signification.[52] If every signified is itself a signifier, and if signifiers refer only to other signifiers, then there is nothing outside the (con)text. "The absence of the transcendental signified extends the domain and the play of signification infinitely."[53]

To extend the play of signification infinitely is to take a decisive step beyond structuralism and its metaphysical commitments. It is to affirm a certain "anarchism" that privileges the openness and "infinite transformations" of textuality over any prospect of enduring insight or judgment.[54] "The meaning of meaning" is henceforth "infinite implication, the indefinite referral of signifier to signifier."[55] Signifiers have no essential meaning, no enduring connection with anything—not even with themselves. Each signifier comes to presence through the play of *différance*, as the fleeting product of its relationship to other signifiers that do not manifest themselves but instead function as the absent, nonrepresentable background from which a given signifier emerges. "The sign which replaces the center . . . is added, occurs as a surplus, a supplement. The movement of signification adds something, which results in the fact that there is always more, but this addition is a floating one because it comes to perform a vicarious function, to supplement a lack on the part of the signified."[56] Every sign, every act of signification, brings with it, if only implicitly and imperceptibly, a totality of signification dispersed through time. But the absence of a center, the lack of an anchor or foundation in something stable outside the system of signification, means that meaning itself is "undecidable": meaning is nothing stable or determinate but instead is an endless succession of determinations of meaning. The totality of signification is itself not totalizable, not reducible to a determinate structure or essence in the traditional sense of (*par*)*ousia* or presence.

Here the endless play of *différance* "exceeds the order of truth," but not in the sense of "a mysterious being" such as Hölderlin's fugitive gods since this would amount to the positing of an essential, ideationally determinate order (a truth) behind the play of differences. The endless play of *différance*, the *procursus* of fleeting intimations of presence that bear the traces of infinite absences, "is thus no longer simply a concept, but rather the possibility of conceptuality, of a conceptual process and a system in general." As in Nietzsche, concepts here are falsifications in that they represent as fixed and determinate what is in reality an endless movement of differences. To represent anything—the world, experience, selfhood, language, text, context—as something to which conceptual determination can ultimately do justice is to overlook the fact that "*différance* is the non-full, non-simple, structured and differentiating origin of differences," and that "differences . . . are effects which do not find their cause in a subject or a substance."[57]

The critique of notions such as subjectivity and substance is one that reduces them from metaphysical causes to mere "effects" of the play of *différance*. This is one point on which Derrida is as influenced by Hume as Nietzsche had been. The tradition conceived of substance and subjectivity as origins or stable grounds. One need only recall the traditional definitions of substance as *hypokeimenon* or *substantia* or Descartes's conception of the self as *res cogitans*. Hume lodged a strong critique of both these notions, arguing that "everything that exists is particular" and drawing the conclusion that the traditional notions of substance and human selfhood as entities with stable existence through time were mere fictions.[58] The self and the objects we experience are simply "bundles of perceptions" rather than beings in which qualities inhere. By the same token, we never experience causal efficacy in the world but instead simply have perceptions of sequences of events or "effects."

Derrida's appeal to the notions of *différance* and the trace exhibits the influence of Hume's antimetaphysical viewpoint. There is no looking "behind" the play of phenomena to find underlying identities or origins. There is only "the limitlessness of play," which is fundamentally prior to all binary oppositions.[59] Our experience and our capacity to render things intelligible can never exceed this limitless play, nor can we locate any meanings that would be autonomous and stable within the play of *différance*. Any entity or relationship whose existence we postulate, any signifier, any element of meaning whatsoever, lacks autonomy: "No element can function as a sign without referring to another element which itself is not simply present. This interweaving results in each 'element'—phoneme or grapheme—being constituted on the basis of the trace within it of the other elements in the chain or the system."[60] It is in this sense that each signifier brings with it an entire, unlimited array of other signifiers that manifest themselves imperceptibly in the mode of absence. The trace, the relation to absent elements of a fleeting presence that is itself never quite a presence, is the fundamental characteristic of all meaning. The trace, this gesture toward absence and undecidability, is "the disappearance of origin . . . a nonorigin" that renders the quest for enduring certainty impossible. To think the trace, "this unnameable movement of *difference-itself*," we must go "beyond the *epistémè*."[61] We must take what Heidegger called a step back from calculative-instrumental rationality to an open, contemplative standpoint that seeks not to master reality but instead to bear witness to it in its endless play of *différance*.

Here again we must ask what kind of seeing or grasping is at work. If all we see is an endless parade of differences, then is meaning altogether indeterminate? Derrida suggests that this conclusion is mistaken, that there is a crucial difference between the indeterminacy of meaning and the undecidability of meaning.[62] To say that all meaning is utterly indeterminate would be to overlook the fact that meaning gets "determined" all the time; Aristotle, for example, determined the meaning of reality as substance (*hypokeimenon*), and Hegel determined the meaning of history when he sketched a program for the realization of absolute spirit. By the same token, the Cartesian-Kantian conception of subjectivity revolves around the notion of intention. Ascribing primacy to the trace or *différance* does not entail that "the category of intention will . . . disappear; it will have its place, but from this place it will no longer be able to govern the entire scene and the entire system of utterances."[63] But if the notion of intention, like all traditional notions of a ground or a center, no longer governs, then what is its exact significance? Is its role subordinate to the role played by other sorts of significations? Does Derrida have some sort of new hierarchy of signification in mind, one that will replace old hierarchies that the "intervention" of deconstruction deems pernicious? In the absence of any kind of authoritative ground or center for discourse, how can deconstruction intervene in a way that avoids the dilemma between quietism and decisionism?

DECONSTRUCTION AND ETHICS

Derrida seeks to affirm two things that appear to be utterly incompatible with one another: the undecidability of meaning and the imperative to intervene in the face of violence and oppression. There is a problem here because, in denying the idea of an authoritative center, Derrida appears to deprive himself of anything like criteria or standards for the determination of meanings to which we ought to ascribe preference or priority over other meanings. This limitation of postmodern approaches that give an absolute priority to forms of discursivity and thereby lodge a total critique of reason—reason is understood here along the same lines as intention, as a phenomenon that does not disappear but which is no longer deemed capable of "governing" the system of signification—is often overlooked because thinkers such as Foucault and Derrida devoted so much energy to decrying concrete injustices in the world.[64] Derrida pursued deconstruction with the aim of countering violence, both metaphysical and political. With regard to metaphysical violence, Derrida argues that "in a classical philosophical opposition we are not dealing with the peaceful coexistence of a *vis-à-vis*, but rather with a violent hierarchy. One of the two terms governs the other (axiologically, logically, etc.), or has the upper hand. To deconstruct the opposition, first of all, is to overturn the hierarchy at a given moment. To overlook this phase of overturning is to forget the conflictual and subordinating structure of opposition."[65] Binary oppositions such as that between reason and unreason, substance and accident, necessary and contingent, universal and particular—all such oppositions assert violent hierarchies in the sense that they purport to reduce the irreducible play of traces to determinate categories and thereby do violence to the phenomena.

But the full range of postmodern writing suggests that there is a deeper and more troubling sense in which the assertion of such hierarchies does violence, and that is in the political realm. Derrida's remarks on the institution of apartheid make it clear that he sees an inner connection between metaphysical and political violence. Derrida states without qualification that racism constitutes "compulsive terror" and that apartheid is institutionalized "evil" and "violence" on a par with the evil of concentration camps.[66] Thus Derrida occupies a standpoint from which he considers judgments about evil and injustice to be entirely legitimate. Derrida offered his remarks on apartheid in an essay written for the catalog of the exhibition Art contre/against Apartheid, which opened in 1983. In this essay, Derrida takes a very clear stand: apartheid is evil. In the face of this evil, the paintings in the exhibition perform a special function: rather than commemorating or representing efforts to end apartheid, the paintings "gaze and call out in silence. And their silence is just."[67] Here Derrida again follows Heidegger, who had first charac-terized the call of individual conscience as silent and had later explored the possibility of a nontotalizing, nonrepresenting, fundamentally open response to the silent call of being. Derrida's appeal to silence also re-flects the influence of Kierkegaard, who had argued for the possibility of a singular relation to God that places the individual above the "universal" realm of ethics and language, that realm within which one can make one-self and one's choices intelligible to other mortals.[68] Derrida for his part focuses on our relationship to the concrete other, in this case the other who has historically been oppressed by apartheid. The question what we are to do about apartheid "awaits an answer only from the future that re-mains inconceivable." What we can say with certainty is that the answer will involve "attempting to speak the other's language without renounc-ing [our] own." This attempt depends on a renunciation of calculative-instrumental thinking, for "what resists analysis calls for another mode of thinking."[69]

This turn away from representational thinking and toward another mode of thinking not only recalls Heidegger's appeal to questioning and contemplative thought; it calls radically into question the entire enter-prise of "juridico-political or juridico-theological discourse, which any more serves only to maintain good conscience." These traditional dis-courses intone piously about human rights but stand idly by while active violence is perpetrated on black Africans. For Derrida this is sufficient to confirm that "the customary discourse on man, humanism and hu-man rights . . . has encountered its effective and as yet unthought limit, the limit of the whole system in which it acquires meaning." This cus-tomary discourse not only does nothing for the oppressed other, it fa-cilitates institutionalized violence against the other. Thus we must aban-don the traditional juridical concept of law altogether and look forward to "the future of another law and another force lying beyond the totality of the present."[70]

In calling for a step back from calculation toward contemplation, Hei-degger had sought to restore a sense of the importance of reverence in the face of being. On several occasions he used the word "releasement" [Gelas-senheit], a term he borrowed from Meister Eckhart, for whom the key to union with God was a suspension of the will and an openness to letting God enter one's soul. Heidegger characterized contemplative thinking as "gentle releasement" that "lets beings be" rather than forcefully projecting conceptual determinacy on them in an effort to gain mastery over them.[71] Heidegger characterized this openness as one that is "responsive" to being.[72] Rather than seeking to accomplish anything concrete, contemplative thinking takes the form of an "awaiting" that "leaves representing entirely alone" and "releases itself into openness."[73]

For Derrida as for Heidegger, this open, awaiting, responsive posture is more primordial than decision and action to the extent that it is their necessary presupposition. Decision and action take place on the plane of calculative-instrumental rationality, with its positive conception of law. But to the extent that action and politics take place "within the general space of . . . the 'trace'," there can be "no decision, and thus no responsibility, without the experience of some undecidability. If you don't experience some undecidability, then the decision would simply be . . . the application of a rule, the consequence of a premiss, and there would be no problem, there would be no decision."[74] Genuine decisions are like Abraham's decision to take Isaac to Mount Moriah; otherwise we are simply talking about the mechanistic pulling of a lever.

But does this call into question the very idea of a rule or a principle, or does it instead problematize *the act of making a decision*? There is a crucial distinction here that Derrida never confronts. Let us say that the principle or rule in question is that we ought never to use animal products for the satisfaction of our desires, and say that I sincerely embrace this principle. Does this mean that every time I choose in accordance with the principle, I am doing something purely mechanical and unthinking, and that my choices are attended by good conscience? Hardly. What it means, particularly in the living contemporary context of a society in which vegans are widely dismissed as kooks and frequently derided for being self-righteous water-walkers, is that one faces constant anguish—not simply in the sense that one suffers the mockery of one's fellow human beings, nor simply in the sense that one is acutely aware that the vast majority of other people are *not* following the principle and hence are perpetuating a regime of animal exploitation that arguably exceeds the magnitude of any human holocaust, but more importantly in the sense that uses of animals are so intimately woven into our cultural practices that pure veganism is a practical impossibility.[75] Thus with every "decision" to eschew the consumption of animal products, one feels not good conscience but a gnawing horror born of a recognition of what is being done to billions of animals *right now* and of the seeming futility of one's decision.

But, Derrida tells us, there can be no decision "without the experience of some undecidability." The experience of undecidability is not simply the recognition that phenomena present themselves to us as what Descartes called "obscure and confused," and that therefore it is difficult to make a decision; the experience of undecidability as Derrida has defined it is the experience of the play of *différance*, the recognition that anything that appears to be stable and present is in fact constituted by an irreducible infinitude of traces. The experience of undecidability is the experience of the founded and hence fictive character of all supposed presences. It is, among other things, a recognition of the impossibility of ethical principles. Traditional thinkers such as Kant would have us believe that responsibility takes the form of freely chosen commitments made by a detached knower with the benefit of rational guidance. This rational guidance takes as its point of departure the idea of the "good will," the will of a rational being possessing inherent moral worth and hence deserving respect; from this principle of the good will there follow certain imperatives for action, such as that I ought to help others in need or that I ought never to tell a lie. The Kantian view treats morality as an endeavor to know principles and act in accordance with them.

In reality, however, responsibility "is heterogeneous to knowledge." Once we are on the plane on which we can speak of knowledge, we have left behind the trace of *différance* and have represented everything in terms of the *idea*. What Kant failed to recognize is that reason and intention cannot function as the "center" for ethical discourse. "The distinction between good and evil doesn't depend on knowledge." And yet Derrida has no trouble proclaiming categorically that apartheid is evil. He suggests that this statement is not justified by knowledge but instead is grounded in the "terrible experience" of a "tragic situation" like that experienced by Abraham.[76] One cannot have such an experience, Derrida suggests, if one is thinking in terms of ethical principles. To experience the anguish of ethical decision in a way that does not reduce ethics to empty rules is to open oneself to a certain kind of experience of the other. Thinkers such as Kant had conceived of our ethical relation to the other as one of equality and reciprocity.[77] But in fact our relation to the other lacks this ideal symmetry. We find ourselves claimed by the other in such a way that we must respond. The essence of this bond with the other cannot be represented as an objective presence but instead is prior to representation and all positive law; indeed, Derrida suggests that it is in our original response to the other that responsibility and freedom are first awakened.[78]

Responsibility as Derrida conceives it is not a matter of holding others responsible. It is a matter of making oneself responsible *to* the other, without any concern for what one might receive in return. "Moral standards should not count or keep account."[79] Instead we must think of responsibility in terms of the vulnerability of the other and the various forms of violence perpetrated on the other. We cannot do so through an appeal to rules or principles because in doing so we would extinguish "the absolute singularity of the other."[80] The mediation of ideas, the appeal to rational considerations, places us at a distance from the concrete call of the other, much in the way in which Benjamin thought that the technological reproducibility of art works destroyed their "aura," the singular claim that they once exercised on us. In order that the other exercise a specifically ethical influence on us, in order that we feel the claim of "an unconditional commandment, so to speak, not to wait" in the face of concrete ethical and political exigencies, we must relate to the other in an unmediated fashion, not as an abstract other in general but rather as "the real thing," as a living, concrete, unique singularity.[81]

Derrida sees in this relation to the singularity of the other the key to a rethinking of ethics. Rather than emphasizing identity or similarity, ethics must be founded on alterity. Ethics must be founded on "*respect* for the other *as what it is*: other."[82] Kant, too, had made respect central to his understanding of ethics, but he thought respect in juridico-positivistic terms that leave no room for the other *as* other. Obligations to others flow from their being rational beings *like us*. Thus the crucial dimension of "letting be," which Derrida borrows from Heidegger, is missing from Kant's view of ethics. But without this dimension of letting be, specifically "the letting be of respect and of the ethical commandment addressing itself to freedom . . . violence would reign to such a degree that it would no longer even be able to appear and be named."[83] This is why "the 1973 verdict [that apartheid is a] 'crime against humanity' . . . continues to have no effect" other than to soothe the consciences of those who celebrate it as a victory over the historical oppression of black Africans.[84] Any such verdict, as the juridico-positivistic assertion of human rights, is ineffectual, at least if it is not born of an authentic recognition of the singular other. Such recognition can never originate in the postulation of a principle such as that of the Kantian good will. What is needed is the complete abandonment of the search for any such center or origin. "The best liberation from violence is a certain putting into question, which makes the search for an *archía* tremble."[85] The search for a unified *arche*, or ground, is predicated on the forgetting of irreducible alterity, the singularity of others and their concrete circumstances. This forgetting facilitates violence under the mantel of humanistic principles. Even though violence can never be eliminated altogether, "*let*[ting] . . . others [be] in their truth . . . [comes] as close as possible to nonviolence."[86] Nonviolence as a regulative ideal therefore depends on the incessant recognition of singular others in concrete circumstances, prior to knowledge, reason, principle, and law. For our relation to the other is "prior to any organized *socius*, to any determined 'government', to any 'law'." Indeed, this relation to the singular other may even be "the very essence of law."[87]

In light of Heidegger's rethinking of the notion of essence, this suggests that law emerges at the level of the *idea* from out of a primordial struggle among nonrepresentable elements. Rather than possessing any solid, unified foundation, law is the product of a violent interplay of forces. "Since the origin of authority, the foundation or ground, the position of the law can't by definition rest on anything but themselves, they are themselves a violence without ground. . . . They are neither legal nor illegal in their founding moment. They exceed the opposition between founded and unfounded."[88] Thus it is a mistake to view any authority, foundation, or law as absolute. Each has what Montaigne recognized to be a "mystical foundation," which is to say that each is in some important sense ultimately groundless.[89] This sense of groundlessness is to be thought together with Derrida's claim that "deconstruction find[s] its force, its movement [and] its motivation . . . in [an] always unsatisfied appeal, beyond the given determinations of what we call, in determined contexts, justice, the possibility of justice." Deconstruction "intervenes" not on the basis of established concepts or determinations of justice, but rather on the basis of the irreducible indeterminacy of *différance*, the claim exercised on us by the singular other, and the possibility of law first opened up by that claim. "Deconstruction is already engaged by the infinite demand of justice," a demand that is infinite in the sense that it is utterly irreducible to principles or clear insight. Justice here is not an abstract conception of justice, such as one that would demand telling the truth in every situation, helping others in need, etc. Rather, "this justice always addresses itself to singularity, to the singularity of the other, despite or even because it pretends to universality."[90]

Not Aporia of Judgment, but Incoherence of Deconstruction

But why and in what sense—or, more precisely, *how*—could an approach to justice that takes singular alterity as its point of departure pretend to *universality*? In his reflection on friendship, Derrida suggests that there are two dimensions of our relation to the other: one that "maintains the absolute singularity of the other" and one that "passes through the universality of the law."[91] These two dimensions correspond to what White characterizes as the sense of responsibility to otherness and the sense of responsibility to act. But where White ascribes a priority to the latter sense of responsibility in ethical and political matters, Derrida conspicuously refrains from doing so, emphasizing instead "the infinite demand of justice" and the essential aporia of judgment—which is to say that judgment can never ultimately be guided or legitimated by clear, universal principles.[92] Derrida takes the traditional conception of friendship as an indication of what happens when we endorse the traditional premium placed on the sense of responsibility to act. He notes that "the *great philosophical and canonical discourses* on friendship . . . will have linked friendship explicitly to virtue and to justice, to moral reason and to political reason." In doing so, these discourses have exercised a "domination" and a "double exclusion" through "the exclusion of friendship between women and . . . the exclusion of friendship between a man and a woman." The canonical discourses on friendship that purport to endorse a universal community united by mutual regard actually perform a systematic exclusion, one that "privileges the figure of the brother" and hence promotes a literal fraternity of man.[93]

This is the same logic that Derrida applies to the discourse of human rights and its implications for apartheid: claims to universality do violence to otherness by purporting to be inclusive while actually facilitating dominance and exclusion. What is needed in the case of friendship, as in the case of apartheid, is "the experience of mourning . . . the moment of loss" that reveals to us the violence done by appeals to generic principles. How, then, are we to understand the statement that even the justice that "always addresses itself to singularity" pretends to universality? Whatever "universality" means here, it is not based on reciprocity; for "the 'who' of friendship moves off into the distance beyond all [such] determinations."[94] Exactly what place, if any, is left for universality in a conception of ethics that privileges singularity is troublingly unclear. One commentator has suggested that the relationship between principles and the sense of obligation that arises out of our relation to the vulnerable, singular other is as follows: "The being-obliged does not depend on the principle. The principle is a distillation, after the fact, of the being obliged. We do not judge the singular in virtue of the principle, but we draft the principle after the fact by excavating the singularity and erecting a relatively hollow schema—or 'principle'—whose cash value is solely the singularities upon which it is drawn."[95] We are not detached subjects who establish abstract principles and only then encounter concrete others and apply principles in our relations with others. Rather, we first encounter concrete others, and on the basis of these encounters we generalize principles cut to the measure of our encounters with others and the sense of concrete obligation that these encounters make possible.

This formulation of the relationship between singularity and universal principles highlights the fundamental limitations and inherently self-contradictory character of a deconstructive approach to ethics. For it begs the question entirely how our original encounter with a violent interplay of forces (Nietzsche, Heidegger, Derrida) or a fluid set of traces (Derrida) gives rise to a peaceful embrace of a specific, vulnerable other. First there is the free play of *différance*, the irreducible abyss of traces, and then, without explanation, there appears the concrete, vulnerable, mortal "other." According to the logic of postmodernism, this other confronts us not as a presence but as a "moveable host of metaphors, metonymies, and anthropomorphisms" (Nietzsche), as just another set of elements in a set of irreducibly polemical discourses. And yet this other somehow presents itself *not* just as another set of elements or forces, but as the kind of being that is sentient, that is vulnerable, that has a world, that, in short, *is like us* and exercises a special sort of claim on us. For all their insistent proclamations of the primordiality of difference and undecidability, postmodern thinkers who express ethical concerns appeal more than anything else to a sense of *identity*. Stones are not mortal, not sentient, not vulnerable. We express no ethical concern for the fortunes of stones. We never treat them as oppressed others. We precisely *do* recognize the mortality and vulnerability of other human beings, even if we do not always respond in the appropriate manner. This is one meaning of Sartre's observation that we find ourselves claimed by the look of other human beings but are not comparably claimed by the in-itself.[96] Clearly the idea of humanity in general is an abstract generalization whose value is limited to the extent to which it can do justice to specific human beings in specific circumstances. But this is worlds apart from the proposition that principles are "relatively hollow schemata."

A reflection on Derrida's views regarding animals, which I will undertake shortly, shows that, if only against his own intention, Derrida bases his entire case against violence toward animals on a sense of identity between humans and animals: like human beings, nonhuman animals are sentient and hence vulnerable. (Identity here does not mean that human beings and nonhuman animals are exactly the same; it means that there is something, some property or set of capacities, that both possess and in virtue of which they are the same in some key respect—in this case, in the respect that they are mortal and hence merit moral concern.) Derrida takes Heidegger to task for classifying animals as "world-poor" in contrast with human beings, who are "world-forming" beings. But Derrida never ventures a word of criticism for Heidegger's having characterized the stone as "worldless." What Derrida and virtually all postmodern thinkers currently writing about the unacceptable violence we do to animals recognize is that animals, *like human beings*, are not simply "traces" or "marks" but are living beings who are different from inert objects such as stones. This is the answer to the question of what kind of seeing or grasping is going on here: we confront not an open sea of traces, but an environment populated in important part by concrete beings who are like us in their capacity to suffer, even though we will never be able to state with absolute, metaphysical precision what the nature of these various beings is nor how they are related to each other or to us. It is our relationship to these beings that confers on us our sense of ourselves and the world; but once we have had this sense of ourselves conferred upon us, we are capable of establishing and employing principles for our conduct. That principles, by their very nature, cannot prescribe their own definitive application is not a news flash. Subscribing, for example, to the principle that we should eschew animal products and animal exploitation altogether is not the end of the problem but only the beginning. There is no knowing a priori just how far we can or ought to go in seeking to live in accordance with this principle, particularly once we have had the insight that *any* action on our part causes the destruction of life, in many cases sentient life. There is no such thing as having definitively and conclusively acted in accordance with a principle.

Instead, principles such as the vegan principle function as regulative ideals for our conduct. But that does not reduce them to "hollow schemata." To see them as such is to make a fundamental mistake in our conception of singularity and its relationship to ethics. Recall Kierkegaard's treatment of the singular exception: it stands higher than the universal. It represents the possibility of a defining relation to God that confers a unique meaning on an individual's life, so unique and inward that the individual cannot communicate it to any other mortal. In invoking the singular exception, the individual undertakes a "teleological suspension of the ethical," a momentary *abandonment of the ethical* in the name of a divine imperative. But this is an abandonment predicated on a knowledge of the ethical sphere of existence: the singular individual recognizes exactly what is being superseded in the moment of exception, hence this individual experiences anguish. In part this anguish is a product of the individual's inability to speak; whereas the hero (the ideal actor in the ethical sphere) can and must speak, can and must communicate with other mortals, the individual claimed by faith and the singular exception rises above the sphere of language (the universal) and is utterly incapable of communicating the nature of the singular exception to others.[97]

Thus, for example, Agamemnon can communicate the nature of his choice to others, whereas Abraham cannot. Agamemnon's predicament is to resolve the apparent contradiction between two ethical duties, that to his daughter Iphigenia and that to his people. Agamemnon recognizes that the former duty must be subordinated to the latter. This all occurs within the sphere of the ethical: Agamemnon can sacrifice his daughter "without moving beyond the teleology of the ethical," and he can do so in a manner that he can make intelligible to others. In fact, "ethics demands that he speak," so that others do not misconstrue his action as unethical or even demonic. Abraham, on the other hand, is called on to do something that from the universal (ethical) standpoint counts as murder or madness. He must sacrifice Isaac, and there is no language available to Abraham that would enable him to communicate this singular exception to others. Abraham is in the predicament that Locke had in mind in invoking the "appeal to heaven": he is cut off from others and any possibility of reasoning or communicating with them about the nature of his decision.[98]

Kierkegaard presented this account of the singular individual as part of a critique of the passionless "present age" and its avid embrace of a Hegelian system.[99] Postmodern thinkers such as Derrida derive inspiration from Kierkegaard's image of Abraham in their own endeavor to counter the totalizing aspirations of a Hegelian system in which identity takes precedence over difference and reason purports to be able to generate foundational principles for conduct. But in doing so, they make a fundamental mistake: they take as canonical for ethics a situation that Kierkegaard defined as exceptional. The singular exception is not simply a situation in which one faces a divine decree that is incommunicable to others. It is, crucially, a situation that places one *at odds* with the rest of humanity. Not only is it a situation in which no principle is being followed, it is a situation for which no principle, not even a "hollow schema," can be articulated. Here ethics, if we can still call it that—and Kierkegaard gives us reason to believe that we cannot—is an infinite array of absolutely unique choices.[100] In making a choice, we can learn nothing from any other choice we have made or might make, since each situation is absolutely incommensurable with all others. Moreover, in making a choice in this specific sense, we place ourselves at a fundamental distance from the concrete others who are the object of postmodern ethical concern. The singular exception demands distance from others precisely where postmodernism would demand proximity as a precondition for a genuine ethical claim. For if there is any proximity or immediacy in choice as Kierkegaard conceives it on the model of Abraham, it takes the form of an immediate relation to God rather than to any mortal being—even if the outward object of choice is another person, say a Regine Olsen.

In this respect Kierkegaard's notion of the singular exception is ill suited to a postmodern rethinking of ethics, an ethics that is concerned to recast the notion of obligation on the basis of the "true world" having become a fable. The deconstructive approach to ethics seeks to model itself on the piety of a Kierkegaardian relationship to God, but it fails to come to terms with the irreducible contradiction between deconstructing the traditional notion of an *arche*, or center (God), and the appeal to Kierkegaardian faith as the foundation of our relation to others. Either there is a center, a "transcendent signified," or our sense of ethics must be based on our concrete encounters with others and the claim that their mortality exercises on us.

Having flatly rejected the former possibility, postmodernism is left with the latter. But there remains the problem posed by the appeal to the trace: how do we distinguish between beings toward whom we have ethical obligations and those toward which we do not? By treating all experience and insight as products of discourse, postmodernism is left with nothing more than the observation that some discourses have asserted the reality of certain sorts of beings and certain sorts of obligations. The primacy of the trace means that there are no authoritative criteria for discriminating among discourses. Poststructuralist thought is committed to the proposition that "the linguistic coordination of action is based on fictions," and the best it can offer by way of ethical conduct is the "concerted deployment of new fictions against whatever fictions are socially in force."[101] This approach to ethics is essentially aesthetic and polemical—aesthetic in the sense that we reduce ethical judgment to a choice among fictions, and polemical in the exact sense in which Nietzsche and Foucault treat ethics as a confrontation between competing discourses. But the evident passion that Derrida brings to his denunciation of apartheid—and, as we shall see shortly, his denunciation of violence toward animals—shows that he is not entirely consistent in treating "human beings" and "animals" as mere traces or effects of *différance*. Indeed, he implicitly treats his own discourses about humans and animals as true and the Enlightenment talk of rights as a fictive cover for exploitation. To this extent, Derrida is caught in a fatal contradiction between two viewpoints: one that exhibits what Habermas calls "the false pretense of eliminating the genre distinction between philosophy and literature," and one that sees the world in the rather traditional terms of different sorts of beings, some of which merit our moral concern because they are like us in respects that are morally relevant.[102]

Even Richard Bernstein, who offers an energetic and insightful defense of many of Derrida's ideas, concludes that Derrida's approach to ethics and justice suffers from this tragic limitation. In expressing ethical concern for the other, thinkers such as Derrida, Lyotard, and Foucault "are led back to the fragile, but persistent 'ideal' of dialogical communicative rationality—an ideal which is more often betrayed than honored."[103] In recognizing the claim that others exercise on us, we recognize—at least in the case of rational others, namely, humans—the imperative to bridge the gap of alterity through appeals to communication, through efforts to attain mutual understanding. Even though these efforts are rarely if ever successful, and even though the underlying ideal of communicative rationality is often "betrayed," the proposition that violence against others is pernicious presupposes both a recognition of the wrongness of violence and a willingness to promote mutual respect and acceptance. Either we follow the polemical terms of Nietzsche's "deconstruction" of the discourse of reason and seek to promote "life-affirming" (which is to say power-promoting) discourses, or we accept Zeus's law of justice and the regulative role of reason in our efforts to respect that law. The deconstructive approach to ethics would like to have it both ways: it would emasculate reason and law while preserving exactly that sense of responsibility that becomes meaningless when rendered autonomous from reason.

Even if reason is not the absolute origin of our sense of responsibility to sentient others, "a *practical* commitment to the avenging *energeia* of communicative reason is the basis—perhaps the only honest basis—for hope."[104] It is fair to say that the moral claim that the other exercises on us is not a claim that we first experience rationally; rather, we feel the claim of the other at what Heidegger would call a prethematic, prerational level.[105] Werner Marx developed this Heideggerian insight into a nonmetaphysical ethical principle according to which moral obligations issue directly from our experience of the mortality that we share with others.[106] The importance of Bernstein's insight into the limitations of deconstructive approaches to ethics is that he recognizes the importance of the endeavor to employ reason and language to communicate, test, and justify our moral judgments. In the face of Derrida's approach to ethics, we are "left with the question: *how can we 'warrant' (in any sense of the term) the ethical-political 'positions' we take?* This is *the* question that Derrida never satisfactorily answers. What is worse . . . he seems to call into question the very possibility of 'warranting' ethico-political positions."[107]

The proponent of a postmodern approach to ethics will respond that the very idea of "warranting" ethical and political decisions is a ruse, a cover for the deployment of discourses of power that seek to extinguish alterity. Derrida himself came very close to saying this when he asserted that "our most and best accredited concept of 'liberty' . . . is indissoluble from [the] concept of sovereignty."[108] Derrida conceives of sovereignty as the ungrounded assertion of power; it is on this basis that he concludes that there are today nothing but "rogue states" in the world.[109] To posit an indissoluble link between liberty and sovereignty is to accept Nietzsche's polemical conception of freedom—the idea that freedom is "essentially the affect of superiority in relation to him who must obey."[110] There is no "warranting" or justifying the distinction between legitimate and illegitimate exercises of power, other than the perspectivist appeal to one's own interest in enhancing the conditions of one's own existence—which is to say, enhancing one's own dominance over others. Apart from the proclamation that violence is bad, postmodern approaches to ethics are virtually indistinguishable from the approaches of Nietzsche and Carl Schmitt, who conceive of discourse in strictly polemical terms and who privilege the singular exception. But approaches such as Derrida's suffer from a limitation that even Nietzsche's and Schmitt's do not: the assertion that we should ameliorate violence against others is undermined by the utter inability to explain, to ground, the turn away from violence and toward at least the striving toward peaceful acceptance of the other.

These are the presumably unintended consequences of privileging the singular exception over reason and ethical principles. If we take Abraham not as exemplary of a horrible exception we might someday have to make to our ethical obligations to others, but as exemplary of the very essence of ethical obligation, then we are left in a situation in which we place ourselves at odds with others, and in which others might view absolutely any and every "ethical" choice we make as murder or madness. It is strange and telling that a number of postmodern thinkers would take a singular act of radical violence (Abraham's readiness to slash his son's throat) as exemplary of the *crux* of ethical obligation.[111] The privileging of the singular exception fails to respect the insight that "the demands of logic, rationality, and transparency . . . coincide with the demands of morality itself."[112] Morality is not itself a product of logic; but once the space of moral obligation is opened up, it is vitally important that we be able to explain our moral choices and discuss them with others. To privilege the singular exception is to place oneself above "the demands of logic, rationality, and transparency." It is, in effect, to give license to absolutely anything—even though one may have good intentions and the "good conscience" that comes from knowing that one would really like there to be less violence in the world.

What is needed for ethics and justice is not an adolescent act of rebellion that consists in demolishing principles in the name of exceptionality.

What is needed is not "to 'give style' to one's character."[113] What is needed is something that Karl Löwith gained from his reading of the Stoics and Jakob Burckhardt, namely, "a sober insight into our real situation: struggle and suffering, short glories and long miseries, wars and intermittent periods of peace."[114] Löwith was not a wide-eyed advocate of totalizing systems or the ideal of a mechanistic ethics. He was a Jew who had to flee his native country and who was driven by "a deep sadness of being [that] poured out of him," a personal ethos of "illusionless acceptance of things as they are, a recognition of the naturalness of the natural, and also a persevering hold on all that was near to him."[115] He knew suffering, and his entire conception of human existence and the imperatives of ethics was informed by this knowledge. He was an advocate of what he called a "cosmo-politics" that recognizes the primacy of the natural world over the specifically human world and acknowledges that human ethics is inscribed within a larger cosmic context.[116]

The Stoics and Kant thought the cosmopolitan standpoint in narrowly anthropocentric terms, as a standpoint that can be occupied only by rational-linguistic beings.[117] With his rethinking of cosmo-politics as the inscription of human action within the larger context of nature, Löwith gave Heidegger's program for a "primordial ethics" a meaning that enables us to move beyond anthropocentrism and recognize a fundamental *kinship* between humans and animals.[118] We share common cause with animals as beings with rich inner lives that matter every bit as much to them as our lives matter to us. The fact that animals cannot articulate this fact to us in terms that we deem acceptable is more a matter of our own limitations than of theirs. Moreover, to "deconstruct" animality and humanity in such a way that these terms come to represent "traces" rather than living, suffering beings is an insult to the dignity of sentient beings. It is an *evasion* of the very sense of responsibility that has increasingly become a focal point of postmodern discourses.

It is one thing to abandon the dream of a metaphysically definitive understanding of nature, human existence, and the similarities and differences between human beings and nonhuman animals. But the retreat from metaphysics should not go to the other extreme and become a *procursus* into the realm of obscurity and confusion. That this is the character of contemporary postmodern approaches to animals will become clear from an examination of some key texts that focus on the problem of violence toward animals. In none of these texts will you find any categorical pronouncements about the moral status of animals—no categorical calls for vegetarianism, let alone for veganism—but merely some general gestures of disapproval of violence toward animals, and the occasional call for animal rights issued by thinkers who have just finished deconstructing the notions of law and right. Given the essential identity between humans and animals as mortal creatures that struggle and suffer, there ought to be no obstacle to a recognition of the moral equality of humans and animals as regards their entitlement to life and the enjoyment of their freedom. Postmodern thinkers are not alone in failing or refusing to acknowledge this moral parity. But they are unique in basing their entire approach to ethics on a conception of difference that, if only against their own intention, undermines the possibility of any kind of moral community.

CHAPTER THREE

"Later here signifies never"

Derrida on Animals

INFINITE RESPONSIBILITY OR INFINITE EVASION?

At the beginning of the previous chapter, I noted a basic difference between traditional (particularly liberal) and postmodern thinkers on questions such as whether it is permissible to kill and eat animals: the former tend to be willing to give a relatively straightforward "yes" or "no" answer to such questions, whereas the latter call for the infinite deferral of any determinate answers. This is not to say that postmodern thinkers of the kind I have been discussing—here I am thinking of Derrida and those thinkers who follow in his path—defer any *response* to such questions, but rather that they defer *responsibility* in the sense of taking any specific, concrete stand. Nor is it to say that all postmodern thinkers will necessarily have the same response to such a question; there is not one set of convictions or conclusions that different postmodern thinkers share, but instead what in a Nietzschean spirit might be called a collection of *styles* of thinking that resemble one another in decisive ways. In particular, postmodern approaches are united in their various attempts to destabilize the notion of autonomous subjectivity that we have inherited from the Western philosophical tradition, a notion that found its culmination in Descartes and Kant. By destabilizing the notion of subjectivity, postmodern thinkers suggest, we undermine the prospect of arriving at clear and enduring principles for action.

As a consequence, the very notion of action becomes radically transformed. Rather than appealing to juridico-political principles for action, which serve "only to maintain good conscience," we rethink action in accordance with the idea that there can be "no decision, and thus no responsibility, without the experience of some undecidability."[1] As I noted in the previous chapter, this conception of action closely follows Heidegger's critique of calculative thinking and his call for a "step back that lets thinking enter into a questioning that experiences—and lets the habitual opening of philosophy fall away."[2] When thinking steps back in this manner from calculation to open contemplation, it becomes "attentive to the truth of being" and "does not effect any results."[3] Rather than seeking to control or affect that which lies beyond and surrounds us, we at least provisionally suspend willing and open ourselves to the call of being. Although we tend to think of Derrida when we encounter the idea of thinking difference, it is from Heidegger that Derrida takes his cue in declaring the priority of difference over identity. Heidegger does not see being as monolithic and determinate but instead suggests that "the same is the same only as [i.e., insofar as it is] the different."[4] The historical identification of being with permanence or presence having been called into question by the "destruction" of the history of ontology first undertaken in *Being and Time*, we become capable of "lending an ear, giving our attention, to that which speaks to us consolingly in the tradition as the being of beings."[5]

Action in the traditional sense thus becomes grounded in a deeper sense of action understood as an attentive listening, a thoughtful responding to being that seeks to correspond to being.[6] Thinking never achieves full correspondence to being but instead is always on the way. That which it heeds is a silent call; hence it would be a mistake to construe the call of being as anything determinate. Questioning, as "the piety of thinking," has a fundamental priority over determinate answers, which issue from calculative, closed rather than open, contemplative thought.[7] This is not to say that action with "results" is abandoned in favor of quietistic repose, but instead that any determination of conduct (or knowledge, for that matter) that truly corresponds to being (to the alterity of what surrounds us) cannot be grounded in detached rationality but must ultimately seek its bearings through the kind of openness that Heidegger conceives as "contemplative" thinking. In such openness, thinking holds back from "representational positing" and lets itself be "claimed by being." This is the meaning of Heidegger's identification of a "primordial ethics" with "a thinking more rigorous than conceptual thinking."[8] This kind of thinking is to guide the formation of the will in practical endeavors such as "the act that founds a political state."[9] In this respect, contemplative thinking has something essentially in common with artistic creativity: both allow human action to be grounded or inscribed in being in such a manner that "what is as yet undecided and measureless" reveals itself to be "the hidden necessity of measure and decisiveness."[10] It is the prospect of such a measure for thinking and hence for action that promises to help human beings respond to the predicament of homelessness, which Heidegger considers characteristic "of contemporary human beings" and which for Novalis is the very essence of philosophy.[11] The overcoming of Cartesian-Kantian subjectivity is the first step toward the prospect of such a homecoming, even if the rift that has opened up between thinking and being can never ultimately be healed.

Derrida follows Heidegger in seeking a more adequate kind of thinking and a more adequate relation to being, although Derrida shifts the terms of the problem so that we are to take our bearings not from a vague sense of "being" but instead from our relation to concrete others and concrete situations. It is in our relation to the singularity of the other that we are to find the kind of measure for thinking and acting that Heidegger sought in the silent call of being. Derrida categorically rejects the suggestion that "pay[ing] attention to the singularity of the other, the singularity of the situation, the singularity of language" constitutes a "relativism . . . with no absolute necessity, or no references to absolutes."[12] The singular other exerts an absolute claim on me that makes it possible to respond in a nonarbitrary way. The nature of singularity is such that my response to the other cannot be generalized into a principle or a form of response that could be known in advance to have application to a variety of different (singular) situations that in some respects appear to resemble one another. Every singularity is absolute, and absolutely every singularity exerts its own singular claim on me—which is to say that every singular other confers its own unique measure on me. Given the logic of the trace, none of these unique measures can be articulated adequately in language. Indeed, according to this logic and the accompanying notion of singularity, measures are never fixed but are always changing.

Nonetheless Derrida and a number of other postmodern thinkers invoke the notion of the universal in their reflections on ethico-political decision and responsibility. Here the appeal to the universal functions as a regulative ideal for achieving mutual understanding and the empowerment of oppressed others. As a regulative ideal, the universal has no concrete content but must instead be given content in concrete circumstances through the particular, often polemical interactions and reflections of specific individuals and groups. Judith Butler, for example, suggests that "the task that cultural difference sets for us is the articulation of universality through a difficult labor of translation" that may prove to be an endless process.[13] Such a radicalized, nonessentialist notion of the universal is needed to prevent existing particular identities from becoming fixed and authoritative; just as a traditional essentialist notion of the universal can function (and has done so, in the judgment of many contemporary postmodern thinkers) to impose Eurocentric conceptions of personhood and justice on all of humanity, the absence of a regulative notion of universality threatens to permit established local identities to become dominant and hence to obstruct the endless process of discursive attempts to transform and revolutionize political identities.

In a similar spirit, Derrida, in an exploration of Kant's cosmopolitan ideal, argues that the phenomenon of forgiveness involves both the unconditional and the conditional, and that these "are absolutely heterogeneous, and must remain irreducible and heterogeneous to one another. They are nonetheless indissociable."[14] Our reflections and choices concerning forgiveness must not be permitted to take place on the level of the merely conditional, which is to say the particular, but must involve some at least implicit appeal to a notion of universality ("the unconditional") that does not possess timeless content but instead has its content conferred on it in the course of historical struggles for recognition and justice.[15] Indeed, given Derrida's unremitting concern for questions of justice, it should not be surprising that justice itself is the very regulative ideal of universality that Derrida appears to have in mind here. "One is never sure of making a just choice; one never knows, one will never know with what is called knowledge. . . . responsibilities are to be re-evaluated at each moment, according to concrete situations." But this is "an entirely different thing from an empiricist, relativist, or pragmatist resignation."[16] The only thing that can qualify our choices and evaluations as nonarbitrary is the regulative function of some sort of unconditionality or universality.

But as I noted in the previous chapter, Derrida identifies the unconditional with the concrete other. Thus in effect Derrida does not so much efface the distinction between universality and singularity as replace the former with the latter. Here universality loses its essential meaning and function as a regulative ideal: if the singular other becomes "absolute," then in each concrete situation I must respond to the claim exercised on me by this specific, concrete other. My response is not arbitrary, inasmuch as my response is tailored to the particular call of this particular other. But unless I can recognize, can make a determination about, what is called for and what is uncalled for in my concrete, unique response to the concrete, unique call of this concrete, unique other, my response will appear to be characterized by an irreducible element of arbitrariness. Saying that "justice demands X in these circumstances," that "this is an unjust situation," or that "this concrete other requires this particular response" needs a basis. For Derrida, this basis is the concrete other and the claim that this other's vulnerability exercises on me. It cannot be any of the "essentialisms of identity" so often associated with liberal humanism.[17]

What each of us has to decide is whether such a conception of (or substitution of singularity for) the universal is meaningful or whether it is an empty if unwitting evasion. It is fair enough to say that "one is never sure of making the just choice." But is it equally fair to say that one is never sure of making an *unjust* choice? The terms of deconstruction would appear to prevent Derrida from affirming the first assertion without also affirming the latter. Thus he is left in the position, to me both highly counterintuitive and utterly tragic, of suggesting that we can never be sure that killing and eating an animal (or, more generally, that using an animal as a delivery device for satisfying human desires) is unjust—*not in one single situation.*

Derrida, the Tradition, and the Question of Capacities

It is by now well established that few, if any, postmodern thinkers escape the historical influence of anthropocentric prejudice on our thinking about animals. Given that the history of this prejudice coincides with the entire history of Western philosophy, it would not be idle to wonder whether such influence can ever be overcome completely.[18] Even thinkers such as Heidegger and Levinas, who make such important contributions to our understanding of the ways in which the other precedes us and constitutes the condition for the possibility of selfhood, reproduce very clearly the influence of anthropocentric prejudice. I have examined the anthropocentric tendencies of these two thinkers at length elsewhere.[19] I return later in this chapter to Heidegger, who figures so prominently in Derrida's reflections on animals and the problem of anthropocentrism. Nonetheless it will be useful to restate briefly the manifestations of anthropocentrism in these and a few other postmodern thinkers since it is against the background of these thinkers' views that Derrida, in some of his last writings, develops his views on our relationships to animals and the ethical exigencies that issue from those relationships. Derrida's reflections not only on the modern thinkers of subjectivity but especially on certain postmodern thinkers of alterity lead him to perhaps the most penetrating insights yet offered by a postmodern thinker into the lives of animals and the horrors that we human beings visit upon them in the name of civilization. But if, as I will argue, even Derrida's insights do not hold the promise of any real justice for animals, then we must consider very seriously the implication that the poststructuralist approach taken by Derrida and thinkers seeking to develop his insights is irretrievably a wrong road, however good its motivating intentions may be.

Common to traditional and some postmodern thinkers is the tendency to think about animals in terms of capacities and to make distinctions between human beings and animals on the basis of possessing or lacking certain capacities. Already in antiquity Aristotle and the Stoics sought to distinguish human beings from animals on the grounds that the former possess *logos* (reason or language), whereas the latter are *aloga* (deficient in virtue of lacking *logos*). In one form or another, this dual prejudice—that animals lack *logos* and that lacking *logos* constitutes an existential deficiency—has continued to manifest its influence on philosophical thinking up to the present. In contemporary liberal thought, which focuses on individuals with interests as the unit of measure for considerations of the moral status of animals, thinkers such as Peter Singer and Tom Regan follow the terms of the traditional reliance on *logos* as the key capacity for determining moral status. This is not immediately apparent in the case of Peter Singer since he follows Jeremy Bentham in appealing to the capacity to suffer rather than to the capacity for thought or speech as the basis for moral considerability. Derrida suggests that Bentham's shift of focus from language or thought to the capacity to suffer "changes everything. It no longer simply concerns the logos. . . . The question [whether animals can suffer] is disturbed by a certain passivity."[20] By shifting the question from whether animals can speak or think to whether they can suffer, Derrida believes, Bentham changes everything by emphasizing the capacity of animals to undergo or be subject to something (namely, suffering) rather than focusing on whether animals are capable of accomplishing anything. Animals are no longer understood as agents but instead are understood as vulnerable beings that can undergo subjection and hence awaken a compassionate response from us. That animals can suffer is a sign that animals share finitude or mortality with human beings and that historical attempts to make a fundamental distinction between the moral status of human beings and nonhuman animals is arbitrary and self-serving.

Singer outwardly appears to hold a view virtually identical to Derrida's as regards the significance of Bentham's appeal to suffering rather than to *logos* as the basis for moral worth. But in fact neither Singer nor Bentham truly "changes everything" in the discourse on animals. Both start out appealing to the capacity to suffer, only to conclude by attributing a superior moral status to human beings on the basis of the human possession and the (supposed) animal nonpossession of reason. In the same famous, oft-cited footnote in which he suggests that the decisive question is whether animals can suffer, Bentham proceeds to argue that it is perfectly permissible for human beings to kill and eat animals inasmuch as animals "have none of those long-protracted anticipations of future misery which we have. The death they suffer in our hands commonly is, and always may be, a speedier, and by that means a less painful one, than that which would await them in the inevitable course of nature. . . . We should be the worse for their living, and they are never the worse for being dead."[21] Suffering per se is not the basis for moral status; instead, one's capacity to suffer is informed in a decisive way by the capacity to contemplate the distant future and, implicitly, to take stock of what one has to lose by dying. If animals lack this capacity, "they are never the worse for being dead." Singer follows this reasoning directly when he proposes that animals cannot have desires about the future and that it is therefore permissible to treat animals as replaceable resources. Even if factory farming is indefensible, Singer states that he "can respect conscientious people who take care to eat only meat that comes from . . . animals" who "have a pleasant existence in a social group suited to their behavioral needs, and are then killed quickly and without pain."[22]

Animals suffer. This is, as Derrida notes, a sign of the fact that mortality is shared by humans and nonhuman animals alike. But where Derrida seeks to challenge any fundamental distinction or limit between human beings and animals, Bentham and Singer persist in drawing a fundamental distinction between humans and animals. This distinction has significant moral implications, in particular that human beings are perfectly entitled to kill and eat animals, at least in certain circumstances (namely, those in which there is no gratuitous or "reasonably" avoidable infliction of suffering, etc.). This appeal to capacities as a means for drawing moral distinctions is even more apparent in the work of Tom Regan, who reserves moral status for beings who qualify as "subjects-of-a-life," those beings possessing "beliefs and desires; perception, memory, and a sense of the future, including their own future; an emotional life together with feelings of pleasure and pain; preference- and welfare-interests; the ability to initiate action in pursuit of their desires and goals; a psychophysical identity over time; and an individual welfare." Regan qualifies this criterion by suggesting that the possession of these capacities is sufficient but not necessary for moral status, which would appear to leave open the possibility of arguing for moral status on some other grounds entirely. But he then states that "it is extraordinarily difficult to give an intelligible account of inherent value in this connection."[23] Regan makes no attempt to offer such an account. Instead he ends up arguing for the moral superiority of human beings over animals on the same grounds as Bentham and Singer, namely, that nonhuman animals have less (if anything) to lose by dying than human beings do. Thus in an emergency lifeboat situation in which somebody must be thrown overboard in order to save the rest of the passengers, not only is it morally appropriate to throw a dog overboard to save a group of humans, it would be morally appropriate to throw *any number* of dogs overboard in order to save just one human life.[24]

A number of influential postmodern thinkers also address the human relationship to and putative differences from animals, with similar results. Levinas expresses a profound ambivalence regarding the question whether animals possess sufficient agency to count as members of the moral community. He writes of a dog he encountered when he was interned in a Nazi labor camp. For Levinas, Bobby, this dog for whom "there was no doubt that [Levinas and his fellow prisoners] were men," was "the last Kantian in Nazi Germany" in spite of the fact that he lacked "the brain needed to universalize maxims and drives."[25] Animals possess transcendence, on Levinas's view; and his encounter with Bobby, the dog in the labor camp, leads him to assert that "there is enough, there, to make you a vegetarian again."[26] But apparently animals do not possess *enough* transcendence to qualify as members of the moral community. Ultimately "the being of animals is a struggle for life. A struggle for life without ethics."[27]

One postmodern response to Levinas is to problematize the very notion of transcendence and to challenge as anthropocentric Levinas's exclusion of animals from the moral sphere. Matthew Calarco rejects the appeal to transcendence altogether, arguing that "Being-for-the-Other and 'holiness' are acts that are purely and wholly immanent to the material world." The language of transcendence hearkens back to an entire history of thinking according to which acts of mind or spirit hover above mere nature. One could see in Levinas's suggestion that the animal possesses transcendence a reassertion of the *nomos-physis* (culture-nature) distinction according to which those beings possessed of something like "spirit" are superior to "mere" nature. In rejecting Levinas's appeal to transcendence, be it in human beings or in animals, Calarco seeks to embrace "a more expansive, fully naturalistic perspective." Calarco supplements this rejection of the language of transcendence with the suggestion that "the underlying logic of [Levinas's] thought permits no such anthropocentrism" of the kind ultimately articulated by Levinas. The appropriate response to Levinas's thinking about animals is not to reject it wholesale, but instead to take it to its logical conclusion—a conclusion that does not permit the anthropocentric move of excluding animals as ethical others. Calarco sees Levinas's ideas as amenable to a revision that leaves fundamentally open the question of who or what may count as an ethical other. Such "agnosticism concerning the 'who' of the Other" obliges us "to proceed from the possibility that *anything*" could turn out, perhaps much to our surprise, to be the kind of other who exercises an ethical claim on us.[28]

In radically extending the scope of possible ethical others, Calarco implicitly follows Derrida's critique of Levinas. Derrida believes that "an ethics like that Levinas attempts" would not "be sufficient to recall the subject to its being-subject, its being-host or -hostage, that is to say, its being-subjected-to-the-other, to the Wholly Other or to every single other."[29] For Derrida, the very fact that Levinas professes to be unsure whether an animal such as a snake can "have a face," that is, whether such an animal can exercise an ethical claim on me, is at best "awkward" and at worst a capitulation to anthropocentric prejudice. Levinas, if only implicitly and unwittingly, reproduces the traditional *nomos-physis* distinction in being unwilling to profess confidence about the capacity of any living being other than a human to be an ethical other. In the face of such anthropocentric prejudice, Derrida proposes that "the only rule that for the moment I believe we should give ourselves . . . is no more to rely on commonly accredited oppositional limits between what is called nature and culture, nature/law, *physis/nomos*, God, man, and animal or concerning what is 'proper to man' . . . than to muddle everything and rush, by analogism, toward resemblances and identities." To deconstruct such oppositional limits is to open for the first time the prospect of seeing nonhuman beings as potential ethical others. The key is not to look for ethical alterity in others who are most like me, but instead to be open to its possibility in those beings that are most *un*like me. "A principle of ethics or more radically of justice . . . is perhaps the obligation that engages my responsibility with respect to the most dissimilar [*le plus dissemblable*, the least 'fellowlike'], the entirely other, precisely, the monstrously other, the unrecognizable other. The 'unrecognizable' [*méconnaissable*] . . . is the beginning of ethics, of the Law."[30]

This invocation of radical alterity as the basis of ethics and the law recalls Derrida's suggestion that our relation to the other is "prior to any organized *socius*, to any determined 'government', to any 'law'" and his anticipation of "the future of another law and another force lying beyond the totality of the present."[31] But this other law, with its "mystical foundation," does not correspond to the "agnostic" opening of the field of ethical alterity proposed by Calarco. Instead, "in talking about the dissimilar, the non-fellow," Derrida understands himself to be "surreptitiously extending the similar, the fellow, to all forms of life, to all species." Thus there is a restriction on the radicalization of alterity: not just anything, but only other "forms of life," may exercise an ethical claim on me. Ethics ties me to all living beings, not only those now alive, but also "dead living beings and living beings not yet born." Do we find ourselves claimed ethically by nonsentient living beings such as trees or ecosystems? Derrida, who reminds us that a concern about animals is evident virtually throughout his writings, leaves this question aside and focuses instead on animals, namely, on *sentient* beings. When Derrida states that ethical fellowship extends to all living beings, he punctuates his assertion with the suggestion that "all animals qua living beings are my fellows."[32]

Derrida never states explicitly that animals are the only nonhuman living beings that can be ethical fellows. But the overwhelming, indeed the virtually exclusive, rhetorical focus on *animals* as ethical others in his writings leaves one with the impression that he is not thinking about plant life in his conception of ethics. One could, in an "agnostic" spirit, leave open the possibility of an ethical relation to nonsentient nature; indeed, I myself have done so in both of my previous books on the moral status of animals, although I do not yet have any clear conception of what it would mean to have an ethical relationship to a tree, to an ecosystem, or to nature as a whole. I am still trying to think through this problem. One difficulty posed by this problem is the fact that sentient beings seem to exercise a specific sort of ethical claim on us that it seems inconceivable for a nonsentient being to exercise on us: *sentient beings can suffer*, and to that extent they merit (as I have argued before and will argue in subsequent chapters) both our compassion and the recognition of rights. It is entirely reasonable to open the field of possible ethical others to nonhuman beings. But there needs to be a reason, or an extrarational occasion or basis that can be articulated rationally, for including a given being in the sphere of moral consideration. To *want* to open the field of possible ethical others without limit is laudable. It is an attempt to avoid the arbitrary and pernicious exclusion of beings that ought to be acknowledged to be ethical others, as when women and people of color were and in many instances still are excluded from full recognition and political enfranchisement. But *actually to open* the field of ethical others without any limit is to do something that undermines the very meaning of ethics, which at most is about living beings and which may ultimately best be thought of as being about sentient beings. Even Derrida stops short of opening the field of ethical others infinitely. What he recommends is "simply an *almost* limitless broadening" of the field of ethical others, thereby expressing an awareness that ethical responsibility is not about just anything whatsoever but is about the "ought" as it pertains to living beings, beings that can fare well or ill in their growth toward the realization of their natural potential.[33]

This limitation in Derrida's approach is not entirely apparent because of his focus on deconstructing all supposed limits. In place of the traditional assertion of binary oppositions such as *nomos-physis* or human-animal, which posit an impermeable limit, Derrida proposes "another logic of the limit . . . *limitrophy*," one that destabilizes all putative boundaries by "*feed[ing] the limit* . . . multiplying its figures . . . making [the limit] increase and multiply."[34] Limits by their nature are never fixed but are instead fluid and shifting. This other logic of the limit leads Derrida to the conclusion that "a thinking of the other, of the infinitely other who looks at me, should . . . privilege the question and the request of the animal."[35] Where the tradition and even some postmodern thinkers have assumed that only humans can train their gaze and make requests, Derrida questions the positing of a limit according to which animals are denied such capacities. A specific focus on the animal here is in part a consequence of Derrida's interest in problematizing or "feeding" the limit between the human and the animal. But it is also something more. It is a specific application of the special privilege that Derrida assigns to living beings in considerations of ethical responsibility. In his last set of seminars on the beast and the sovereign, Derrida stresses a certain commonality between the beast and the sovereign, namely, that both inhabit "a world that is . . . undeniably common to both of them." This commonality consists in the fact that both the beast and the sovereign are living beings subject to death.[36] Here it is not simply a matter of Derrida having expressed himself elliptically, thereby leaving open the possibility that nonliving beings, which are not subject to death, might be ethical others. Notwithstanding the logic of limitrophy, Derrida makes a clear distinction between non-living and living beings. "In the former case, the other, the element of the other, is nonliving, inanimate anonymity (the earth or the sea); in the latter case, the other is living and is in each case a singular organism [*un organisme singulier*], a beast or a cannibal."[37] Living beings, unlike nonliving beings such as the earth or the sea, are *singularities*. This is what qualifies living but not nonliving beings as at least potential ethical others.

And yet in spite of this characterization of living beings generally as singularities, Derrida's virtually exclusive focus in discussing the ethical significance of nonhuman living beings is animals and their capacity to suffer. He calls for "a zoo-anthropological politics," a politics oriented specifically on animals and human beings.[38] Nonetheless, Derrida resists the suggestion that he is basing membership in the moral community on the possession of capacities. Instead, he suggests, he is trying to do two things. First, he is trying to shed light on a historical process of human self-assertion in the course of which human beings have attributed certain capacities to themselves by means of denying those very capacities to animals. The capacity for ethical responsiveness, which Derrida, following Heidegger, links to responsibility, will figure centrally in Derrida's argument. Second, instead of asserting that animals do in fact possess ethically significant capacities that have historically been denied to them, Derrida wants to call into question the attribution of these capacities to human beings. Here the capacity for relating to things "as such" and the ability to relate to death will figure prominently. A guiding commitment is the belief that basing moral status on the possession or lack of certain capacities constitutes "an immense disavowal, whose logic traverses the whole history of humanity."[39] As Cary Wolfe notes, for Derrida this disavowal is a product of "a panicked horror at our own vulnerability, our own passivity—in the end, our own mortality."[40] Rather than attribute agency to animals, we are led to believe, Derrida will call into question the agency of human beings. At the same time, Derrida devotes a great deal of effort to intimating that animals may possess certain capacities that have historically been considered both ethically significant and exclusive to human beings, such as the look, a relation to death, and, at least implicitly, the capacity to respond.

One thinker whom Derrida criticizes for denying animals the capacity to respond is Lacan. For Lacan, an animal is not "a subject of the signifier" because it lacks "the locus of the Other." Thus an animal can "pretend" but not "deceive"; it cannot, for example, "cover up its tracks." Nor can it respond, inasmuch as "the response of the other" is a function of speech.[41] Like the tradition before him, Lacan conceives of response in contrast with (mere) reaction. Aristotle characterizes human action in terms of deliberative choice and denies this capacity to animals, arguing that their behavior is not rational but instead is determined by appetite or desire.[42] Human beings are able to step back from various possible goals or ends and evaluate them rationally. Animals, in contrast, can (at best) seek the appropriate means for satisfying given desires but cannot step back from these desires and evaluate their desirability within the larger context of a whole life. Animals, on this view, are locked in an eternal present.[43] For Lacan, as for Aristotle and the Stoics, what fundamentally distinguishes human beings from animals is the possession of *logos*. Thus, for example, the bee dance does not qualify as a language but is merely a "code, or a system of signalling" due to "the fixed correlation of its signs to the reality that they signify. . . . the message remains fixed in its function as a relay of the action, from which the subject detaches it as a symbol of communication itself."[44] Given Lacan's exclusion of animals from the sphere of language and subjectivity, this view of the bee dance would presumably hold for all supposed animal communication.

Derrida notes that Lacan's view has decisive and perhaps surprisingly orthodox implications for the moral status of animals. The Lacanian "subversion of the subject" simply "move[s] from one disavowal to another" and constitutes "a stagnant confirmation of inherited thinking, its presuppositions, and its dogma."[45] That the animal is imprisoned in the imaginary and lacks access to the symbolic order, that the animal lacks desire and the unconscious, that animals can be gregarious but not social—all these commitments on Lacan's part are reflections of the traditional prejudice that human beings can "respond" but that animals can merely "react." In the end, Lacan "will have founded all 'responsibility' . . . on the distinction, which [Derrida finds] so problematic, between *reaction* and *response*."[46] Because "the animal . . . is confined to the fixity of the innate . . . whereas man . . . is not so confined," Lacan believes that "what is proper to man . . . is the Law, the relation to the Law (with a capital L)." Any fellowship with animals, the possibility of which Derrida wants to explore as the basis for an ethical relation to animals, is categorically excluded by Lacan, who conceives of fellowship in rigidly anthropocentric terms. It is in this context that Derrida asks whether "one only [has] duties toward man and the other man as human" and raises the possibility that my most genuine ethical responsibility is to those who are "*le plus dissemblable.*"[47]

There are other postmodern thinkers, such as Giorgio Agamben, who have written about animals but whose views have been shown to be beset with the same sorts of anthropocentric limitations as those of Levinas and Lacan. Calarco observes that a great many postmodern ("continental") thinkers reproduce the same "anthropocentric value hierarchy" articulated by the tradition. In spite of the anthropocentrism of much of Agamben's writing, Calarco believes that the later Agamben's wholesale abandonment of the human-animal distinction can pave the way toward the development of "a non-anthropocentric ontology of life-death . . . a kind of relational ontology" that holds the promise of addressing the persistent problem of violence against animals.[48] In *The Open: Man and Animal*, Agamben's aim is to stop the "anthropological machine" that "functions by means of an exclusion" that has historically subjugated not only animals but also groups of humans such as Jews. Agamben seizes on the very drawing of distinctions as the source of the problem: we draw the human-animal distinction in order to confer on ourselves a privileged proximity to the divine.[49] Implicit here is the suggestion that we might do best to dispense with such distinctions altogether. I do not examine Agamben's thought here in any detail because I consider such an approach to be fundamentally misguided. As I have argued before and will continue to argue in the remainder of this book, I believe that there are fundamental differences between human beings and animals that confer certain crucial responsibilities on humans of which animals, the vast majority if not all of them, are incapable. The desire to efface the human-animal distinction is laudable to the extent that it is born of a desire to recognize and do justice to the holy alliance that prevails among all vulnerable, mortal beings. But it is misguided inasmuch as it does violence to important differences between human beings and animals, differences that confer on human beings special responsibilities toward animals that animals simply do not appear to be capable of taking on toward themselves, other animals, or human beings.

None of this is to say that animals categorically cannot "respond" to each other or to human beings. It is to say—and here I assume that anyone sensitive to the subtleties of difference should find it unobjectionable—that response can take many different forms, of which response in the sense of taking ethico-political responsibility is just one. It is response in this specific sense that I think animals lack—although, as I have argued throughout my writings on animals, I do not believe that this lack has the least significance for the moral status of animals. Many animals respond in a wide variety of ways to other animals, including human animals. When nonhuman animals respond, it is most often, and perhaps always, in the mode of an emotional response. This is not to denigrate the responses of animals, but rather to suggest that they appear to lack a certain form of reflective rational interplay with their emotions that Aristotle tried to specify when he made a distinction between deliberative choice (*proairesis*) in humans and appetite or desire (*epithymia*) in animals. Even Aristotle expressed a sensitivity to the sophistication of animal agency, when in the zoological texts he attributed a variety of forms of intelligence to animals.[50] But he denied ethico-political agency to animals on the grounds that they were *aloga*. It is beyond question that *logos* can take many forms; Porphyry hastens to point out that, on a sufficiently broad conception of *logos*, many animals (indeed, all sentient ones) unquestionably are capable of a variety of mental operations that help to secure their survival and even make them capable of establishing a sense of community with other animals and human beings.[51] But even Porphyry maintains that animals possess "a great inadequacy," namely, "that no animal has a manifest aim for, or progress in, or desire for, virtue."[52] Animals do not contemplate the ethical or political good as such—which is precisely what thinkers such as Derrida *are* doing when they see deconstruction as having an ethical function.

The history of anthropocentric prejudice has led many people to assume that because nonhuman animals lack the capacity for abstract reflection and hence cannot contemplate explicit sets of generally applicable social rules, animals do not find life meaningful. The assumption is that participation in meaning is an all-or-nothing affair: either a being is capable of appreciating a wide variety of forms of meaning, including abstract representations that can be expressed in linguistic form, or that being is excluded from the sphere of meaning altogether and its life is characterized essentially by reaction rather than response. To suppose that human beings are the only living beings who can respond rather than merely react is to subscribe to the thesis of human exceptionalism, according to which human beings are morally superior to all nonhuman beings because only human beings possess the cognitive apparatus that makes it possible for life to matter. Only human beings, on this view, can care about life. Any being for which life is not meaningful is a being that stands to lose nothing by losing its life.

A typical proponent of this endeavor to proclaim human exceptionalism in contemporary thought is Peter Carruthers, who argues that nonhuman animals are categorically excluded from moral consideration because they cannot engage in abstract reflection. On Carruthers's view, to be a beneficiary of moral concern, one must be able to contemplate and agree with others on abstract social rules, and one must be able to think about one's first-order experiences such as pain. Because animals cannot engage in abstract reflection, Carruthers argues, animals neither can take on responsibilities nor have rights; for Carruthers, who presents a standard contractualist position, a being either has both rights and obligations or has neither. Moreover, because animals cannot think about their first-order experiences, their pains are all nonconscious and hence morally insignificant. On the basis of these claims, Carruthers concludes that inflicting harm on animals is perfectly permissible provided that there is at least slight human benefit to be derived from the practice; in particular, Carruthers dismisses as naive and misguided any misgivings we might have about practices such as factory farming and animal experimentation.[53]

Carruthers's position regarding the permissibility of excluding animals from direct moral consideration follows from his claim that animals are incapable of having desires about the future, engaging in long-term planning, and other forms of mental life that depend on the capacity for abstract reflection.[54] In many respects Carruthers's view of animal behavior is like that of Descartes, who viewed animals as biological mechanisms without any subjective awareness. Descartes offers the example of vision: "Animals do not see as we do when we are aware that we see, but only as we do when our mind is elsewhere. . . . In such a case we too move just like automatons."[55] Every visual experience of an animal, in other words, is like certain visual experiences I have when I am experiencing highway hypnosis: I am driving on the highway, lost in thought, and after a while I realize that for some time I have been braking, accelerating, and changing lanes in a manner consistent with the flow of traffic even though I have no memory of having done any of these things. I "saw" the brake lights on the car in front of me and I braked appropriately, but I was not consciously aware of this act of vision.

For Descartes and Carruthers, this is the form that *every* perceptual experience in a nonhuman animal takes, and it betokens a complete incapacity for the kind of inner awareness that is characteristic of a being for whom experience is meaningful. On this view, nonhuman animals are unable to think about and evaluate the various contingencies with which they are confronted; instead, animals simply react to stimuli in their environments, without any subjective awareness of what is happening and without the capacity to take anything like a deliberative stand on the exigencies they face.

Work in ethology in recent generations has provided evidence that many nonhuman animals have subjective states of awareness and that their lives matter to them, even if their lives do not matter to them in exactly the ways in which life can matter to a being that possesses the capacity for abstract reflection and linguistic communication. The evidence of contemporary ethology is not absolutely dispositive inasmuch as, for reasons sketched by Thomas Nagel, there can be no definitive proof that nonhuman animals possess subjective awareness and the ability to evaluate and take a conscious stand on their lives. As Nagel points out, the subjective encounters that different sorts of animals have with the world are informed to a great degree by the kinds of perceptual and cognitive apparatus they possess; and to the extent that these apparatuses vary from species to species, there is no way human beings can ascertain with certainty exactly what the subjective experience of a member of another species is like.[56] But Nagel never questions the proposition that many nonhuman animals have subjective experiences of the world, that *there is something it is like* to be, for example, a bat. The upshot of Nagel's challenge is not to reject the proposition that life matters for many non-human animals, but rather to caution us about the limits of our ability to arrive at definitive descriptions of the inner workings of animal behavior. The fact that very few animals can communicate their experiences to us in language that we can understand (and that will satisfy the criteria of traditional scientific inquiry) by no means obviates the task of investigating animal minds; it simply makes the task more difficult.

Even though it seems impossible in principle to provide absolutely incontrovertible evidence that many animals have rich subjective lives and that their lives matter to them just as our lives matter to us, ethological research has made it increasingly implausible to suppose that human beings are the only beings for whom experience is meaningful. Take the example of the broken-wing display of the piping plover. When a plover becomes aware of a potential predator near its young, the plover will lure the predator away by fluttering and dragging its wings along the ground, as if it were injured. This behavior is often accompanied by loud squawks on the part of the plover, as if to draw additional attention to itself and away from its young. Once the plover has drawn the intruder a sufficient distance from the nest, the plover flies back to the nest to tend its young. Plovers are able to distinguish between benign and dangerous intruders and are able to modify their behavior depending on the behavior exhibited by the intruder. The piping plover appears to have a clear goal, some sort of understanding of what is involved in deceiving another being, and the ability to adapt its specific behavior to the exigencies of the particular situation.[57]

Various animals exhibit compassion, helping behavior, and other socially valuable sorts of behavior.[58] Marc Bekoff has done extensive research to discover the elaborate social rules that govern canid play, an activity that involves empathy and a sense of fairness.[59] There are clear rules governing play among dogs, and a dog who violates these rules is liable to be excluded from play by the other dogs. Even if the dogs do not grasp the sense of fairness at work here in terms of context-free, linguistically articulable rules, it is nonetheless indicative of a sense of give-and-take among individuals and an awareness of the goals and expectations of the activity. Such an activity can be described in narrowly behavioristic terms, without any later reference to subjective states of awareness, but the plausibility of such an account is undermined by the fairly obvious if not definitively provable fact that dogs appear to derive a tremendous amount of enjoyment from playing—just as human beings do. By the same token, it may not be possible to provide incontrovertible proof to a skeptic that ravens entertain something like conscious intentions when they endeavor to share food with strangers, but that is exactly what some researchers have proposed as the most parsimonious explanation of this behavior.[60] The same holds for phenomena such as the capacity of animals like New Caledonian crows to manufacture and use tools to remove insects from crevices.[61]

Frans de Waal argues that social cooperation in animals provides the evolutionary building blocks of morality. His research with capuchin monkeys suggests that they may have a rudimentary sense of fairness: capuchins appear to protest when researchers offer a low-value reward such as a piece of cucumber rather than a high-value reward such as a grape when a capuchin who has been trained to expect the high-value reward performs a task correctly. But this sense of fairness is rudimentary in the sense that it appears to be egocentric rather than disinterested: a capuchin protests only when she or he receives the low-value reward, not when a conspecific receives it. De Waal believes that this egocentric form of fairness is the evolutionary precursor to other forms of fairness such as the ideal of complete impartiality. It is this sense of impartiality, de Waal observes, that appears to be unique to human beings. "We have moral systems and apes do not."[62] What even apes lack is the ability to take on responsibilities. De Waal recognizes that the ability to respond is not identical with the ability to take on a responsibility. Animals possess many of the necessary components of morality, particularly other-regarding affects such as compassion. But they lack the capacity for what Aristotle and Porphyry alike conceive as virtue as such. For de Waal this means that it makes no sense to extend "principles of justice to animals" because animals cannot become "full members of society."[63]

De Waal excludes animals from full moral consideration and argues that our primary moral obligations should be to our fellow human beings. He offers as support for this conclusion the contention that he knows "of no animal rights advocate in need of urgent medical attention who has refused such attention. This is so even though all modern medical treatments derive from animal research: anyone who walks into a hospital makes use of animal research then and there. There seems to be a consensus, therefore, even among those who protest animal testing, that human health and well-being take priority over almost anything else."[64] Now what exactly does this observation show? For de Waal it shows that even the writer of this book agrees that from a moral standpoint, the very practices such as animal testing that I protest are in fact perfectly acceptable—or that they would be perfectly acceptable as long as we did our best to minimize the pain and suffering endured by animals in the course of experimentation. De Waal fails to see a very obvious alternative explanation: that there is often a tragic conflict between our moral insights, which are a product of detachment from particular affiliations and commitments, and our egocentric impulses, which we share with animals such as capuchins. We do all sorts of things that we ought not do. Doing these things does not show that we agree that they are right. It shows that we are subject to what Gary Francione calls "moral schizophrenia."[65]

What is most relevant in de Waal's thinking for the present discussion is his focus on capacities and his acknowledgment that even apes appear to lack the impartial standpoint that is the core of, or at least the regulative ideal for, ethical judgment. This suggests that only human beings are capable of forming and living in accordance with strict ethical obligations, and it opens up the possibility of detaching the capacity to have obligations from the capacity to have rights so that nonhuman animals can be acknowledged to be bearers of rights even though they cannot be held responsible for respecting abstract rules of conduct. Derrida and contemporary postmodern thinkers who follow him tend to overlook this fact because they lodge a wholesale critique of liberal humanism and eschew any focus on capacities. Wolfe dismisses any "mining for ethical 'universals' that . . . would attempt to counter [the] threat [of ethnocentrism] by uncovering first principles of ethics."[66] Humanist principles give rise to rights that are "middle class" and "white" and hence render it "impossible to make good on the desire for difference and heterogeneity."[67] These are highly controversial and, as I will argue in the next chapter, highly dangerous claims that have become conventional wisdom in postmodern circles. Kelly Oliver suggests that the humanist conception of rights is inherently exclusionary, that by its very nature it does violence to oppressed groups such as women, people of color, and animals. Implicitly following reasoning offered by Marx in *The German Ideology*, Oliver maintains that appeals to abstract universals such as rights simply preserve existing disparities of power.[68] Calarco dismisses liberal humanism as inherently anthropocentric and believes that the discourse of animal rights "is in fact another form of identity politics or has had precisely the effect of further fragmenting the left."[69]

Wolfe, Oliver, and Calarco, all of whom are deeply influenced by Derrida, are united in their dismissal of humanism and the language of rights, and they are united on the same left grounds. I am not convinced that one must embrace left politics in order to develop a more adequate animal ethics. I am not even sure what the term "left" means, given the infinity of traces, many of them mutually conflicting, that constitute its use. But to the extent that "left" functions as a declaration of the priority of difference over identity or universality in ethico-political discourses, as I think it does in the writings of the postmodern thinkers under discussion, I am convinced that embracing left politics is a wrong road, however noble the motivating intentions. Moreover, I believe that many postmodern thinkers, particularly Derrida and those exploring his *Holzwege*, implicitly acknowledge the priority of identity over difference in their expressions of moral concern for animals.

Consider Derrida's suggestion that ethics and justice, properly conceived, are most fundamentally concerned with what is most dissimilar or most unfellowlike (*le plus dissemblable*); his belief that "the 'unrecognizable' . . . is the beginning of ethics, of the Law"; and his contention that "so long as there is recognizability and fellow, ethics is dormant," particularly when we think the recognizable and fellowship in strictly human terms.[70] This last contention is what Wolfe has in mind when he suggests that ethics must always be recognized to be founded on a fundamental *aporia* and that any understanding of ethics in terms of principles and rational judgment reduces ethics "to the mechanical unfolding of a positivist calculation."[71] If we seek to base our sense of ethical commitment on abstract principles (such as rights), and if we extend the range of our ethical commitment only to what is entirely familiar (i.e., to only those beings we already consider to be sufficiently like us), then we fail to recognize the essential openness of all ethical questions and the corresponding openness of the range of potential ethical others. Hence the rejection of abstract conceptions such as rights and the supposed rejection of any consideration of capacities.

But even on Derrida's view, notwithstanding his proclamations to the contrary, identity has a certain priority over difference, and capacities matter. For in arguing that we must seek to embrace the radically other, Derrida makes it clear that his guiding aim is not polemical but instead is the forging of some kind of solidarity through the recognition of identity (or at least similarity) underlying apparent differences. As noted above, Derrida states that "what I am doing is simply an almost limitless broadening of the notion of the fellow. . . . I am surreptitiously extending the similar, the fellow, to all forms of life, to all species."[72] The aim is to preserve differences while finding common ground. The common ground as regards our ethical obligations toward animals is that animals, like human beings, are mortal: they suffer and die, just as we do. Derrida and Derridians outwardly disavow the relevance of capacities in considerations of moral status because they recognize the ways in which capacities such as language and reason have historically been used as means for excluding not only animals but women, people of color, and so on from full moral consideration. But at the same time, these thinkers appeal to the capacity to suffer, which bespeaks sentience, as the basis for moral considerability. In fact, sentience appears to be the implicit sine qua non for these thinkers in determining which beings count as morally significant. Derrida flirts with the possibility that nonsentient life is part of the moral community, but he never follows up on this possibility. Instead he gives a special privilege to animals, if only through the rhetorical focus of his speaking and writing.

Similarly, Calarco points toward the possibility of letting absolutely anything count as a member of the moral community; but he never suggests how anything other than sentience, the capacity of a conscious being to suffer in the course of its struggle to realize its natural potential, could be morally relevant. We could, in an "agnostic" spirit, leave open the possibility that we could find ourselves claimed by the ethical call of a nonsentient being. I have nothing to say for or against such a *logical* possibility. But as a *pragmatic* principle, this makes about as much sense as leaving open the possibility that ethics could turn out to be about exercising dominance over others rather than about seeking peaceful solidarity or mutual tolerance. It reminds me of Locke's story about a prince in Brazil who had "an old parrot . . . that spoke, and asked, and answered common Questions like a reasonable Creature" and did so in excellent French. Locke states that if the prince's story can be relied on as accurate, then we ought to recognize the parrot to be rational in the same sense that human beings are rational.[73] In other words, if a creature such as a parrot could do precisely what Descartes denies it can do, namely, use language in the same way that most human beings can, then there would be no basis for concluding that the parrot was any different in relevant respects than a human being.[74] Similarly, if someday we were to discover that the earth or the sea were exercising an ethical claim on us, then we would have to acknowledge that until that moment we had misunderstood the sorts of capacities the earth or the sea possesses and that in fact the earth or the sea is like us in being a member of the moral community.

As far back as antiquity there is ample acknowledgment of the possibility that birds possess *logos* in some form, even if not in exactly human form. Aristotle, of all people, suggests that birds possess the unique distinction among animals of having the kind of tongue that facilitates communication and probably even the sharing of information.[75] Thus we understand what it would mean to extend moral consideration to a bird; and doing so would not be much of a stretch from current thinking, given what we now know about the sophisticated mental abilities of a variety of birds including parrots and corvids. But we do not understand what it would mean to extend moral status to all life, whether sentient or non-sentient—unless, of course, we embrace biocentrism rather than zoocentrism, and even then it is extremely difficult if not impossible to articulate what it would mean to have a direct moral obligation to a nonsentient being. But that appears not to be what Derrida and Derridians want to do. Their recurring emphasis on suffering and mortality makes this clear, as does Derrida's focus on the capacity for "auto-affection" in animals, "the aptitude to being capable of affecting itself, of its own movement, of affecting itself with traces of a living self, and thus of *autobiograparaphing* itself [*s'autobiograparapher*, signing or initialing one's own biography] as it were."[76] Derrida equivocates here as to whether he is attributing this ability to "the essence of the living" or more narrowly to "the animal in general," and it is worth asking whether it seems reasonable to suppose that nonsentient beings can "sign or initial their own biographies." This converges with the question whether nonsentient beings can "respond" in the sense that Derrida has in mind when he asks the question, "and say the animal responded?" The logic of the trace and the deconstruction of binary oppositions forbid us to assert categorically that nonsentient nature cannot respond and that it therefore lies fundamentally outside the scope of human responsibility. But Derrida does not offer us the slightest hint as to what it would mean for nonsentient beings to respond. Nor, as I have suggested, does he seem to be very concerned with such a possibility. Instead he takes his lead from Bentham and focuses on the capacity to suffer, a capacity that Derrida implicitly treats as the hallmark of mortality.

That this remains Derrida's central focus is not immediately apparent because he outwardly eschews considerations of capacities and devotes much of his attention to critiquing other thinkers and the particular capacities to which they have appealed in seeking to maintain a fundamental distinction between human beings and animals. In this connection Derrida's *Auseinandersetzung* with Heidegger is of special significance since it both illuminates Derrida's own unwitting appeal to capacities and shows how Derrida seeks to make vulnerability rather than agency the fundamental criterion for moral considerability.

HEIDEGGER'S VIEWS ON ANIMALS

In *Anthropocentrism and Its Discontents*, I examined the confrontation between Heidegger and Derrida on the question of animals and their moral status. Since then several sets of lectures by Derrida on animals have been published and merit examination.[77] These recent publications do not, however, change anything in the basic terms of Derrida's views on animals nor in the overall character of his critique of Heidegger. It is by now well known that Heidegger's views on animals are unequivocally anthropocentric. Why, then, is Derrida so preoccupied with Heidegger on the animal question? My answer in *Anthropocentrism and Its Discontents* was that "Derrida's critique of Heidegger is motivated primarily (if not entirely) by his mortification at Heidegger's silence about the Nazi death camps."[78] An additional reason is that Derrida takes his philosophical bearings from Heidegger more than from any other thinker. Heidegger initiates a critique of the metaphysics of subjectivity that Derrida seeks to radicalize through his reflections on the logic of the trace.

Karl Löwith once observed that even Heidegger, notwithstanding his critique of Cartesian subjectivity, "continue[s] to proceed, like Descartes, within the Christian tradition" that Nietzsche identified as the source of modern subjectivism.[79] Heidegger seeks to invert the traditional conception of the relationship between the individual and the social whole. Descartes and Kant, for example, conceived the human being as a detached, knowing agent of experience that could enter into social relations with other agents. Much of the focus of twentieth-century phenomenology was on making a case for the proposition that the human individual is not autonomous in the first instance but instead emerges from a social context that precedes any individual. Thus, for example, Heidegger advances a concept of human Dasein as "always already" immersed in a set of cultural practices, and Sartre argues that the possibility of individual consciousness is predicated on the "look" of the other. But notwithstanding this ontological priority of community or others in the formation of individual consciousness or agency, Heidegger develops his notion of human existence in terms that reproduce certain fundamental Platonist prejudices of Christian dualism. This is evident not only in the emphasis he places on faculties or capacities that he attributes exclusively to human beings, but in the way in which he seeks to make a fundamental distinction between the human body and the bodies of nonhuman living things.

In the "Letter on 'Humanism,'" Heidegger makes two interrelated statements that prove to be decisive for his conceptions of humans, animals, and the difference between the two: that "ek-sistence . . . is proper only to the human being" and that "the human body is essentially other than an animal organism."[80] "Ek-sistence" is a term that Heidegger coins in an attempt to capture what he takes to be the uniqueness of the subjective experience of human beings. It is a revision or development of the notion of human existence (Dasein) that Heidegger had earlier introduced in *Being and Time*. There he had written of the "ecstatic" character of human temporality, by which he meant that time is not something in itself, not a time line or "pure sequence of nows" lying outside of human beings. Instead temporality takes the form of horizons of past, present, and future toward which we move and from which we return in rendering things and situations present. The present is never simply the present in the sense of a moment that is simply before me. Instead, temporality must be understood in terms of the Greek term *ekstatikon*, which "means stepping outside of oneself [*Aus-sich-heraustreten*]. It is affiliated with the term 'existence'. It is with this ecstatic character that we interpret existence, which, viewed ontologically, is the original unity of being outside of oneself that comes toward itself, returns to itself, and makes present. . . . Essential to every ecstasis is . . . *a carrying away toward something*. . . . We call that toward which each ecstasis in itself is open in a definite way *the horizon of the ecstasis*."[81] Where in *Being and Time* Heidegger conceives human Dasein as an ongoing project of making things present by constantly being carried toward and back from the horizons of the past and future, in the "Letter on 'Humanism'" he emphasizes the horizonal-ecstatic character of human temporality by recasting the notion of existence as ek-sistence. To be ek-sistent is to be capable of being carried away, of being carried beyond oneself in such a way that one forges the present out of one's relationship to the already disclosed past and the open future rather than encountering the present as something wholly imposed on one from outside. One can recognize the extent to which the present is a matter of interpretation, reinterpretation, disavowal, and transformation in accordance with possibilities that one has inherited and in accordance with exigencies for action that are disclosed through an ecstatic relation to the future.

In this sense, "the future has a priority in the ecstatical unity" of temporality. To the extent that the meaning of human care is being-towards-death, as Heidegger argues in *Being and Time*, the future has priority in the sense that it represents the possibility of resolutely drawing one's life together into an authentic whole in accordance with exigencies of action disclosed in the *Augenblick*, or moment of vision.[82] Human ek-sistence is "open" in the sense that we are capable of stepping outside of ourselves, outside of what immediately presents itself to us, and gaining what might be called contemplative distance from ourselves and our relationship to the past, present, and future. We thus are able to relate to possibility as such, which is to say that we can survey various possibilities that have been disclosed by our historical-cultural past and take a stand on which one(s) are best suited to the exigencies of the present moment. In stating that "ek-sistence is proper only to the human being," Heidegger is committing himself to a very traditional proposition: that only human beings possess openness to possibility as such, and hence that only human beings possess the kind of freedom that is constitutive of genuine agency and the capacity for response and responsibility.

Starting with Aristotle, the tradition has maintained that human beings but not animals are capable of reflecting on different possible goals and of choosing from among them. Animals, in contrast, are not able to reflect on ends but instead are simply able to pursue various means for achieving a fixed range of material goals, such as providing themselves with food and shelter and dealing with natural adversaries. Heidegger characterizes this capacity on the part of human beings, and its lack in animals, in terms of the human capacity to relate to death. In *Being and Time* he makes a fundamental distinction between an ordinary, everyday conception of death as the demise of the body and an existential conception of death as an active relating to the range of possibilities that have been disclosed for us. Death in the latter sense, which Heidegger calls being-towards-death, is the active relationship any human individual can take on to the openness of the future and the task of rendering that future concrete by making a concrete choice. It is possible for any human individual to confront the lack of totality in its own life and take a stand that promises to draw one's life together into a whole. "That which makes up the 'lack of totality' in Dasein . . . is a 'not-yet' which any Dasein, as the entity which it is, has to be." To become what one is, one must take a stand on what one is—there is no pregiven truth about one's life until one asserts that truth on the basis of what one sees in the *Augenblick*. To be human Dasein is to possess this capacity. But we typically evade the burden of responsibility to unify our lives in a way that would fulfill the historically disclosed responsibility that we encounter in the moment of vision. "For the most part, Dasein ends in unfulfillment, or else by having disintegrated and been used up. . . . proximally and for the most part Dasein covers up its ownmost being-towards-death, fleeing *in the face* of it."[83]

In the essay "What Are Poets For?" Heidegger develops the notion of seeing characteristic of the *Augenblick* in terms of "the open," a notion that he borrows from Rilke's Eighth Duino Elegy. The distance we have from death enables us to relate to it in a manner that is unavailable to any animal. For Rilke, this means that the animal has a relationship to the open and a freedom that human beings fundamentally lack:

With all its eyes the creature sees
the open. Only our eyes are
as if reversed and surrounded
by snares, which block their free departure.[84]

We are able to see the open, "what lies outside," only by gazing into the
face of the animal. The animal is free in virtue of inhabiting the open
and being "free from death." An animal relates to its own existence as
something "infinite," inasmuch as its existence is "ungrasped and without
a view of its condition." Where

> human beings see the future, [the animal] sees
>   everything
> and itself in the midst of everything and healed
>   [*geheilt*] forever.

Lacking any distance from the world that it inhabits, the animal has a
seamless relation to things that enables it to relate to things freely. Human beings, in contrast, have critical distance from the world and hence
are subject to death in a way that animals are not. Rilke concludes the
Eighth Duino Elegy by asking,

> Who turned us around like this, such that we,
> whatever we do, have the bearing
> of one going away? Like one who, on
> the last hill that shows him his entire valley
> one more time, turns, stops, lingers—,
> thus we live and are always taking our leave.

Heidegger follows the terms of Rilke's characterization of human beings and animals, except that where Rilke situates animals in the open,
Heidegger believes that animals lack the kind of openness that would
permit them to relate to beings as such. To have the bearing of one who is
constantly taking leave, constantly looking back at things from a distance,
is on Heidegger's view to have had things disclosed for oneself. This is
the bearing of one for whom home is always at a distance, and for whom
the prospect of drawing one's life together into an authentic whole is
always a regulative ideal. Rilke's open is an infinite one in which animals

dwell without any limits. For Heidegger, "where something is encountered, a barrier comes into being."[85] For the Heidegger of *Being and Time*, this encounter is primordially an encounter with death—an encounter that, for Heidegger as for Rilke, is exclusive to human beings. Thus Heidegger and Rilke differ on the basic meaning of the open: Rilke believes that animals inhabit the open freely, whereas Heidegger recasts the notion of the open so that it becomes synonymous with "the unconcealedness of beings" proper to human Dasein. Understood in this way, what Rilke calls the open is really "closed up, unlightened, . . . incapable of encountering anything unusual, or indeed anything at all."[86] Whatever freedom Rilke attributes to animals, it is not the freedom towards death that Heidegger sees as uniquely human and as the basis for authentic choice. "Plant and animal do not will because, muted in their desire, they never bring the Open before themselves as an object" and hence do not find themselves in need of healing the rift between self and nature—precisely because that rift never occurs.[87]

What Rilke characterizes as freedom is something he thinks the child has in common with animals: the animal dwells in an eternal present,

> As when a child
> sometimes becomes lost in the silence and gets
> shaken back.

We envy animals and children, Nietzsche tells us, because they lack memory and thus play "in blissful blindness between the hedges of past and future."[88] The freedom of the animal and the dreaming child is freedom *from* death, from the burden of responsibility to temporalize the disparate moments of one's life ecstatically so that they come to constitute a coherent whole that is responsive to the exigencies with which one is confronted. Freedom as Heidegger conceives it is freedom *towards* death and hence toward possibility.

With the existential conception of death, Heidegger seeks to shed light on a manner of relating to the world that he, like many figures in the tradition before and after him, considers to be unique to human beings. Death in the existential sense discloses "the possibility of the impossibility of every way of comporting oneself towards anything, of every way of existing." There is no essential content to human existence, no transmundane measure or formula for human choice. Instead, we find ourselves in the groundless position of having to take a stand on previously disclosed possibilities. Dasein is being toward possibility, where possibility "knows no measure at all." "Possibility of impossibility" is an expression that Heidegger acknowledges to be obscure, and it is one that Derrida employs in similarly obscure fashion on a number of occasions. One sense of this expression is that the choice one makes in the mode of authenticity is, like the choice made by Kierkegaard's knight of faith, utterly unintelligible and inexplicable to others; from the standpoint of others, the choice may well appear absurd and in that sense "impossible." Inasmuch as the choice that one makes in the mode of authenticity is not reducible to any principles, guidelines, or rules articulable in the mode of average intelligibility, it falls outside the scope of possibility in any ordinary sense. The call of conscience, which draws authentic Dasein to this choice, "*discourses solely and constantly in the mode of keeping silent.*"[89]

A related sense of this expression pertains to the fact that when we are brought before death in an authentic manner, we are brought before the bounds of intelligibility. In *Being and Time*, Heidegger characterizes being-towards-death as a way of relating to possibility that occurs in the orientation or mood (*Befindlichkeit*) of anxiety. In "What Is Metaphysics?" he contrasts anxiety with everyday moods such as boredom and love, ascribing to anxiety the privilege of bringing us face-to-face with "the nothing," the ground of all intelligibility and hence of the possibility of encountering beings as a whole. "We can never comprehend absolutely the whole of beings in themselves," but "we certainly do find ourselves in the midst of beings that are somehow unveiled as a whole."[90] To find ourselves in the midst of beings as a whole on the basis of an encounter with the nothing is to encounter our own finitude, our own limits. It is to see possibility as "thrown," which is to say that possibility does not subsist independent of human Dasein but instead becomes disclosed through, and thus in a fundamental sense is a function of, human discursivity. To come face-to-face with our own finitude is to grasp possibility as such (namely, as contingent), to see that our possibilities are circumscribed, and to become capable of metaphysical questioning. To confront the possibility of an impossibility is to question and think metaphysically.

Metaphysical questioning is different than asserting a definitive metaphysical position. Our encounter with the nothing is the condition for the possibility of wonder and the "why?" that makes us "inquire into grounds and ground things." As noted earlier, Heidegger gives a fundamental priority to questioning over arriving at determinate answers. To "inquire into grounds and ground things" is fundamental to the human condition. Even deconstruction is an inquiry into grounds that attempts to give an account, however provisional and subject to revision such accounts must always be, of phenomena such as language, human experience, and ethics. On Heidegger's account, human Dasein is "metaphysical" in the sense that "going beyond beings occurs in the essence of Dasein." This "going beyond beings" is what Rilke has in mind when he says that we see the open, whereas the animal simply dwells within it. We have a certain distance from beings as a whole, in virtue of which we are comparative wanderers always in search of home. To relate to beings as a whole is to grasp beings "as such." In virtue of our finitude, "we can never comprehend absolutely the whole of beings in themselves," hence we must be alert "to the constantly lurking possibility of deepest error."[91]

Heidegger makes a great deal of the "as such" in distinguishing human beings from animals, and this proves to be a focal point in Derrida's critique of Heidegger on animals. In *The Fundamental Concepts of Metaphysics*, Heidegger argues that animals are "world-poor" in comparison with the capacity of human beings to "form" world, in the sense that animals are strictly confined within their environments and cannot augment the scope of things to which they relate. Animals relate to given exigencies of nourishment, shelter, and dealing with adversaries in the mode of "captivation" (*Benommenheit*), which signifies a "fundamental *lack* [*Genommenheit*] *of any consideration* [*Vernehmen*] *of something as something.*" Animals are not closed off from things, as a machine or an inert object might be. They have a sense of openness, but this openness is, as Rilke described it, the immediacy of being delivered over to things (*Hingenommenheit*). Thus, for example, "the world of the bee is confined to a definite domain that is rigid in its scope. . . . The worker bee knows the blossoms it visits, with their color and scent, but it does not know these blossoms *as* stamens, it does not know the roots of the plants, it does not know anything like the number of stamens and leaves. By comparison, the human world is rich."[92]

In denying animals the capacity to relate to something as something, Heidegger is denying them the capacity to engage in the kinds of interpretive activities identified in *Being and Time* as the locus of meaning. Essential to the production, transformation, disavowal, and reappropriation of meaning is the ability to relate to something as something. This is the ability to relate units of meaning to other units of meaning and to the *topos* of meaning as a whole. Heidegger describes such relating as occurring on two levels, both of which presuppose the kind of disclosedness of beings of which Heidegger believes animals are fundamentally deprived. One level is the level of the "apophantic 'as.'" Aristotle recognized that a distinctive use of language consists in making assertions about things. In making an assertion, we relate in a very specific sense to something as something: we reduce a rich context of engaged activity to a statement about how a given subject relates to a given predicate or quality. An assertion is "*a pointing-out which gives something a definite character and which communicates*."[93] Aristotle characterizes the assertion as apophantic *logos*. "Apophansis" comes from "apo," meaning away from, and "phaino," meaning to bring to light.[94] Apophantic *logos* focuses narrowly on something that it displays apart from the larger context. To make an assertion such as "the picture on the wall is hanging askew," one must have a determinate sense of a number of things: pictures, this particular picture, walls, this particular wall, the various states that count as "hanging askew," and this particular state of hanging askew. Apophantic *logos* involves relating to each of these things and states "as such" and consists in binding and separating units of meaning.[95]

Heidegger acknowledges that *logos*, or discourse, often takes this form, but he denies it the privilege that Aristotle ascribed to it. Assertions do point things out, but "the determination that occurs in an assertion is never a primary discovering . . . never a primary and original relation to beings."[96] Apophantic *logos* lets things be seen in the specific mode of their presence-at-hand, which means that by the time we present something apophantically it has been cut off from the larger context of significations and interrelationships from which it derives its meaning.[97] To show something in its presence-at-hand is to represent or depict it as something static, thereby eliding the dynamic context from which the thing or situation depicted has been taken. The units of meaning being related to one another in an assertion are abstract, and we relate to them "as such."

In his critique of the traditional conception of language as present-at-hand strings of words, Heidegger situates assertion against the background of what he considers to be a more original form of discourse, one characterized not by the apophantic "as" but by the hermeneutic "as." Our primary mode of vision is not a detached staring at present-at-hand objects. Instead, at the level of engaged practice, in which we are involved in tasks and projects, our seeing is always a "circumspective" looking for the appropriate means toward the ends we are pursuing. Circumspective seeing is interested, whereas detached staring at the present-at-hand is disinterested. When we form and modify relationships between things in engaged activity, our seeing "understands circumspectively" in the sense that we already grasp a totality of meaningful interrelationships and look with the aim of finding and using whatever will help us to proceed with the task at hand.[98] The heremeneutic "as" lets us see the suitability and the unsuitability of different means for different aims. Where detached staring and the apophantic "as" are oriented on present-at-hand objects (which need not be physical objects but are often abstract objects of meaning), circumspection and the hermeneutic "as" are oriented on the practical dimension of readiness-to-hand. One of Heidegger's key aims in Division I of *Being and Time* is to argue that relating to things in the mode of presence-at-hand is a derivative mode of relating to things, one that involves detachment from the totality of meaningful interrelationships. It is the tradition's failure to see that assertion and presence-at-hand have this founded character that prevented it from seeing the primacy of engaged practice over the kind of detached, objectifying staring characteristic of science.

In stating that animals lack the as such, Heidegger denies them the capacity for apophantic *logos*. In suggesting that animals are comparatively world-poor, he is equivocating on the question whether and to what extent animals are capable of the hermeneutic "as." For human beings to possess the hermeneutic "as" is for them to be able to develop meaning in seemingly limitless ways. To the extent that interpretation, which always involves the "as" in one form or the other, is always about the world, human beings are "world forming." Animals, by comparison, are world-poor in the sense that their capacity for interpretation (to the extent that it is appropriate to attribute this capacity to them) is strictly limited to the concrete material exigencies that they encounter in their natural environments. As Kant argued against Descartes, animals are not merely machines but instead have mental representations and feelings; they have a conscious relationship to their environments.[99] Heidegger implicitly follows Kant's reasoning in proposing that it would be a mistake to suppose that animals lack world altogether. It is not the case that the animal is completely deprived of world, which would mean that animals have no subjective sense of things. Instead, "animals have less" world than do human beings.[100] An inert object such as a stone, on the other hand, is not a living being and lacks all experiential apparatus; hence it would seem to make perfect sense to say that stones are "worldless." They have no relationship to things whatsoever. With the thesis of the animal's world-poverty, Heidegger is trying to articulate in his own language a commitment shared by the vast majority of philosophers in the West at least since Aristotle: that human beings possess capacities for language and abstract reflection that disclose the world to us in ways that it cannot be disclosed to nonhuman animals. In particular, the kinds of disclosure of which human beings are capable give rise to the possibilities of response and responsibility.

But Heidegger never fully explores his commitment to the world-poverty of the animal. In particular, he never explicitly addresses the question whether it makes sense to attribute interpretive activity to animals. His characterization of interpretive activity in Division I of *Being and Time* pertains to the formation and development of teleological relationships on a number of levels. On the most basic level, we explore, develop, and make use of relationships between useful tools, practices, and the like. At higher levels of sophistication, we integrate these lower-level practical activities within the larger framework of life concerns and overarching projects. Heidegger is relatively clear in denying, if only in an indirect manner, the latter to animals: in treating animals as beings that merely "perish" whereas human Dasein "dies," Heidegger is making a categorical distinction between beings that are incapable of drawing their whole lives together into a meaningful whole and those that are so capable. Death in the existential sense is possible only for those beings capable of anxiety, the unique power of which is to bring us face-to-face with our world as such, which for Heidegger is the same as bringing us face-to-face with ourselves as being-in-the-world.[101] Only those beings capable of relating to possibility as such—only those beings capable of ek-sistence—experience death in the existential sense. Thus animals "are," but they do not exist in the sense of relating actively to the openness of the future and the task of drawing their lives together into a meaningful whole.[102]

Heidegger never resolves the tension between his recognition that life extends beyond human Dasein and includes plants and animals, and the sharp distinction he draws between beings capable of death and all other beings. On the one hand, he acknowledges that we have not yet come to terms with "all that is puzzling about living creatures."[103] On the other hand, he characterizes life as "a kind of Being to which there belongs a Being-in-the-world" and maintains that nonhuman living beings are "separated from our ek-sistent essence by an abyss."[104] Heidegger's thesis of the world-poverty of the animal must be interpreted against the background of this tension. On the one hand, for example, a honeybee "knows" the flower's stamen in the sense that the bee is able to discriminate which part of the flower yields nectar and which parts to not; the bee never wastes time seeking to collect nectar from, say, the stem of the flower. This capacity would seem to presuppose at least a basic capacity to employ the hermeneutic "as": if a bull "knows" to fight with its horns rather than its tail, this would seem to involve a sense of the "serviceability" or "in-order-to" of horns and tail. But on the other hand, vision operates in animals in a fundamentally different manner from the way in which it operates in human beings. An animal's ability to see is a "capacity," but the human ability to see, which would presumably include the circumspection that guides our practical dealings with the ready-to-hand, "ultimately has an entirely different relationship to possibility [*Möglichkeitscharakter*] and an entirely different kind of being."[105] Moreover, animals such as bees never establish decontextualized knowledge of things such as stamens, petals, and stems, and bulls never establish decontextualized knowledge of things such as horns and tails, because they lack language and hence are "never placed freely into the clearing of being."[106] This, in turn, means that nonhuman animals are incapable of establishing principles.[107] They are also, for the same reason, incapable of experiencing the original wonder of philosophical questioning.

Heidegger's remarks about the ontological status of the human body show that, even if he never confronts this tension in his thinking about animals, he ultimately gives a decided preference to the proposition that we are separated from animals by an abyss. In the "Letter on 'Humanism,'" Heidegger roundly criticizes the traditional conception of the human being as a rational animal, arguing that any conception of the *animalitas* of humans presupposes (and misses) the ek-sistent character of human understanding. Thus Descartes was wrong to suppose that the bodies of humans and animals are essentially the same in being mechanisms. Not only does this characterization fail to do justice to the phenomenon of life, but "the human body is something essentially other than an animal organism."[108] However we are to understand human embodiment, we must avoid any facile identification of human and animal bodies on the basis of shared or similar physiology. In this connection Heidegger goes so far as to assert that an essential difference prevails even between the bodies of human beings and apes. "Conventional wisdom tells us that the hand is part of our bodily organism. But the hand can never be defined as a bodily organ for grasping or be explained in these terms. The ape, for example, possesses organs for grasping, but it does not have a hand. The hand is infinitely different than, separated by an essential abyss from, all organs for grasping such as paws, claws, or talons. Only a being that speaks, i.e., thinks, can have a hand."[109]

In associating the human hand with *logos*, with the capacity for speaking and thinking, Heidegger follows a long tradition of thought that extends at least as far back as Aristotle.[110] Like the tradition before him, Heidegger is trying to capture what he takes to be the uniqueness of human beings, that which separates us even from apes "by an abyss." His belief that animals, presumably including apes, lack the capacity to form principles is of a piece with Frans de Waal's belief that apes do not form moral systems. But Heidegger differs from de Waal in characterizing the difference between humans and animals such as apes as "abyssal." In doing so, notwithstanding his passing suggestion that living beings "are in a certain way most akin to us," Heidegger effectively denies any real kinship between human beings and nonhuman living beings.[111] Only human beings, as linguistic beings, are "the shepherds of being" in the sense that they can hear and respond to the appeal (*Zusage*) made to us by being.[112] Thus what Heidegger says about the hand finds its counterpart in his remarks about the capacity to respond: in both cases, agency depends on, indeed is conceived fundamentally as, the capacity to *think*. In denying animals hands, and in implicitly denying them ears, Heidegger is denying them the "as such" and the capacity to think. And it is here that Derrida situates the crux of his critique of Heidegger's views on animals.

DERRIDA'S CRITIQUE OF HEIDEGGER

Derrida is severely critical of Heidegger for arguing that human beings are capable of relating to something as something and that animals are not. This denial of the "as" to animals is, Derrida maintains, an act of violence. It implicitly amounts to the assertion that human beings have a *right* to language and that animals lack this right. Defending such an assertion, Derrida believes, is "humanist arrogance" tantamount to "defending a serial killer pedophile." The idea that animals lack language and convention altogether is "crude and primitive" in that it fails to consider the possibility that there might be less than fully developed signifiers to which animals have access. The categorical denial of capacities such as language to animals reflects Heidegger's adherence to the anthropocentrism of the tradition; Heidegger merely describes the animal "as it appears to us" and thereby overlooks the "absolute singularity," the "irreducible multiplicity," of animals. Genuine thinking, Derrida urges, must get beyond the limits of this kind of anthropocentric prejudice.[113]

Derrida's critique of the traditional assumption that animals cannot respond is an attempt to question the traditional prejudice that animals lack the "as such" and hence language. The tradition has assumed that animals are not linguistic beings and hence cannot "respond" in a manner that would enable them to take on responsibilities and hence to count as full members of the moral community. The tradition has assumed that animals can merely "react." Heidegger follows thinkers from Aristotle onward in asserting this distinction, suggesting that the animal's lack of the "as such" and hence of apophantic *logos* limits animals to mere "behavior" (*Benehmen*). Human beings, in contrast, are capable of "conduct" (*Verhalten*) in virtue of possessing the capacity for reasoning (Aristotelian *nous* or *noein*). Apophantic *logos* provides human beings with the kind of "orientation" that makes action rather than mere behavior possible.[114]

With regard to this kind of thinking, Derrida states that his "hesitation concerns only the purity, the rigor, and the indivisibility of the frontier that separates—already with respect to 'us humans'—reaction from response and in consequence, especially, the purity, rigor, and indivisibility of the concept of responsibility that is derived from it."[115] Can we really make a legitimate distinction between reaction and response even in our own case, let alone in attempting to distinguish ourselves from animals? Thinkers such as Lacan and Heidegger found the notion of responsibility on the capacity to respond, a capacity that has been understood to be distinct from the capacity to react. These thinkers assume that response plays a central role in human life and do not pay any attention to the fact that human beings, too, often react—that human behavior is often driven by appetites, much in the way that Aristotle believed all animal behavior is driven. To react is to be passive rather than active. Aquinas wrote that animals *non agunt sed magis aguntur*: they do not act but rather are acted upon.[116] In problematizing the active-passive dichotomy of response and reaction, Derrida is calling radically into question the notion of human action and the historical assumption that human beings are fundamentally active whereas animals are fundamentally passive. At the same time, Derrida is following Heidegger in conceiving of thinking as a primordial form of action. Derrida recognizes that this strategy "risks . . . casting doubt on all responsibility," but he justifies this risk on the grounds that this fundamental dimension of doubt is "the unrescindable essence of ethics, decision, and responsibility." In asserting that decision and ethics are based on clarity and certainty, the tradition suppresses the dimension of "reactionality in the response."[117] To acknowledge what the tradition has disavowed here is to avoid reducing ethical choice to the sort of automatic recursive procedure that could be performed by a computer. It is to recognize that ethical choice and genuine responsibility depend on "the experience of some undecidability." "By its essence a decision is exceptional and sovereign." Nonetheless, Derrida states that what is needed is "another concept of the political," one that would distinguish his own position from the one advanced by Carl Schmitt.[118] How this other concept of the political could embrace singularity without having the pernicious decisionistic consequences examined in previous chapters, Derrida never tells us.

Derrida's point in deconstructing the response-reaction distinction is not simply that we have attributed to ourselves too much agency, but that we have attributed too little agency to animals and perhaps to life generally. We are confronted with the task of "developing another 'logic' of decision, of the response and the event. . . . It would therefore be a matter of reinscribing this *différance* between reaction and response . . . within another thinking of life, of the living, within another relation of the living to their ipseity, to their *autos*, to their own autokinesis and reactional automaticity, to death, to technics, or to the mechanical [*machinique*]."[119] This logic of decision is one that would not characterize decision in terms of apophantic *logos* but would instead give prominence to the fundamental undecidability at the root of all responsibility. It would take its bearings not from determinate judgments nor even from clearly identifiable feelings about others and their vulnerability, but instead from the irreducible singularity of every living being and concrete situation. This logic would no longer think life as "mere" life in contradistinction to human existence, but instead would attempt what Calarco calls an "ontology of singularities."[120] Such an ontology would proceed from a Nietzschean recognition that every singular living being is a multiplicity of forces or agencies and from a recognition of the "autodeictic" and "autotelic" character of animals, their capacity to relate to themselves and their own particular purposes.[121]

To characterize animals in these terms is to attribute to them the sorts of capacities to relate meaningfully to their environments and to engage in acts of self-determination that Heidegger, following the tradition, denies to animals. Heidegger reproduces the traditional strict either-or between response and reaction, thereby lumping animals together with plant life and placing both on the opposite side of an abyss from human beings. Derrida clearly recognizes that animals are in some respects very much like human beings and in other respects unlike human beings. His aim is like Nietzsche's: not to elevate humanity above the rest of nature, but to show how the tradition has overvalued human existence. At the same time, Derrida deliberately avoids any step in the direction of eliminating the human-animal distinction. Calarco finds this refusal on Derrida's part "to be one of the most dogmatic and puzzling moments in all of his writings."[122] Wolfe attempts to show the reasonableness of Derrida's refusal to abandon the human-animal distinction by noting that for Derrida, the abyss that separates humans from animals is one that also separates different sorts of living beings from one another.[123] In other words, the abyss separating human beings from animals has no special privilege but is simply another instance of the irreducible and mysterious ways in which dogs differ from cats; one cat differs from another cat; one human being differs from another human being; and even the way in which, in virtue of the play of the trace, one human being or dog or cat differs from itself.

By acknowledging that animals possess the capacity for self-determination, Derrida opens up the possibility of according to animals their proper status as morally significant beings. At the extreme, we could even open ourselves to the possibility that animals participate in "question and response" and can find themselves claimed by the *Zusage* of language that Heidegger reserved exclusively for human beings.[124] To the extent that this is a genuine possibility, the suggestion that an ape fundamentally lacks hands is the "most significant, symptomatic, and seriously dogmatic" statement that Heidegger makes about animals.[125] To suppose that human hands are fundamentally different from paws, claws, and the like is dogmatically to assert a difference in kind that does not (obviously) prevail in reality. It is to deny that there can be any such thing as "animal conduct."[126]

By the same token, to suppose that death is fundamentally different in humans and animals is dogmatically to exclude animals from the sphere of mortal beings. Heidegger attributes being-towards-death exclusively to human beings. By comparison, all other living beings merely "perish." Notwithstanding his efforts to characterize bodily organs as having capacities rather than being mere equipment or mechanisms, Heidegger never makes a single remark acknowledging that animals suffer and die and that we therefore are ethically bound to animals.[127] Heidegger expresses a vague awareness that life and death go together. But Derrida's analysis makes it clear that Heidegger seeks to drive a wedge between life and death in the case of nonhuman living beings. Heidegger's later discussions of the fourfold include a characterization of mortality that includes human beings and excludes animals. Heidegger defines mortality as the capacity to heed the call of Being and to speak in response.[128] In *Being and Time* Heidegger anticipates this later distinction when he states that "death, in the widest sense, is a phenomenon of life."[129] "Death in the widest sense" refers to mere biological demise, in contrast with the existential conception of death as being-towards-death. Heidegger grants that animals die in a biological sense but not in an existential sense. Derrida directly challenges this bifurcation and implicit hierarchization of life into mortal and nonmortal beings when he defines finitude as an "alliance of death and the living."[130] Where Heidegger reserves the notion of finitude for linguistic beings who can relate to possibility as such, Derrida reminds us that animals share with us the struggle for survival and the capacity to suffer, which ought to render them beneficiaries of ethical concern.

Derrida notes that "the common condition of both beast and sovereign, qua living beings, is to be exposed to death, and to a death that always risks coming back from *who* to *what*, to reduce *who* to *what*, or to reveal the 'what' of 'who.'"[131] Given a historical prejudice according to which the political sovereign, as a secularized version of the divine sovereign, possesses the *ius vitae ac necis* (the right of life and death) absolutely over his subjects, one might almost be excused for forgetting that the sovereign is, after all, a living being rather than something supernatural.

Similarly, prejudice of the kind articulated by Heidegger might lead one to suppose that animals do not really "die" but instead merely "perish," which would mean that animals are never a "who" that becomes a mere "what" upon dying but are instead never anything more than an inert "what." Just as the sovereign is not above life and death, animals are not beneath them. Derrida sees in Heidegger's distinction between death and perishing a pernicious mechanism for human self-assertion and the exclusion and subjugation of animals. Here again Derrida equivocates between wanting to admit animals into the sphere of mortals and challenging Heidegger's claims about human exceptionalism. Derrida asserts that "it's not at all certain in any case that man has a relation to death or an experience of death *as such*, in its possible impossibility, or that one can say, properly, in the proper sense and simply, calmly, that the animal is deprived of it."[132] With regard to the first of these uncertainties, Derrida states that, "against Heidegger, we never have access to our own death *as such*." To have access to death as such, "it is not enough . . . to utter the word 'death.'" In other words, not only is it "not at all certain" that we have a relation to death as such, we simply do not. Nor, Derrida implies, have any of us ever "encountered the world as such."[133] Here Derrida is intent on leveling down the distinction between humans and animals asserted by Heidegger and the tradition before him: not even humans are really capable of experiencing their death as such, nor, perhaps, *anything* "as such."

In calling this capacity into question, Derrida, if only unwittingly, is undermining the very possibility of philosophical reflection in which he himself is engaging. The critical distance that makes it possible to apprehend and describe, for example, the logic of the trace, or to affirm or deny that human beings are capable of the "as such," depends crucially on the capacity to contemplate things as such. For all his anthropocentric tendencies, even Heidegger recognizes that to relate to beings as such is *not* to "comprehend absolutely the whole of beings in themselves." The same holds, *mutatis mutandis*, for our experience of death. In this experience, we do not grasp some transcendent meaning of our lives, nor do we literally "see" our biological demise or what lies beyond it.[134] Relating to death as such in the existential sense involves a distinctive way of seeing the range of possibilities that have been disclosed and of seizing on that one "ownmost" possibility that one considers most adequately to define oneself and one's place in the world under given circumstances. This conception of choice is, as I have suggested, essentially decisionistic—which makes it virtually the same as the conception of choice invoked by Nietzsche and poststructuralism.

If there is something wrong with Heidegger's characterization of the relationship between human beings and animals, it is not that he attributes the "as such" to human beings. It is that Heidegger too hastily denies modes of understanding to animals in an effort to maintain an impermeable boundary between the human and the animal. In addition to challenging the attribution of certain capacities to human beings, Derrida challenges the historical denial of these capacities to animals. He is concerned in particular with Heidegger's denial that animals have access to the "as such" generally and to death as such in particular. To attribute the "as such" exclusively to human beings is, Derrida implies, to do violence to animals by excluding them from the realm of mortals. Faced with such an exclusion, Derrida says that he would rather strive to be immortal or a-mortal like animals than to be "mortal" like a human being. But what he really wants is to include animals within the realm of mortals. To deny animals the "as such," to classify them as world-poor, "would be to deprive them of the other as other, of this alterity in general." This alone would effectively and violently exclude animals from the moral community. By the same token it would deprive animals of any capacity for intelligibility, thereby making it impossible to explain what we now know to be a great variety of modes of engaged activity in animals in anything other than behavioristic or mechanistic terms. Derrida correctly notes that this categorical denial of modes of intelligibility in animals, which is driven by "the presupposition of an absolute difference between the beast and the human," is "crude and primitive."[135] At least since Darwin, if not since Porphyry, we know or have had reason to know that differences between human and nonhuman animals are best conceived as differences in degree rather than as differences in kind, and that many animals exhibit capacities that the tradition has long reserved exclusively for human beings.

Nonetheless, Derrida suggests that he is less interested in attributing capacities to animals that they have heretofore been considered not to possess than in questioning our accustomed certainty that human beings possess those qualities.[136] In addition to questioning the supposition that human beings can relate to death (let alone to anything) as such, Derrida challenges Heidegger's thesis that human beings are world-forming whereas animals are world-poor and stones worldless. If, as Novalis observed, philosophy is a kind of homesickness or searching for home, then are we human beings not in some sense worldless or world-poor, just like a stone or an animal?[137] Is Celan's "Die Welt ist fort, ich muss dich tragen" ("The world is gone, I must carry you") not definitive of the human condition?[138] If the world, like Hölderlin's fugitive gods, has abandoned us, are we not left in a desolate condition in which each of us is left to "carry" or bear the other?[139] This would mean that the animal is not alone in being deprived or captivated, and in being "deprived of deprivation itself" in the sense of being blind to its own limits. It would mean that we human beings are similarly blind and deprived.[140] Heidegger's suggestion that human beings are world-forming whereas animals are world-poor would be yet another expression of human self-assertion, yet another evasive denial of our vulnerability and the fate we share with animals that takes the form of elevating ourselves by denigrating the animal other.[141]

Human beings in the West have long conceived themselves as an intermediate form of existence between gods and animals. This is no longer controversial. This manner of thinking informs the writings of thinkers from Aristotle to Pico to Heidegger. In contemporary thought there is a range of responses to the inadequacy of this approach to the human condition. As I noted at the outset of *Animals and the Moral Community*, perhaps the most highly influential approach today is to argue that animals possess many if not all of the sophisticated cognitive abilities that have traditionally been considered to be possessed by human beings alone.[142] Such an approach is laudable in its intention to give animals their due, to ascribe to them the capacities that have historically been deemed necessary and sufficient for membership in the moral community. But this approach goes wildly wrong, in my judgment, by seeking to level the differences between human beings and animals altogether. In *Animals and the Moral Community* I criticized contemporary attempts to attribute abstract conceptual ability and intentionality to animals on the grounds that they attribute to animals more sophisticated cognitive abilities than at least the vast majority of animals appear to possess. These contemporary approaches thereby re-create animals in our own image rather than letting animals be the beings that they genuinely are. What these approaches fail to recognize is that the degree of cognitive sophistication a being possesses is completely irrelevant to that being's moral status; all that matters morally is whether the being is sentient, whether it has internal states of awareness that make life meaningful for that being.[143]

Because he devotes most of his attention to challenging the attribution of capacities such as the "as such" to human beings, Derrida outwardly appears to be doing something quite different from contemporary thinkers who attribute intentionality to animals. Derrida and those seeking to develop his ideas continually stress the violent character of attributing certain capacities to humans and denying them to animals, the upshot being that we should abandon any appeal to capacities altogether. But in the end Derrida bases his entire case for the moral status of animals on a capacity—the capacity to suffer. He attempts to avoid the clear implication that he is appealing to capacities by characterizing suffering not as a capacity, which implies power, but as a condition of passivity. When Bentham asks the decisive question, "Can [animals] suffer?" the meaning of the term "can" "changes sense and sign. . . . 'Can they suffer?' amounts to asking 'Can they *not be able?*' "[144]

In one sense this characterization seems perfectly reasonable: Suffering is less an activity than a condition that we endure passively. We do not perform suffering; it happens to us. But in another sense this characterization of suffering is a diversionary tactic that lures our attention away from the fact that not just any being, but only a being possessing subjective states of awareness, is mortal and can evoke our compassion. Derrida follows Bentham in considering suffering to be decisive for the question of moral status, and in believing that animals have a claim on our compassion.[145] Derrida does sometimes make vague gestures toward our kinship with the living in general. But as I have noted, he never develops these gestures. He never suggests, for example, that plants or stones merit our compassion. He never asks, "and say the sea (or the tree) responded?" Derrida ultimately does not embrace the "agnostic" approach to ethical alterity recommended by Calarco, and for good reason: he recognizes, if only implicitly and against his own intention, that suffering is a capacity and that only certain kinds of living beings are capable of it.

Suffering is a condition of which only those beings are capable who are also capable of states of self-awareness and some kind of conscious life project, even if we humans might consider that self-awareness and that project to be significantly diminished or dim in comparison with our own. As I will argue in the next chapter, conceiving moral status simply in terms of the capacity to suffer, and conceiving the nature of ethical connection in terms of compassion, tell only part of the story of what it means to be ethically bound to another mortal being; what this account leaves out is a recognition of the fact that each morally significant being has the same right as any other not to be interfered with in its pursuit of its own goals. Derrida and Derridians fail to recognize that compassion is one crucial moment in establishing a moral connection to others, but that it is not sufficient by itself to ground the moral life. These thinkers mistakenly assume that rights are by their very nature a tool for domination; and while these thinkers often suggest that rights may have some temporary pragmatic value, they envision a utopian future in which the language of rights is forever left behind. Such a view assumes a strict binary opposition between capacities and rights, on the one hand, and suffering and compassion, on the other. But to the extent that suffering is indeed a capacity, even if it is not the power to produce something, this opposition proves to be a false dichotomy. This, in turn, invites a reconsideration of the grounds on which postmodern thinkers seek to dispense with capacities and rights talk altogether. What is truly distinctive in Derrida's discussion of suffering is not his attempt to avoid the language of capacities, but rather the way in which he draws attention to passivity and vulnerability as a fundamental characteristic of beings possessing moral status. In the next chapter I argue that vulnerability and compassion constitute one indispensable dimension of morality, but that they are insufficient by themselves as an account of the moral life.

Rather than taking a clear stand on the question whether we should continue to affirm differences between human beings and animals or simply deny them altogether, Derrida problematizes the human-animal boundary. He shifts (or purports to shift: is mortality not a kind of essence?) from an essentialist ontology to an "ontology of singularities," one that makes it possible to show that what prevails between different beings is not an array of essential differences but rather fundamentally "undecidable" ones. It now becomes possible to see the differences between humans and animals as both vast and infinitesimal. The differences are vast inasmuch as different singular realities are absolutely irreducible to one another, and infinitesimal inasmuch as we share the fundamental condition of finitude or mortality with animals. The term "human" encompasses a multiplicity of forms of life that are in some respects like and in other respects decidedly unlike the forms of life encompassed by the term "animal." That the sphere of the living is constituted by multiple singularities is obscured by the play of language, which gathers diverse singularities together under abstract categories or terms such as "man" and "animal." The term "animal" does violence to a multitude of living singularities by treating them as if they were all essentially the same as one another.

Derrida proposes employing the neologism "animot," a contraction of "animal" and "mot" (word), to signal this violent character of language. The *animot* is "neither a species nor a gender nor an individual [but rather] an irreducible living multiplicity of mortals."[146] Language does violence to this irreducible multiplicity by concealing singularities under symbolic rubrics. At the extreme, language does its violence by lumping singularities together under universal concepts, thereby leveling genuine distinctions between the singularities. When we speak univocally of "man" or "humanity," we do this kind of violence. (Is Abraham just another 'man'? Is Sarah?) By the same token, we do violence to animals by grouping them all together under the general term "animal." We ignore the infinite differences between the many different singular living beings when we use this term. In doing so, we surreptitiously deny animals certain capacities for self-determination and represent animals to ourselves as objects under our control. Any thinker who unquestioningly accepts the characterization of "man" as an agent and "animal" as a patient reproduces this violence. Heidegger, for example, speaks univocally of *the* animal and thereby denies powers or capacities such as death to the animal.[147]

Even a neologism such as "animot," as a figure of language, cannot avoid altogether the problem of violence, the "crime" that we commit when we group "all nonhuman living creatures within the general and common category of the animal." (Here Derrida once again conflates animals and the living, thereby eliding the question of capacities.) What the term "animot" *can* do is draw attention to this violent character of language. The suffix "mot" means "word." Every utterance of "animot" immediately "bring[s] us back to the word" and "opens onto the referential experience of the thing *as such*, as what it is in its being, and therefore to the stakes involved in always seeking to draw the limit, the unique and indivisible limit held to separate human from animal." At stake here is "a thinking . . . that thinks the absence of the name."[148] The term "animot." Derrida believes, holds the promise of reminding us that animals are never simply "animals" but instead are irreducible, suffering singularities that lie beyond the reach of any language.

At the same time, the term "animot" calls into question "the unique and indivisible limit" traditionally assumed to prevail between human beings and animals, thereby leading us to "another logic of the limit" that Derrida names "limitrophy."[149] In place of traditional binary oppositions such as man-animal, we are to conceive of limits as fluid and mobile. The Greek "trophe" signifies food, nourishment, or cultivation. Limitrophy is a logic according to which boundaries are never fixed and impermeable but instead are constantly on the move and constantly in question. Our aim, Derrida suggests, should be neither to efface nor to ascertain the limit between humans and animals, but instead to enhance or augment it. We must acknowledge "heterogeneities and abyssal ruptures as against the homogeneous and the continuous." We should avoid the "sinister connotations" of biological continuism and acknowledge what "even animals know": that we constantly experience "something like a discontinuity, rupture, or even abyss between those who would call themselves men and what so-called men, those who name themselves men, call the animal."[150] Notwithstanding his criticism of Heidegger's assertion that the ape lacks a hand, Derrida even suggests that "the gap between the 'higher primates' and man is in any case abyssal," just as "the gap between the 'higher primates' and other animals" is abyssal.[151]

Wolfe suggests that with this kind of statement, Derrida is not trying to highlight the uniqueness of the divide between humans and animals but is instead characterizing that divide as just one among many that prevail among the irreducible multiplicity of living beings.[152] I cannot agree. Implicit in Derrida's writings on animals is a recognition that human beings possess capacities that put them in a position to take responsibility for themselves, each other, and animals. Apart from the open question whether animals can respond, which as I have argued is designed to challenge the traditional supposition that animals can merely react, Derrida never seems to take completely seriously the prospect of animals *actually taking responsibility* for themselves or others. Derrida seems keenly aware that there are a number of important ways in which human beings exhibit capacities and engage in activities that most if not all animals simply do not. One thinks here of sophisticated cognitive operations such as conceptual abstraction, the formation of principles, and perhaps the extraordinary violence of which human beings continually show themselves to be capable. All these operations would appear to depend on our capacities for reason and language. But Derrida is profoundly ambivalent about the historical attribution of *logos* to humans and its denial in animals. The more we have learned about animal capacities and behavior, the less clear the line has become between human beings and animals. By now it has become not only nearly impossible but, more important, irrelevant to try to specify an impermeable boundary between human and animal capacities. Anticipation of future contingencies, tool use, nuanced communication, resourcefulness in adapting to unforeseen contingencies, teaching one's young, altruistic behavior—none of these can any longer be claimed to be the exclusive possession of human beings.

The prospect of drawing a clear, immobile line between humans and animals is made all the more futile by the ambiguity of the term "logos": in its efforts to reserve *logos* for human beings, the tradition, led by Aristotle, has conceived *logos* in terms of intentionality and linguistic predication.[153] But this definition has been challenged throughout the history of philosophy as being anthropocentric and unduly narrow. In antiquity Plutarch and Porphyry are distinctive in having sought to broaden the notion of *logos* so that it comes to signify the capacity of any being capable of conscious perception to come to grips with its environment by seeking the advantageous and avoiding the harmful.[154] They thereby problematize the boundary between the human and the animal in a manner that anticipates Derrida.

But these thinkers also see basic differences between human beings and animals, Porphyry noting that human beings are distinctive in pursuing moral virtue. Porphyry's point in problematizing the human-animal boundary is not to deny differences between humans and animals altogether, but rather to argue that these differences are neither absolute nor morally significant. This appears to be one implication of Derrida's discussion of animals as well: that whatever differences prevail between human beings and animals, they are not indicative of metaphysical (or in any other sense insuperable) boundaries, and that these differences are not the basis for the human assertion of superiority over animals. If anything, these differences confer special responsibilities on human beings. In particular, for Derrida, we must open ourselves to the suffering of animals in a manner that evokes our compassion. Once our sense of compassion toward animals has been activated, we will see that "it is necessary to set up rules so that one cannot do just whatever one pleases with nonhuman living beings" and in particular that we must "reduce, little by little, the conditions of violence and cruelty toward animals."[155] Derrida never so much as hints that animals can take an active role in the amelioration of this violence. Nor does he offer any clear sense of what sorts of rules need to be established in this connection. He does, however, give us a clear sense of what these rules will *not* entail: anything like the recognition of rights, and anything like obligations of vegetarianism or veganism.

DERRIDA'S EVASION OF VEGANISM

Derrida's deconstruction of the traditional notions of subjectivity and rights leads him to a conception of responsibility as an incalculable response to the suffering of others. Responsibility is not a general sense of obligation that can be established from a standpoint of detached reflection. Instead it is a concrete response to a singular other in specific circumstances. Responsibility must be performed over and over again without end. Both the who and the what of responsibility cannot be determined or ascertained in advance but must be encountered in a Kierkegaardian-Heideggerian *Augenblick*. What Derrida envisions here is a conception of responsibility that is detached from the traditional conception of autonomy: "The relation to self, in this situation, can only be *différance*, that is to say alterity, or trace."[156]

But the others who exercise a claim on us through their vulnerability and suffering, the others to whom we are obligated to respond, are not simply human and are not simply traces. Derrida recognizes that animals are concrete living beings hidden by the cloak of language, that these beings suffer, that we are not entitled to be indifferent to their suffering, and that some kind of concrete response is called for. This is one implication of Derrida's deconstruction of the traditional distinction between reaction and response: that it is violently reductive to classify animals as beings that can merely react, when it is patently clear that animals exhibit a rich variety of modes of "autotelic" conduct that indicate activity rather than mere passivity. Another implication is that we human beings often merely react, even though we characterize ourselves as beings whose distinctiveness lies in responding rather than merely reacting. The Cartesian-Kantian notion of subjectivity ignores this fact, representing human existence in terms of agency and denigrating animals either as machines (Descartes) or as "things" (Kant). Derrida's deconstruction of the reaction-response distinction reminds us that we share a great deal in common with animals, and that we have committed a grievous act of violence by representing animals as our inferiors.

Yet another implication of Derrida's deconstruction of the reaction-response distinction is that we must not fall back on general rules or principles in making political and ethical choices. Properly understood, responsibility is "a responsibility without limits, and so necessarily excessive, incalculable, before memory."[157] Responsibility in this sense "requires not blindly trusting . . . axioms" that treat ethics as the simple following of objective rules. The proposition that the predicament of animals demands strict veganism of human beings would presumably be such an axiom. As I noted early in the previous chapter, Derrida distances himself from the call for universal vegetarianism (and a fortiori for veganism) when he states that he is "not recalling [the violence that traditional philosophy has done to animals] in order to start a support group for vegetarianism, ecologism, or for the societies for the protection of animals."[158] Elsewhere he states that he does "not believe in absolute 'vegetarianism,' nor in the ethical purity of its intentions—nor even that it is rigorously tenable, without a compromise or without a symbolic substitution." Elizabeth Roudinescu adds that "even as we fight against violence, it is necessary to acknowledge that there will never be an end to it. The prohibition against killing animals seems to me impossible to put into practice in our societies, and in any case it is not desirable. . . . [T]he excess of prohibitions of every kind often generates forms of violence no one expected."[159] Even forms of protest such as the demand for animal rights exercise violence. Violence against animals is so interwoven into the philosophical and religious roots of our society that "acknowledged forms of ecologism or vegetarianism are insufficient to bring it to an end, however more worthy they may be than what they oppose."[160]

What this all amounts to is the suggestion that calls for vegetarianism may be well intended, but they nonetheless are impossible to implement and simply reproduce violence. The abdication of responsibility expressed in these ideas is breathtaking. We have an "obligation to protect the other's otherness," but apparently this obligation does not entail refraining from destroying the other.[161] Derridians often brush off the suggestion that deconstruction leads to irresponsibility. David

Wood dismisses the criticism that Derrida's views are "negative, nihilistic" with the observation that Derrida "converts the condition in which we find ourselves from a negative to a positive one" by articulating a notion of "responsibility that exceeds all calculation."[162] Calarco suggests that "Derrida's writings on animality have been badly misread in most cases," although he declines to name those readers he considers to have offered "egregious misreadings."[163] I suspect I am one of those readers. In *Anthropocentrism and Its Discontents*, I criticized Derrida for failing to take the enormous problem of animal suffering anywhere nearly as seriously as he appears to have taken the Holocaust.[164] If Derrida or any other postmodern thinker can get to the point of asserting the *axioms* that suffering is bad and that we have an obligation to show compassion toward others who suffer, then rejecting as impossible or violent the principle that we ought to refrain as far as possible from consuming or using animals is nothing more than an evasion of responsibility. I must agree with Paola Cavalieri when she states that "ethics is too serious a matter to be subject to such maneuvers" and that "Derrida simply erases the problem of the value of animal life by dismissing philosophical vegetarianism."[165]

Derrida is right to observe that eliminating violence against animals altogether is impossible. But that should not be taken as basis for inaction. Even David Wood, who for the most part is highly supportive of Derrida's thought, sees the inadequacy of Derrida's dismissal of vegetarianism. The idea that responsibility is fundamentally open and indeterminate leads Derrida to part "company with vegetarianism." What Derrida fails to recognize is that "vegetarianism, like any progressive position, can become a finite symbolic substitute for an unlimited and undelimitable responsibility—the renegotiation of our Being-toward-other-animals. . . . Derrida's ambivalence toward vegetarianism seems to rest on the restricted, cautious assessment of its significance; one which would allow vegetarians to buy good conscience on the cheap."[166]

There is a sort of conventional wisdom about the supposed moral self-righteousness of vegetarians and particularly vegans, and I will wager that this wisdom is possessed primarily if not exclusively by individuals who are not vegans. The conventional wisdom goes like this: To be a vegetarian, all you have to do is stop consuming animal flesh and you will be morally pure. To be a vegan . . . here the wisdom rapidly breaks down because, as anyone who has seriously thought about veganism knows, it is ultimately impossible to "be" a vegan. Vegans eschew not only the consumption of animal flesh, which requires killing animals, but also uses of animals as delivery devices for food, clothing, and the satisfaction of other (for example, labor or medical) needs. Uses of animals are so deeply and imperceptibly woven into the fabric of human society that most of us are unaware of the many products and processes that employ animals. Moreover, many people simply do not care about animals and cannot be relied upon to stop using and killing them. Animals taste good, they make life much more pleasurable and convenient than it would be without their use, and, most important, they are fundamentally incapable of speaking on their own behalf to protest the egregious ways in which we treat them.[167] In the face of these facts, each of us has a choice: we can strive to approach veganism as a regulative ideal, or we can fall back on the detached insight that responsibility is "incalculable" and refrain from returning to the sphere of concrete action. Ethical vegetarians eschew animal flesh on the grounds that killing animals is a default of our "obligation to protect the other." Ethical vegans recognize that even uses of animals that do not lead directly to their deaths constitute violent subjugation, and that we have an obligation to seek as far as possible to avoid such uses of animals.

The conventional wisdom, as it manifests itself in contemporary postmodern thought, takes the form of supposing that if we embrace a principle or imperative that can be stated straightforwardly, we are inevitably performing a "positivist calculation" and hence failing to take our responsibility seriously. The supposition is this: "Absolutism functions only as an attempt at domination; that is, accept this rule and you won't be required to think ever again!"[168] One might conceivably lodge this criticism against a vegetarian; to suppose that only those practices that directly involve killing animals are morally wrong is to fail to see that the problem of violence against animals goes far beyond direct killing, and that in many instances of animal use that do not lead directly to killing (such as egg production or experimentation), we eventually kill the animals anyway. Once one recognizes the wrongness of violence, which even Derrida and Derridians concerned about animals recognize, one ought to be led immediately to the conclusion that one can take steps to ameliorate this violence even if it cannot be eliminated altogether.

I believe that one reason Derrida and others do not take veganism seriously is that, if only subliminally, they appreciate the burdensome character of such a responsibility. As I stated in "Animal, Vegetable, Miserable," to become a vegan is to embark on a very difficult journey.[169] To take this task seriously is to remind oneself constantly of the myriad ways in which we do unnecessary violence to animals for the sake of our own pleasure and convenience, and to be constantly mindful of the obligation to make very deliberate choices about a great many things that people typically take for granted. Only someone who has not lived as a strict vegan, which means living in the mode of constantly trying to reduce the extent of one's participation in violence against animals, could come to the conclusion that embracing veganism signals the end of thinking and the end of responsibility. It is simply the beginning.

In previous chapters I raised the question how thinkers who give a fundamental priority to difference over identity can, without contradicting their own presuppositions, come to the conclusion that violence is bad. I suggested that there is a kind of vision involved in arriving at this conclusion. This vision cannot disclose the absolute truth, if there is one, about each and every singular living being we encounter in our experience. But it can disclose elemental truths about existence that serve as the ground of general principles for action. Karl Löwith once observed that we must accept a certain "resignation concerning ultimate meaning" in life but that experience nonetheless discloses "some kind of permanence in the very flux of history, namely, its continuity," which can serve "as the common standard of all particular historical evaluations." Reflection on history gives rise to "a sober insight into our real situation: struggle and suffering, short glories and long miseries, wars and intermittent periods of peace."[170] The same is true of our reflection on our relationship to nature, which is what Löwith appears to have had in mind in calling for a "cosmo-politics" that would recognize the human historical world to be inscribed within a larger cosmic whole.[171]

It is from the standpoint of such a cosmo-politics that it becomes possible to see not just human suffering but the suffering of nonhuman sentient beings as regrettable and worth seeking to ameliorate. As I argued in *Animals and the Moral Community*, a sense of felt kinship with animals first gives rise to a sense of compassion toward them; the intercession of reflection should then lead us to the insight that animals not only merit our compassion but also have a right not to be caused the kind of suffering that we needlessly inflict on them every day. In this connection I cannot agree with Wood when he suggests that Derrida "converts the condition in which we find ourselves from a negative to a positive one."

To "respond" to the suffering of animals by characterizing our responsibility as "incalculable" is in effect to do nothing at all. It is to dwell in the negative moment of reflection when what is urgently called for is a positive return to the sphere of concrete action. The very same form of vision that leads anyone, postmodern thinkers included, to the insight that the suffering of animals is deplorable is the same form of vision that can and ought to ground a concrete, genuinely positive response to that suffering—particularly in light of the fact that few, if any, people thinking, speaking, writing, and reading about the moral status of animals today can legitimately claim to *need* to consume and use animals.

Here, I think, we find the limits of postmodernism in regard to the moral status of animals. Postmodern thinkers implicitly rely on a certain kind of insight in arriving at the proposition that the suffering we cause animals is deplorable. That proposition expresses a general commitment that transcends individual "animots" and particular cases of suffering. The only way anyone, postmodern or otherwise, can arrive at such a general principle is by means of the very kind of sight that postmodernism seeks to debunk as a dream of human subjectivity. In this connection the notion of an "ontology of singularities" proves to be irreducibly oxymoronic. Singularities by their very nature are irreducible to any kind of general principles or categorizations. Any postmodern thinker who decries violence against animals is, if only against his or her own intention, invoking a notion of animal life according to which different individual animals share certain capacities and sorts of experience in common with one another. Naturally this does not mean that the generalizations we make about animals can capture the utter uniqueness of any given individual animal, any more than the generalizations we make about human beings can capture the uniqueness of individual human beings. But this is not the purpose of the kinds of generalizations we make when we argue, for example, that certain sorts of animals are capable of suffering and that we have an obligation to ameliorate that suffering.

The purpose of such generalizations in ethics is not to efface individuality but rather to facilitate the formation of principles that articulate and remind us of our responsibilities toward sentient life. Here is an example of what can happen in the absence of such principles: Leonard Lawlor embraces Derrida's call for compassion toward animals and argues that such compassion involves a "renunciation of sovereignty" over animals. Lawlor states that he is "trying to find a way to make animals, all of them, be worthy of being members of a moral community," by getting human beings to "restrain ourselves in relation to them." But Lawlor considers our restraint toward singular animal others to be compatible with "eating the animals *well*," that is, with "a kind of vegetarianism that is compatible with a minimal carnivorism." Because "evil and violence, radical evil, cannot be reduced, cannot be eliminated from the roots of life itself . . . we must affirm that violence may be necessary in order to institute anything like unconditional hospitality." Thus we are permitted to "welcome others into ourselves" in a very literal way, namely, by eating them. "You have to eat, after all." Lawlor states that he is "a practicing vegetarian, but at holidays [he eats] meat."[172]

Again, I find this reasoning stupefying: Violence is ineliminable; hence the effort to ameliorate it is futile. So go ahead and eat animals, provided that your conduct is regulated by "a kind of asceticism."[173] The problem with this reasoning is not, as Wood suggests, that it fails to take deconstruction to its logical conclusion.[174] It is rather that this reasoning *succeeds* in taking deconstruction to its logical conclusion. The "aporetic ethics" recommended by Derrida and Derridians expresses a vital moment in the dynamics of ethical responsibility: the moment in which we take in what is going on around us, recognize that the complexity of existence vastly outstrips our grasp, and feel the claim exercised on us by beings that share suffering and mortality with us. But ethics requires more than this. For all its talk of the moment of "response," this approach to ethics fails to heed the imperative to act in the mode of sacrificing oneself (one's leisure, one's convenience, and perhaps even one's life) for the sake of others. Genuine hospitality toward animals is simply not compatible with eating or using them. Another kind of response is needed.

CHAPTER FOUR

Animal Rights and the Evasions of Postmodernism

THE LIBERAL EVASION OF ANIMAL RIGHTS

Do animals have a right not to be eaten by human beings? Do they have a right not to be used as instrumentalities by humans? If they do have such rights, are these part of a larger constellation of rights such as the right to procreate freely without the interference of human beings? If animals have rights, what is the basis for their possession of rights? Do all or only some animals have rights? Do those animals that have rights all have the same rights, or do different animals have different rights? Is the very idea of rights "metaphysical," hence nothing more than a vestige of thinking that is both antiquated and pernicious, as some have alleged?[1] Or is the idea of rights worth defending, and capable of being defended, without any recourse whatsoever to metaphysical conceptions of subjectivity and the like?

This is merely an adumbrated sketch of the issues surrounding the idea of animal rights, and yet it makes amply clear the complexity of the problem of ascribing rights to animals. Not all thinkers who reject the discourse of animal rights are postmodern in their basic philosophical orientation. Postmodern thinkers, as we have seen, see the rejection of rights talk as a corollary of the endeavor to destabilize traditional notions of agency and subjectivity. Some contemporary liberal thinkers, on the other hand, seek not to reject the discourse of rights altogether but instead to preserve the notion of rights as an entitlement exclusive to human beings. These liberal thinkers accept the traditional notions of agency, responsibility, and legal and moral personhood, but they contend that none of these concepts properly applies to nonhuman animals. Thus these thinkers consider the idea of rights to be an indispensable legal and moral concept in the sphere of human relations, but they consider the extension of rights to anyone or anything nonhuman to be incoherent and even pernicious.

These thinkers argue that the problem with extending rights to animals manifests itself on two levels, one pertaining to the task of clarifying the philosophical basis for ascribing rights to animals, and the other pertaining to the untoward consequences for human beings of extending rights to animals. Regarding the former aspect of the problem, jurist Richard Posner characterizes philosophical discourses on animal rights as "inherently inconclusive" on the grounds that "there is no metric that enables" the various approaches to animal rights "to be commensurated and conflicts among them to be resolved." The kind of "metric" that Posner has in mind would establish conclusively how, for example, approaches such as utilitarianism and deontology could be reconciled with one another. Such a metric would thereby resolve all conflicts between the various approaches to ethics. Posner offers this assessment of animal rights discourse as "inconclusive" in the course of a discussion in which he categorically opposes the ascription of rights to animals. Posner rejects as "weird" and "insane" any ethical theory that so much as hints that the life of an animal might be equal to or superior to that of a human being, for example, a theory according to which the life of a healthy chimpanzee has greater ethical value than that of a human being who has a severe mental disability. He repeatedly appeals to what "most people" believe, to what "most of us" or "any normal person" would say.[2] In doing so, Posner seeks to discredit not only the philosophical idea of animal rights (which, I am willing to stipulate, "most people" in contemporary society probably do find "weird") but also the sentiments that underlie it.

What Posner fails to acknowledge is that the lack of a unifying "metric" that he invokes to discredit the idea of animal rights is actually a feature of ethical theories generally: there is no universally agreed upon metaethical standpoint that can resolve all conflicts between different theories. And yet Posner seems to have no problem with the idea of attributing rights to human beings. Indeed, he expresses the concern that human rights could become threatened by the elevation of animals to a moral status comparable to that of human beings.[3] Here the anthropocentric basis of Posner's approach to rights becomes clear. He sees legal rights as "instruments for securing the liberties that are necessary if a democratic system of government is to provide a workable framework for social order and prosperity." Rights bearers are "actual and potential voters and economic actors. Animals do not fit this description." Rights, on Posner's view, are legal mechanisms for coordinating the economic and political activities of human beings; hence they have no applicability to animals except insofar as they promote *human* interests.[4] The idea of community between human beings and animals has "tinsel wings," and the whole idea of animal rights is a "siren song" that engenders "deep revulsion" in anyone who traces out its full implications.[5]

Richard Epstein spells out even more clearly the anthropocentric ideology underlying this conception of rights. At least as far back as Roman law, animals have been conceptualized legally in ways that promote the advancement of human civilization. Against this background, the idea of animal rights is revealed to be "the indulgence of the rich and secure." Moreover, human beings have historically been viewed as bearers of rights because they were recognized in Roman law to have been born in a state of natural freedom. For the Romans, this meant that human beings should be treated as legal persons because they are natural persons. But animals were never "natural persons"; hence there is no basis for treating them as legal persons. Here, Epstein suggests, the analogy between the rights of slaves and women and the supposed rights of animals breaks down: restrictions on the freedom of women and slaves were lifted once it was recognized that they were humans, just like free men, and thus that differential legal treatment was untenable. But, Epstein argues, there is no comparable sameness between humans and animals; hence no "restoration of some imagined parity" between the two through the extension of legal personhood to animals is possible.[6]

Epstein, like Posner, is content to accept the conventional wisdom, the wisdom of "most people," that animals are subhuman things—things that feel and have some capacity for action, but things nonetheless. And like Posner, Epstein considers "troubling" the prospect of viewing animals as bearers of rights; indeed, "the whole discussion gets creepy" when we contemplate the possibility of valuing the life of a healthy chimpanzee more highly than that of "a profoundly retarded child."[7] To a person such as me, who believes that animals have moral status comparable to that of human beings, Epstein would not have the same reaction as Posner (either that I am "insane" or that "in my heart of hearts" I do not really believe what I say I believe) but instead would dismiss my view as an "indulgence of the rich and secure."

Epstein, like Posner, relies on a widespread, historically entrenched set of sensibilities about the relative value of human beings and animals and marshals these sensibilities as justifications for privileging human beings over animals. Posner treats as an unassailable basis for thinking about our ethical obligations to ourselves vis-à-vis other species the proposition that "it is because we are humans that we put humans first. If we were cats, we would put cats first, regardless of what philosophers might tell us. Reason doesn't enter."[8] Posner's suggestion recalls that of the pre-Socratic philosopher Xenophanes, who said that "if cattle and horses or lions had hands . . . horses would draw the forms of the gods like horses, and cattle like cattle, and they would make their bodies as they each had themselves."[9] In other words, the impulse to relate to one's own kind as preeminent in the cosmos is a natural one that is not exclusive to human beings.

When Posner suggests that "reason doesn't enter," he means that our deepest moral convictions are not products of reason or philosophical arguments but instead are rooted in sentiments. "Our preferring human beings to other animals" is not rationally justified but instead is "a fact deeply rooted in our current thinking and feeling, a fact based on beliefs that can change but not a fact that can be shaken by philosophy." Posner treats the human conviction of superiority over all other beings as one of those "tenacious moral instincts" against which "ethical argument is and should be powerless." He leaves open the logical possibility that we could experience a fundamental change in our feelings about animals, and he rightly recognizes that such a change would bring with it an entirely "new morality." But he considers the prospect of our abandoning this conviction to be far-fetched. He states that his views about human superiority are "deeper than any proof" inasmuch as they are based on "a moral intuition deeper than any reason."[10] His continual appeals to what "most people would say" suggest that he considers his moral intuitions about animals to be in the mainstream.

What Posner fails to recognize, in his haste to justify his tenacious sentiments about the moral status of animals, is that we should *never* treat any of our moral intuitions as impervious to rational scrutiny. Posner makes what has become a very common mistake in his analysis of the nature of moral convictions: he assumes that because our moral convictions do not have their origin in reason, reason therefore has nothing to say about those convictions. Here the legitimacy of the analogy between rights for women and slaves, on the one hand, and rights for animals, on the other, becomes clear. As Epstein recognizes, a set of tenacious moral intuitions once led people to accept a fundamental moral and legal difference between masters and slaves, and one between men and women. But rational reflection led to the recognition that we were being inconsistent in our application of the moral intuition that people born naturally free ought to be accorded legal and moral personhood; reason led us to recognize that women and slaves deserved legal and moral personhood for the same reasons that free men had been accorded such personhood. The origin of human rights was a sentiment, a deeply held moral intuition, that certain sorts of living beings ought to be treated in certain ways; the intercession of reason enabled us to recognize that we had acted on this intuition in highly selective ways, and this recognition led to a change not only in our laws but in the way we *feel* about abrogating the rights of certain human beings.

What Posner fails to recognize, in other words, is that sentiment and reason are not autonomous faculties that have no influence on one another. Placing one's moral intuitions above rational scrutiny and declaring that one need not offer any rational justification makes it just a little too easy to rest satisfied with moral convictions that, when viewed from outside, start to look unacceptably self-serving. Posner, like Epstein, is very clear that his moral intuitions about human superiority are self-serving. But by disburdening himself of the need to subject these intuitions to rational scrutiny, Posner puts himself in the comfortable position of never having to confront the potential wrongness of his intuitions. There are only two things that might force someone like Posner to change his moral views: either some (to Posner) inexplicable and "insane" change in his basic sentiments about animals, or a sea change (again, inexplicable and insane) in his society's guiding intuitions about the moral status of animals.

We can and ought to perform the same kind of rational reflection on our intuitions about animals that our culture has performed on our intuitions about women and slaves. To anyone inured to the long-standing prejudice of human superiority, the idea of a cosmic community that transcends human beings will indeed appear to be borne on "tinsel wings." Every zoo, every circus, every fast food restaurant, many an experimentation lab, and much of the body of Anglo-American law would appear to testify to the proposition that animal rights are a product of someone's naive fancy. From within the fabric of moral intuitions about our own superiority, it just seems right to privilege ourselves and our own interests over those of nonhuman animals. But when we establish some critical distance from these intuitions, and when we go back to the ancient idea of being born in a state of natural freedom, it becomes possible to recognize the sheer arbitrariness of considering ourselves to be cosmically superior to animals. What we should learn from Xenophanes's observation about the manner in which we have drawn our gods is that it is perfectly *understandable* that we have drawn them in human form, *not* that it is perfectly *legitimate* that we have done so. The fact that cows or horses would have drawn the divine in bovine or equine form is not a demonstration that we have been justified in conceiving the divine in anthropocentric terms; it is a subtle reminder that we are different than nonhuman animals in not having had to do so.

As I argued at length in *Animals and the Moral Community*, our ability to reflect rationally on our desires and intuitions sets us apart from most if not all nonhuman animals. It puts us in a position to recognize a fundamental kinship with animals, a kinship forged out of the mortality that we share with them. None of this is to say that our sense of kinship with animals has its origin in reason. On the contrary, it originates in a feeling of vulnerability and mortality that we share with other sentient beings. Posner's suggestion that we are right to privilege ourselves over nonhuman animals amounts to the assertion that our selfishness and disregard for animals are justified. But this sense of selfishness often comes into conflict with our moral obligations toward others, and part of the work of reason consists in subjecting our selfish inclinations to scrutiny. As regards our relationship to animals, much of the work of reason in this connection consists in undoing a set of prejudices that long ago became reified into tenacious "moral convictions."

One need not be postmodernist to see a tremendous danger here: that if a person or a culture refuses to listen to reason (or, in the words of Hesiod, to "listen to justice"), there is nothing we can do to force the recognition that animals were born naturally free in very much the same sense in which human beings were born naturally free. Posner insists that expressing a preference for our own species is not a "mere 'prejudice' in a disreputable sense akin to racial prejudice or sexism."[11] Why or in what sense is it not a disreputable prejudice? Posner gives no direct answer to this question. His implicit reasoning seems to be at one with Epstein's: we benefit materially from treating animals as instrumentalities.[12] That this is at least part of Posner's reasoning is evident from his identification of his own moral position regarding animals as "soft-utilitarianism."[13]

And yet Posner is quite energetic in seeking to demonstrate the inadequacy of utilitarianism as a way of thinking about the moral status of animals, not to mention the problem he alleges about the need for a "metric" to reconcile all the different moral theories with one another. Posner even goes so far as to dismiss as "sheer assertion" Peter Singer's claim that we ought to care about the suffering of all beings that can suffer.[14] Posner's desire to preserve the subordinate status of animals is not arbitrary in the sense that it is random or groundless; there is a clear logic to his endeavor to preserve the subordinate status of animals. But Posner's position is arbitrary in the extreme inasmuch as Posner refuses to recognize the pernicious inconsistency in his endeavor to treat humans and non-human animals as morally distinct sorts of beings. Moreover, Posner's evident willingness to treat different sorts of animal as morally distinct from one another further reflects the arbitrariness of his position.

To treat human beings as having been born naturally free and hence deserving of legal personhood while denying animals legal personhood on the grounds that they were not born naturally free is to misunderstand at a fundamental level the concept of freedom. Aristotle had equivocated on the concept of freedom when he posited a strict either-or between deliberative choice (*proairesis*) and behavior determined by appetite (*epithymia*): either rational evaluation of and selection from among desires, or behavior strictly determined by those desires. Human beings, possessed of *logos*, were capable of the former, whereas animals, which for Aristotle were *aloga*, were consigned to the latter—all of which is to say that humans are free whereas animals are not.[15] With few exceptions, this prejudice about "free" human beings and "unfree" animals has persisted virtually unmodified until very recently in Western philosophy and ethology. Schopenhauer recognized that animals possess both understanding and will; he suggested that the main difference between humans and animals is that human beings are capable of abstract reflection on the things that they understand whereas animals are not. For Schopenhauer, as for thinkers such as Plutarch, Porphyry, and Montaigne before him, animals are unquestionably born naturally free. No longer satisfied with the historical appeal to the black box of "instinct" as way of explaining animal behavior, much of contemporary ethology has been devoted to exploring the ways in which different sorts of animals actively evaluate and negotiate the exigencies that confront them in their lived environments.[16] It is on this basis that Derrida challenges the traditional either-or of conduct and behavior and characterizes the activity of animals as "autotelic."

In light of what has become overwhelming evidence that many animals relate deliberately and actively to their environments even if they may not be capable of abstract reflection and moral agency, the sorts of considerations and justifications offered by some liberal thinkers for opposing animal rights ring hollow, as do their reasons for believing that there is nothing wrong with showing preference for certain sorts of animals over others. Posner makes a telling remark in this connection: that he is "much taken with Richard Rorty's . . . answer to the question of which animal species we are prepared to admit as members of our community," namely, those animals whose faces sufficiently resemble our own that we could imagine having a conversation with them.[17] Rorty suggests that it is on this basis that "we send pigs to slaughter with equanimity, but form societies for the protection of koalas." The fact that "pigs rate much higher than koalas on intelligence tests" shows that our preference for koalas is not based on any kind of rational consideration; indeed, it shows that "rationality . . . is a myth."[18]

Consider for a moment what Posner (and Rorty) would have us believe: that "we" send pigs to slaughter with equanimity; that "we" are prepared to admit as members of our community only those animals that resemble us in certain ways; that if reason were really at work in our evaluations here, "we" would see an inconsistency between the fact that pigs are more intelligent than koalas and the fact that we eat the former but not the latter, and "we" would not be willing to continue eating pigs but might consider eating koalas instead; and that reason really plays no role whatsoever in our evaluations. "We" are guided purely by intractable sentiments such as "pigs are things to eat and koalas are not."

Who is this "we" to whom Posner incessantly refers? I cannot find myself in it, nor am I confident that "equanimity" is quite the right characterization of most people's attitudes toward the slaughter of pigs. If people really had such a sense of equanimity, they would not spend so much effort maintaining themselves in a state of blissful ignorance about the husbandry practices of firms such as Smithfield Farms, and fewer people would make such a show of obtaining "free-range" meat and supporting animal welfare measures. Some people do exhibit utter indifference toward animal slaughter, but my sense is that many more people exhibit what Gary Francione calls "moral schizophrenia": they have a deep sense that something is profoundly wrong with animal slaughter, but that sense is overwhelmed by the kind of selfishness that leads some very intelligent people to take the position that "this is just what we do, and reason plays no role."

Moreover, it is by no means clear that some monolithic "we" feels toward pigs the way Posner and Rorty say we do. More than a few people in our culture relate to pigs as companion animals. A dear friend of my wife's had an iguana as a companion animal for many years and was devastated upon his demise. There may be something comforting in making categorical assertions about what "we" do and do not find acceptable, but such assertions are wildly at odds with the fact that people differ on these questions. In the face of these differences, one can respond that there is no accounting for taste, one can dismiss certain of these differences as "insane," or one can dig a little deeper and start asking questions such as whether we ought to base the sorts of moral and legal entitlements we accord different sorts of animals on our personal inclinations. Thinkers such as Posner try to prevent us from asking these sorts of questions by seeking to make such questions look incoherent. They thereby leave us in a situation in which anything goes, as long as "we" or "most of us" find it acceptable.

There is a strategy at work here. It consists in characterizing certain questions or statements as products of confusions about our concepts. I will have more to say in the final section of this chapter about this strategy, since it has become highly influential among some postmodern thinkers. In particular, I will show that, even though it involves impassioned talk of "deflections" and "evasions," this strategy can itself be a form of evasion and has functioned as one in some discussions of animal rights. Before doing that, however, I would like to make a final observation about the motivation underlying the liberal evasion of animal rights, as I believe it has a great deal in common with the postmodern evasion of animal rights. I noted above that liberal criticisms of the notion of animal rights present two main sorts of challenges, one of them being a challenge to the possibility of articulating a coherent philosophical basis for ascribing rights to animals. The other sort of challenge concerns the practical problems that would arise if we were to abandon our historical claim to dominion over animals. By anyone's account, our form of life would change radically if we were to accord basic rights to animals. From our current, entrenched anthropocentric perspective, it is virtually impossible to envision what life would be like if we were to accord rights to animals. A great many questions would need to be answered. I alluded to some of these at the beginning of this chapter. Would all animals have rights? Exactly which rights would they have? Would all animals have the same rights as one another? What would we do in cases of seemingly irreducible conflict between the rights of animals and the rights of human beings?

Thinkers such as Posner and Epstein cite the difficulty involved in answering these types of questions as grounds for concluding that we should not accord animals rights. Posner asks, for example, whether we would be required to prevent predatory animals from killing other animals, what kinds of habitats we would be required to provide for rights-bearing animals, and whether animals would have a right to reproduce.[19] Epstein asks whether, if we give Medicare to human beings, we would also need to provide it to chimpanzees, and how we would determine the appropriate distribution of scarce resources among human beings and animals.[20]

These are indeed difficult questions. They are questions that a number of people who take animal rights seriously have been thinking about for some time. We are confronted here not only by some very tricky practical questions, but at a more fundamental level by a demand on the human imagination to envision a world in which we actively respect nonhuman animals. Only in such a world will we find the will to resolve difficulties of the kind raised by Posner and Epstein. In the world that most of us currently inhabit, questions such as whether we ought to prevent predation in wild nature tend to bring thinking to a grinding halt. But they need not have this effect. If one starts from the proposition that we live in a cosmic community with all sentient beings and that this sense of community imposes duties of nonharm on us, then it becomes possible to think concretely about the nature and extent of these duties. Some thinkers committed to the ideal of cosmic community have sketched proposals for making restitution to nature in instances in which we encroach upon it, for example, when we destroy habitat in order to construct homes for ourselves.[21] Others have added the consideration that the extent of our duties to animals is a function of our involvement with them, such that our greatest duties are to "those sentient animals that we have made vulnerable and dependent by (for instance) destroying their habitats, breeding them, or confining them," whereas our least duties are to animals in the wild with whom we have virtually no contact.[22]

Under the constraints of anthropocentric ideology, it is very difficult to arrive at clear answers to questions such as exactly how we ought to compensate animals we have displaced when we encroach upon their habitat, or what the precise mechanics of a worldwide shift to veganism would be. With regard to the latter question, which is often answered with the objection that it would be impossible to produce sufficient plant stuffs to feed the world's population, it is worth considering "the prodigious waste of grain that is fed to intensively farmed animals," not to mention the extensive use of fossil fuels and chemical fertilizers, the massive deforestation and concomitant soil erosion, and the production of greenhouse gases in the raising of animals for human consumption.[23] The United Nations Food and Agriculture Organization reports that fifty-three billion land animals are raised worldwide for human consumption every year. The extreme inefficiency of meat production is well documented; for example, a calf must be fed twenty-one pounds of protein to produce one pound of meat for human consumption, and the production of that one pound of meat consumes 2,500 gallons of water.[24] Cessation of animal husbandry to satisfy human desires would put at our disposal a wealth of resources for the production of food, clothing, and other commodities. It would also help to reverse the trend of deforestation and reduction of species diversity that has been caused by cattle grazing.[25] Seen in this light, the claim that a shift to a vegetarian diet would have catastrophic environmental consequences is not simply speculative; it belies logic—especially when one considers that a substantial proportion of the world's population is already vegetarian.[26] Indeed, finding sufficient resources for the satisfaction of human needs seems to be much less problematic than changing our attitudes and commitments. The task posed for human contemplation, rather than the instrumental task of figuring out specific answers to specific practical problems, will prove to be decisive in the endeavor to embrace veganism as an ethical imperative.[27]

Until we have undertaken the task posed for contemplation, which calls on us to employ our imagination to envision a world in which we live with animals rather than against them, we simply will not be in a position to give definitive answers to many of the concrete practical questions posed by thinkers such as Posner and Epstein. What is important to note here is that the question whether animals deserve rights is in no way dependent on our ability to give clear answers to every last one of the relevant practical questions. Indeed, the order of priority is exactly the reverse: we must have established an abiding commitment to the proposition that animals deserve rights before we can address the practical questions involved in actually according them rights.

Here it becomes even clearer why thinkers such as Posner and Epstein want to deny the analogy to women and slaves. To acknowledge the legitimacy of the analogy is to put oneself in the position of having to recognize that comparable sorts of practical objections were raised against the possibility of extending full citizenship rights to slaves and women as Posner and Epstein raise against the extension of rights to animals. The crux of the argument for denying an analogy between women and slaves, on the one hand, and animals, on the other, is that women and slaves were moral agents whereas animals are not. Epstein thus finds it "troublesome . . . to assume that animals are entitled to limited rights on a par with human beings while denying that they are moral agents."[28] It has been almost thirty years since Tom Regan debunked the speciesist prejudice involved in asserting that all and only moral agents merit rights. It is remarkable that some thinkers who believe in the notion of rights for human beings still commit the speciesist mistake of supposing that there can be moral agents but not moral patients, and that the former but not the latter can be bearers of rights. And it *is* a mistake, one that even a little rational reflection will reveal to be a mistake, if only we allow ourselves the indulgence (or is it merely an "indulgence of the rich and secure"?) of supposing that reason can help us to identify and rectify some of our moral errors and inconsistencies.

What thinkers such as Posner and Epstein fail to acknowledge is that the same sorts of considerations they offer as grounds for denying animals rights could be offered as reasons for denying rights to all of humanity. Indeed, comparable considerations were offered as reasons for privileging free men over women and slaves. It is not all that long ago that quite a few people in my country resisted giving women positions of authority in the work world because doing so would displace men, who were considered to be the natural breadwinners. What makes the prospect of according animals rights so frightening to some people is the implications of the sheer number of animals compared to the number of human beings: to accord rights to animals, the reasoning goes, would so profoundly encroach on the prerogatives of human beings that our very way of life would be destroyed. Again, one can easily picture this kind of objection having been raised against the emancipation of the slaves in the United States. And again, the analogy is illuminating: in both cases, the opposition to the extension of rights derives from a fear that the hegemony and material prosperity of those who already enjoy rights will be seriously undermined. Thus it is not surprising that Posner and Epstein both offer cheerful assurances that animals are much better off being the property of human beings than they would be as autonomous bearers of rights. Posner suggests that treating animals legally as commodities has the "liberating potential" to protect animals, and Epstein suggests that domestication has benefited animals by sparing them the "solitary, poor, nasty, brutish, and short" existence to which they would be subject in wild nature.[29] What neither Posner nor Epstein adds is that in being removed from the supposed Hobbesian hell of a natural existence, animals are delivered into another Hobbesian hell: that of the autocratic sovereignty of human beings. Nor does Posner or Epstein offer the slightest defense of the suggestion that the natural existence of animals is a living hell and that being subject to human dominion has "liberating potential." Marc Bekoff has done a great deal to dispel the myth that wild nature is "red in tooth and claw" *tout court*, and Gary Francione established long ago that the regime under which animals have the legal status of property simply functions as a set of mechanisms for the exploitation of animals.[30] If anything is "weird" in all this, it is that a thinker such as Posner could suggest that the same regime of animal ownership in which we send pigs to slaughter "with equanimity" has the "liberating potential" to protect animals. Again I refer the reader to the work of Gary Francione, who has shown that the promise of animal welfare is an utterly hollow one.[31] That this promise is hollow is one of the reasons why it is important for us to acknowledge that animals have rights.

The fact that a number of liberal thinkers eschew the idea of animal rights is important to take into consideration when examining the postmodern disavowal of animal rights. For while there are certain key differences, the two approaches have something in common: *they both limit their proclamations of concern for animals to considerations that do not push us out of our comfort zones.* We should care about animals, we should feel their pain as we feel our own, just as long as doing so imposes no categorical obligation on us to treat animals in ways that are ultimately inconvenient for us. Troubled by animal slaughter? Purchase meat from producers who kill their animals "humanely," if it makes you feel better. Bothered by the conditions in which animals are kept prior to slaughter? Buy "free range" meat—again, only if it makes you feel better, not because you have any affirmative moral obligation to do so. Compunctions about using animals in medical experimentation? Would you rather have us perform the experiments on human beings? And anyway, wouldn't it be an act of totalitarian force to impose prohibitions on people in regard to the use of animals? In this connection, the anti–animal rights position and the postmodern approach amount to the same thing: feel-good ethics. In the one case we make ourselves feel good by extending animals no more consideration than we feel like extending to them; in the other we make ourselves feel good by stressing the importance of responding to the ethical claim exercised on us by vulnerable animal others, a claim that we assure ourselves need not terminate in anything like a categorical prohibition on killing or using animals.

Consider the postmodern logic as regards the killing of animals, a logic that can be applied *mutatis mutandis* to other uses of animals: death is part of life; the problem of animal slaughter is so pervasive that it is far beyond anyone's control; control (like agency) is a construction and hence an illusion in any case; the logic of the trace makes it impossible to articulate principles that could apply to many different instances, inasmuch as each individual instance is incommensurable with any other; therefore, there can be no general prohibition on the killing of animals to satisfy human desires, and any attempt to realize one is both futile and misguided. Here the precise logic of postmodernism differs from the logic of anti–animal rights liberalism, which is simply inconsistent in its use of reason in determining who properly counts as a bearer of rights. But the two approaches are united in offering people ways of thinking about their relationships to animals that demand all too little of us. Writers such as Michael Pollan and Jonathan Safran Foer are the standard-bearers for this attitude toward animal ethics in the contemporary popular imagination.[32]

But these two approaches differ in their respective attitudes toward reason. Notwithstanding Posner's insistence that "reason doesn't enter," the liberal standpoint involves a merely "immanent" critique of reason whereas the postmodern standpoint undertakes a "total" critique.[33] Liberal thinkers who accept the ideas of agency, rights, and duties implicitly accept the proposition that reason has a role to play in moral and political life. They also implicitly accept the proposition that reason is capable of reflecting on its own nature and limits, in the tradition of Kantian critique. Posner is making a rational claim when he asserts, for example, that the origin of our moral convictions is sentiment rather than reason. He is equally making a rational claim when he seeks to defend the institution of human rights while denying rights to animals—even if the original sentiment underlying this distinction is not purely rational. Postmodern thinkers, on the other hand, lodge a "total" critique of reason in the sense that they seek to undermine altogether the potential of reason to work progressively toward the realization of a just society. With this rejection of reason comes the rejection of anything like universalizable norms and a fortiori the notion of rights. Recall the Nietzschean conception of justice that guides postmodern thought, if only against the postmodernist's own intention: "The active, aggressive, arrogant man is still a hundred steps closer to justice than the reactive man" in virtue of his unbridled will to assert "supreme mastery on earth."[34] Bereft of any sense of objectivity (even in a fallibilistic Habermasian sense) and any commitment to reciprocal exchange between equals, the total critique of reason is inseparable from pointedly polemical conceptions of truth and justice. In place of any hope of progress through dialogue toward the realization of a "(counterfactual) universally shared, posttotalitarian moral ethos," the poststructuralist ethos leaves us, Richard Wolin has observed, with a tragic array of "evasions, equivocations, and denials."[35] The evasion of animal rights is a case in point.

DERRIDA'S EVASION OF RIGHTS

In an exploration of Derrida's writings on animals, Leonard Lawlor repeats two interrelated claims about the notion of rights that we have encountered before: that the regime of rights simply reproduces the violence that it purports to oppose, and that its tendency to reproduce violence is born of its fundamentally exclusionary nature. We establish rights by identifying a class of bearers of rights—let us call them "persons"—and then we use that classification to confer privilege on rights-holders and to exclude and subjugate non–rights-holders. From the postmodern standpoint, the logic of rights is the same as the logic of discourses generally: perspectival, polemical, exclusionary. Rather than seek to admit animals into the moral community by reiterating a logic of exclusion, Lawlor suggests, the approach advocated by Derrida is one according to which we try "to find a way to make animals, all of them, be worthy of being members of a moral community" by getting human beings to "restrain ourselves in relation to them." It is imperative that we "change our relationship [to animals] into one of friendship" and that we exhibit compassion toward them.[36]

This is what we are being told: that extending the scope of rights so as to include animals would simply reproduce a violent logic of exclusion, and that therefore the best approach is to awaken a sense of compassion in ourselves that can serve as the ground of a friendship relation between human beings and animals. What we are never told is exactly how including animals in the sphere of rights-holders functions to exclude anyone or anything that merits moral status. The implicit logic appears to be that the only way to decide which animals to include is to employ criteria such as some minimal level of cognitive functioning or some minimal degree of similarity to human beings such as (Rorty) having a face that looks like it could become engaged in a conversation with us. Thus the danger would be ever-present that we would deem certain animals not to be sufficiently like us to merit moral consideration, and we would deny those animals rights. But as Gary Francione and I have both argued at length, the question is not whether a given animal is sufficiently like a human being to merit inclusion in the moral community. Francione rejects "similar-minds theory" and argues persuasively that the sole criterion should be whether an animal is sentient.[37] I have argued that sentience, which includes the capacity to suffer, is part of a complex set of experiential capacities possessed by living beings that have purposes and goals that they pursue just as we pursue our own, even if not all sentient creatures are capable of engaging in abstract reflection on those purposes and goals. It is difficult to see just how extending rights to animals—say, the right not to be killed and eaten by human beings—could do violence to animals, provided that we avoid the evident pitfalls of similar-minds theory.

Even more to the point, I simply find it incomprehensible how anyone could make an impassioned case for regarding animals as our friends, or for acknowledging that we and animals are inextricably referred to one another in a condition of "precarious life," and yet continue to eat meat and engage in a variety of other uses of animals that, at least for most anyone reading this book, could easily be avoided altogether.[38] Derrida and a number of postmodern thinkers writing under his influence have suggested that the ideal of peaceful interrelationships with nonhuman animals is illusory inasmuch as violence against animals is ultimately ineradicable. They also argue that, to the extent that responsibility is fundamentally openness, the animal rights approach is untenable because it closes us off from concrete encounters with singular others. As regards the prospect of a declaration of rights for animals, Derrida states that he does "not believe in the miracle of legislation."[39] The idea of simply legislating vegetarianism or veganism would be a fruitless endeavor.

This much should be uncontroversial: that simply seeking to force people to change their relationships with animals is hopeless and misguided. By anyone's account, the only way to bring about a real change in our treatment of animals is to change how we value the lives of animals; and the only way to do that is to change people's feelings, their affective assessments, of animal life. As I argued in *Animals and the Moral Community*, what is needed is a felt recognition of our essential kinship with animals. But does this by itself mean that juridical notions such as rights have no role to play in securing and protecting the moral status of animals, let alone of human beings?

At certain moments even Derrida seems not to think so. He states that "the concept of human rights" is one for which he has "the greatest respect but which . . . must be relentlessly analyzed, reelaborated, developed, and enriched (historicity and perfectibility are in fact essential to it)."[40] Rights are a kind of principle. As I noted near the end of the previous chapter, to conceive of principles as recursive mechanisms that we apply mindlessly is to misunderstand their nature entirely. To suppose that rights can be applied easily and straightforwardly, or that the respective rights of various rights-holders will automatically and transparently reveal themselves to be mutually compatible and free of so much as a hint of conflict, is to adhere to a simplistic conception not only of rights but of our living relationship to them. Kant makes this point very clearly when he states that no group of people should ever "commit itself by oath to a certain unalterable set of doctrines. . . . A contract of this kind, concluded with a view to preventing all further enlightenment of mankind for ever, is absolutely null and void, even if it is ratified by the supreme power, by Imperial Diets and the most solemn peace treaties."[41] Rights by their nature are conceived and applied through a historical process of enlightenment. Properly understood, they could never be grasped adequately as correlates of "a positivist calculation."

That Derrida, if only against his intention to transform ethics into a sense of irreducible openness to singular alterity, expresses a recognition of a potential place for rights in the transformation of our moral relationship to animals is clear from his assertion that "the mutation of relations between humans and animals *will not necessarily or solely* take the form of a charter, a declaration of rights, or a tribunal governed by a legislator." Derrida goes on to state that "although animals cannot be placed under concepts like citizen, consciousness linked with speech, subject, etc., they are not for all that without a 'right.' "[42] Thus the concept of right (but not rights in the plural[43]) is of some relevance to the predicament of animals, although neither Derrida nor any of his followers ever spells out the exact role and relevance of the notion of right to that predicament. Cary Wolfe states that a universal declaration of animal rights is "long overdue" but explains that the significance of the discourse of animal rights is purely "rhetorical." "Rhetorical" here refers to a specifically Rortyean pragmatism, in which "the rules of the game are ungrounded, unchecked, and uninsured by anything else."[44]

Given Derrida's insistence on the priority of irreducible singularity over any kind of general principle, the rules of the game *must* be ungrounded. We are returned to the problem examined above of having to rely on ungrounded prejudices ("we" think of koalas but not pigs as our friends) as a basis for the ways in which we treat animals and, for that matter, other human beings. "The difficulty of ethical responsibility is that the response cannot be formulated as a 'yes or no'; that would be too simple. It is necessary to give a singular response, within a given context, and to take the risk of a decision by enduring the undecidable. In every case, there are two contradictory imperatives."[45]

The implicit if unintended upshot of Derrida's logic is this: for every imperative to conduct ourselves peacefully toward others, there is a corresponding imperative to conduct ourselves violently. If I pose as an imperative that we must never kill and eat animals, or that we seek as far as humanly possible to avoid uses of animals, the contradictory imperative would be to eat or use animals. Presumably Lawlor's call for "minimal carnivorism" would be one form of such a contradictory imperative.[46] In previous chapters I asked the question on what basis we ought to opt for peace over violence. The answer was that, in a framework according to which "the rules of the game are ungrounded," there is no basis whatsoever for preferring peace over violence—hence the problem (or rather one of the many problems) with which Nietzsche leaves us and Derrida's ambivalence between "two contradictory imperatives." Indeed, one would do well to wonder whether, in making such a suggestion about contradictory imperatives, Derrida, if only against his own intention, actually gives license to precisely that "humanist arrogance" that he invokes as the basis for dispensing with conceptual tools such as the discourse of rights.[47] For it virtually invites us to see the use and consumption of animals as being compatible with offering them our hospitality.[48] One can easily imagine an anti–animal-rights liberal making such a suggestion.

Decisionism Revisited: We Dispense with Rights at Our Own Peril

To give priority to singularity over universality is not necessarily, Derrida seems to believe, to dispense with the latter altogether. In "Force of Law," Derrida hints that deconstruction's call for justice involves universality.[49] But as I noted in chapter 2, to subjugate the universal to the irreducibly singular is to beg the question altogether what universality can mean and what role it can play in ethics. At best its meaning becomes radically transformed in a way that no one has come close to explaining, and at worst it loses its meaning altogether. The notion of universality has historically been conceived in terms of rationality. Derrida notes that claims involving an "always" find their origin in reason. One can easily imagine Derrida dismissing calls for universal vegetarianism or veganism as products of such a conception of reason. And it is easy to understand why Derrida finds it necessary to reject such calls: the objectification of detached contemplation "de-vitalizes," which is to say that the "gaze" of rationality is inseparable from a regime of domination in which life becomes "neutralized either by death or by captivity."[50]

This is the "major failure of logic" on which the extension of rights to animals is based: to the extent that the "rights of man . . . [are] systematically dependent on a philosophy of the subject of a Cartesian or Kantian type," and inasmuch as the Cartesian-Kantian subject is a subject bent on the domination of nature (where "nature" broadly conceived includes women, people of color, animals, earth and sea, etc.), the putative extension of rights to animals can only be a ruse for the reproduction of a system of dominance and submission. "There are indeed 'animal rights' . . . but they do not forbid the killing of animals in general, be it for the production of meat for food, or for experimentation and dissection." The "reason" that advances the idea of rights "is not one" but instead purports to be one in order to conceal "the force of the stronger."[51]

Thus, notwithstanding "the strong sympathy that [the] Universal Declaration of Animal rights elicits from" Derrida, he sees the idea of such a declaration as "radically *problematic*" in presupposing that concepts such as selfhood and freedom have been made completely clear—to say nothing of his concern that such concepts are ultimately nothing more than polemical devices for the exercise of power.[52] It is in this spirit that Dominic LaCapra urges us to "displace the notion of rights in the direction of competing claims." Nonetheless LaCapra criticizes Coetzee's Elizabeth Costello for seeking to ground her ethical relation to animals in sympathy, arguing that "sympathy . . . requires supplementation by norms and processes linked to forms of sociopolitical practice."[53] In doing so, LaCapra, if only unwittingly, sheds light on the ultimate incoherence of postmodern approaches that proceed from a strong critique of humanism only to marshal key humanistic concepts in the service of ethics.[54] Even Derrida's views exhibit this incoherence; alongside assertions of the radical primacy of singularity, one finds Derrida making statements such as "it is necessary to set up rules so that one cannot do just whatever one pleases with nonhuman living beings."[55] For what is a "norm" or a "rule" if not a principle for action that has been subjected to rational scrutiny? As we have seen, so-called norms that have not been subjected to rational scrutiny—norms to which we adhere where "reason doesn't enter"—are nothing more than arbitrary expressions of prejudice. They are nothing more than assertions of perspectives of power—exactly the terms in which Derrida characterizes the notions of reason and rights. Once again we are confronted with the choice between a total critique of reason and an immanent one.

In the end Derrida opts for the former. He eschews the embrace of rights and instead characterizes the distinction (and, implicitly, the ethical relationship) between human beings and nonhuman animals as a "site of decision."[56] Like all ethical problems, the problems posed by our relationship to animals irreducibly involve "the risk of a decision."[57] As noted near the end of chapter 1, the language of decision recalls Carl Schmitt's politics of the exception, with its radical rejection of rationally grounded norms. That Derrida recognizes the pernicious implications of the politics of the exception is clear from the fact that he asserts his intention to develop "another concept of the political," one that dispenses with Schmitt's conception of sovereignty altogether.[58] LaCapra implicitly follows Derrida in calling for "a major paradigm shift" away from "'rights' discourse" and toward "a notion of basic claims of beings in an interactive network of relations that places sovereignty in question."[59] What neither Derrida nor LaCapra nor anyone else seeking to develop a postmodern conception of the political seems to have recognized is that Schmitt's notion of sovereignty, with its fundamentally polemical character, is inseparable from any political orientation that proceeds from a total critique of reason and a consequent rejection of rationally scrutinized norms. The reflection on Nietzsche's perspectivism undertaken in chapter 1 showed that the idea of a politics of "competing claims" in which sovereignty (the unilateral imposition of power that is unanswerable to any rationally secured norms) plays no role whatsoever is a contradiction in terms.

Friedrich Hayek sought to illuminate the dangers of the sovereign exception in *The Road to Serfdom*.[60] That the central planning that is the target of Hayek's critique and the notion of decision to which Schmitt and Derrida appeal both involve a rejection of general norms should serve as a warning to anyone who would seek to realize a utopian political ideal by rejecting norms that express an "always."[61] Schmitt accurately characterized political decision as being irreducibly at odds with rationally certified norms when he stated that "looked at normatively, the decision emanates from nothingness."[62] The sovereign decision on the exception is by definition a suspension of norms. Its sovereignty consists in standing outside "the normal case," hence outside rational articulation.[63] Hayek shows that the rejection of fixed principles leads directly to an irreducible dimension of arbitrariness; where "power [is] limited by no fixed rules," its expression knows no bounds, and those who wield it are ultimately answerable to no one.[64]

It is for this reason that Hayek argues for the importance of the rule of law in society. Hayek follows A. V. Dicey's definition of the rule of law as "the absolute supremacy or predominance of regular law as opposed to the influence of arbitrary power, and excludes the existence of arbitrariness, of prerogative, or even of wide discretionary power on the part of government." The rule of law is "a permanent framework of laws" designed to prevent "*ad hoc* action" on the part of the government. The rule of law "safeguards that equality before the law which is the opposite of arbitrary government." Hayek recognizes that the problem with a decisionistic conception of choice is that it confers arbitrary power on the decision-maker. The function of clearly articulated principles (a framework of laws) is to prevent the government from exercising coercive power over the citizens, or at least to limit that coercive power as much as possible.[65]

Ronald Dworkin illustrates the significance of the rule of law by explaining its proper role in Supreme Court decision making.

> It is essential to the rule of law that [Supreme Court justices] accept the constraints as well as responsibilities of the jurisprudence of principle. They must rely on principles that they honestly think provide a persuasive justification for our actual constitutional traditions. They must set out the principles on which they rely in their opinions transparently; and they must apply those principles consistently across all the cases that come before them. They must not invent arbitrary exceptions when these principles yield results they find uncongenial.[66]

Adherence to clearly articulated principles, the judicial doctrine of stare decisis, and so on provide the best guarantee that law will be "*prospective, open, and clear*," that the law will be applied impartially to all, and that people will thereby have reasonable expectations regarding the consequences of their conduct.[67]

There is a direct parallel here between law and morality. To dispense with principles (norms, rules, etc.) that govern a variety of cases of like kind is to arrogate to oneself the prerogative to "invent arbitrary exceptions." This prerogative prevails wherever "reason doesn't enter" and "the rules of the game are ungrounded." The origin of ethical principles is not some detached transcendental standpoint. It is a felt sense of lived kinship with other sentient beings. Once that sense has been awakened, it becomes possible to develop principles that articulate that sense in rational terms. Indeed, it is more than possible. It is vitally important that we develop such principles, to guard against the tendency to revert to an egocentric (anthropocentric) standpoint that isolates us from our kinship with other sentient life.[68] I take Lawlor's "minimal carnivorism" to be an example of the problem of anthropocentric arbitrariness. Lawlor states that he is "a practicing vegetarian, but at holidays [he] eat[s] meat."[69] One can imagine the following sort of scenario: In general I am a vegetarian or vegan. But now it is Thanksgiving, and Grandma has prepared a festive holiday turkey for dinner. Naturally I wouldn't want to offend Grandma by refusing to eat what she has so laboriously prepared—not to mention the fact that it tastes so damn good! What doesn't come into question in such a situation is whether I ought not to offend the turkey.

Now why am I, in such a scenario, in general a vegetarian or vegan? Lawlor's answer to this question sheds light on the limits of the postmodern approach to animals. For the most part, his discussion leads to the conclusion that we ought to have compassion and establish a "friendship" relation to animals.[70] But as noted above, Lawlor identifies his real motivation as "a kind of asceticism." To embrace vegetarianism or veganism on ascetic grounds is specifically *not* to engage in the practice out of any direct concern for animals. It is, as Porphyry so eloquently demonstrates, to be a participant in the "Olympics of the soul," that process of soul purification in which we escape the prison house of embodiment and find union with the divine.[71] What Lawlor proposes is a comparable if secularized form of spiritual practice: I refrain in general from eating meat as part of a regimen of spiritual discipline, not for the sake of animals themselves. If my vegetarianism or veganism *were* motivated by a direct concern for animals, then my living concern would become formalized into a principle and I wouldn't go looking for opportunities to disregard my concern (Lawlor calls these opportunities "holidays").

A fundamental confusion of a number of thinkers writing in the wake of Derrida is to suppose that the discourse of rights is inseparable from a set of metaphysical commitments about the human self and its ability to establish clear and enduring knowledge about reality. As I noted at the beginning of this chapter, some thinkers allege that the discourse of rights is "metaphysical" and hence that it must be dismantled along with the metaphysical humanism in which it is grounded.[72] Many of these thinkers treat as unproblematic the retention of some notion of universality in ethics once we have become "posthumanist," even though, as I have noted, they give no clear indication what universality can mean or what specific role it can play in an ethics based on recognition of the other. Typically we are given only negative formulations, such as the following: "It is important to stress that this notion of universal consideration does not make the positivist claim that all things or all life forms *do* count; nor does it supply any positive claim concerning *how* various beings or relational structures might count. On both points, an ethics of universal consideration requires us to keep the question wide open."[73]

An ethics of this kind is caught in the dilemma between paralysis and arbitrariness that I discussed near the end of chapter 1. Observing that ethics has an irreducibly aporetic dimension is one thing, but an ethics that refuses to take a positive, principled stand is as good as meaningless. To remain at all times "wide open" is to be prepared for the possibility that anything could become an object of ethical concern. It is to refuse to make any discriminations for fear of exercising exclusionary violence, which amounts to taking no ethical stand at all. In refusing to make any positive assertions about the proper beneficiaries of ethical concern, this approach is scarcely distinguishable in its concrete application from an approach that acknowledges no proper beneficiaries of ethical concern.

Postmodern thinkers place themselves in an untenable position regarding ethics by making an odd supposition: that the notion of subjectivity must be conceived in specifically metaphysical terms, hence that all the relevant concepts will have been made completely clear. Anyone who accepts the critique of metaphysics initiated by Nietzsche and Heidegger and elaborated by Derrida, so the thinking goes, will immediately see the need to dispense with liberal-humanist notions of selfhood, agency, autonomy, responsibility, equality, and reciprocity. Thinkers who follow this line of reasoning assume that the critique of the Cartesian *res cogitans* and the Kantian transcendental subject leave us bereft of all the subsidiary notions employed by Enlightenment thinkers. What we are left with is an assessment of rights as nothing more than "shrewd rhetoric."[74] Thinkers of this stripe also sweep aside the concern about arbitrariness that I have expressed. "'Relativism is a bogus charge levied by those who think they have a corner on philosophical foundations."[75] Not surprisingly, in offering this flimsy ad hominem response when confronted with a central failing of postmodernism, Wolfe cites the authority of none other than Richard Rorty.

The distinction between an immanent and a total critique of reason makes it abundantly clear that one can untether notions such as selfhood and responsibility from the metaphysical moorings that they were once thought to have. The postmodern thinkers under discussion are united in undertaking a total critique of reason that completely undermines traditional notions of agency, responsibility, and rights. And yet at the same time, these thinkers employ reason in order to lodge this critique. They marshal reason in the service of irrationality, thereby leaving themselves in the position of espousing what Husserl referred to as "the rationality of 'lazy reason.' "[76] The problem is not solved by noting that postmodern thinkers are aware that they rely on reason. Richard Bernstein correctly suggests that "it is a slander" to allege that Derrida "undermines and ridicules any appeal to rational argument. . . . He does *not* 'reduce' all logic and argumentation to disguised rhetorical tropes."[77] But even Bernstein has to acknowledge, as noted in chapter 2, that Derrida never explains *"how we can 'warrant' (in any sense of the term) the ethical-political positions we do take."* Derrida, in short, fails to provide us "with an orientation for avoiding the abyss of nihilism that he so desperately wants to avoid."[78] Indeed, in his last lecture course on animals, Derrida devotes a great deal of attention to deriding the endeavor of thinkers such as Heidegger to attain a sense of orientation.[79]

At the end of chapter 2, I made the following suggestion: that given the essential identity between humans and animals as mortal creatures that struggle and suffer, there ought to be no obstacle to a rational recognition of the moral equality of humans and animals as regards their entitlement to life and the enjoyment of their freedom. There is no reason to suppose that "fundamental moral rights" must be conceived as "ontologically grounded entities."[80] It is not at all clear why taking our bearings from our shared mortality with nonhuman animals, an orientation that itself may well be inscribed within a larger sense of commonality with the living generally, should involve the least "force" or "arbitrariness."[81] Nor is it clear why there should be any problem with formalizing this sense of shared mortality into a set of principles that include the proposition that eating or using animals is morally wrong. It is particularly troubling to see people who have no need to use or consume animals, who disregard the moral standing of animals purely or primarily out of pleasure and convenience, refuse to acknowledge the wrongness of these practices. John Coetzee suggests that "our ethical impulses are prerational" and that "all that a rational ethics can achieve is to articulate and give form to ethical impulses."[82] Coetzee's view is very much like Posner's: our ethical "impulses" are extrarational and intractable, and all that reason can do is spell them out while leaving them completely unmodified. Such a conception of the relationship between reason and impulse fails to recognize the potential of reason to scrutinize our prerational impulses and see whether they are warranted. Some of our impulses are merely selfish appetites that need to be forsaken in our endeavor to do justice to our relationships and obligations to others. To take the position that my ethical impulses just are what they are is to give voice to lazy reason. It is to rationalize an egotistical (or, in the case of our relationship to animals, an anthropocentric) perspective and to fail (or simply refuse) to see that rational reflection can change the way we feel about things.

ANOTHER FORM OF POSTMODERN
EVASION: CORA DIAMOND

Many postmodern thinkers are united not only in their evasion of rights but also in their implicit commitment to the proposition that our prerational impulses are invulnerable to rational scrutiny. A number of these thinkers set up a strict either-or between "traditional" philosophical argumentation and an acknowledgment of the condition of vulnerability and suffering that each of us shares not only with other human beings but with nonhuman animals. They place the appeal to rights on the side of philosophical argumentation and maintain that the genuine ground of ethical commitment lies within the reach of those who adequately acknowledge the obscurity of many of our concepts and what Cora Diamond, following John Updike, calls "the difficulty of reality." Diamond follows Simone Weil in arguing that people like me, who seek to attribute rights to animals, are beset with a conceptual confusion—that we misunderstand concepts such as "justice" and "rights." Justice and rights, on Diamond's view, "come from . . . different conceptual realm[s]" and exhibit "a difference in grammar." Justice concerns "a responsiveness to the relentless treatment of vulnerable" beings, whereas "rights remain within the sphere in which we are sharing things out, exchanging this for that, balancing this right against that."[83] Diamond's goal is to defend Weil's claim that "when genuine issues of justice and injustice are framed in terms of rights, they are thereby distorted and trivialized."[84] But in fact Diamond's (and Weil's) argument, while motivated by a sincere concern to uncover the lived ground of rational articulations of principles of justice, shows something else altogether: that the complete bifurcation of feeling and reason, the endeavor to treat them as autonomous domains that have no interaction with one another, leads to the very kind of conceptual confusion that Wittgensteinian thinkers pride themselves in overcoming. And, more important, Diamond's argument leaves animals in a more vulnerable position than they would be in if we were to embrace and seek to clarify the idea of animal rights.

Diamond contrasts "moral debate, in which the livingness and death of animals enter as facts that we treat as relevant in this way or that," and the lived acknowledgment of animals "as presences that may unseat our reason." This opposition between moral debate (and philosophical argumentation more generally) and the experience of living presences is a corollary of "the difficulty of reality," namely, that there are "experiences in which we take something in reality to be resistant to our thinking it, or possibly to be painful in its inexplicability, difficult in that way, or perhaps awesome and astonishing in its inexplicability." Diamond gives as an illustration of the difficulty of reality the torment and isolation experienced by Coetzee's Elizabeth Costello when she contemplates the Holocaust and considers the ways in which our treatment of animals may be very much like the Holocaust.[85] The "painful inexplicability" of such events makes any accounting for them in terms of "facts" and "reasons" an ultimately fruitless endeavor. Reason simply reifies the pain, horror, and irreducibility of such presences, leaving them "distorted and trivialized."

But we must not ignore these horrors. Diamond invites us to consider Elizabeth Costello's appeal to "poetry, rather than philosophy, as having the capacity to return us to [a more adequate] sense of what animal life is. . . . '[D]ebate' as we understand it may have built into it a distancing of ourselves from our sense of our own bodily life and our capacity to respond to and to imagine the bodily life of others."[86] There is undoubtedly something right in Diamond's suggestion that poetry has a special role to play in awakening a felt appreciation of life, struggle, and suffering. Schopenhauer observes that the artist's grasp of the inner nature of things is instinctive and prerational rather than purely conceptual. The distinction of tragedy, the highest form of poetry in Schopenhauer's estimation, is that it conveys a sense of "the terrible side of life," that of conflict and suffering.[87] The poet does so by evoking in us a sense of our inner connectedness to the world-will, which is to say our relationship to everything in the world that participates in struggle and suffering. One might even push this contrast between philosophy and art further and follow Schopenhauer in seeing music as the preeminent medium for awakening in us a sense of the horrors of existence.

But none of this should lead us to suppose that poetry or any other artistic form is "better" than philosophy when it comes to establishing a sense of moral connectedness with animals. Philosophy and art approach the world in different but complementary ways. Each is suited to illuminating certain dimensions of existence but not others. Schopenhauer notes that "philosophy is nothing but a complete and accurate repetition and expression of the inner nature of the world in very general concepts, for only in these is it possible to obtain a view of that entire inner nature which is everywhere adequate and applicable."[88] Philosophy achieves something that neither poetry nor any of the other arts can, namely, the rational articulation of certain universal truths of existence (e.g., as Schopenhauer and Löwith both recognized, that willing is inseparable from suffering). It is through such rational articulation that we become able to recognize that certain feelings give rise to certain sorts of responsibilities. Schopenhauer for his part uses philosophical reflection to proceed from a felt sense of kinship with animals to the assertion of duties of "heavenly" or "eternal" justice toward animals.[89] But he would be the first to say that philosophical abstraction does not disclose for us our participation in the world-will and our inner connectedness with other suffering beings. That connectedness is disclosed through our will and its affects and is given forms of expression in art that it is not the purpose of philosophy to provide.

Diamond's criticism of philosophy as being out of touch with "the difficulty of reality" is directed at a particular conception of philosophical argument. There are ways of doing philosophy to which Diamond's critique has little if any applicability. (Presumably her own approach to philosophy would be one such way.) There is no reason to suppose that philosophy must by its very nature be out of touch with the horrors of existence. Those approaches to philosophy that seek to ground all philosophical insights in the autonomy of reason, as if reason could arrive at the truth of existence without any consideration of our embodied encounter with the world around us, are most susceptible to Diamond's critique. Wolfe suggests that the approach that is the object of Diamond's critique is one that "hew[s] to the protocols of analytic philosophy."[90] Approaches to philosophy that maintain an openness to the irreducible complexity and torment of reality would presumably be more adequate in recognizing the limits of philosophy and the inability of concepts to capture the complete truth of existence.

But again, none of this is to say that concepts and conceptual analysis have no role to play in establishing a sense of the moral status of animals. (Not all philosophical analysis is "analytic" in the specific, historically conditioned sense gestured toward by Wolfe.) Does the idea of rights ineluctably "distort and trivialize genuine issues of justice and injustice"? If we conceive of rights exclusively as mechanisms for regulating exchange and for meting out abstract entitlements, and if we conceive of justice and injustice in terms of the suffering and evil experienced by mortal creatures and the response these (ought to) evoke in us, then it may be fair to say that "the difference between justice as Weil conceives it and justice thought of in terms of rights is a difference in grammar."[91] Weil believes that "justice consists in seeing that no harm is done to men," whereas rights talk pertains to situations in which someone cries, "Why has somebody else got more than I have?" Weil's conception of justice is like Schopenhauer's, except that she explicitly limits its scope to human relationships; she admits no constraints on our will apart from "material necessity and the existence of other human beings around us." She writes a great deal about the problem of "affliction" but does not utter a word about the extraordinary ways in which we afflict animals. To the prospect of extending the scope of her analysis to include animals, if indeed she would be willing to extend the list of constraints on our will so as to include the imperative to respond to the affliction of animals, Weil would presumably say that granting them rights would do them no good. To offer the afflicted the vocabulary of rights "is to offer them something which can bring them no good and will inevitably do them much harm," inasmuch as "rights are dependent upon force" and the afflicted lack the power of enforcement.[92]

Weil's confinement of considerations of justice to human beings and her narrow definition of rights as mechanisms for regulating economic exchanges are both anthropocentric limitations that stand in need of conceptual clarification. Diamond seeks to extend some of Weil's considerations to human-animal relationships, but she nonetheless reiterates a central confusion in Weil's discussion: the idea that because "the cry of hurt of someone to whom evil is done is altogether different from someone's outrage at getting less than what he takes to be his fair share of something," it follows that the language of rights properly applies to the latter but not to the former.[93] The confusion consists in supposing that because rights are mechanisms for protecting interests, and because the suffering of the afflicted is something to which we ought to respond prior to any abstract consideration of facts, interests, reasons, and so forth, rights have no logical connection with the problem of affliction.

But the appeal to rights need not be construed in such unduly narrow terms. Weil dismisses rights for their "mediocrity" and calls the idea of natural right a "lie."[94] There is, however, a relatively straightforward way to understand the interrelationship between rights and living presences: in an ideal world in which everyone responded in exactly the right way to the cry of affliction, it might make sense to treat rights as superfluous. In such a world it would not be necessary to point out that it is unjust to cause others to suffer or to ignore their suffering, nor would there be a need to construct legal personhood as "an artifact" for the protection of beings who suffer.[95] Diamond acknowledges in passing that "the language of rights is, one might say, meant to be useful in contexts in which we cannot count on the kind of understanding of evil that depends on loving attention to the victim."[96] Given the world in which we live, and given the extraordinary affliction that animals suffer at our hands, the language of rights would appear to be absolutely indispensable in the endeavor to release animals from their state of affliction.

Nonetheless, Diamond is quite right to state that "without [loving] attention . . . there is no perceiving the evil of genuine injustice."[97] Simply confronting people with the proposition that animals merit rights is, by itself, a fruitless endeavor. What is needed is a kind of soul conversion that can change the sensibilities of people who staunchly deny having any "mystical, panmoralistic" sense of being part of a cosmic whole whose moral beneficiaries include any beings other than humans.[98] Such a change in sensibilities is needed to motivate people to acknowledge and respect the rights of animals. That animals *have* rights, however, is not dependent on people acknowledging these rights. The fact that animals share life, sentience, and struggle with us, that they are in this respect "absolutely identical with us," is sufficient by itself for a rational recognition that animals merit rights.[99] Or rather it *should* be sufficient. The unremitting refusal of the vast majority of humanity, including quite a few philosophers who profess concern for the plight of animals, to acknowledge that animals are the kind of "living presences" that merit our full moral respect stands as a testimonial to the urgent need for a recognition of animal rights. Poetry *and* philosophy so far seem to have failed utterly to soften the hearts of very many people. That itself is a "difficulty of reality."

It is right to say that the language of rights by itself is not sufficient for the liberation of animals from their servitude. But Diamond's suggestion that a language different from that of rights "is needed . . . by the victims of such evil, or those who speak on their behalf," is potentially misleading.[100] For it could be construed to mean that the language of rights is not really even necessary—that some other kind of language is really all we need in order to find and live in accordance with our proper relationship to animals. The kind of language that Diamond presumably has in mind is poetic language or, more broadly, the language of art that Schopenhauer recognized to be capable of addressing us at the level of our affects and not simply at the level of our intellect.

The languages of art can certainly make a contribution to our appreciation of the predicament of animals. But there is no reason to suppose either that poetry has a special priority in this connection or that the ascription of rights to animals "can bring them no good and will inevitably do them much harm." One of the major pitfalls of the philosophy of language in the wake of Wittgenstein is to suppose that nature is simply a kind of linguistic construction or set correlates of linguistic phenomena. To suppose that all our ways of relating to things are linguistic is to miss something of which Schopenhauer was keenly aware: that we have an immediate, visceral relation to all other beings that struggle and suffer, and that any kind of language simply distances us from nature. Even poetic language distances us from the world, which is why Schopenhauer privileged music over poetry and specified music without words as the most direct expression of our relation to the world-will.[101]

Poetic language has the potential to bring us back into touch with the inner nature of things, in a world in which not only reason and language but a variety of institutional forces (capital, technology, bureaucracy, etc.) and our own sense of our superiority over nonhuman nature constantly divert our attention away from our essential sameness with animals and our essential continuity with the world-will. Experience shows that all the language in the world, be it poetic or philosophical, is not sufficient to awaken the kind of experience of evil and affliction that leads to a change in people's values and behavior. What is needed is a face-to-face encounter with evil and affliction, the kind of encounter in the face of which one cannot turn away, one that permanently haunts us. As regards animals, what is needed is what Diamond calls a "fellow-creature response." She opposes this response to the endeavor to "defend animals' rights on the basis of an abstract principle of equality."[102] But again, why portray this as a strict either-or? An abstract principle of equality is entirely applicable here, even if it is insufficient by itself to motivate a change in people's feelings and values. Moreover, such a principle has tremendous potential to protect animals precisely where we cannot rely on people (including ourselves) to maintain at all times the full visceral sense of our shared mortality with animals. Seen in their best light rather than in the light in which they manifest themselves too often, moral principles are conceptual tools that enable us to preserve a felt sense of connectedness with and desire to respond in appropriate ways to others. These principles remind us of our own most deeply held commitments in those moments when fear, fatigue, or selfish appetite obscure our sense of what is ultimately most important to us.

Thus there is no reason to suppose that "the abstract appeal to the prevention of suffering as a principle of action" must unavoidably encourage "us to ignore pity, to forget what it contributes to our conception of suffering and death, and how it is connected with the possibility of relenting." Understood in a more living and less reified sense than the one to which we are accustomed, principles have the power to *reawaken* our sense of pity, to *remind* us of what it contributes to our conception of suffering, and how it is connected with the possibility of relenting. That none of this emerges in Diamond's discussion gives me pause to wonder whether there is more than conceptual confusion at work here—whether there is an anthropocentric evasion comparable to that seen in postmodern thinkers such as Derrida. Diamond believes that "images of fellow creatures are naturally much less compelling ones than images of 'fellow human beings' can be."[103] But are they? "Much less"? "Naturally"? And for whom? Is this a legitimate characterization of a "fact"? Or is it exactly the kind of "deflection" of a difficulty of reality that thinkers such as Diamond and Stanley Cavell seek to avoid?[104]

Diamond notes that one aspect of the difficulty of reality is that "so far as we keep one sort of difficulty in view we seem blocked from seeing another."[105] A prime example of this phenomenon is the way in which our preoccupation with human affliction tends to blind us to (and vastly underestimate) the colossal problem of animal affliction. To assume confidently, as so many people do, that animal suffering is less significant than human suffering is to engage in a tragic deflection. It is worth taking very seriously Elizabeth Costello's suggestion that "anyone who says that life matters less to animals than it does to us has not held in his hands an animal fighting for its life."[106] For it reminds us of the tremendous difficulty involved in trying to appreciate the specific contours of the life of a being with whom we cannot converse in our own language, and it likewise reminds us of the fact that animals struggle, suffer, and go to great lengths to defer death—exactly as we do.

Diamond suggests that a related aspect of the difficulty of reality is that any attempt "to bring a difficulty of reality into focus . . . is inextricably intertwined with relations of power between people."[107] This again is true but potentially misleading. At the end of chapter 1 I examined Foucault's conception of discourse as inherently perspectival and polemical. It would be naive to suppose that speech situations are not mediated through dynamics of power. But matrices of power include beings other than human, linguistic agents. The fact that fifty-three billion land animals are killed worldwide each year for human consumption—one can scarcely imagine the number if we include sea creatures—provides irrefutable evidence that animals are subjected on an almost incomprehensible scale to human caprice. And this is to say nothing of the deplorable conditions under which many of these animals are confined prior to slaughter. As I argue in the latter half of the next chapter, the human, all too human, conflicts that confront us are entirely real and tragic; but the more we focus on them in isolation from the larger cosmic context in which they play themselves out, the less we focus on—the less we acknowledge and take responsibility for—the suffering and death that we cause animals and that we could avoid if only we would demand a little more of ourselves.

If ethics is above all a concern for the other, particularly for the vulnerable other, then animals ought to be at least as much an object of our ethical concern as our fellow human beings. That this moral equation of humans and nonhuman animals strikes so many people as counterintuitive or simply wrong is a reflection of a deeply rooted anthropocentric prejudice that I first examined in *Anthropocentrism and Its Discontents*. In that text I showed that the dominant voice in our culture as regards human-animal relations has since Greek antiquity been one according to which human beings are fundamentally superior to animals, and according to which animals either have no direct moral worth or have less moral worth than human beings. But our history also includes occasional voices of discontent about this anthropocentric prejudice. Pythagoras, Empedocles, Plutarch, Porphyry, Montaigne, and Schopenhauer all express radical insights into the prospect of what the contemporary thinker Elisabeth de Fontenay calls "pathocentrism," an approach to moral community oriented on feeling rather than on a purely rational recognition of our continuity with and obligations toward animals.[108] Such an approach holds the promise of expanding the scope of our moral concern to include all creatures that feel and struggle and die.

The thinkers I have just named recognize that the historical focus on *logos* (reason and language) as the necessary and sufficient criterion for membership in the moral community is an evasion motivated by human selfishness. And yet, or rather for precisely this reason, the words "animals [are] our fellows in mortality" continue to ring hollow for the vast majority of humanity.[109] First we must dig beneath the superstructure of rational abstraction and feel our essential kinship with nonhuman animals. This task is difficult for many people in industrialized nations today because our contact with animals is severely limited; and where we do have such contact, it is mediated through institutional mechanisms such as pet ownership and zoo confinement, which participate in and reinforce a global ideology of human dominion over animals and the rest of nature. But it is possible to overcome the distorting influence of this deep-rooted ideology, if only we can engage in the kind of selflessness in our encounters with animals that we expect of ourselves in our ethical encounters with our fellow human beings. One must be genuinely open to animals in a way that eludes rational description but at least roughly corresponds to Heidegger's call to "let beings be."[110]

Once that "pathocentric" ground of kinship has been disclosed, it becomes possible to recognize with regard to animals exactly what Weil implicitly recognizes about human beings but refuses to articulate: that we are referred to them in a relation of shared mortality in virtue of which they have rights and we have obligations. Rights are not a "lie." They are simply the rational expression of our recognition that we *ought* to care for other beings who share the condition of mortality with us, and there is no reason to suppose that they presuppose any metaphysical foundation whatsoever.[111]

CHAPTER FIVE

Toward a Nonanthropocentric Cosmopolitanism

HISTORICAL COSMOPOLITAN IDEALS

The ideal of civil society that prevails today owes a direct debt to Enlightenment thinkers such as Kant, who sought to articulate the importance of notions such as autonomy, equality, reciprocity, and mutual respect for any viable system of political decision making. But our contemporary ideal owes an equal if indirect debt to an ancient cosmopolitan ideal according to which human beings are morally superior to all other natural beings and hence enjoy a natural prerogative to use nonhuman beings to satisfy human needs and desires. Kant does not invent the cosmopolitan ideal but simply modifies it in accordance with the liberal humanist notion of the individual that had developed through the reflections of the Christian humanists in the Renaissance and those of Descartes and the social contract thinkers in modernity. Thus to the extent that the ancient cosmopolitan ideal is fundamentally anthropocentric, it should come as no surprise that Enlightenment cosmopolitanism and our contemporary ideal of civil society are likewise anthropocentric.

For the Western philosophical tradition this posed no problem since the tradition conceived of society as being concerned exclusively with human relationships and activities. And for many people today, this still poses no problem whatsoever. But for anyone concerned with the fortunes of nonhuman animals, it has become a matter of serious controversy whether the concept of society or community should ultimately be restricted to human beings, particularly given the fact that so many of our activities and cultural practices involve the subjection and exploitation of animals. For if social relationships and responsibilities are conceived in exclusively human terms, then, in accordance with the ancient cosmopolitan ideal advanced by the Stoics, animals are categorically excluded from the sphere of justice, and nothing we do to animals can be classified as unjust. According to early Greek writers such as Hesiod, human society originated in a "golden age" in which human beings shared a fundamentally peaceful existence not only with one another but also with animals. Human beings lived as if they were gods, without having to struggle for their existence, and without having to kill and eat animals.[1] Only after a sort of fall from grace did human beings become violent toward one another and toward animals, and only then did it become necessary for Zeus to impose *dike* or the law of justice and peace. According to Hesiod, Zeus thereby placed all human beings in the sphere of justice and expressly excluded all animals—apparently on the grounds that animals were not capable of "listen[ing] to justice."[2] Ovid, too, offers a *Verfallsgeschichte*, the beginning of which is a golden age in which humans and animals lived together in a sort of paradise.[3] To the extent that the historical roots of our received conception of justice lie in an ideal of peaceful coexistence with animals, it strikes me as odd that our conception of justice categorically excludes any consideration of animals. Or perhaps it is the other way around: given that our traditional conception of justice has no implications whatsoever for our treatment of animals, it ought to strike us as odd that Hesiod and Ovid characterized our original and putatively ideal condition as one in which we were friends and companions of animals.

The history of the West is marked by a conspicuous tension between fanciful depictions of a peaceful ideal state and the *factum brutum* of violence. Our history is not simply one of violence among human beings, but also and perhaps even more significantly a history of human violence toward animals. Every year fifty-three billion animals are slaughtered for the sake of the welfare and enjoyment of human beings, and our traditional principles of justice do not raise the least scruple against such practices. If we are to take the interests and the fate of animals seriously, we will need a more exacting conception of justice than the one we have inherited. As even Rawls recognized, a robust conception of obligation toward animals would presuppose "a theory of the natural order and our place in it."[4] And yet Rawls claims that the concept of justice pertains exclusively to relations among human beings. Like the Stoics before him, Rawls maintains that, to the extent that animals lack the capacity to enter into contracts and assume obligations, it is impossible in principle to do an injustice to an animal; for Rawls it is utterly meaningless to speak of justice or injustice with regard to animals.

I take this tension in Rawls's thought to be an indication that even Rawls, if only against his own intention, sees his theory of justice against the background of a more fundamental theory of the natural order and our place in it. For Rawls this appears to be a theory according to which human beings have a superior place in the cosmos and animals an inferior one. Rawls, in other words, simply gives modern expression to the Stoic doctrine of cosmopolitanism. On the Stoic view, material goods such as animals are mere *adiaphora* or "indifferents," and animals were created specifically for the sake of human beings.[5] Of course there is a basic difference between Rawls and the Stoics: Rawls conceives of the world in secularized, presumably godless terms, whereas the Stoics presume the cosmos to have been ordered by the gods. But with regard to the moral status of animals, this difference is insignificant. Regardless of whether a traditional theory of the cosmos and our place in it presupposes a creator-god, the implications for animals are the same. Like the earlier view of human beings as created in the image of a God or gods, the modern, secularized view still conceives of humanity as in certain respects godlike.[6] In both cases the conviction that human beings are godlike serves as the basis for a moral hierarchy of living beings in which rational beings (humans) are superior and nonrational beings (animals) inferior. The supposedly superior beings enjoy the prerogative, indeed the right, to use the supposedly inferior beings as they see fit.

As I have noted, the contemporary cosmopolitan ideal has its roots in an ancient theory of the cosmos. The crux of this theory is found in the writings of Aristotle. In the *Politics*, Aristotle proclaims the superiority of human beings over animals: "After the birth of animals, plants exist for their sake, and . . . the other animals exist for the sake of man, the tame for use and food, the wild, if not all, at least the greater part of them, for food, and for the provision of clothing and various instruments. Now if nature makes nothing in vain, the inference must be that she has made all animals for the sake of man."[7] In texts such as *De anima* and the *Politics*, Aristotle denies animals reason and the capacity to form beliefs, and he excludes animals from moral-political community on the grounds that they lack these capacities. Aristotle presupposes a natural hierarchy in which humans are superior to all nonrational beings and may use such beings in any way they see fit for the satisfaction of human needs and desires. The use of animals, like all use of nonrational beings, liberates human beings from material need and facilitates our striving for *eudaimonia*. *Eudaimonia* is dependent on rational contemplation or *theoria*, an activity that makes human beings godlike—contemplation places us, as Heidegger might put the point, in the nearness of the gods.[8] According to Aristotle, animals have no capacity for contemplation, hence no share in *eudaimonia*.[9] Animals are "inferior in their nature to men" and are categorically excluded from virtue and politics.[10]

Like Aristotle, the Stoics presuppose a cosmos hierarchically structured in terms of degrees of perfection. According to the Stoics, the world itself is the highest perfection. The world is rationally ordered, and its perfection can be grasped only by rational beings. Thus only human beings and gods can actively participate in the true good that characterizes the cosmos; all other beings, such as animals and plants, are inferior to (less perfect than) rational beings. According to Seneca, "the Good [is] non-existent" in plants and animals "because there is no reason there . . . that alone is perfect which is perfect according to nature as a whole, and nature as a whole is possessed of reason."[11] This is a decisive commitment that informs the dominant voice in the entire history of Western philosophy, ancient as well as modern: only those beings that can apprehend or contemplate the good *are* intrinsically rather than merely instrumentally good. In Stoic thought, the influence of this prejudice finds expression in the doctrine of living in accordance with nature (*kata physei*). The meaning of living in accordance with nature varies with the being in question and its place in the cosmic hierarchy. Animals are moved by immediate perceptions and impulses; "for them it is sufficient to eat and drink and rest and procreate, and whatever else of the things within their own province the animals severally do." But for human beings, "to whom [God] has made the additional gift of the faculty of understanding, these things are no longer sufficient. . . . For of beings whose constitutions are different, the works and the ends are likewise different."[12] For human beings, material welfare is a necessary but not a sufficient condition for living in accordance with nature. The endowment of reason makes human beings capable of moral conduct, and according to Cicero such conduct is "the sole thing that is for its own efficacy and value desirable, whereas none of the primary objects of nature is desirable for its own sake."[13] Plants and animals count as such "primary objects" and exist for the sake of human beings.[14] On the Stoic view, the world itself is also an object. To the extent that the world is an object of contemplation, it exists for the sake of gods and humans alike. But because the gods are by nature self-sufficient, the world, to the extent that it is a means for the satisfaction of bodily needs, exists for the sake of human beings. Thus animals and other nonrational beings are "destined for service," in order that human beings may be freed for reflection on "the divine administration of the world."[15]

According to Stoic cosmology, such contemplation is the essence of cosmopolitanism, and cosmopolitanism is the highest level of existence. This anthropocentric vision of ideal existence influences the entire subsequent history of European thinking about the status of human beings and animals in the cosmic scheme. In medieval Christianity this influence is especially evident in the thought of Saint Augustine and Saint Thomas Aquinas, although it is also apparent in the writings of such thinkers as Origen, Saint Basil, John Chrysostom, and even Saint Francis of Assisi. Like his predecessors the Stoics, Augustine maintains that animals have no access to divine truth because they lack reason.[16] Thus "human beings are superior" to animals; and animals, like all nonrational beings, exist "to serve us in our weakness."[17] Because animals were not created in God's image, we are entitled to kill them for the satisfaction of our needs. And we may do so without the least scruple, inasmuch as we share no "community of rights" with animals. "We can perceive by their cries that animals die in pain, although we make little of this since the beast, lacking a rational soul, is not related to us by a common nature."[18] Augustine's denial of a community of rights with animals is a restatement of the Stoic prejudice that all and only rational beings are members of the sphere of justice, and that nothing we do to nonrational beings such as animals can possibly be construed as an injustice.

Like Augustine, Aquinas sees human beings as the crown of creation and maintains that animals exist for the satisfaction of human needs. Humans are rational beings who possess free will and stand in the nearness of God. Animals, on the other hand, lack both reason and freedom; thus their behavior must be guided by the hand of God.[19] On Aquinas's view, "all animals are naturally subject to man.... For the imperfect are for the use of the perfect: plants make use of the earth for their nourishment, animals make use of plants, and man makes use of both plants and animals. Therefore it is in keeping with the order of nature that man should be master over animals.... Since man, being made in the image of God, is above other animals, these are rightly subject to his government."[20] From this follows Aquinas's well-known conviction that our duties with regard to animals are in fact duties toward humanity; the only reason to avoid cruelty to animals is that being cruel to animals makes us more likely to be cruel to our fellow human beings.[21] Apart from this anthropocentric restriction, Aquinas recognizes no limits on what we may do to animals to satisfy our desires: "It is not wrong for man to make use of [animals], either by killing or in any other way whatsoever."[22] Thus Aquinas advances a cosmopolitan ideal according to which animals have no direct moral status but are merely resources and instruments for the practice of virtue.

In the Enlightenment the cosmopolitan ideal develops in accordance with Kant's program for religion within the limits of reason alone. Kant and other modern cosmopolitan thinkers adhere to the Stoic-Christian prejudice that animals are "lower" beings that are not only practically but also morally inferior to humans. The replacement of God with secularized human reason as the ultimate basis for moral as well as metaphysical truth does nothing to change the moral status of animals; the traditional assumption of human divinity and the resulting sense of superiority over animals remain unshaken.

This assumption of human superiority is central to Kant's cosmopolitan ideal:

> In the system of nature, a human being (*homo phaenomenon, animal rationale*) is a being of slight importance and shares with the rest of the animals, as offspring of the earth, an ordinary value (*pretium vulgare*). ... But a human being regarded as a person, that is, as the subject of a morally practical reason, is exalted above any price; for as a person (*homo noumenon*) he is not to be valued merely as a means to the ends of others or even to his own ends, but as an end in himself, that is, he possesses a *dignity* (an absolute inner worth) by which he exacts *respect* for himself from all other rational beings in the world.[23]

All natural beings, to the extent that they are natural beings, possess "ordinary" [*gemeinen*], which is to say "slight" [*geringen*] worth. Here Kant presupposes a hierarchy of value according to which nonrational beings have an inferior status in the cosmos. Nonrational beings are "things" with merely instrumental or relative value, whereas rational beings are "persons" and possess worth "above all price."[24] In the Kantian cosmos, those beings possess the highest moral worth who can recognize their own intrinsic worth and be recognized to possess such worth. Beings that make value distinctions are fundamentally superior to beings that do not make value distinctions; and given that the making of value distinctions is a rational activity on Kant's view, human beings possess a worth that is incomparable to that of all other beings in the world.

The worth of rational beings is not merely quantitatively but is in fact qualitatively superior to that of all nonrational beings. Absent the discovery of nonhuman rational beings in the universe, a possibility that Kant explicitly entertains, this means that human beings are fundamentally the "lord[s] of nature."[25] To the extent that animals cannot contemplate abstract notions such as that of absolute worth, they are categorically excluded from the sphere of moral beings. Human beings possess reason, which makes possible mutual respect among moral agents and progress in our moral striving. The apex of such striving is the realization of a cosmopolitan condition in which all rational beings live "in accordance with [an] integral, prearranged plan" that "nature has as its highest purpose."[26] In accordance with this plan and purpose, "violence will gradually become less on the part of those in power, and obedience towards the laws will increase. There will no doubt be more charity."[27]

And yet in this supposedly ideal society human beings will have no duty of charity toward animals but at most a duty of compassion that forbids "violent and cruel treatment of animals." Like Aquinas, Kant sees a causal relationship between cruelty toward animals and cruelty toward our fellow human beings. The less cruelty we exhibit toward animals, the more respect we will show to human beings. Kant's view of charity is an extension of his view of friendship: "*Friendship* (considered in its perfection) is the union of two persons through equal mutual love and respect." Because no "morally good will unites" human beings with animals, there can be neither friendship nor charity shared between the two.[28] Indeed, there can be no direct duties of any kind on the part of a person toward a mere thing. Our duty of compassion toward animals is in no way an indication of respect for animals, inasmuch as animals are mere means and hence not the kind of beings toward which it is possible to have respect.

And to the extent that we find it relatively easy to exploit animals without feeling any pangs of conscience, Kant's assurance that violence on the part of those in power will gradually become less in a cosmopolitan state has little if any significance for the fortunes of animals: the remarkable extent of animal exploitation in contemporary society stands as a testimonial to our ability to excuse our acts of animal cruelty as we assert and congratulate ourselves for our "civilized" humanity. Thus, for example, "when anatomists take living animals to experiment on, that is certainly cruelty, though there it is employed for a good purpose; because animals are regarded as man's instruments, it is acceptable."[29]

The idea of "a good purpose" is unequivocally anthropocentric in considerations of this kind. Notwithstanding his tepid assertion of indirect duties toward animals, Kant really conceives of ethics as a system of exclusively human relationships concerned with "human beings' duties to one another"; even "the question of what sort of moral relation holds between God and human beings goes completely beyond the bounds of ethics and is altogether incomprehensible for us."[30] Ethics is that part of morality that deals exclusively with the good for human beings, whereas the subject matter of morality as a whole is the good per se; morality as a whole encompasses relations between humanity and God but excludes relations between human beings and animals. For Kant our moral relation to God is literally "incomprehensible" inasmuch as it is not reducible to conceptual understanding but presumably requires recourse to something like faith. This means that, in effect, animals are banished not simply from the sphere of moral relationships and duties among human beings, but from the sphere of morality altogether. *For practical purposes,* indirect duties toward animals are as good as no duties.

Two things should be noted about Kant's cosmopolitan ideal. First, Kant sees ethics as an exclusively human affair that does not take its bearings from God as a transcendent being. As a postulate of pure practical reason, God serves as an immanent, purely conceptual model "of practical perfection, as an indispensable rule of moral conduct, and as a standard for comparison."[31] In accordance with this secularized conception of God and the idea of perfection that comes with it, ethics takes no cognizance of the interests of animals whatsoever. Second, even though Kant's concepts of God and the human good are secularized and immanent, they are strongly influenced by ancient conceptions of the good, divinity, and the relationship between gods and human beings. Like his predecessors in antiquity, Kant understands the good as a possibility that is accessible only to rational beings. Only those beings capable of reflecting on the good, which for Kant are moral agents, merit genuine moral status. For Kant as for the Stoics, the moral status of a being is determined by that being's proximity to the divine. Animals are much further removed from the divine essence than human beings are, hence animals have a putatively lower moral status than humans—provided that animals can be said to have any moral status whatsoever. Regardless of whether God is understood to be a transcendent being or simply a postulate of pure practical reason, the implications for the moral status of animals are the same: animals are mere things, means for the satisfaction of the needs and desires of beings that are capable of contemplative activity.

COSMIC JUSTICE

We are heirs to this anthropocentric way of thinking; animals are its victims. Whether or not we still believe in God, we must forever renounce the arrogance of asserting our superiority to and dominion over animals. The warrant traditionally invoked for regulating human-human and human-animal relationships has been an ideal of God as a perfect being and measure for human striving; a corollary of this image of God has been the proposition, often repeated in the history of Western philosophy, that God created animals expressly for the sake of human beings. But have we really understood ourselves as made in God's image? Or have we instead fashioned an all too convenient image of God that is consonant with our own desires? For what has ultimately been decisive in the moral sphere in our tradition is precisely the well-being of *human* beings; the cosmos that we have outwardly conceived as theocentric is in fact utterly anthropocentric. We have done less to understand ourselves as having been made in God's image than to make God in our own. The recognition of this anthropocentric prejudice brings with it the need to rethink the notion of the divine. Kant sees the inappropriateness of basing moral judgments on considerations of material welfare and calls instead for an ethic based on the principle of respect. But he limits the principle of respect to rational beings, which is to say to human beings. In effect, on Kant's view, the respect that human beings have for themselves and other human beings is a secularization of reverence for God, where both human beings and God are understood to be fundamentally linguistic-rational beings. Once again, for Kant as for the Stoics, morality has direct implications only for beings capable of the *logos*.

It is a fundamental mistake of the Western tradition to have posited language and reason as conditions for moral worth. The tradition was right to deny these capacities to animals (to most if not all of them, at any rate), and it was also right to consider these capacities to be conditions for the possibility of taking on moral obligations. But there is no logical connection between these capacities and moral worth. So it should not be surprising that not one single representative of the tradition has explained or justified this supposed connection; instead such a connection is dogmatically presupposed and used as a justification—or rather, as an excuse—for the widespread exploitation of animals. This is why the traditional concept of justice, as it has been understood by thinkers such as Rawls, is ill-suited to the task of animal liberation. This task demands a radical rethinking of the concept of justice and a corresponding rethinking of the notion of dwelling.

This recalls Rawls's assertion that "a correct conception of our relations to animals and to nature would seem to depend upon a theory of the natural order and our place in it."[32] Karl Löwith gestures toward such a theory of our place in the natural order when he writes that "human community cannot be in order when it is not in tune with the cosmos [*kosmosartig verfaßt*]." To appreciate the proper place and vocation of human beings, we must think "cosmo-politically in the literal sense of the term." This requires us to acknowledge that the world is not merely the human world, that there is a "pre- and suprahuman world of sky and earth, which stands and maintains itself utterly on its own [and] infinitely eclipses the world that stands and falls with human beings. . . . [It] does not belong to us, but rather we belong to it." Löwith begins here to uncover the nonanthropocentric potential of the notion of world, a potential ignored by the Stoics and Kant alike. When contemplated in relation to this suprahuman world of earth and sky, "the world of [human] Dasein . . . [is] not the ordered cosmos, but is instead our world of being with others [*Mitwelt*] and our environment near and far, which has a kind of order only insofar as it is centered on concernful human beings."[33] When this anthropocentric sense of order refuses to acknowledge its debt to a deeper, cosmic sense of order, we encounter the problem of hubris, a refusal to acknowledge the ultimately subordinate place of human beings in the larger cosmic scheme of things. Whereas ethics has traditionally been understood fundamentally in terms of human world and human relationships, Löwith's teacher Martin Heidegger saw the possibility of a more primordial ethics in which freedom is conceived as "letting beings be" and which "ponders the abode of human beings."[34]

This sense of abode or dwelling needs to be thought in terms of Löwith's cosmo-political ideal, so that Heidegger's idea of "dwelling in the truth of being" is seen to signify dwelling within the order of a suprahuman nature, and his ideal of the human being as the "shepherd of being" is understood in a nonanthropocentric sense.[35] If the specifically human notion of justice is oriented on reciprocal rights and corresponding duties, the cosmic notion of justice takes its bearings from a fundamental asymmetry between human beings and animals—and perhaps from the asymmetry between human beings and nonhuman living beings generally. This asymmetry consists in the fact that it is possible—and, I argue, morally incumbent upon human beings—to recognize that we have fundamental obligations toward animals (and perhaps toward nonhuman nature generally) in spite of the fact that animals (and nonhuman nature generally) are fundamentally incapable of taking on reciprocal obligations toward us. The tradition was right to proclaim that moral agency requires the capacities for reason and language, and to proclaim that nonhuman animals are incapable of being moral agents. The central mistake of the tradition was to assume that because animals cannot be moral agents, they cannot be beneficiaries of direct moral concern either. Thus it becomes imperative to develop a notion of asymmetrical duties toward animals, that is, duties with no corresponding rights that we can assert against those beings toward whom we have these duties. The sphere of specifically human goods, which Kant calls "ethics," does include certain asymmetrical duties, such as those we are generally assumed to have to so-called marginal cases such as people with severe mental disabilities; but that sphere cannot ultimately accommodate the full range of asymmetrical duties. This failing of the tradition is due to a speciesistic prejudice whose abandonment makes possible the establishment of a new and more adequate conception of justice. To recognize the arbitrariness of excluding animals from the sphere of morality or the good is to begin to understand the notion of "the abode of human beings" in a truly cosmo-political sense, and in turn to begin to realize such a sense of dwelling. To do so would be to take a decisive step in the direction of what Heidegger calls "the piety of thinking."[36]

But Heidegger himself did not conceive of this piety in animal-friendly terms, at least not explicitly. In this connection, as noted in chapter 3, Derrida maintains that Heidegger repeats the "anthropo-teleological" prejudice of the tradition in excluding animals from death in the phenomenological-existential sense and hence from the sphere of responsibility.[37] Heidegger denies that animals, as nonlinguistic beings, have any sense of death as such, and for Heidegger this means that animals do not possess freedom and cannot take on any kind of responsibility. For Derrida this means that Heidegger effectively belittles animals by reducing their deaths to the status of merely passing out of existence, rather than viewing the death of an animal as an event with any real moral gravity. Thus it is ironic that even Derrida scrupulously avoids making any definitive claims about the right of animals not to be eaten by human beings. The closest Derrida comes to making any such pronouncement is a rather tepid statement at a conference to the effect that "I am a vegetarian in my soul."[38] In his soul. To my knowledge, Derrida was neither a vegan nor a vegetarian. Moreover, even though Derrida purports to believe that "we must reconsider in its totality the metaphysico-anthropocentric axiomatic that dominates, in the West, the thought of just and unjust," he punctuates his remarks about the wrongness of killing animals with the qualification that he is "not recalling this in order to start a support group for vegetarianism, ecologism, or for the societies for the protection of animals."[39] For Derrida, any definitive claim about the moral status of animals, such as a categorical call for veganism or even vegetarianism—indeed, any definitive moral claim about anything at all—would bring the activity of questioning, which is essential for authentic responsibility, to a standstill. In taking such a stand, Derrida does exactly what he charges Heidegger with doing, namely, failing to take genuine responsibility. Derrida is outraged by Heidegger's involvement with National Socialism and with Heidegger's persistent silence on his role in Nazism, and as a result Derrida misconstrues Heidegger's views on animals in a way that confuses Derrida's own thinking.[40]

It is fair to say that Heidegger is unconcerned with animals as moral beings and that he is far from believing that human beings should have anything like respect for animals. Clearly Heidegger places higher cosmic worth on humans than on animals. But this has nothing to do with why Heidegger excludes animals from the existential phenomenon of death. The reason he excludes animals from death in the existential sense is that "animals do not relate to beings as such," that is, animals lack the essential capacities for understanding and ek-sistence, that way of being in the world in which human beings relate to themselves, to others, and to possibility as such.[41] Herder and Schopenhauer recognized that animals lack the "Besonnenheit" or reflective awareness that makes freedom and responsibility possible, although both thinkers acknowledged a fundamental continuity between human beings and animals.[42] Heidegger implicitly follows this line of thought: The lack of reflective awareness in animals signifies an essential "captivation [Benommenheit]. . . . *The animal as such does not stand in an open relation to beings. Neither its so-called surroundings nor its own self are [in the] open [for it] as beings.*"[43] Animals have their own kind of openness to beings, but this is an "openness [in the mode] of submission [Hingenommenheit]" to things in contrast with the kind of openness that makes freedom or "letting beings be" possible.[44] To describe human beings as world-forming and animals as comparatively world-poor, as Heidegger does, is to acknowledge that not animals but rather only human beings are "addressed by being" and stand "in the light of being," that is, that not animals but only humans "ek-sist" and "experience death as death."[45] Thus "an animal can never be 'evil.' . . . For evil presupposes spirit. The animal can never get out of the unity of its determinate rank in nature. . . . The animal is not capable of dealing with principles."[46]

As noted in chapter 3, Heidegger maintains that "this comparison between animals and humans in terms of world-poverty and world-formation does not give license to estimations or evaluations of perfection and imperfection—quite apart from the fact that such estimations are hasty and inappropriate." Thus we must approach the question of the relative worth of humans and animals with caution: "Is the essence of human beings higher than the essence of animals? All this is questionable in the very posing of the question."[47] In other words, the essential differences between human beings and animals have no moral significance but simply amount to the fact that human beings can experience existence and death as such, because only human beings, in virtue of their reflective awareness, stand in the light of being, can grasp principles, and are therefore capable of making choices in a manner that is impossible for animals. Both in the human social sphere and in the cosmic sphere, reflective awareness or ek-sistence is the condition for the possibility of taking on duties. From the cosmic standpoint, a lack of ek-sistence is not a basis for the denial of rights, provided that the prospective beneficiary of rights in question is a conscious being.

And yet Heidegger's thinking remains anthropocentric to the extent that he retains much of the old prejudice concerning the proximity of human beings to the gods. Although in the "Letter on 'Humanism'" he seeks to call this proximity into question, he ultimately proclaims a special relationship between mortals, which he conceives as human, and gods; moreover, he conceives of the "abode of mortals on the earth" in terms of the capacity for "dwelling," which he considers to be unique to human beings.[48] "But 'on the earth' already means 'under the sky.' Both of these *also* mean 'remaining before the divinities' and include a 'belonging to human beings' with one another.' By a *primordial* oneness the four— earth and sky, divinities and mortals—belong together in one."[49] This does not mean simply that human beings stand in closer proximity to the gods than do animals, but rather that animals do not stand in proximity to the gods at all. Thus Heidegger repeats the mistake of the tradition to the extent that he confuses proximity to the gods with the ability to *think* this proximity. In this connection it is noteworthy that he does not say one single word on behalf of the moral status of animals but instead treats animality as a sort of abstract counterconcept to the human.

One thinker who does not view animals in these terms is the Neoplatonist Porphyry, who rejects the Stoic commitment to the cosmic superiority of human beings over animals. In place of the ideal of an anthropocentric cosmopolitanism, he develops an ideal of cosmic justice that is well suited to the establishment of a nonanthropocentric cosmopolitanism. According to Porphyry, justice consists in "restraint and harmlessness toward everything that does not do harm." This includes all animals, at least those endowed with voice (*phone*), inasmuch as they participate in the *logos* of nature; but it excludes plants inasmuch as they are incapable of perception and hence have no share in the *logos*. Given their capacities for memory and perception, animals are rational beings and in this sense participate in the *logos*. Porphyry anticipates an objection that Gassendi will later make against Descartes when he argues that participation in the *logos* need not involve the full-blown linguistic ability possessed by human beings.[50] Such a nonlinguistic conception of the *logos* is the key to developing a cosmic sense of justice and cosmopolitanism, in that it opens us to the prospect of an essential kinship not simply between human beings and gods, but between conscious beings generally and the divine. Where Aristotle and Kant reject the possibility of friendship between human beings and animals, Porphyry sees such friendship as a corollary to the essential cosmic kinship that unites humans and animals.[51] Porphyry reminds us of the Golden Age, in which "friendship and perception of kinship ruled everything [and] no one killed any creature, because people thought the other animals were related [*oíkeíos*] to them." Porphyry stresses that in Egyptian tradition animals were beloved of the gods and that, when we acknowledge the bond of kinship that prevails between humans and animals, "the friend of the genus will not hate the species."[52]

Porphyry's account of the way in which animals participate in the *logos* and his view of the resulting kinship between human beings and animals provide the basis for a nonanthropocentric notion of community with animals and a conception of justice that calls on us to refrain from harming any conscious being that poses no harm to us. Porphyry recognizes that killing conscious beings is sometimes unavoidable, as when we defend ourselves against a deadly animal or human adversary; and he suggests that we may well have a right to kill in such situations. But he is clear that we have no such right in our relations with harmless creatures.[53]

A reader could hardly be reproached for inferring from Porphyry's arguments and from the title of his text that he is an advocate of universal vegetarianism. After all, when he lists the things without which human beings cannot survive, he names "air and water, plants and crops" but makes no mention of animal flesh. And yet Porphyry does not argue that all human beings ought to practice vegetarianism. He writes that "my discourse will not offer advice to every human way of life: not to those who engage in banausic crafts, nor to athletes of the body, nor to soldiers, nor to sailors, nor orators, nor to those who have chosen the life of public affairs, but to the person who has thought about who he is and whence he has come and where he should try to go." Porphyry's arguments are directed in Neoplatonist fashion to those among us who aspire to take part in "the Olympics of the soul," those who would seek to transcend the conditions of embodiment toward an ideal of spiritual purification.[54] Indeed, the Neoplatonist strain in *De abstinentia* stands in an uneasy tension with the many passages in which Porphyry presents what modern thinkers would call a direct-duties approach to animals: on the one hand we are told that practices such as eating meat arouse our passions and therefore are incompatible with the aspiration to achieve spiritual enlightenment, while on the other hand we are told that animals are beloved of the gods and that we should respect the inherent dignity of animals. It remains for the contemporary reader to resolve this tension, and in particular to confront the question whether Porphyry's reasons for excluding so many people from the duty to eschew animal flesh have any force within the context of contemporary society and consciousness.

Notwithstanding this limitation in his views, Porphyry points the way toward a revision of the Stoic doctrine of *oikeiosis* or belonging. The Stoics conceived of *oikeiosis* as a stepwise progression in the notion of community, in which all but the final stage are possible for animals as well as for human beings. The first stage of *oikeiosis* takes the form of pure autoaffection and begins at birth: "Immediately upon birth . . . a living creature feels an attachment for itself, and an impulse to preserve itself and to feel affection for its own constitution and for those things which tend to preserve that constitution, while on the other hand it conceives an antipathy to destruction and to those things which appear to threaten destruction." The second stage of *oikeiosis* involves a broadening of the sphere of belonging to include love for one's offspring. These first two stages show that the Stoics conceive of *oikeiosis* as the expansion of affection to ever-larger circles of belonging, beginning with the individual's relation to itself and progressing to concern for one's offspring as extensions of oneself. The Stoics also recognize that members of some species of animals form mutually beneficial bonds with creatures that are not their immediate family members, and that some animals participate in cross-species symbiosis.[55]

But the Stoics believe that in animals, the capacity to expand circles of belonging is sharply circumscribed. They maintain that only human beings can expand the range of *oikeiosis* beyond the first two levels, by employing reflection to recognize a higher potential than that exhibited by the filial bond in animals. According to Hierocles, "the outermost and largest circle [of *oikeiosis*], which encompasses all the rest, is that of the whole human race. . . . It is the task of a well-tempered man, in his proper treatment of each group, to draw the circles together somehow towards the center."[56] Unique to human beings is a universal sense of belonging that obligates each of us to treat strangers far removed from our inner circle as if they were closely related to us. Cicero describes the characteristics of this third level of *oikeíosis* in the following way: "Nature has endowed us with two roles [*personae*], as it were. One of these is universal, from the fact that we share in reason and that status which raises us above the beasts; this is the source of all rectitude and propriety [*decorum*], and the basis of the rational discovery of our proper functions. The second role is the one which has been specifically assigned to individuals."[57]

On the Stoic view, both of these *personae* are unique to human beings and are requisite for the true good of which only human beings are capable. Porphyry shows us how we might dispossess ourselves of the anthropocentric core of Stoic thinking by conceiving of the universal persona of human beings as the source of an essential kinship between human beings and animals, where the Stoics presuppose an essential enmity between humans and animals. The affirmation of our inner kinship with animals will enable us to develop an ideal of justice that is both necessary and sufficient for a nonanthropocentric cosmopolitanism, a cosmopolitanism in which we actively acknowledge the cosmic equality of humans and animals and eschew our regrettable history of animal exploitation.

CONTEMPORARY COSMOPOLITANISM: A CRITIQUE

Contemporary disputes over the proper nature and terms of cosmopolitanism have some highly revealing implications for the endeavor to achieve a nonanthropocentric cosmopolitanism. Like the larger debates about the political in the past generation, these disputes over the terms of cosmopolitanism are fundamentally anthropocentric and take the form of disagreements over the viability of classical liberal notions such as agency, equality, and universal principles in the endeavor to respect and/ or empower disenfranchised segments of humanity. A key focal point of these disputes is whether cosmopolitanism ought to concern itself first of all with the fortunes of individual agents or instead with the fortunes of groups, be the identities of those groups racial, ethnic, religious, geographic, or economic—or some combination of these.

Like Kant before them, contemporary thinkers in the liberal tradition take as their point of departure the notion of universality as a regulative ideal for coordinating the actions of diverse agents on a worldwide scale. Martha Nussbaum argues that this ideal demands looking past local and national allegiances and affirming common aims that underlie difference. Nussbaum understands cosmopolitanism as "allegiance . . . to the worldwide community of human beings" and sees in the affirmation of universally shared human qualities and values the best prospects for overcoming the factionalism that was a concern of the Stoics.[58] The primary operative value for Nussbaum, as for Kant, is respect for others; for example, for an American to "love or attend to" an Indian, it is necessary to attain "a human identity that transcends these divisions. . . . The world citizen must develop sympathetic understanding of distant cultures and of ethnic, racial, and religious minorities within her own. She must also develop an understanding of the history and variety of human ideas of gender and sexuality." In doing so, the cosmopolitan becomes uprooted from her familiar surroundings and accustomed way of doing and valuing things and thereby enters into "a kind of exile—from the comfort of assured truths, from the warm nestling feeling of being surrounded by people who share one's convictions and passions."[59]

But does Nussbaum's cosmopolitan manifest concern for animals? The fact that Nussbaum follows and develops Rawls's model of justice makes it unsurprising that she equivocates on this question and ultimately gives a fundamental priority to the interests and fortunes of human beings over those of animals. Not only does her characterization of the concerns of the cosmopolitan focus more or less exclusively on our relationship to other human beings, but she frames her discussion of the capabilities approach to justice in pointedly anthropocentric terms. Nussbaum considers it "clear that there is no respectable way to deny the equal dignity of creatures of species across species," inasmuch as many animals possess capacities that qualify them as agents rather than as mere instrumentalities for the satisfaction of human needs. Animals, on Nussbaum's view, are "direct subjects of the theory of justice"; but because "the members of the consensus" that we seek to reach in ethical and political matters are "all human," this "consensus is an anthropocentric idea." The crux of this anthropocentric idea is the proposition that whereas justice requires us to secure certain capabilities for all human beings *equally*, it requires us to secure certain capabilities for animals only to a degree of *adequacy* to be determined, presumably, through the process of consensus making. We ought to secure the vital capabilities of animals according to "a high threshold of adequacy."[60]

But this does not prevent us from subordinating the interests of animals to those of humans in situations in which we consider the sacrifice to be urgent, or at least reasonable, precisely because we need only secure the "adequate" realization of animal capabilities, not the realization of capabilities equal to that enjoyed by human beings. Why not? For several reasons. First, beings that are mentally more sophisticated are more capable of suffering harm than those that are mentally less sophisticated; thus the harm posed by death "seems less grave" to the latter beings than to the former. Because we are held to a standard of adequacy with regard to animals but to one of equality with regard to humans, we can justify "the painless death of [a free range] animal" but not that of, say, a mentally impaired but still sentient human being.[61] Second, on Nussbaum's view, "where humans are concerned, the idea of equal dignity is not a metaphysical idea," whereas where animals are concerned it is; and given that "the question of equal dignity [for animals is] a metaphysical question on which citizens may hold different positions while accepting the basic substantive claims about animal entitlements . . . the idea of cross-species dignity is not a political idea that can readily be accepted by citizens who otherwise differ in metaphysical conception."[62] The Rawlsian form of political liberalism endorsed by Nussbaum seeks to remain neutral as regards substantive claims about the good, focusing instead on providing the procedural conditions necessary for different human political agents to pursue their interests. Thus members of a liberal polity may disagree about the moral status of animals and their basic entitlements.[63]

Nussbaum argues that animals should be recognized to have basic entitlements, such as the entitlement not to be killed gratuitously for sport, but she never explains how she can argue for some entitlements on liberal grounds but not for others.[64] What she does tell us is that she is keenly interested in avoiding conflicts with major religions regarding animals, which reminds us of the fundamentally anthropocentric orientation and hence the limits of political liberalism as regards the moral status of animals and the prospects for achieving a nonanthropocentric cosmopolitanism. "A truly global justice . . . requires looking . . . at the other sentient beings," but ultimately "the pursuit of global justice requires the inclusion of many people and groups who were not previously included as fully equal subjects of justice: the poor; the lower classes; members of religious, ethnic, and racial minorities; more recently, women." "Looking at the other sentient beings" does not prohibit us from using them in various forms of entertainment such as horse racing, it does not prohibit us from killing them (painlessly, of course) to provide food for humans, it does not prohibit us from experimenting on animals (as long as we seek to "improve the lives of research animals"), and it by no means requires us to decry any practice that harms animals as long as it is undertaken in the name of religion.[65] Thus in accordance with the terms of political liberalism as articulated by Rawls and developed in the direction of capacities by Nussbaum, animals are not genuinely recognized to be subjects but instead remain instrumentalities for the satisfaction of human needs.

Kwame Anthony Appiah offers a comparably anthropocentric vision of cosmopolitanism. He models cosmopolitanism on the Golden Rule, the idea "that we should take other people's interests seriously, take them into account." Like Nussbaum, Appiah embraces an ideal of universality that can relate all of humanity in a global community. He recognizes that in important respects this ideal remains a regulative ideal lacking concrete content, and he suggests that "we can live together without agreeing on what the values are that make it good to live together; we can agree about what to do in most cases, without agreeing about why it is right." Cosmopolitanism is an ideal of human beings living together in harmony even where they do not agree on underlying values. The mechanism for achieving this harmony is not the operation of timeless reason but instead active engagement in conversation and persuasion. The goal here is not consensus, which remains elusive, but rather "help[ing] people to get used to one another." What people share in common is "concepts such as good and evil, right and wrong." Conversation and persuasion help us to clarify these ideas and render them concrete, with the aim of "temper[ing] a respect for difference with a respect for actual human beings." Both forms of respect give rise to obligations to strangers, although Appiah believes that our first allegiances are properly to those closest to us.[66]

On Appiah's view, both strangers and those closest to us are human beings. Whatever forms of concern or tolerance our shared humanity may require of us with regard to other human beings, animals are excluded from the sphere of concern, and presumably from the sphere of justice, because they are *aloga* and hence incapable of the conversation and persuasion that Appiah places at the center of his cosmopolitan ideal. Thus there is no reason to suppose that there should be any necessary agreement on the question whether it is "cruel to kill cattle in slaughterhouses where live cattle can smell the blood of the dead . . . because applying value terms to new cases requires judgment and discretion." Such questions, like moral questions generally, are "essentially contestable."[67] The anthropocentric terms of Appiah's cosmopolitanism make such a conclusion unsurprising but nonetheless troubling. Even though he maintains that reason cannot produce substantive moral universals that would be clear and compelling to everyone, he nonetheless assumes that human beings can converse with and persuade one another "about what to do in most cases" and thereby "live in harmony." Appiah tacitly assumes the same thing as Rawls and Nussbaum: a vision of humanity that includes conceptions of agency, equality, mutual respect, and something like reasonableness. Even though Appiah stresses that there is no one thing that it means to be reasonable, he implicitly presupposes a shared conception of reasonableness as the basis for living in harmony and respecting difference. We are entitled to disagree about the acceptability of industrial slaughterhouses, and our disagreement is implicitly reasonable. It is difficult to imagine Appiah countenancing comparable disagreement about, say, the acceptability of trafficking in human slaves.

Notwithstanding this anthropocentric limitation, Appiah's approach has the advantage of recognizing that while universality plays an important role in securing cosmopolitan harmony, this universality is formal and empty until it is given concrete content through discursive practices. Seyla Benhabib takes this conception of universality as the point of departure for her reflections on what she calls "another cosmopolitanism," one in which "the universalist standpoint . . . views the moral conversation as potentially including all of *humanity*. . . . every person, and every moral agent, who has interests and whom my actions and the consequences of my actions can impact and affect in some manner or another is potentially a moral conversation partner with me." But where Appiah casts suspicion on the power of reason to ground conversation, Benhabib argues that each of us "has a moral obligation to justify [our] actions with reasons" to other participants in the discursive process or to their representatives. The goal of cosmopolitanism is not simply to realize or concretize universals, but rather to "mediate moral universalism with ethical particularism" and to "mediate legal and political norms with moral ones" so as to bring about "dialogic universalism." "Universal principles of human rights . . . precede and antedate the will of the sovereign. . . . The tension between universal human rights claims and particularistic cultural and national identities is constitutive of democratic legitimacy. Modern democracies act in the name of universal principles, which are then circumscribed within a particular civic community."[68]

Thus for Benhabib cosmopolitanism is the endeavor, on a worldwide scale, to find a balance between universal ethico-political principles and the rightful claims of particular groups or communities. Those undertaking this endeavor must acknowledge a basic "paradox of democratic legitimacy," namely, that there is an irreducible tension between "a promise to uphold human rights . . . and the will of democratic majorities." This paradox cannot be overcome, but "its impact can be mitigated through the renegotiation and reiteration of the dual commitments to human rights and sovereign self-determination."[69] This tension between universal principles of justice and the good, on the one hand, and the claims of particular groups, on the other, is the central focus, if only implicitly, of most if not all approaches to cosmopolitanism in contemporary thought. Liberally minded thinkers tend to give a special primacy to the universal even where, like Benhabib, they argue that the universal must derive its content from discursive attempts at persuasion or consensus making and that the particular cannot properly be subsumed under the universal but instead must be brought into something like a dialectical mediation with it. For her own part, Benhabib seeks to bring the universal and the particular into balance with one another by means of "democratic iterations," which are "complex processes of public argument, deliberation, and exchange through which universalist rights claims and principles are contested and contextualized, invoked and revoked, posited and positioned, throughout legal and political institutions, as well as in the associations of civil society." Such iterations are "a dialectic of rights and identities."[70] Working toward a dialectical relationship between universal human rights claims and particularistic sovereignty claims (such as the respective claims of different nations), cosmopolitanism undertakes "an immanent critique of the tradition of moral and legal universalism" that promises to "undermine the logic of exclusions and to expose the self-contradictions of liberal universalism."[71]

Benhabib seeks to "situate" the universal in relation to concrete cultures, values, and practices, just as she has sought to situate the self as an ever-evolving product of difference and cultural specificity.[72] But in certain key respects, particularly as regards the fortunes of animals, her cosmopolitanism remains squarely within the anthropocentric tradition. This is most evident in Benhabib's conception of universalism as "dialogic": participants in the process of democratic iterations are fundamentally linguistic beings capable of showing "*universal moral respect* and *egalitarian reciprocity.*"[73] Naturally this by itself does not exclude animals as beneficiaries of ethico-political discourse. Benhabib acknowledges that "there may be beings to whom we *owe* moral obligations and who may become moral victims by virtue of being impacted by our actions but who cannot represent themselves: sentient beings capable of pain, such as animals. . . . [T]he moral interests of those who are not full participants in moral discourses ought to be and can be effectively represented in discursive contexts through systems of moral advocacy."[74] But her central concern is to extend her situated universalism "to all of *humanity*," and one must seriously question her suggestion that animals "can be effectively represented in discursive contexts through systems of moral advocacy." In the absence of a substantive commitment to the inclusion of animals as members of the moral community with a moral status essentially equal to that of human beings—precisely what Nussbaum refuses to grant because it is a "metaphysical" commitment on which reasonable people can disagree—it seems far-fetched to suppose that animals will spontaneously find advocates in linguistic beings whose own interests so often and so extensively conflict with their own interests.

That Benhabib is ultimately no more willing than Nussbaum to make room for this kind of *substantive* commitment is suggested by Benhabib's criticism of David Held's cosmopolitan principles for giving "not only a vision of justice but one of the good as well."[75] To give a vision of justice without giving a vision of the good is to sketch *procedural* principles that promote the empowerment of different human agents to act on their own respective conceptions of the good; these procedural principles include equality, reciprocity, and mutual respect. But, as noted above, such a procedural vision of justice is neutral as regards particular *substantive* conceptions of the good. This leaves animals in the position of having to wait for the good graces of a linguistic-moral agent to act on their behalf, and of being beholden to the ability and willingness of human beings to set aside self-serving prejudice and to try to envision life and the good from the standpoint of an animal. Procedural principles of justice work to the advantage of those beings who are in a position to act as agents in an ethico-political context and leave nonlinguistic beings vulnerable and subject to human anthropocentric prejudice. The fact that a thinker such as Nussbaum is inclined to argue that the ideal of human equality is nonmetaphysical, whereas the ideal of human-animal equality is a metaphysical one about which reasonable individuals can disagree, is an indication that any conception of cosmopolitanism that takes its bearings from human linguistic-moral agents rather than from a principle of respect for sentient life is doomed to subject animals to exactly the kind of exclusion that Benhabib seeks to avoid in the case of human relations.

Contemporary cosmopolitan thinkers are considerably more concerned with the exclusion of human beings than they are with the exclusion of animals from empowerment in the ethico-political sphere. This is true even and perhaps especially for those postmodern thinkers who argue that the liberal focus on autonomous individuals and the articulation of universal principles serves an enthocentric prejudice and in effect functions to exclude disempowered groups from full moral and political consideration. This strong critique of political liberalism takes a number of forms, but its various proponents are united in rejecting the standpoint of the autonomous individual as an Enlightenment fiction that fails to acknowledge the operation of difference in constituting the various and always shifting identities of individuals and groups. Poststructuralism, these thinkers argue, has shown that the very way in which we characterize political subjects or actors is itself a political process; as Foucault argued, representation is not objective but instead always serves interests of power.[76] By focusing on power and the cultural practices, particularly discursive ones, that constitute and transform group identities, poststructuralist thinkers are led in the direction of arguing that instead of seeking the sort of overlapping consensus recommended by Nussbaum, the proper function of political discourse is to radicalize the process of representation in a manner that empowers disenfranchised groups rather than assimilating them into some hegemonic total vision of the human. "The objective should be not just the legitimation of minority discourses but also the minoritization of the body politic as such. . . . [I]t is only ethically and politically appropriate that minority discourses take a lead, in the form of ongoing coalitions, in producing radical change." The operative assumptions here are twofold: that every identity is in principle "heterogeneous and fissured from within," and that the true function of the political is to facilitate the transformation of minority identities so as to "[unsettle] the binary matrix" of traditional liberal representation and bring about "the generalization of heterogeneity over the entire body politic so that there will be a time when binarity will be no more."[77]

This focus on difference rather than stable, all-encompassing identity takes many forms in contemporary postmodern discourse, but a guiding if typically unstated premise of discourses of this sort is that politics is *polemical* in the strict sense of the term: properly understood, political discourses need to promote a certain conflict rather than promoting harmony. Thus, for example, Paul Rabinow gestures toward a "critical cosmopolitanism" built on Marilyn Strathern's call for a conception of politics as "oppositional . . . suspicious of sovereign powers, universal truths," and respectful of difference.[78] The aim of such a cosmopolitanism would be to examine critically the relations of power and discourse between anthropologists and the "others" they study, with an eye toward militating against the forceful imposition of ethnocentric prejudices in the process of representing the others being studied by anthropology. This anthropological aim has a more general implication for cosmopolitanism as an ethico-political ideal, namely, that the various "others" in the political realm, particularly those who have been marginalized by traditional ethnocentric (which is to say Eurocentric) prejudices, need to become empowered to explore their own identities and possibilities on their own terms. Indeed, according to the terms of poststructuralist thinking, identity and possibility ultimately converge with one another.

Taken to its logical extreme, this radical rethinking of cosmopolitanism actually leads to a conception of "pluralized forms of popular global political consciousness."[79] The radicalization of the political renders it irreducibly plural; hence cosmopolitanism in the singular would amount to a hegemonic imposition of a single sense of identity on a plurality of processes of political self-assertion. Nonetheless a number of poststructuralist approaches to cosmopolitics make a place for the universal in political discourses; the universal here "exceeds the pragmatic demands of the specific context" but "must not . . . be permitted to programme political action, where decisions would be algorithmically deduced from incontestable ethical precepts."[80] "The task that cultural difference sets for us is the articulation of universality through a difficult labor of translation" that may prove to be an endless process.[81] Such a radicalized, nonessentialist notion of the universal is needed in political discourse to keep existing particular identities from functioning hegemonically to prevent the exploration of alternative understandings and ways of being. "A plurality of situated cosmopolitanisms" promises to promote "the variously willed and forced detachments from local and restrictive identities" and hence to give rise to "a vivid spectrum of diverse dialectics of detachment, displacement, and affiliation."[82]

To the extent that the most marginalized peoples arguably constitute "the immense majority of the world population," it should not be surprising that so many contemporary thinkers advocate a polemical model of political discursivity: existing liberal institutions and discourse would appear neither to have taken the needs and interests of marginalized peoples into account nor to be capable of doing so. Any monolithic approach to cosmopolitanism would thus appear simply to reproduce and reinforce both the thinking and the institutions that perpetuate the marginalization of most of the world's population. To the extent that "a politics of exclusion [is embedded] into the heart of nineteenth-century European liberal theories and practices with respect to empire," the "deracinated" and universalistic approach of liberalism is bound to perpetuate the "infantilization" of "whole peoples."[83] What is needed, then, is something that Kant professed to recognize but to which he never ultimately did justice: a recognition of the particular and the ways in which it must be brought into relation with the universal rather than simply being subsumed under it. David Harvey takes Kant's remarks on the importance of local geography to their logical conclusion, arguing that any cosmopolitanism worth its name must be focused on social movements and founded on the "construction of an entirely new and different geography (practically as well as conceptually) around relational principles of belonging that entail a completely different definition of space and place to that contained either in the Kantian or Heideggerian schemas."[84]

In a similar spirit, Boaventura de Sousa Santos and César Rodríguez-Garavito call for a "subaltern cosmopolitanism," an approach to cosmopolitanism that "aims to empirically document experiences of resistance, assess their potential to subvert hegemonic institutions and ideologies, and learn from their capacity to offer alternatives to the latter." A commitment to subaltern cosmopolitanism is implicit in the approach of any cosmopolitan thinker who believes that "top-down" approaches are destined to fail because they impose a totalizing vision of the political on a diversity of local processes of identity formation. The "bottom-up" approach recommended by de Sousa Santos and Rodríguez-Garavito seeks to promote justice, in particular "counter-hegemonic projects seeking to subvert interstate hierarchies and borders."[85]

But who, exactly, counts as a subject or participant in such "counter-hegemonic projects"? Will "our cosmopolitan quest for universal justice" include a sustained and authentic commitment to justice for animals?[86]

Or do the plural, dialectically informed cosmopolitanisms of postmodernity offer animals no better prospects than does liberalism, with its "lure of a transcendental guarantee"?[87] Common to the various postmodern and liberal approaches to cosmopolitanism is a commitment to *discursive* processes for the formation and transformation of political identities and possibilities. This is particularly clear in Rawlsian political liberalism and Habermasian discourse ethics; but it holds equally for any approach that emphasizes "the grammar of representation" and focuses on "the problem of the formation of collective subjectivities in the modern world by consideration of the material, institutional, and discursive bases" for the construction of identity.[88] Nothing in principle excludes animals from considerations of justice as we human beings seek to transform our identities and realize possibilities for resituating our always already situated senses of autonomy. But to the extent that "cosmopolitanism generally invites a description from the perspective of the participant as he or she negotiates a dense array of affiliations and commitments," it seems at best wildly wishful thinking to suppose that animals will be recognized without further ado as full participants in the never-ending process of cosmopolitan identity-transformation—precisely because "participants" are conceived by liberals and postmodernists alike as *linguistic* agents.[89]

It is beyond question that a primary concern of many of the postmodern thinkers of cosmopolitanism is the dialectical overcoming of the hegemonic influence of global capital on local, marginalized communities and the concomitant realization of a new relationship to nature.[90] Some advocate a move toward "socialist cosmopolitanism," while others focus on a more general conception of "social justice" whose beneficiaries are women, "Blacks, Latinos, American Indians, poor people, lesbians, old people, [and] the disabled."[91] Apart from the occasional passing suggestion that animals and/or nature generally can be(come) political subjects, one finds little if anything of concrete value in contemporary writings on cosmopolitanism as regards the fortunes of animals. In liberal thought this is a product of the endeavor to secure procedural fairness for human beings by refusing to articulate any first-order substantive conception of the good. In postmodern thought this is a product of a specifically discursive (and polemical) conception of the formation and transformation of political identities. In both cases animals are an afterthought precisely because they are *aloga* and hence are not conceived as fully empowered ethico-juridico-political agents. Animals cannot speak on their own behalf and hence are incapable of being liberal actors or participants in acts of polemical resistance to established institutional power structures. Iris Marion Young is quite right when she suggests that "in order to be a useful measure of actual justice and injustice, [a theory of justice] must contain some substantive premises." Young believes that these premises must be "about social life," and she correctly observes that such premises are "usually derived, explicitly or implicitly, from the actual social context in which the theorizing takes place."[92]

The question remains what sort of substantive premises are needed to ground a theory of justice that is not simply about *social* life but encompasses all of *sentient* life. As things stand today, I do not believe that postmodern conceptions of cosmopolitanism are in any better situation than liberal ones to provide an answer to this question, precisely because both approaches take as their point of departure "the actual social context in which the theorizing takes place"—a context that by its very nature does not make room for nonhuman animals as primary "participants." Notwithstanding the assurances of liberals and postmoderns alike that animals are or can be genuine beneficiaries of justice, both approaches are beset with a certain anthropocentric prejudice that can be overcome only by situating our conception of social justice within the larger context of what I refer to as "cosmic justice," a conception of justice whose substantive basis I have sought to develop in terms of "cosmic holism."[93] The human, all-too-human wars and struggles for recognition are urgent and entirely real. The ideal of cosmic justice seeks not to devalue these struggles but rather to place them in a larger world context that we have tended to repress from the beginnings of civilization up to the present.

The imperative of cosmic justice is one that requires a Herculean effort of us: to look past ourselves and see ourselves as part of a larger cosmic whole that in recent generations has, incorrectly in my judgment, been dismissed as merely an immanent product of human discourses (and hence as just another effect of power and discursivity) rather than being seen as the living measure of our own self-understanding and the ultimate source of any authentic conception of justice. Such an act of selflessness is the absolute precondition for the possibility of a nonanthropocentric cosmopolitanism.

CHAPTER SIX

Cosmopolitanism and Veganism

COSMIC HOLISM AND COMMUNITY WITH ANIMALS

The ideal of cosmic justice, of duties of justice not simply to our fellow human beings but to all sentient life, finds its ground in a cosmic holism according to which we are bound in an essential kinship relation with all beings that suffer and struggle to realize their natural potential.[1] The revision of the Stoic doctrine of *oikeiosis* that I proposed in the previous chapter is a corollary of cosmic holism and an essential precondition for asserting duties of justice toward animals. The Stoics recognized that all sentient beings have a natural affinity for their own kind—first for their own bodily integrity, and then for their offspring and certain other conspecifics. But the Stoics failed to acknowledge the possibility of kinship between species, opting instead to erect an absolute barrier between human and nonhuman beings on the grounds that only human beings can take on the "universal persona." There is a tragic irony in the Stoics' characterization of the third and highest level of *oikeiosis*: where one ought to be able to expect the standpoint of universality, a standpoint characterized by reason, to disclose our fundamental ethical relationship to all beings that share in mortality, the Stoics instead consider the scope of ethical belonging to encompass all and only those beings who possess *logos* in the specifically human sense of predicatively structured reason and language. They thereby construe as a metaphysical brick wall a set of relationships that have emerged through historical contingency, much in the way that Aristotle construed the exclusion of women and slaves from citizenship as their cosmic fate rather than recognizing it to be a freely chosen act of subjugation.[2] The universal persona as the Stoics conceive it is not universal at all but instead is highly selective and hierarchizing; it presupposes and reinforces a sense of the cosmos as a place in which beings that participate in language and reason in the specifically human sense are fundamentally superior to beings considered to be *aloga*.

The anthropocentric limits of cosmopolitanism as it is traditionally understood are evident in its unremitting focus on the capacity for a certain kind of citizenship. One might think that contemporary thought had disencumbered itself of this kind of anthropocentric prejudice, but in fact it has not. Diogenes Laertius, when asked where he came from, said, "I am a citizen of the world [*kosmopolítes*]," thereby intending to express his sense of belonging to a larger cosmic whole of specifically linguistic beings.[3] Virtually without exception, the postmodern thinkers examined in the previous chapter conceive of the task of rehabilitating cosmopolitanism as one of enfranchising women and other historically oppressed groups of human beings, animals being a mere afterthought. Liberal thinkers likewise explore the prospects of cosmopolitanism in specifically anthropocentric terms; Richard Wolin is exemplary of this tendency in seeing in "the spirit of cosmopolitanism" the potential "to sketch valid, cross-cultural norms of international behavior and citizens' rights."[4] While much has been done in the past generation to debunk the myth that only human beings possess subjective awareness and that animals are mindless machines, thinking about the moral status of animals remains in a troubling state of stagnation. More precisely, we suffer from what Gary Francione has called "moral schizophrenia."[5] We have become increasingly willing to think, write, and speak of animals as genuine beneficiaries of direct moral concern, but we persist in using animals in a remarkable variety of ways that cause them suffering and abrogate their freedom of self-determination.

A genuinely nonanthropocentric cosmopolitanism is one that acknowledges the moral parity of human beings and animals. Such an acknowledgment brings with it the recognition that the traditional notion of citizenship, tethered as it is to the notion of linguistic agency, is ill suited to the full inclusion of animals in the sphere of moral concern. In the sphere of social justice, which encompasses ethico-political relations among human linguistic actors, the traditional notion of citizenship may prove to function very well—subject to the qualifications and criticisms of that notion examined in the previous chapter. In the sphere of cosmic justice, which encompasses all sentient beings, we must radically rethink the notion of citizenship so that it accommodates a notion of agency that does justice to the manifest ways in which a great variety of animals actively relate to their environments. Cosmic justice must be predicated on the acknowledgment that animals are beneficiaries of direct and full ethical concern, even though they themselves are incapable of participating in the forms of life that constitute deliberative ethical discourse. It is here that the Herculean act of selflessness to which I referred at the end of the previous chapter finds its place: we must treat animals as fully enfranchised members of the moral community, even though from our restricted and impoverished standpoint as linguistic actors animals appear to be completely silent. We must use our supposedly superior intelligence to find ways to envision the agency of animals so as to render ourselves unable to ignore the ethical claim that they constantly exercise on us—a claim that we occasionally purport to acknowledge but which we must learn to acknowledge constantly.

Rawls is quite right to suggest that a sense of our moral relationship to animals demands "a theory of the natural order and our place in it."[6] Our conception of the natural order underlies and ultimately determines our sense of moral connectedness to, or separation from, nonhuman animals. Aristotle was profoundly ambivalent in his reflections on our proximity to animals. On the one hand, he recognized in his zoological treatises a great many cognitive affinities between human beings and a wide variety of animals. But on the other hand, in his psychological, political, and ethical writings he characterized animals as *aloga* and categorically excluded them from the ethico-political sphere.[7] The Stoics dispense with this ambivalence altogether, proclaiming that animals are utterly incapable of scrutinizing their perceptions and gaining control over their impulses. Only human beings are capable of the rational abstraction that facilitates contemplation of the divine *logos*; animals, like all nonhuman sublunary beings, exist expressly for the sake of satisfying human physical needs.[8]

As noted in the previous chapter, the Stoics set the terms of discourse for the entire subsequent history of Western philosophy regarding the respective places of human beings and animals in the order of nature. They conceive kinship in terms of rationality rather than sentience, thereby arrogating to human beings a place alongside the gods and subordinating animals to the status of mere instrumentalities. In *Animals and the*

Moral Community I called for an abandonment of the historical endeavor "to attribute to ourselves quasi-divine status and prerogatives by distinguishing ourselves from the rest of nature" and a concomitant "revisioning of the cosmopolitan ideal" that would involve "acknowledg[ing] our mortality and the fundamental limitations that we share with animals." In particular I argued for a *moral equivalence* between human beings and animals, one of the most important consequences of which is universal veganism as a strict ethical duty.[9] The central purpose of this chapter is to explore and make a case for that consequence.

A nonanthropocentric conception of the universal persona of *oikeiosis* is one according to which we see the fundamental *sameness* of all sentient beings—not sameness with regard to specific physical form, mental capacities, or subjective encounter with the world, but with regard to the fact that the basic terms of life and death are essentially the same for all sentient beings. Humans and animals are, existentially, in exactly the same predicament: both must survive and give life meaning (regardless of whether that meaning can be articulated predicatively) in the face of the constant yet indeterminate threat of death. Nonetheless we flatter ourselves with repeated and insistent proclamations that human suffering counts more than animal suffering inasmuch as we can give meaning to our suffering in ways that animals cannot. We continue to repeat the old story, told even by the likes of Bentham and Schopenhauer, that we have more to lose by dying than animals because only we can contemplate the remote past and the distant future. I would wager that the vast majority of the world's human population continues to subscribe to the increasingly implausible proposition that human lives "have greater intrinsic value [than those of animals] because they are worth more *to their possessors*."[10]

Such statements are remarkably self-serving, not to mention ludicrous on their face. Anyone who has seen an animal struggle to preserve its life can have no doubt that animals care about their lives every bit as much as we care about ours. Any supposition to the contrary has no basis in fact and is designed to rationalize a regime of animal exploitation that has its roots in a view of the cosmos that places human beings at the center. This view originally took the form of a divinely ordered cosmos in which humans were to aspire as much as possible to be like the gods (or God) and as little as possible like "mere" animals. With the flight of the gods in modernity, human beings have usurped the role once thought to be occupied by God: that of the ultimate arbiter of both truth and goodness. In both phases of this history, animals have been virtually excluded from moral consideration; and even where thinkers such as Bentham assign a place to animals in the moral community, that place has virtually without exception been an inferior one—again, on grounds of self-serving, speciesistic bias.

It would be wrong to call speciesism arbitrary; it has functioned historically to the tremendous material advantage of the vast majority of humanity. (One would do well to wonder whether it has functioned to our spiritual advantage as well. I have serious doubts about that.) But speciesism is nonetheless ethically completely indefensible, at least if we conceive of ethics in nonanthropocentric terms. Recall the terms of the golden age stories related by Hesiod and Ovid: We originally lived in peace with one another and with animals. But owing to a fall from grace the genesis of which remains unexplained, conflicts ensued and Zeus found it necessary to bestow the law of justice on human beings. But Zeus intended the law of justice to govern relations only among human beings because only human beings were capable of "listen[ing] to justice."[11] The purpose of justice was to maintain peace among human beings, animals being excluded on the grounds that they could not comprehend the reasoning that lies at the core of this quid pro quo conception of justice: that the only way to avert the violence that had descended upon the world was for individuals to respect one another's person and property.

The belief underlying this logic is that peace is preferable to a state of violence. Zeus's law of justice was intended to restore—as far as possible, given the known proclivity of human beings to violence—the peace and safety that had been known in the golden age. We human beings owe one another respect—not in the sense that human beings possess inherent worth and merit respectful treatment simply because they are the kind of beings they are, but rather in the sense that I can demand nonviolent treatment from you only to the extent that I am willing to treat you in like manner. "Respect" thus becomes a purely instrumental term, and justice becomes a contractual expedient for the preservation of peace—but peace only among human beings, because animals have been excluded from the equation in advance. This conception of justice anticipates Epicurus's contractualist conception of justice, according to which principles of justice are voluntary agreements designed to promote mutual advantage.[12] Such a conception of justice leaves no room for animals, being based as it is on the notions of linguistic agency, deliberation, and explicit consent.[13] This conception of justice makes it impossible to say that taking advantage of animals is unfair, because fairness becomes a procedural matter of sheer reciprocity among linguistic agents. If animals cannot take advantage of us in ways comparable to the ways in which we have built our entire civilization by taking advantage of them, then there is nothing "unfair" in our treatment of animals, even if we might concede that there is something morally wrong with that treatment.

The contractualist notion of justice advanced by thinkers from Hesiod to Rawls is based on exactly this reasoning. It places no demand on us to give animals their due as we expect to be given ours. It leaves animals in the precarious position of being subject to the good graces of moral agents who may elect to evaluate the moral status of animals in a wide variety of ways, depending on the "theory of the natural order and our place in it" that the agent in question feels like employing or to which the agent is prereflectively inured. If that theory is one according to which animals are fundamentally inferior to human beings, then the question of justice toward animals cannot arise precisely because a justice relation presupposes that the parties to the relationship are in *some* fundamental sense equal.

The cosmic holism that I advocate seeks to confront and overcome a seeming contradiction: that humans and animals are cosmically and existentially the same, and that nonetheless human beings systematically take grievous advantage of animals. Cosmopolitanism as it is traditionally conceived seizes upon a manifest *difference* between human beings and animals—the possession or lack of predicative rationality—and ignores the essential *sameness* of the two. The central failing of this cosmopolitan ideal and its ideological twin, the contractualist conception of justice, is that they base their commitments on a capacity that is not ultimately decisive for the question whether a given being can be a beneficiary of justice. There are a great many vulnerable, sensitive, meaning-creating beings in the world who cannot speak on their own behalf, at least not in a manner that captures the attention of very many human beings. Cosmic holism and its correlate, a nonanthropocentric cosmopolitanism, recognize and respect the fact that these vulnerable, subjugated beings not only merit just treatment but may have a stronger claim to just treatment than do the linguistic beings who have subjugated them from time immemorial. If we truly believe that peace is better than violence, if we are authentically committed to the principle of *ahimsa*, then we recognize that peaceful interrelationships are not the kind of arrangements that we respect simply in order to gain something. We act peaceably toward others because we care about them, because we respect their selfhood and have compassion for their predicament. The most authentic way to act peaceably toward another is to do so selflessly, without regard for what we might receive in return.

This what I meant at the end of *Animals and the Moral Community* when I stated that "we truncate the notion of justice by restricting it to the human sphere."[14] There is something cosmically *unfair* about taking advantage of a being who cannot defend himself or herself. The simple fact that we are able to herd, manipulate, enslave, and kill practically any kind of animal does not mean that we are *entitled* to do any of these things. Of course, many people take the view that we need not offer any kind of justification for our treatment of animals, that the question of entitlement is a red herring. Anyone who takes this position is engaging in a colossal and tragic evasion. Recall Posner's suggestion, examined in chapter 4, that the thinking that would equate animal exploitation with human slavery exhibits "a sad poverty of imagination" and his charge that "the philosophical discourse on animal rights is inherently inconclusive because there is no metric that enables utilitarianism, Romanticism, normative Darwinism, and other possible philosophical groundings of animal rights to be commensurated and conflicts among them resolved."[15] These sorts of statements not only are highly questionable on their face but reflect a complete failure to acknowledge animals as beings who share fully in vulnerability and mortality.

What makes Posner's charge about the inherent inconclusiveness of animal rights discourse questionable is not that such discourse is in fact "conclusive," at least not in the sense that it "commensurates" all "possible philosophical groundings" and "resolves all conflicts among them." What makes Posner's charge questionable is that he holds animal rights discourse to a standard that no ethical discourse, regardless of the subject matter, can possibly attain. As Gary Francione has put the point, "we cannot have mathematical certainty about our moral views—whatever they may be—concerning capital punishment, affirmative action, abortion, or animal rights."[16] I have often had the experience of being challenged to give a definitive answer to an entire array of specific ethical questions pertaining to our treatment of animals: Do insects count as moral subjects, and if so, how can I justify practices such as driving or mowing my lawn? If my child were in desperate need of a medicine or a medical procedure that would not be available in the absence of animal experimentation, would I refuse the medicine or the treatment? If I am truly committed to respecting animals as moral subjects, am I not betraying that commitment by benefiting from technological advancements whose development involved the use of animals? What, if anything, am I to do about unwanted mice or cockroaches in my living space? If I have the opportunity to rescue a stray cat but am convinced that cats are obligate carnivores, so that taking in this cat would involve me in the perpetuation of killing sentient beings for the sake of other sentient beings, what am I supposed to do? These are all very difficult questions that await resolution, and some of them may never ultimately be resolved with mathematical precision. To use that fact as a basis for alleging that moral concern for animals in incoherent is to misunderstand, perhaps deliberately, the nature of moral obligation. Moral reflection is not a recursive procedure that a computer could be programmed to perform. Instead it begins, as Rawls recognized, with a global sense of nature and the place of human beings in it. The biggest challenge for moral reflection as it pertains to the human-animal relationship is to establish and begin to dwell within a sense of the cosmos that does not make hierarchical discriminations between different sorts of sentient beings. It is against the background of such a sense that we can begin to answer the many specific questions that plague us in our efforts to reenvision the world as a place in which human beings treat animals as we wish to be treated ourselves.

Many years ago I attended an academic conference at which a well-known philosopher gave a talk comparing several different theories of animal rights. I arrived a few minutes into the talk, and as I entered the room I heard the speaker say, "Well, now, according to this theory I can't wash my dishes or take a shower, so clearly that theory won't do." These words have always stuck in my memory because they strike me as an excellent example of how *not* to think about the moral status of animals. It is undoubtedly the case that a theory that prohibited us from washing our dishes or showering would throw many people's lives into upheaval; one can easily imagine all the other things we would be forbidden to do on such a view. But whether a theory or approach would inconvenience us is not the proper measure of its legitimacy. We need to learn to put before our own interests those of others who suffer from a fundamental disadvantage in comparison with us, those who have historically been disen-franchised and exploited. In the sphere of human relations, this principle has gained increasing acceptance at least in word if not in deed. Cosmic justice for animals requires the extension of this principle to the sphere of human-animal relations.

I do not know to which ethical theory that speaker was referring, but it would appear to be the theory according to which we ought to have reverence for all life. This is the view to which Albert Schweitzer pur-ported to subscribe, but it is not the view that I am proposing here.[17] We owe cosmic justice not to just any living beings, but to beings possessing subjective awareness, those whose capacity for suffering is not the sine qua non of moral status but instead is part of an ensemble of characteris-tics possessed by beings for whom life is meaningful. That is why I stated in chapter 3 that the response-reaction distinction, traditional though it may be, is worth defending, even if it needs to become more nuanced. Sentient beings respond to their environments; these responses take var-ious forms, some of them involving predicative thought and some not. Plants and a variety of other nonsentient living beings react. Inert beings such as stones do neither. The reason a theory prohibiting dishwashing or showering "won't do" is not that such prohibitions make life diffi-cult or unpleasant for human beings; it is that such a theory sketches the scope of ethical concern too broadly. By the same token, a theory that assigns full moral status only to linguistic agents sketches the scope of ethical concern too narrowly. Members of the moral community are sen-tient beings who can be harmed or impeded in their conscious endeavors to survive and make sense of the world. As I suggested in chapter 3, the day the earth or the sea responds—one could just as well say a plant or a stone—will be the day we need to rethink radically the notion of ethical obligation.

THE VEGAN IMPERATIVE

The central failing of postmodernism as regards the moral status of animals is one that it shares with almost all liberal approaches: it can-not make sense of, hence it holds back from embracing, the principle that eating, enslaving, or otherwise doing avoidable violence to one's kin is fundamentally wrong. If liberalism has done a better job than postmodernism of at least paying lip service to this principle as it pertains to the sphere of *human* relations, that is because liberalism stops short of a total critique of reason and thus remains in the position of being able to articulate principles. But almost without exception, neither liberalism nor postmodernism has taken this principle seriously as it pertains to our relationships with *animals*.[18] This is because liberalism and postmodernism alike ultimately privilege human beings and the social sphere over sentient beings and the cosmic sphere. This myopia brings with it tragic consequences for animals. The United Nations Food and Agriculture Organization reports that fifty-three billion land animals are killed annually for human consumption worldwide. That means that every single year nearly nine thousand times as many land animals are killed for human consumption as there were Jews who perished in the entire Holocaust. That number excludes a comparably unimaginable number of sea creatures. It also takes no account of the presumably billions of animals who are subjugated and sometimes killed as beasts of burden, as experimental objects, as obstacles in land development projects, and as captive living toys for human entertainment.

When I drew the analogy between our treatment of animals and the Holocaust in "Animal, Vegetable, Miserable," I received a small number of enraged criticisms for having belittled the Holocaust by comparing the fate of so many Jews to that of "mere" animals.[19] I had noted Isaac Bashevis Singer's characterization of our treatment of animals as "an eternal Treblinka" in the short story "The Letter Writer," in which a man unexpectedly finds himself able to recognize a mouse scuttling across the floor to be "a child of God" and a "holy creature" who shared in humanity's struggle for existence.[20] In invoking Singer's analogy I had absolutely no intention of belittling the hideous fate of the Jews. Instead my intent was to draw attention to the way in which, when we occupy the anthropocentric standpoint, we do something that is arguably much worse: we belittle, indeed we ignore, the fate to which we condemn a virtually incalculable number of sentient, meaning-seeking creatures, and we fail to appreciate the fact that this sacrifice of innocents is so woven into our everyday practices and values that we tend to shudder at the characterization of this regime as being in any way comparable to large-scale human tragedies. As I have noted a number of times already, we find it relatively easy to disregard or undervalue the suffering to which we subject animals because animals cannot make their appeals to us in words. That inability,

as I argued in *Animals and the Moral Community*, has no significance whatsoever for the moral status of animals. We make a tragic mistake with hor-
rific consequences for animals if we infer from that inability that animals
matter less than humans in the cosmic scheme of things.

In *Precarious Life*, Judith Butler explores a conception of ethical responsibility based on a Levinasian recognition of "the precariousness of the
other."[21] Butler mentions in passing that animals are not to be understood on the traditional model of beings that are out of control, thereby
intimating that the tradition has done a disservice to animals by characterizing them as reaction machines.[22] Her central point, however, is
not to shed light on animals as subjects of urgent ethical concern but
rather to criticize a common mode of "bestializing" humans by comparing them to mere animals. Her central, virtually exclusive aim is to "return us to the human." The focus of her discussion of "ethical outrage"
is specifically human relations, which should not be surprising given the
fact that she takes Levinas as her point of departure. Butler stresses the
importance of "words" as the vehicle for conveying ethical outrage.[23] In
this respect, Butler's approach shares the same limitation as the liberal
and postmodern approaches I examined in the previous chapter: it places
animals and their vital interests at a distance and construes animals primarily as vehicles for "returning us to the human."

It may very well be the case that we grasp our own humanity by con-
trasting our own existence with what we conceive to be the existences
of animals. But it is a fundamental mistake to proceed from this rather
mundane fact to the conclusion that "animals make us human," at least
if in so concluding we ultimately take animals—if only against our own
intention—as means for finding our own humanity. Kelly Oliver tends
in this direction when she asserts that "the constitution of our humanity is dependent on animal pedagogy" and goes on to suggest that there
are ways of "eating and dissecting the teacher . . . in more thoughtful and
less violent ways."[24] There is no consideration here whether eating and
dissecting the animal teacher might just plain be wrong. Is that omission
perhaps a sign that animals are not being acknowledged fully, that the
expression of concern for animals as vulnerable others is at best ancillary
to a more pressing interest in the fate of human beings?

One may take the view that the focus of Butler and others on the
importance of words is not to be taken lightly, that words are an indispensable medium for the human engagement with all ethical exigencies.

That, too, is undoubtedly the case. But words alone are not enough, and the unremitting focus of liberal and postmodern thinkers alike on linguistic discourse threatens to divert our attention from the fact that our innermost connection with animals is extralinguistic, that it takes the form of kinship that is first of all felt rather than thought or discursively described. When we return from that primordial encounter in which we feel our essential sameness with all sentient life, our return must surely take linguistic form. But to experience that feeling of kinship and make a genuine place for it in the living context of our valuations and actions, we need to *stop* talking and let beings be by silently dwelling among them. Only then are we in a position to translate our felt kinship with animals into concrete principles for action.

The single most fundamental principle to be derived from a primordial encounter with animals is that of ethical veganism, the principle that we ought as far as possible to eschew the use of animals as sources of food, labor, entertainment, and the like, inasmuch as eating, enslaving, or otherwise doing avoidable violence to one's kin is fundamentally wrong. To care about animals as our kin is to find utterly unacceptable any hierarchization of the moral worth of different sentient beings, and to endeavor to treat them as far as possible as we would treat our fellow human beings. As Gary Francione has aptly pointed out, this does not mean that animals are entitled to things such as driver's licenses or voting rights.[25] But it does mean that they are entitled to peaceful treatment by human beings, which means that they are entitled not to be eaten, used as forced field labor, experimented upon, killed for materials to make clothing and other commodities of use to human beings, or held as captive entertainment. Some thinkers believe we should assume that animals give their implicit consent to be used in such practices if the practices are of significant value to human beings. But what we really ought to do in such situations is assume that animals *do not* give their consent. To do otherwise is to act in a pointedly self-serving way. It is to offer a blanket rationalization for a system of exploitation that benefits human beings and simply harms animals.[26]

There are a number of anthropocentric responses to the vegan imperative as I have articulated it. One is based on the traditional prejudice that human life is more important than animal life, that the death of a human is a greater loss than that of an animal inasmuch as human beings have greater opportunities for satisfaction than animals. But as I have argued, the lives of animals matter to them every bit as much as our lives matter to us; each sentient being's life matters to it to an incalculable degree. Another response is that certain uses of animals do not harm them but in fact benefit them. One form this response takes is the suggestion that certain kinds of animals would not exist if they were not bred and maintained for domestication, and that it is better for such animals to exist as domesticated than not to exist at all. Another form of this response is the suggestion, offered by Bentham and others, that animals experience a much less horrible death at our hands than they would suffer in wild nature. And yet another form of this response is that many domesticated animals appear to be perfectly happy; for example, a sheep wandering around in a field does not appear to be suffering in any way and is assured of nutritious food and proper treatment.

Each of these challenges to the vegan imperative is advanced from the myopic standpoint of anthropocentrism. It is by no means clear that it is better to exist in a state of captivity than not to exist at all. Slaves, as Rousseau recognized, can become so accustomed to the deprivation of their freedom that they behave as if slavery were a perfectly acceptable condition for them, even though slavery is inherently at odds with the slave's true nature as a free, self-determining being.[27] To think otherwise is to endorse at least implicitly the Aristotelian reasoning according to which the slave benefits from being held as a slave. Nor is the question what is in an animal's interest a clear and straightforward one, particularly given that anthropocentric prejudice inclines us strongly to see our treatment of animals as largely, if not entirely, benign. And the proposition that we do animals a favor by killing them and sparing them the horrors of a natural death is based, as the work of Marc Bekoff and others has shown, on an unrealistically one-sided view of nature as "red in tooth and claw" (Tennyson) that ignores the many ways in which animals enjoy life and cooperate with one another.[28] In short, all these anthropocentric responses assume a little too quickly that human uses of animals actually make animals better off, when in fact human beings are the primary, if not the exclusive, beneficiaries.

The vegan imperative pertains to a wide variety of uses of animals, but the problem of killing animals merits an additional word. There is extraordinary arrogance in the often cheerful suggestion that animals are better off for being killed by human beings. The logic appears to be this: death is inevitable; a less painful or distressing death is better than a more painful or distressing one; death at the hands of human beings is less painful or distressing, hence more "humane," than a natural death. But what is really being asserted here? Can we quantify the respective amounts of pain or distress involved in different sorts of death? Assuming that such a calculus is even possible, can we trust ourselves to perform it in an objective and dispassionate way, particularly given our well-established penchant for animal flesh? And, most important, what makes us think we have the right to decide who dies, how they die, and when they die? That we arrogate to ourselves this prerogative is all the more awful to contemplate given the fact that very few, if any, members of the human race can legitimately claim that their survival depends on the consumption of animal products.

There is one additional criticism of the vegan imperative that merits consideration: that the imperative as I have presented it equivocates on the strictness of our duties toward animals by employing the qualification "as far as possible" and referring to "avoidable" violence. Thus the imperative would appear to leave a great deal of room for discretion about what constitutes "necessary" uses of or ways of treating animals. But in fact this is less a criticism of the imperative than an index of the difficulty of conceptualizing and living in accordance with it. Only on a crudely positivistic conception of imperatives or principles is living in accordance with them reducible to Cartesian clear and distinct insight. As I noted in previous chapters, veganism presents itself as an infinite task, one that the terms of existence make ultimately unfulfillable and that must therefore be seen as a regulative ideal for our conduct. Living in accordance with the vegan imperative is not like turning on a light switch. It is like delving ever deeper into uncharted territory.

It is worth adding here that the nature of principles is such that there is no reason to believe that all the rights of the respective parties must be mutually compatible. If every being has a right to preserve its own existence, I do not see how we can say that either party to a literal face-to-face life-and-death struggle is categorically wrong to kill another in preservation of its own life. In such a case there simply seems to be a conflict of rights. Now if this is true, then there is at least one sort of case in which deadly violence cannot be avoided. But that has little if anything to do with the vegan imperative, inasmuch as precious few human beings ever find themselves in a situation in which it is literally a matter of their life or an animal's. And yet we treat every case of conflict between our own interests and those of animals as what Gary Francione calls "burning house cases," that is, as if our lives really did depend on the subjugation of animals—even though for the vast majority of us they do not.

To see the vegan imperative as a regulative ideal is to start by acknowledging Schopenhauer's insight into the inevitability of suffering and destruction in the world, and to recognize that the endeavor to act peaceably toward animals is an endless task that is not fulfillable once and for all. All willing, as Schopenhauer observed, is bound up with suffering and destruction; and yet willing is the essential condition of existence. We literally cannot live without inflicting harm, and some of that harm will be inflicted on sentient beings. Unless we choose the path of the Jain priest and decide to permit ourselves to die, we are left in the condition of having to try to minimize the destruction that we cause. Critics of veganism sometimes take this as a sign that vegans are arbitrary and selective regarding the beings toward whom they exhibit concern—for example, that vegans are arbitrary in showing concern for "warm, fuzzy" creatures such as cats and dogs whereas they exhibit no particular concern for the many mice and other creatures who are killed in mechanized harvesting operations. Anyone who has such an attitude is not taking the vegan imperative seriously. A principled commitment to nonviolence toward animals that finds its motivation in a sincere sense of felt kinship simply cannot accommodate such a contradiction. Genuine felt kinship moves us to delve ever deeper into the endeavor to live peaceably with animals. It so moves us in spite of the fact that we cannot know in advance exactly how the principle should be applied in every specific contingency, and in spite of the fact that fidelity to the vegan imperative provides no guarantee that we will not encounter some irreducible conflicts.

VEGANISM AND THE ETHICS OF DIET

This leaves us with the question how veganism as an ethical principle is to be realized. For all the bad press he has received in contemporary academic circles, Descartes has an excellent methodological rule: start with what is simple, and proceed from there to the complex.[29] For the vast majority of the world's population, and certainly for the vast majority if not all readers of this book, a comparatively simple starting point is the question whether it is acceptable to eat animals. (Other comparatively clear starting points pertain to clothing, animal experimentation, holding animals in captivity, etc.) What makes us think it is morally acceptable to eat our kin? Derrida notes that people have a particular abhorrence at the thought of being eaten by cannibals; for Robinson Crusoe, the worst kind of death would take the form of being eaten by a member of one's own kind. Derrida also asks the question whether "every carnivorous human being is not secretly an anthropophage" (an eater of human beings) who avoids recognizing the essential identity of meat eating and anthropophagy only "by the detour of a repression."[30] Derrida thereby invites us to consider whether eating animals is comparable to the prospect of eating human beings. But he leaves this in the elliptical form of a question and stops conspicuously short of concluding that meat eating—or eating human beings, for that matter—is fundamentally wrong.

One diagnosis of Derrida's (or anyone else's) refusal to embrace veganism, even though he professes to deplore the various forms of violence that are perpetrated on animals and human beings alike, is that the logic of the trace reveals the infinite complexity and irreducibility of singular cases to a simple formula. Human beings, not being the masters of language, are simply not in a position to articulate abstract principles that could govern absolutely any particular life contingency. But as I have argued, to take this view of principles is to misunderstand at a basic level both how they are formulated and how they can become applied in concrete circumstances. From the standpoint of a cosmic holism that opens us to our essential kinship and shared struggle with animals, the prospect of eating animals should fill us with the same kind of revulsion that Crusoe feels at the prospect of being eaten by other human beings. One simply does not eat one's own kind, one's kin. From the standpoint of cosmic holism, a meal containing meat would be what Ovid vividly calls "a Thyestean banquet," the moral equivalent of the meal that Atreus surreptitiously prepared for his brother Thyestes in an act of revenge, a meal that consisted of Thyestes's own children.[31] There is nothing about the logic of the trace that in any way undermines the meaning, nor mitigates the force, of the proposition that killing and eating animals is a practice that should fill us with the same kind of horror and revulsion that we ought to feel when we contemplate the story of Atreus and Thyestes. The rare, Donner Party–like situation in which we absolutely must consume another sentient being in order to survive *may* constitute an exception to the vegan imperative. But whether or not it does, such a situation should still fill us with revulsion, and in any case it is not typical but instead is the kind of "burning house" case that all too often diverts our attention from our real motivation for eating animals.

Thus a different diagnosis of the refusal of Derrida and others who care about animals to embrace veganism recommends itself: people do not like to be pushed outside their comfort zones. They prefer to live in accordance with "feel-good ethics," ethical gestures and commitments that feel good to assert but which demand relatively little of us in their concrete realization. Being a vegetarian means different things to different people. The strictest kind of vegetarian is one who will not under any circumstances consume animal flesh. Depending on where you happen to find yourself, and particularly if you find yourself away from home and in unfamiliar circumstances, it can be very difficult to avoid animal flesh altogether; and the less familiar the cultural context into which you place yourself, the more difficult this can be. Less strict vegetarians have a convenient solution in such situations: they simply allow themselves to eat a little meat, assure themselves that this consumption is insignificant in the large cosmic scheme, and promise themselves that they will return to their vegetarian regimen as soon as they are in more familiar or more convenient surroundings. There is an even less strict viewpoint—I have heard people give expression to it more times than I can count—according to which being a vegetarian means not consuming red meat at home.

All these approaches fall short of embracing the vegan imperative. Even the so-called strict vegetarian still consumes eggs and dairy products, and some self-styled strict vegetarians consume fish and other sea creatures. What the vegan imperative demands is a delving ever deeper into the questions of what constitutes violence toward animals and how human beings can do a better job of avoiding it. Committing oneself to the vegan imperative demands that we push ourselves out of our comfort zones and that we stop worrying about what people will think, how we will negotiate the social niceties of accepting a dinner invitation from nonvegans, and what we will do if we end up in some remote locale that is far from vegan-friendly and in which we may have to search for some time in genuine hunger until we find something suitable to eat. Feel-good ethics permits us to talk the talk of moral concern without doing the hard work of reenvisioning our daily lives, changing our habits, and enduring what is sometimes a great deal of personal inconvenience. Ethical veganism is fundamentally incompatible with the feel-good approach to the moral status of animals.

The vast majority of postmodern and liberal thinkers alike who profess concern for animals stop conspicuously short of embracing anything like the vegan imperative, let alone ethical vegetarianism. Their professions of concern strike me as instances of feel-good ethics: express concern for animals, eat a little less meat, perhaps purchase free-range meat, make a donation to the Humane Society, and express some more concern for animals. Life goes on essentially as before. That the people to whom I am referring typically respond with protests that they have been misunderstood is not only unconvincing, it is unsurprising. This is a tragic, if well-intentioned, case of evasion. Indeed, the entire postmodern approach provides a symptomology of evasion every bit as troubling as the evasions of liberal thought. How can one continue to eat animals when for most, if not all, of us the practice is completely unnecessary? The answer is simple: because we are accustomed to eating them, because it is convenient to do so, and because we like the taste.

The move from vegetarianism to veganism is more difficult for many people to comprehend than the call for vegetarianism. Not long ago I got into a discussion with a well-known American political philosopher about the ethics of diet. This person was not a vegan or vegetarian and posed a series of challenges to me that seemed intended to reduce my vegan commitments to absurdity. If animals are going to die anyway, what difference does it make if we kill them in order to eat them, particularly if we raise them in comfortable circumstances and kill them without pain or trauma? What is so bad about taking milk and eggs from animals, particularly if we raise the animals "humanely" rather than in factory farming circumstances, and given that these acts of taking do not involve killing animals? This person did everything possible to minimize the supposed harms of raising animals for human use and consumption and to try to make my views look ridiculous. What this person did *not* do was try to think about the problem from a nonanthropocentric standpoint such as that of the free subjectivity of an animal. Nor did this person stop (as far as I could discern) to wonder whether the insistence on posing these questions from the anthropocentric standpoint carried with it an a priori guarantee that the answers would all provide justifications for the human husbandry and consumption of animals. In the very way the questions were posed there was an entire set of presuppositions about the supposed rudimentariness of animal interests and the prerogative of human beings to use animals. These presuppositions excluded in advance any possible comprehension of the proposition that taking substances such as milk and eggs from animals is an act of violence.

That under existing productive relations the commodification of milk and eggs involves violence against animals—the same holds for silk, wool, leather, and the like—is now completely beyond dispute. (Just do an Internet search for the term "rape rack.") The harder question is whether such commodification constitutes violence regardless of the conditions under which it is performed. The political theorist mentioned above pressed the point that the production of milk and eggs for human consumption need not take the form that it currently takes. That is technically correct. But it misses the larger point that using animals as delivery devices for food (and clothing, etc.) to be consumed by humans, viewed from the standpoint of cosmic holism and in the light of felt kinship, is a perverse idea. Again, what makes us think that such practices, even in the friendliest circumstances, are compatible with our moral concern for animals as individual subjects? A corollary of the vegan imperative is the principle that if you would not do something to a human being, there is a strong presumptive claim against doing it to an animal. I permit myself the liberty of supposing that most anyone would find abhorrent the prospect of confining human beings and using them as sources of, say, milk. What makes us think we are any more entitled to do this to a cow or a goat?

The anthropocentric answer to this question is that a cow or a goat does not have the same comprehension a human being would of what is happening to it, and therefore that the cow or the goat is not harmed as a human in comparable circumstances would be. If "does not have the same comprehension" means that the cow or the goat cannot conceptualize the situation and think about it in predicative terms, that is one thing. But to assume that this means in addition that animals have no appreciation of their predicament is to congratulate ourselves too hastily on our cognitive superiority to animals, and to presuppose that animals must be able to think consciously about their predicament in order for it to constitute a predicament. (If I am a shopkeeper and I short-change a child who does not realize that she is being short-changed, I am still doing something morally wrong.)[32]

This is why measures such as California's Proposition 2 do not present a compelling case for the idea that human beings really care about the fortunes of animals. This measure, passed by a nearly two-thirds margin in 2008, calls for sufficient space for veal calves, egg-laying hens, and pregnant pigs to be able to get up, lie down, extend their limbs, and turn around freely. Such a measure reinforces very nicely the anthropocentric drive to use animals. It allows people to feel good about the husbanding and consumption of meat and eggs, by letting us assure ourselves that the confinement on which both animal husbandry and Proposition 2 are predicated is "humane." What people voting for the measure seem not to have taken seriously is the question whether the confinement (not to mention the killing) of animals to benefit human palates is morally justified. People seem to have been too busy congratulating themselves that veal calves and pregnant sows will finally be able to turn around in their stalls. They are, after all, just animals.

Shortly after the publication of "Animal, Vegetable, Miserable," the *New York Times* published a handful of letters, one of whose authors suggested that I "might feel less lonely as an ethical vegan . . . if [I] recognized that [I have] allies in mere vegetarians (like me), ethical omnivores and even carnivores."[33] Elsewhere the author of this letter suggests that we think of animal welfare measures on the analogy of improving conditions for slaves: opposing animal welfare measures, measures designed to improve the conditions in which we confine animals, is like being opposed to giving slave children shoes or teaching slaves to read.[34] After all, isn't a slave with shoes better off than a slave without shoes? Seen within the narrow utilitarian constraints imposed by that author, such a proposition is hard to deny. But its moral force is mitigated almost entirely when viewed against the background of the fact that slavery itself, like the confinement of animals in the service of human convenience and pleasure, is categorically wrong.

My purpose in writing "Animal, Vegetable, Miserable," indeed my purpose in writing everything I have written about the moral status of animals, has not been to "feel less lonely as an ethical vegan." It has been to try to shed light on the fact that, whatever one may think about the worthiness of animal welfare measures, such measures by their very nature stop short of according animals full respect. Indeed, as Gary Francione has exhaustively demonstrated, animal welfare measures not only presuppose a regime of animal exploitation, they function in practice to make people feel better about exploiting animals.[35]

Nonvegans often react defensively when the proposition is put to them that animal welfare measures are simply not sufficient for the expression of genuine, nonanthropocentric concern for animals. This defensive reaction is yet another evasion of the vegan imperative. Rather than assessing the merits of ethical veganism, nonvegans who react in this way seem to be exhibiting a desire to incriminate the vegan messenger for taking some kind of moral high ground, thereby countering an authentic moral appeal with an ad hominem dismissal. I cannot help but wonder whether such a reaction is born of a repressed intimation that the husbanding and consumption of animals is at odds with our cosmic kinship with them. The failure or refusal to acknowledge others is not unique to the animal rights debate; to be human is to engage in such refusals and evasions all the time. To point out such an evasion is not to take some moral high ground. It is to try to do a better job of coming to grips with reality and do justice to the vulnerable beings who populate it.

A Critique of the Deep Ecology of Meat Eating

A resourceful if ultimately uncompelling argument in favor of meat eating (and, by extension, of the consumption of other animal products) proceeds from the premise that predation is an essential feature of the natural world to the conclusion that we flatter ourselves inappropriately by supposing that we can or should seek to remove ourselves from the eternal cycles of predation. On this view, the desire to establish a peaceful relationship with animals is a product of the very history of anthropocentric prejudice that the call for ethical veganism seeks to overcome. The aspiration to live a vegetarian or vegan existence is born of a desire to separate ourselves from nature rather than identifying ourselves with it. According to this critique of vegetarianism and veganism, cosmic holism is actually compatible with meat eating and the consumption of other animal products. One can, many proponents of this position maintain, be a sincere advocate of animal rights and still eat meat. Indeed, according to many formulations of this view, one *ought* to eat meat.

One of the most famous sources of inspiration for this line of reasoning in contemporary thought is Aldo Leopold, who proposes that whatever "tends to preserve the integrity, stability, and beauty of the biotic community" is fundamentally "right." Leopold presents a version of cosmic holism according to which experiences that "remind us" of the "man-earth relation" have "value," and according to which there is value in certain forms of hunting. Hunting is perfectly compatible with the endeavor to "get back to nature," as long as our hunting practices are not trophy oriented nor facilitated by undue gadgetry, and as long as they are undertaken with respect for biotic community.[36] Such respect is compatible with the capacity to "mourn the death of another," even when we ourselves have caused that death in the course of hunting for sport.[37]

According to this reasoning, it is possible to kill an animal even while we respect it; indeed, respect for animals and involvement in the cycles of predation are inseparable from one another. James Hatley argues that "our ethical discourse is obsessed by its abhorrence of predation" and that we need to begin to see ourselves as part of the eternal cycles of predator and prey. Hatley urges us to take seriously Wendell Berry's call to undo our culture's repression of "the slipperiness, the bewilderment, and so the very wildness of the distinction between the human and the natural." We must undo a repression: like Leopold before him, Hatley stresses the need to remember something that our culture has sought to forget—that even though we are in some sense set apart from the rest of nature by our capacity for reflective consciousness and our endeavors to insulate ourselves from natural threats, we are nonetheless part of nature. Hatley offers the possibility of being the prey of a wild animal as the preeminent inspiration to this act of memory. "Finding ourselves in the position of being prey to an animal predator is a telling case of the natural world's provoking discomfort, difficulty, and danger within a human and humane context. Hardly anything could be more intimate than becoming the food, and so the very body, of another animal in the wild. . . . We may be able to suppress predation, but we can hardly undo it."[38]

By taking seriously the prospect of being the prey of some predatory animal, we remedy a colossal misunderstanding of ourselves as existing fundamentally outside the natural context of predatory activity. We undo the "arrogant and presumptuous forgetfulness of our irretrievable involvement in all other flesh, in a community shared with nonhuman others," thereby putting ourselves in a position to "find ourselves addressed by . . . an aspect of our own goodness that we would otherwise forget." Our misunderstanding of our relationship to nature is reflected in the basic way in which we have appropriated nature. "In truth, our appropriation of nature does not so much eliminate predation as codify it in asymmetric terms: we make over the space in which we live *as if* humans had become inedible and everything else is revealed to be more or less available for ingestion." The asymmetry here consists in the supposition that we are predators and never prey, that in essence we are different from other natural beings. We thereby fail to acknowledge that "we only get to be a human, or a bear, or a microbe by eating others!" We rectify this misunderstanding, and presumably attain a more adequate relationship to the natural world, by establishing a "covenant" with predatory species in which "we find ourselves continually in transition between two spaces—one in which predation is asymmetrical and the other in which predation is reflexive."[39]

The word "covenant" signifies an enforceable promise. The promise that Hatley has in mind appears to be a commitment not to see ourselves as separate from nature, but instead to see ourselves as enmeshed in a cycle of moving back and forth between separation from nature and immersion as potential prey in nature. Our promise is, at least symbolically, to offer ourselves to predatory animals as their sustenance, just as animals and other living things are our sustenance. Hatley's focus is on one side of this reciprocity—our making ourselves available to predatory animals. About the other side of this reciprocal relationship he says very little. He states that "without the ingestion of the other's flesh, human flesh would quickly be no flesh at all," which might lead one to conclude that Hatley, like Leopold, sees no problem with human predation of animals as long as a certain reciprocity is respected. But Hatley also states that "vegetables . . . too must be considered part of the order of flesh." He thus leaves open the question of diet. Presumably one may eat meat without the least scruple, provided that one obtains it in accordance with our covenant with nature: if it is natural and appropriate for us to be prey, reciprocity would seem to imply that it is comparably natural and appropriate for us to be predators. But opting for a vegetarian diet could also be accommodated by Hatley's conception of reciprocity, inasmuch as "in eating vegetables, one is eating matter that has been nourished by the decaying bodies of animals, even the human animal, as well as plant matter."[40]

Dominique Lestel has recently taken this logic of reciprocity one step further by arguing not only that meat eating is permissible but that it is incumbent upon us. Where Hatley places emphasis on the importance of giving ourselves to predatory animals, Lestel stresses the importance of being able to receive as well as give. Lestel models his ethic of carnivorism on the "ethically positive approach" of indigenous peoples such as the Algonquin. The positive character of this approach is evident in the fact that "when the Indians kill their prey, they thank its 'spirit' for the 'gift' it has given; and they do all this in such a way as to ensure that the species itself continues to proliferate and its members live in good conditions." It is a mistake to see predation as aggression; on the contrary, predation is "one of the principles" of "the harmony and justice" that govern "the energies that circulate in the world." Eating animals is not simply "a biological necessity" but reinforces a cosmic relationship of "mutual dependence." In eating animals, "I accept my share in the compromise inherent in my animality." This acceptance "constitutes a posture of humility in comparison with the vegetarian, who purports to occupy a position above the animality to which, for all that, the vegetarian belongs."[41]

Thus where the vegetarian would prefer to forget that we are animals and exist subject to the eternal cycles of predation, Lestel, like Leopold and Hatley, stresses the importance of reminding ourselves of the true conditions of our existence.[42] "I do not claim that nature pushes us to kill, but rather that predation has occupied a central place in the world ever since carnivores have existed, and that only with difficulty can one consider the everyday condition of so many living beings to be a perversion or take it for granted that human beings can be moral [by being] *against* nature." Lestel has "infinite respect for animals"; argues vehemently in his writings for an end to "invasive animal experimentation"; and calls for only "limited, ritual consumption of meat."[43] His point is not to declare open season on animals but instead, like Leopold and Hatley, to explore an ethics of reciprocity born of a recognition of our true place in nature—a place that confers on us both prerogatives and urgent ethical responsibilities.

For Lestel these ethical responsibilities include the obligation to recognize the subjectivity of animals and the fact that animals share with us in the struggle to survive and confer meaning on experience. The "ethical carnivore" does not take meat eating lightly but instead undertakes this practice with full appreciation of the "infinite debt" that we owe to animals.[44] To eat meat ethically is to "consume it with [a] mixture of pious reverence and anxiety." To consume meat in such a ritual fashion is not to do so as part of one's everyday practices but instead to do so with the specific intention of celebrating our own animality and the sacrifice that the animal we eat has made on our behalf. The purpose of meat eating is not to promote human health, and the amount of meat we consume is not to be dictated (at least not exclusively or primarily) by environmental considerations. Lestel recommends a pious modesty in the amount of meat we consume, but he cautions us against the aspiration to eliminate the consumption of meat from our diets altogether. "One can perfectly well advocate a drastic reduction in the consumption of meat without necessarily *suppressing* it." The reason not to suppress the consumption of meat altogether is that "a life without [some] violence" toward animals "would lose something that is essential to a life truly worth having been lived."[45]

The ethic proposed by Lestel is not one based on compassion or equality but instead is "an ethic of shared life. . . . The question of suffering is entirely secondary," even though it is never legitimate to make an animal suffer. Thus Lestel's views regarding the proper ethical relationship between human beings and animals exhibit a certain tension: on the one hand he maintains that we must not endeavor to eliminate violence altogether from our relationship to animals, while on the other hand he expresses compassion for animals and decries at least the needless infliction of suffering on them. Lestel seeks to resolve this tension by emphasizing the importance of preserving a dimension of violence in our relationship to animals, while decrying practices such as factory farming and invasive animal experimentation. The function of our "ritual" consumption of meat is to inflict the least violence possible on animals while still affirming our own animality and our "metabolic" continuity with all other living beings.[46]

It is our animality and our continuity with all living beings, Lestel argues, that the advocate of ethical vegetarianism endeavors to forget. Lestel distinguishes three types of vegetarian: the political vegetarian, who rightly lobbies against the "ignominy" of factory farming; the "personal" vegetarian, who refrains from eating meat simply because she or he does not like it; and the ethical vegetarian, who succumbs to the "Bambi syndrome" in embracing an ideal of complete peace with animals. Lestel directs his critique exclusively at the ethical vegetarian, who reasserts the humanist "thesis of human exceptionalism" and mistakenly "believes that human beings can place themselves above the evolution of all other species."[47] In representing human beings as essentially different from nonhuman animals, which are enmeshed in the eternal cycles of predation and are unable to entertain the prospect of a life without violence, the standpoint of the ethical vegetarian amounts to "a politics of apartheid between human beings and other animals." The truly consistent ethical vegetarian is "profoundly hostile to life" in seeking to eliminate cruelty from the world, inasmuch as "the sole means for satisfying [the ethical vegetarian's pacifistic aspiration] would be to suppress all animal life on earth."[48]

This aspiration to eliminate suffering is born, Lestel believes, of a fundamental misunderstanding of the significance of predation and our relation to it. The ethical vegetarian sees things in unduly anthropocentric terms in supposing that animals have an interest in not being killed. "The vegetarian's fundamental postulate, according to which the animal's good is never to be hunted and not to be eaten, is less apparent" than the ethical vegetarian would have us believe. Animals themselves do not consider "being killed" to be "an ethical scandal," so why should we consider it to be one? The ethical vegetarian would like to forget that life is fundamentally inseparable from violence and cruelty. The ethical vegetarian purports to love animals but really "loves a highly idealized animal, an animal that is ultimately no longer very animal."[49] The ethical vegetarian engages, to use Nietzsche's terminology, in a denial of life.

Lestel offers one additional criticism of the ethical vegetarian that shows the continuity of his approach with that of some other writers in the deep ecology tradition: he challenges the vegetarian's categorical distinction between animals and plants. Recall Hatley's characterization of plant life as belonging to the domain of "flesh." The intent behind such a characterization is to deconstruct any supposed boundary between different types of living things, and ultimately to challenge the traditional thesis of human exceptionalism. Lestel tries to catch the ethical vegetarian in a contradiction by challenging the proposition that it is more legitimate to kill a plant than to kill an animal. He asks how we can be so sure that plants do not suffer. And he maintains that even though "plants may not be able to think, they nonetheless engage in calculation and respond appropriately to the problems they encounter." Plants relate actively to their environments, have interests, and pursue those interests; we ought not to view them simply as objects at the disposal of human beings. For those of us who cannot take seriously the proposition that plants suffer and have subjective lives that in essential respects are indistinguishable from the lives of animals, Lestel proposes that an appreciation of "the temporality of vegetation" will disclose for us "the intelligence" of plants.[50]

In offering this characterization of plant "experience," Lestel implicitly follows others who have sought to deconstruct the traditional response-reaction distinction. As I noted in chapter 3, Derrida and others seek to challenge the traditional presupposition that only human beings respond and that animals merely react. Lestel devotes a great deal of energy to showing the absurdity of the prejudice that animals are machines that merely react.[51] And like some postmodern thinkers, he extends the postmodern critique of the response-reaction distinction by suggesting that not only animals but also plants actively respond to their environments. Lestel thereby makes the same mistake as Kelly Oliver, who maintains that "even plants respond to their environment and even to human voices or touch." Oliver undermines the response-reaction distinction completely by proposing that "living beings are responsive beings."[52] To erase the distinction between animals and plants in this manner is to ignore the clear preponderance of scientific evidence. While we cannot state with apodictic certainty that plants lack sentience, the overwhelming weight of scientific evidence casts tremendous doubt on this possibility. Plants lack central nervous systems, nociceptors (pain receptors), and other morphological features associated with the capacity for sentience. To make a plausible case for plant sentience, one would have to do a lot more than simply note that plants exhibit changes that correspond to changes and contingencies in their environments.

The proposition that plants respond seems less a serious claim than an instance of what happens when the deconstructive impulse is given free rein. Remember that deconstruction's modus operandi is to locate a traditionally accepted distinction and show how it undermines itself. The guiding principle is that if a given distinction lacks an incontrovertible metaphysical foundation, that distinction is a mere construction. But a distinction such as that between plants and animals—or, as I shall argue shortly, between human beings and other animals—does not need a metaphysical foundation in order to tell us something important about reality. That does not mean that such distinctions are impervious to revision or refinement. It simply means that one does not have to identify a precise and immovable dividing line to recognize and discuss manifest differences between two modes of life. Even Aristotle recognized that the line between plant and animal is not absolutely clear.[53] But he also recognized important differences between the two that we dismiss only at the risk of misunderstanding what it means for an animal to be an animal.

In particular, to say that all living beings respond is to misconstrue altogether the phenomenon, and the importance, of the notion of subjective awareness and freedom. Many traditional thinkers err by attributing free agency to human beings alone and characterizing animals as reaction devices whose movements are strictly determined by their appetites. We now know that this way of distinguishing between human and nonhuman animals is a distortion motivated by anthropocentric prejudice. But the solution is not to dismiss the distinction altogether. It is to do a better job of employing it. This includes acknowledging the ways in which many animals consciously encounter and assess their environments and choose from among different possible courses of action. It also includes acknowledging that human beings are not fully conscious beings and that much of our behavior is determined by factors other than rational reflection. Human and nonhuman animals alike sometimes respond and sometimes react.

But this provides no basis for leaping to the conclusion that plants are capable of responding. The suggestion that plants do possess this capacity seems to lack any basis either in science or in our face-to-face encounters with the plant world. (Such a suggestion, a Wittgensteinian would say, involves a confusion in our concepts.) The ascription of conscious agency to plants—suffering, intelligence, decision making—is a product of a simple confusion between instances of what John Searle calls "*intrinsic intentionality*, which are cases of actual mental states, and . . . *observer-relative ascriptions of intentionality*, which are ways that people have of speaking about entities figuring in our activities but lacking intrinsic intentionality."[54] We have a tendency to describe various nonconscious entities and systems as if they were acting consciously and deliberately. For example, we say that "the car doesn't want to start" or " petunias like full sun." We talk metaphorically, *as if* cars and petunias had conscious desires and preferences and could act on them. But this does not mean that machines or plants have any subjective awareness.

To suggest otherwise is fanciful. And in the case of thinkers interested specifically in challenging the view that human beings should adopt as far as possible a peaceful relationship with animals, it is to employ a rhetorical "Aha! Gotcha!" maneuver intended to reduce the vegetarian's or vegan's argument to absurdity. Shortly after I published "Animal, Vegetable, Miserable," the New York Times published an article entitled "Sorry, Vegans: Brussels Sprouts Like To Live, Too" that appears to have been written in exactly this spirit.[55] Once again: the day the earth or the sea (or a Brussels sprout) responds is the day we need to rethink ethics as it pertains to relationships between individuals. There may be ecocentric ethical principles that govern our relationship to the plant world. But what I am discussing is the ethics of relationships between individuals, specifically between human and animal individuals. There is currently no settled understanding of how zoocentric and ecocentric ethics relate to one another, nor of how conflicts between the two ought to be resolved. So far in my work I have given priority to the former because I believe that sentient beings can be harmed in ways that nonsentient beings cannot. As I have noted already, I take the capacity to suffer not to be the sole or preeminent basis for granting this priority to sentient beings, but rather to be a conspicuous indication of a larger ensemble of capacities possessed by conscious, free, meaning-making beings and lacked by plant life.

Lestel punctuates his critique of ethical vegetarianism with the suggestion that "vegetarians ultimately play a very positive role" inasmuch as they "deliver a message of fundamental importance to the carnivore that the latter would do wrong not to hear. For eating meat is never a trivial matter."[56] In this respect Lestel has something fundamentally in common with the advocate of ethical vegetarianism or veganism: he sees a fundamental kinship between human and nonhuman animals, he acknowledges the agency and the worth of sentient animals, and he calls for a cessation to practices such as factory farming and invasive animal experimentation. Like thinkers in the deep ecology tradition such as Leopold and Hatley, Lestel stresses the importance of "remembering" our animality by acknowledging our essential continuity with the entire living world. On Lestel's view, we *must* eat meat in order to engage in this primordial act of recollection.

But *why* must an acknowledgment of our essential animality involve the consumption of meat, ritual though it may be? What form is such ritual consumption to take, and what is the special power of killing, mastication, and ingestion such that they will confer on us a sense of reverence for the beings we are destroying? The only hint offered by Lestel comes in the specific traditions to which he appeals in making his case for carnivorism: the Algonquin, the Cree, and the Sioux, all of them indigenous cultures far removed from our own cultural situation and consciousness.[57] It is worth asking exactly what relevance the cosmologies of these cultures have to our own endeavor to ground our ethical commitments in cosmic holism. *Must* cosmic holism make a place for killing and eating animals? Or is it instead the case that the cosmic consciousness of certain cultures was fundamentally shaped by the fact that they *had* to consume animals in order to survive? It would be extraordinarily ill-advised to follow the example of a culture that had to engage in certain acts of violence, when we ourselves simply do not need to engage in them.

What, then, about Lestel's claim that we must eat meat in order to remember our animality? Leopold, Hatley, and Lestel are united, and quite right, in arguing that the Western philosophical tradition has produced gross misunderstandings of human beings, nonhuman nature, and the relationship between the two through its persistent endeavor to cultivate a sense of human exceptionalism. Lestel's claim is that we cannot retrieve a sense of our true humanity and its proximity to the predatory world of nature unless we consume at least some meat. But again, why suppose that eating meat will have the magical effect of restoring to us a sense of our immersion in and obligations toward nature? Lestel sees meat eating as a way of asserting our continuity with the rest of nature. On Lestel's view, the vegetarian reproduces the error of humanism in supposing that human beings can do something that no other living being can, namely, remove themselves from the violent cycles of predation; we simply reassert the logic of human exceptionalism by endeavoring to raise ourselves above the rest of nature. Lestel thus believes that the ethical vegetarian, if only unwittingly, perpetuates a logic that historically has given human beings license to subjugate animals.

But everything turns here on the term "exceptionalism." Historically it has functioned as an assertion of human superiority over the rest of nature. We seize on the capacity for *logos* (reason or language) as unique to human beings, we take that uniqueness as a sign of our moral superiority over animals and the rest of nature, and on that basis we arrogate to ourselves the prerogative to use animals and the rest of nature as instrumentalities for the satisfaction of human needs and desires. But to the extent that the ethical vegetarian asserts a kind of exceptionalism, it is of a different order altogether. The "exceptionalism," if one can really call it that, of the ethical vegetarian or vegan is not one according to which human beings are superior to other animals and enjoy prerogatives that other animals lack. On the contrary, the ethical vegetarian or vegan recognizes that human beings possess the capacity to articulate and strive to live in accordance with principles, a capacity that even Frans de Waal has recognized to be absent in nonhuman animals.[58] The mistake of the tradition is to suppose that our being unique in possessing this capacity entitles us to exclude nonhuman animals as full beneficiaries of ethical principles, whereas the ethical vegetarian or vegan recognizes the self-serving inconsistency of this exclusion. The ethical vegetarian or vegan recognizes that the capacity to form principles confers obligations on human beings to act on behalf of nonhuman animals, and in particular to refrain from inflicting harm on animals wherever possible.

Thus Lestel provides us with a caricature of ethical vegetarianism or veganism. The vegan imperative does not involve any supposition that human beings are superior to other sentient beings but instead is founded on the recognition that our capacity for reflection imposes burdens on us that no other sentient being appears to be capable of assuming. Nor does an affirmation of the vegan imperative involve the aspiration to eliminate violence or predation from the world altogether. Embracing the vegan imperative involves a Schopenhaurian insight into the inevitability of destruction, suffering, and death in the world. It also involves the Schopenhaurian endeavor to reduce suffering in the world, against the background of a clear recognition that suffering is the basic condition of existence. This is where ethical veganism parts company with Lestel's conception of an "infinite debt" to animals: rather than capitulating to the inevitability of suffering and predation in the world, the ethical vegan takes the position that we make a grievous moral mistake by contributing to the world's suffering when we can avoid doing so. Reducing all life to the amorphous category of "flesh" is fundamentally incompatible with such an expression of moral concern for animals, as is the proposition that human life is somehow diminished by the aspiration to eschew all violence toward animals.

Ultimately it is not the ethical vegan but the advocate of carnivorism who is speciesist. Recall the terms of Zeus's imposition of the law of justice, discussed near the beginning of this chapter: the law of justice was designed to regulate human relationships in the interest of averting violence. The basic principle was that peace is preferable to violence. Zeus was able to impose the law of justice on human beings because he saw that they were capable of "listen[ing] to justice"; that is, human beings could recognize the operative principle and use it as a basis for evaluating their desires and actions. Animals were not bound by the law of justice because they could not comprehend it. Thus human beings became bound by obligations that animals could not assume. The vegan imperative involves a recognition of the core principle that peace is preferable to violence. It also involves a rectification of the speciesistic character of Hesiod's and Ovid's formulations of the law of justice; rather than asserting that human beings have duties of nonviolence only toward other human beings, the vegan imperative asserts that human beings have duties to act peaceably toward all sentient beings, even those who cannot reciprocate. Where the tradition sees justice as a utilitarian quid pro quo, cosmic holism sees justice in terms of natural entitlements that sentient beings have regardless of whether they can give as much as they get.

What makes the "ethical carnivore" speciesist is the assumption that it is perfectly permissible to inflict violence on animals in situations in which it would not be permissible to inflict violence on human beings. A consistent ethical carnivore would be willing to accept violence among human beings along with human violence toward animals. If the operative assumption is that human life is somehow diminished if it lacks some participation in the natural cycles of predation, then why stop at killing animals? Why not participate in violence against human beings as well? After all, Aristotle notes that one of the basic ways to obtain slaves is through hunting.[59] Why endorse the hunting of animals but not the hunting of human beings, except by dint of speciesistic prejudice? Lestel will presumably respond by saying that he is not advocating the hunting of animals, and this may be true in the everyday sense of the term. But in essence that is exactly what he is suggesting when he advocates the ritual slaughter and consumption of animals. The so-called ethical carnivore's speciesism consists in assuming not simply that human life should involve some ritual violence, but that this violence should be exercised on nonhuman animals rather than on human beings. The ethical vegan recognizes that, even though violence cannot be eliminated from life altogether, what makes human life most worth living is the aspiration to reduce as far as possible the amount of violence we inflict. We remind ourselves of both our humanity and our infinite debt to animals not by engaging in violence, ritual or otherwise, but rather by seeking to *reduce* violence in the world.

A Concluding Word About the Ethics of Diet

The vegan imperative calls for a radical rethinking of our relationship to sentient beings and an act of self-sacrifice on the part of humans. Veganism is much more than the refusal to eat animals; it has implications for how we work, how we clothe ourselves, how we entertain ourselves, and how we heal ourselves. Nonetheless, I would like to conclude with some thoughts about our culture's relationship to animals as food because this particular use of animals seems to me to pose the single greatest obstacle to an embrace of the vegan imperative. It is difficult to find a cultural practice that people take more seriously, and as more definitive of their identity, than eating. It is in this spirit that Noëlle Chatelet characterizes eating as "speaking of oneself, degree zero" and suggests that "morality finds in food the ideal pretext for maintaining itself."[60] Thinkers from Rabelais and Montaigne to Grimod de la Renyière and Brillat-Savarin to Roland Barthes and Michel Onfray have seized on food as an essential focal point for understanding and celebrating the human condition. And virtually without exception, thinkers in this tradition have celebrated the consumption of animal products as integral to the cultivation of our humanity. The vegan imperative demands that we step back from this cheerful celebration and ask some hard questions about the ideology of consuming animal products.

It is no secret that many people love to consume animal products. A key dimension of the historical discourse of gastronomy is its blithe treatment of this practice as an unquestionable human prerogative. Pascal Ory notes that "gastronomy is neither 'good' cuisine nor 'haute cuisine.' It is the subjection of eating and drinking to a rule (*nomos*), such that eating and drinking are transformed into an 'art of the table.'"[61] Cuisine, on this view, is more than mere sustenance; it is "the complex place of . . . metamorphosis."[62] Our capacity for rational reflection on eating makes the consumption of food something fundamentally different (and higher) for us than it is for animals. We are capable of developing what Montaigne called a "*science de la gueule*" (a science of the gullet) and what Dick Humelbergius Secundus called a "stomachical metaphysics."[63] To the extent that the consumption of animal products has played a prominent role in the historical discourse of gastronomy, the endeavor to confer scientific or metaphysical validity on our gustatory preferences has at the same time been the effort to provide a transcendental deduction of animals as food.

This effort takes its bearings from a tradition of thinking that extends from Aristotle to Mill and beyond, according to which human beings are capable of pleasures that no animal can enjoy. Aristotle distinguishes between pleasures that accompany "the activities of thought" and those that accompany bodily activities, and he argues that the former are clearly superior to the latter. To the extent that animals are *aloga*, they are incapable of both the contemplative activity that is essential to a truly good life and the pleasure that accompanies contemplation.[64] Mill reiterates this hierarchization of pleasures in stating that "a beast's pleasures do not satisfy a human being's conceptions of happiness. Human beings have faculties more elevated than the animal appetites, and when once made conscious of them, do not regard anything as happiness which does not include their gratification." Mill has in mind here "the pleasures of the intellect, of the feelings and imagination, and of the moral sentiments," which he believes have "a much higher value as pleasures than [do] those of mere sensation."[65] Pleasures of the intellect, imagination, and feelings are so superior to those of the body that, Mill believes, "it is better to be a human being dissatisfied than a pig satisfied."[66]

It never occurs to thinkers such as Mill that many nonhuman animals may actually enjoy "pleasures of the intellect, of the feelings and imagination, and of the moral sentiments" because both of these thinkers assume dogmatically that animals are fundamentally incapable of thought, higher feeling, and moral sensibility. From this assumption thinkers such as Mill derive the prejudice of human exceptionalism that Lestel rightly decries: that because human beings are capable of forming principles, human beings are morally superior to nonhuman animals. This prejudice motivates much of the historical discourse of gastronomy.

The influence of this prejudice is perhaps clearest in Brillat-Savarin's blunt assertion that "animals feed themselves," whereas "only man, possessed of mind [*l'homme d'esprit*], knows how to eat."[67] Only man is capable of subjecting his eating practices to a regulatory *nomos*. Only man is capable of transforming the otherwise mundane activity of eating into a science of cuisine governed by "the rules of geometry."[68] Only man can "[improve] upon a sensual drive, transforming it for good into art," thereby rendering the ordinary sublime.[69]

It is no accident that the historical discourse of gastronomy is laden with references to the human prerogative to consume animal products. Brillat-Savarin argues not only that human beings are alone in knowing how to eat but that this capacity is a clear indication of our superiority over animals. Only human beings possess a tongue with sufficient discriminatory taste to attain the sublime, and only human beings are omnivorous; animals, by comparison, are strictly "limited in their tastes." Like the Stoics before him, Brillat-Savarin takes this supposed superiority of human sensibility to be a sign that animals were created expressly for the sake of satisfying human desires. "By divine right, man is the king of nature, and everything the earth produces was created for him. . . . Therefore why not make use, at least with appropriate moderation, of the goods that Providence has to offer us . . . particularly if they exalt our acquaintance with the author of all things!"[70]

Brillat-Savarin stresses the importance of cuisine as a focal point for the cultivation and assertion of human community. The study of gastronomy and the cultivation of culinary taste promote conviviality and cosmopolitanism. Brillat-Savarin's presupposition that animals exist for the sake of human beings gives rise to an unequivocally anthropocentric conception of kinship: human beings bond with one another through culinary rituals that involve the consumption of animal products; animals, in being treated as objects of consumption, are categorically excluded from the circle of kinship. Brillat-Savarin sees in the invention of fire the prospect of cooking animal flesh.[71] A host of writers in the gastronomic tradition implicitly follow Brillat-Savarin in celebrating the superiority of human beings over animals, and in treating the consumption of animal products as essential to the cultivation of human community. Indeed, even a cursory examination of the literature on gastronomy makes woefully implausible Jean-Robert Pitte's claim that innovations such as nouvelle cuisine were predicated on a "worship of nature."[72] If anything, gastronomical writing celebrates the human subjugation of nature.

Remarks about pigs and geese play an exemplary role in deciphering the ideology of traditional gastronomy. Brillat-Savarin's contemporary Grimod de la Renyière characterizes the pig as "the animal that is most useful to man" and expresses delight and wonder at the fact that every last part of the pig can be used to gratify "our sensuality."[73] Grimod thus echoes the sentiments of the Stoic Chrysippus, according to whom "the pig, that most appetizing of delicacies . . . was created for no other purpose than slaughter, and god, in furnishing our cuisine, mixed soul in with its flesh like salt."[74]

Grimod offers a similar assessment of the goose and its fattened liver, lamenting the fact that the bird must be treated cruelly but seeing redemption in the animal's courage in the face of its fate: "Stuffed with food, deprived of drink, and set near a large fire before which it is nailed by its feet to a plank, this goose passes, it must be admitted, a rather unhappy life. This would be a completely intolerable torture for it, if the idea of the fate that awaits it did not serve as a consolation. But this perspective makes it endure these evils with courage . . . it resigns itself to its destiny and does not permit itself to shed so much as a tear."[75] Like the pig, the goose is destined for slaughter. Moreover the goose takes existential satisfaction in the knowledge that its suffering and slaughter serve the higher good of human pleasure. One could add to Mill's claim about men and pigs the corollary that a pig or a goose that is slaughtered (and perhaps tortured beforehand) for human enjoyment is better in the cosmic scheme than one that dies a natural death. After all, a meal centered on "quail stuffed with foie gras" lets "everyone [leave] transfigured by the experience."[76] Everyone, that is, except the quail and the goose, who have simply been destroyed in the name of the superiority of human taste.

Roland Barthes recognizes the terms of the power dynamic underlying many of our culinary practices, and he undertakes an "archaeology" of gastronomy.[77] This leads him to see that our gustatory practices have global moral significance. Barthes suggests that eating steak rare "represents both a nature and a morality," namely, the morality of "bull-like strength." Steak "is the very flesh of the French soldier, the inalienable property which cannot go over to the enemy except by treason." Steak, like wine, is part of a "sanguine mythology," a mythology according to which we realize our highest potential as human beings through bloodshed and "the brutality of meat."[78] The morality of steak and wine is the morality of a gastronomic Thrasymachus, for whom might makes right and the subjugation of animals is *le propre de l'homme.*

Barthes recognizes the essential violence of Western ways of eating, lamenting at one point the fact that the partridge we eat has to pay for our pleasure with its life.[79] Barthes sees the knife and fork as symbols of "the murder of food" and contrasts these with chopsticks, which outwardly hold the promise of a more peaceful and harmonious way of relating to food. "By chopsticks, food becomes no longer a prey to which one does violence (meat, flesh over which one does battle), but a substance harmoniously transferred; they transform the previously divided substance into bird food and rice into a flow of milk; maternal, they tirelessly perform the gesture which creates the mouthful, leaving to our alimentary manners, armed with pikes and knives, that of predation." But the promise of chopsticks, like the symbolic significance of steak and wine, proves to be part of a mythology: "The chopsticks exist because the foodstuffs [have already been] cut into small pieces," i.e., the use of chopsticks presupposes the very violence that the use of knife and fork recall directly. Chopsticks "never violate the foodstuff"; they are "the alimentary instrument which refuses to cut."[80] And yet they participate every bit as much in a regime of domination and murder as the knife and fork. They simply do a better job of concealing the violence on which their use is predicated.

The larger mythology to which knife, fork, and chopsticks alike belong is one of human superiority over the rest of nature. It is a mythology according to which the subjection and slaughter of animals for the satisfaction of human desires is regrettable but unavoidable. One might suppose that the critique of human exceptionalism undertaken by postmodernism would have brought with it a debunking of this utterly polemical conception of our relationship to food. And yet we cling insistently, indeed desperately, to an ideology according to which the sentient beings we husband and consume are "just dumb animals," and according to which it is an affront to the dignity and autonomy of human individuals to suggest that animals might possess a moral worth anywhere near that of the sophisticated beings who want to eat them.

What would need to happen for people to establish critical distance from this ideology and to begin to appreciate the fact that animals are our kin and should not be husbanded or consumed? Marcela Iacub proposes that we must experience a tragic event that dislocates us from the comfort of our familiar presuppositions. The trauma of this experience forces us to see something crucial that we were not able to see prior to the tragic event. For Iacub, the dislocating experience was learning about the prosecution of a man in France who had had sex with a pony. This man could have killed and eaten the pony without any legal sanction; but sex with the pony was considered prima facie to have constituted an act of violence, regardless of whether in fact the pony might have enjoyed the experience. Reading about the prosecution of this man led Iacub to the tragic realization that French law at least purports to care about the suffering of animals but treats with blithe disregard the killing of animals. This in turn led Iacub to recognize that there is "metaphysical, economic, [and] moral" significance to killing an animal that clearly "does not want to die!"[81] On the basis of this recognition, Iacub stopped eating meat.

Our capacity to insulate ourselves from trauma and evade insights that place great demands on us poses the single greatest obstacle to a recognition of the dignity and nobility of animals and the importance of making fundamental changes to our diet as well as to a host of other cultural practices. It is clear that rational insight by itself is not sufficient to bring about a fundamental change in our sensibilities and values. Iacub is right to suggest that some kind of dislocating experience is needed for us to reevaluate our most deeply held convictions. As regards animals, my first such experience was reading about the treatment of pigs in Sinclair's *The Jungle* when I was a teenager. Reading that book opened up a sense of horror in me that has persisted to this day. It completely changed the way I see the world and the place of human beings and animals in it.

Anyone who experiences that sense of raw horror will never again be able to look at animals as food—nor, for that matter, to look at them as instrumentalities for the satisfaction of human desires that could easily be satisfied through other means. What a pity that we are so good at rendering ourselves insensitive to the moral claim that animals exercise on us.

NOTES

INTRODUCTION

1. Here as in my other writings, I use the term "animals" as shorthand for "nonhuman animals" and the terms "humans" and "human beings" to refer to human animals.

2. Gary Steiner, *Animals and the Moral Community: Mental Life, Moral Status, and Kinship* (New York: Columbia University Press, 2008), p. 163.

3. Jacques Derrida, Cerisy Conference, 1993, cited in David Wood, "*Comment ne pas manger*—Deconstruction and Humanism," in *Animal Others: On Ethics, Ontology, and Animal Life*, ed. H. Peter Steeves (Albany: SUNY Press, 1999), p. 20.

4. The first of these books was *Anthropocentrism and Its Discontents: The Moral Status of Animals in the History of Western Philosophy* (Pittsburgh: University of Pittsburgh Press, 2005); the second was *Animals and the Moral Community*, cited above. I refer to both throughout the present book.

5. Hilary Putnam, *Ethics Without Ontology* (Cambridge: Harvard University Press, 2004), p. 121.

6. Richard J. Bernstein, "Introduction," in *The New Constellation: The Ethical-Political Horizons of Modernity/Postmodernity* (Cambridge: M.I.T. Press, 1991), p. 11.

7. The classification of specific thinkers as adherents of particular varieties of postmodernism is fraught with danger: Is Foucault a poststructuralist? For his own part, Foucault simply tells us that "in France, certain half-witted 'commentators' persist in labelling [him] a 'structuralist,'" and that he has "been unable to get into their tiny minds that [he has] used none of the methods, concepts, or key terms that characterize structural analysis."

Michel Foucault, *The Order of Things: An Archaeology of the Human Sciences* (New York: Vintage Books, 1973), p. xiv. I prefer to avoid as much as possible the classification of specific postmodern thinkers according to particular rubrics, because these rubrics threaten to reify the uniqueness of particular postmodern thinkers' aims and methods and, more important, because doing so diverts attention from the fact that no postmodern approach, be it phenomenological, structuralist, or poststructuralist, seems capable of articulating clear and abiding principles for ethico-political conduct. As a result, in this book I often refer to postmodernism generally where some readers might prefer that I specify poststructuralism. In doing so, I follow the practice of writers such as Wolin and Dosse, who acknowledge that postmodernism is a network of different approaches but who nonetheless often refer to postmodernism generally when their remarks apply more properly to poststructuralism. See Richard Wolin, *The Seduction of Unreason: The Intellectual Romance with Fascism from Nietzsche to Postmodernism* (Princeton: Princeton University Press, 2004), and François Dosse, *History of Structuralism*, vol. 1: *The Rising Sign, 1945–66*, trans. Deborah Glassman (Minneapolis: University of Minnesota Press, 1998).

8. Michel Foucault, *The History of Sexuality*, vol. 1: *An Introduction*, trans. Robert Hurley (New York: Vintage, 1980), p. 159.

1. The Use and Disadvantages of Nietzsche for Life

1. Cary Wolfe, *Animal Rites: American Culture, the Discourse of Species, and Posthumanist Theory* (Chicago: University of Chicago Press, 2003), p. 69.

2. Alain Boyer, "Hierarchy and Truth," in *Why We Are Not Nietzscheans*, ed. Luc Ferry and Alain Renaut, trans. Robert de Loaiza (Chicago: University of Chicago Press, 1997), p. 14.

3. Vincent Descombes, "Nietzsche's French Moment," in *Why We Are Not Nietzscheans*, p. 83.

4. See Francis Bacon, *The New Organon*, ed. Lisa Jardine and Michael Silverthorne (Cambridge: Cambridge University Press, 2000), Book I, aph. 124, p. 96.

5. Descombes, "Nietzsche's French Moment," p. 83.

6. André Comte-Sponville, "The Brute, the Sophist, and the Aesthete," in *Why We Are Not Nietzscheans*, p. 54.

7. Wolin, *The Seduction of Unreason*, p. 221f.

8. Ibid., p. 223.

9. Some postmodern thinkers even deny outright any commitment to the task of liberation. Foucault, for example, concludes the first volume of *The History of Sexuality* with the assertion that "the irony of this deployment [of discourses about sex] is in having us believe that our 'liberation' is in the balance." Foucault, *The History of Sexuality*, 1:p. 159. But if one is serious in treating the prospect of liberation, of an amelioration of suffering and oppression, as a fanciful illusion, then how can the kind of discourses on power in which one is engaged amount to anything more than Heideggerian *Gerede* or idle talk?

10. Pierre-André Taguieff, "The Traditionalist Paradigm—Horror of Modernity and Antiliberalism: Nietzsche in Reactionary Rhetoric," in *Why We Are Not Nietzscheans*, p. 203.

11. Jacques Bouveresse, *Le philosophe chez les autophages* (Paris: Les Éditions de Minuit, 1984), p. 72.

12. Comte-Sponville, "The Brute, the Sophist, and the Aesthete," p. 59.

13. See Hesiod, *Works and Days* 105–213, 275, and Ovid, *Metamorphoses*, book 1, lines 90–162. For a more detailed discussion of Hesiod and Ovid on the five ages of man and the advent of justice, see Steiner, *Anthropocentrism and Its Discontents*, pp. 43ff.

14. Arthur Schopenhauer, "On the Doctrine of the Indestructibility of Our True Nature By Death," in *Parerga and Paralipomena*, vol. 2, trans. E. F. J. Payne (Oxford: Clarendon Press, 2000), sec. 141, p. 281f. See also Arthur Schopenhauer, *The World as Will and Representation*, vol. 1, trans. E. F. J. Payne (Indian Hills, Colo.: Falcon's Wing Press, 1958), sec. 27, p. 149, and sec. 29, p. 164f.

15. Schopenhauer, "Additional Remarks on the Doctrine of the Vanity of Existence," in *Parerga and Paralipomena*, vol. 2, sec. 146, pp. 287, 290.

16. Schopenhauer, *The World as Will and Representation*, vol. 1, sec. 59, p. 324.

17. Ibid., p. 326; *On the Basis of Morality*, sec. 19.

18. On the Enlightenment conception of historical progress as a secularized version of Christian eschatology, see Karl Löwith, *Meaning in History* (Chicago: Phoenix Books/University of Chicago Press, 1962).

19. Schopenhauer, *The World as Will and Representation*, vol. 1, sec. 54, p. 281; see also sec. 59, p. 324.

20. Friedrich Nietzsche, *The Birth of Tragedy*, in *Basic Writings of Nietzsche*, trans. Walter Kaufmann (New York: Modern Library, 1992), sec. 3, p. 42.

21. See Schopenhauer, *The World as Will and Representation*, vol. 1, sec. 56, p. 307.

22. Ibid., sec. 52, pp. 256, 263. Cf. Georg Wilhelm Friedrich Hegel, *Introductory Lectures on Aesthetics*, trans. Bernard Bosanquet (London: Penguin, 1993), pp. 94–97. Consistent with the priority he ascribes to music over poetry, Schopenhauer states that the purest form of music is music without words. Schopenhauer, *The World as Will and Representation*, vol. 2, trans. E. F. J. Payne (New York: Dover, 1958), chap. 39, p. 450.

23. Schopenhauer, *The World as Will and Representation*, vol. 1, sec. 62, p. 341.

24. Ibid., sec. 63, p. 350; sec. 66, p. 370.

25. Friedrich Nietzsche, *Daybreak: Thoughts on the Prejudices of Morality*, trans. R. J. Hollingdale (Cambridge: Cambridge University Press, 1982), Book IV, sec. 210, p. 133.

26. Immanuel Kant, *Critique of Pure Reason*, trans. Norman Kemp Smith (New York: Humanities Press, 1950), at A313/B370–A315/B372, p. 310f.

27. See, for example, Friedrich Nietzsche, "On the Prejudices of the Philosophers," sec. 5, and "Our Virtues," sec. 228, in *Beyond Good and Evil*.

28. Aristotle, *De Interpretatione* 1, *Metaphysics* 6.4; Descartes, letter to Mersenne, November 20, 1629.

29. Friedrich Nietzsche, "Of First and Last Things," in *Human, All Too Human: A Book for Free Spirits*, trans. R. J. Hollingdale (Cambridge: Cambridge University Press, 1987), vol. 1, sec. 11, p. 16.

30. Friedrich Nietzsche, "The Philosopher: Reflections on the Struggle Between Art and Knowledge," in *Philosophy and Truth: Selections from Nietzsche's Notebooks of the Early 1870's*, ed. and trans. Daniel Breazeale (Atlantic Highlands, N.J.: Humanities Press International, 1992), sec. 84, p. 33.

31. Friedrich Nietzsche, "On Redemption," in *Thus Spoke Zarathustra: A Book for All and None*, trans. Walter Kaufmann (New York: Viking Press, 1972), Second Part, p. 140.

32. Friedrich Nietzsche, "On Truth and Lies in a Nonmoral Sense," in *Philosophy and Truth*, pp. 82. 83.

33. Nietzsche, *Daybreak*, Book 2, sec. 119, p. 124.

34. Friedrich Nietzsche, "How the 'True World' Finally Became a Fable: The History of an Error," in *Twilight of the Idols*, in *The Portable Nietzsche*, ed. and trans. Walter Kaufmann (New York: Penguin, 1982), p. 485. See also "Skirmishes of an Untimely Man," sec. 34, p. 535: "The 'beyond'—why a beyond, if not as a means for besmirching *this* world?"

35. Friedrich Nietzsche, *The Will to Power*, trans. Walter Kaufmann and R. J. Hollingdale (New York: Vintage, 1968), Book Three, sec. 579, p. 310f.

36. Ibid., p. 311.

37. Nietzsche, *On the Genealogy of Morals*, Third Essay, sec. 1, in *Basic Writings of Nietzsche*, p. 533.

38. Nietzsche, *The Will to Power*, Book Three, sec. 579, p. 311.

39. Nietzsche, *On the Genealogy of Morals*, Second Essay, sec. 7, p. 505.

40. See Nietzsche, "Our Virtues," in *Beyond Good and Evil*, sec. 229, p. 348: "Almost everything we call 'higher culture' is based on the spiritualization of *cruelty*, on its becoming more profound . . . What constitutes the painful voluptuousness of tragedy is cruelty."

41. Nietzsche, *The Birth of Tragedy*, sec. 5, p. 50; sec. 4, p. 45; sec. 5, p. 46.

42. Ibid., sec. 5, p. 46; sec. 6, p. 52.

43. Nietzsche, "Skirmishes of an Untimely Man," in *Twilight of the Idols*, sec. 10, p. 519f.; sec. 21, p. 527.

44. Friedrich Nietzsche, "On the Use and Disadvantages of History for Life," in *Untimely Meditations*, trans. R. J. Hollingdale (Cambridge: Cambridge University Press, 1987), sec. 10, p. 123; *The Birth of Tragedy*, sec. 8, p. 61, and sec. 7, p. 59.

45. Nietzsche, *The Birth of Tragedy*, sec. 13, p. 87.

46. Ibid., sec. 11, p. 78; sec. 15, pp. 94, 96; sec. 15, p. 96; sec. 16, p. 104; sec. 5, p. 52; "Attempt at a Self-Criticism," sec. 5, p. 22.

47. Nietzsche, *The Birth of Tragedy*, sec. 18, p. 110.

48. David Hume, *A Treatise of Human Nature*, 2d ed., ed. L. A. Selby-Bigge (Oxford: Clarendon Press, 1981), Book 1, Part 4, sec. 6, p. 252; see also appendix, p. 634.

49. Ibid., Book 1, Part 4, sec. 6, p. 262. See also Book 3, Part 3, sec. 4, p. 610: Questions of virtue, too, are grammatical.

50. Nietzsche, *The Will to Power*, Book Three, sec. 550, p. 295; see also sec. 551; sec. 484–85, p. 268f.; Book Two, sec. 370, p. 199.

51. Ibid., Book Three, sec. 552, p. 299. Here Nietzsche makes the point in regard to God or nature, but it applies *mutatis mutandis* to human agency.

52. Nietzsche, *Beyond Good and Evil*, "On the Prejudices of Philosophers," sec. 12, p. 210.

53. Ibid., sec. 16, p. 213.

54. René Descartes, *Discourse on Method*, in *The Philosophical Writings of Descartes*, vol. 1, trans. John Cottingham et. al. (Cambridge: Cambridge University Press, 1985), Part 6, p. 142f (translation altered).

55. Nietzsche, *Beyond Good and Evil*, "On the Prejudices of Philosophers," sec. 16, p. 213f.

56. Hume, "Abstract," in *A Treatise of Human Nature*, p. 658.

57. Nietzsche, *Beyond Good and Evil*, "On the Prejudices of the Philosophers," sec. 17, p. 214.

58. Ibid., sec. 19, p. 217. See also *Human, All too Human*, vol. 2, part 1, sec. 17, p. 218: "Not 'an immortal soul,' but *many mortal souls.*"

59. Nietzsche, *The Will to Power*, Book Three, sec. 581, p. 312.

60. Nietzsche, *Beyond Good and Evil*, "Our Virtues," sec. 230, p. 351f.

61. Hume, *A Treatise of Human Nature*, Book 2, Part 3, sec. 3, p. 415. Cf. Book 3, Part 1, sec. 2, p. 470: "Morality, therefore, is more properly felt than judg'd of."

62. Nietzsche, *The Gay Science*, trans. Walter Kaufmann (New York: Vintage, 1974), Book Five, sec. 356, p. 303.

63. Nietzsche, "On the Despisers of the Body," in *Thus Spoke Zarathustra*, p. 34.

64. Nietzsche, *The Gay Science*, Book Five, sec. 354, p. 297.

65. Ibid., Book One, sec. 1–2, pp. 74–76; Book Four, sec. 290, p. 232.

66. Nietzsche, "Skirmishes of an Untimely Man," sec. 14, p. 522.

67. Nietzsche, *The Will to Power*, Book Two, sec. 254, p. 148.

68. Nietzsche, "The 'Improvers' of Mankind," in *Twilight of the Idols*, sec. 1, p. 501.

69. Nietzsche, *The Will to Power*, Book Four, sec. 863, p. 459.

70. Ibid., Book Two, sec. 401, p. 216f.; sec. 254, p. 148; sec. 258, p. 149.

71. Nietzsche, "What Is Noble," in *Beyond Good and Evil*, sec. 259, 258, p. 392f.

72. Nietzsche, *The Gay Science*, Book Four, sec. 299, p. 240. See also sec. 335, p. 265: If you seek to "experience [your] own judgment as a universal law," you show "that you have not yet discovered yourself nor created for yourself an ideal of your own."

73. Nietzsche, *Daybreak*, Book One, sec. 14, p. 16.

74. Nietzsche, "What Is Noble," sec. 260, p. 395.

75. Nietzsche, *The Gay Science*, Book Five, sec. 343, p. 280; see also Book Three, sec. 124; Book Four, sec. 283, p. 228.

76. Nietzsche, *The Will to Power*, Book Four, sec. 854, p. 458.

77. Nietzsche, "Morality as Anti-Nature," in *Twilight of the Idols*, sec. 3, p. 488f.

78. Walter Benjamin, "The Work of Art in the Age of Mechanical Reproduction," in *Illuminations*, ed. Hannah Arendt (New York: Schocken Books, 1968), p. 241.

79. Nietzsche, *On the Genealogy of Morals*, First Essay, sec. 16, p. 490; "Natural History of Morals," in *Beyond Good and Evil*, sec. 200, p. 302; "Skirmishes of an Untimely Man," sec. 45, p. 549.

80. Nietzsche, "The 'Improvers' of Mankind," sec. 2, p. 502f.

81. Nietzsche, "Preface," in *On the Genealogy of Morals*, sec. I, p. 451.

82. Nietzsche, *Beyond Good and Evil*, "On the Prejudices of Philosophers," sec. 19, pp. 217, 215.

83. Nietzsche, "The Four Great Errors," in *Twilight of the Idols*, sec. 7, p. 499.

84. Nietzsche, *Beyond Good and Evil*, "On the Prejudices of Philosophers," sec. 19, p. 217.

85. Martin Heidegger, "Letter on 'Humanism,' " in *Pathmarks*, ed. William McNeill (Cambridge: Cambridge University Press, 1998), pp. 269–71.

86. Nietzsche, *Beyond Good and Evil*, "On the Prejudices of Philosophers," sec. 22, p. 220.

87. Nietzsche, *The Will to Power*, Book Two, sec. 400–401, pp. 216–18.

88. Ibid., secs. 259–60, p. 149f. See also "Schopenhauer as Educator," in *Untimely Meditations*, sec. 4, p. 148: "I am concerned here with a species of man whose teleology extends somewhat beyond the welfare of a state."

89. Nietzsche, *The Will to Power*, Book Two, sec. 462, p. 255. See also Nietzsche's criticism of "anti-natural morality" in "Morality as Anti-Nature," sec. 4, p. 489f.

90. Nietzsche, *On the Genealogy of Morals*, Second Essay, sec. 11, p. 512.

91. Descombes, "Nietzsche's French Moment," p. 90.

92. Carl Schmitt, *Political Theology: Four Chapters on the Concept of Sovereignty*, trans. George Schwab (Chicago: University of Chicago Press, 2005), pp. 53ff.

93. Ibid., p. 15.

94. Karl Löwith, "The Occasional Decisionism of Carl Schmitt," in *Martin Heidegger and European Nihilism*, trans. Gary Steiner (New York: Columbia University Press, 1995), p. 144.

95. Carl Schmitt, *The Concept of the Political*, trans. George Schwab (Chicago: University of Chicago Press, 1996), p. 53.

96. Löwith, "The Occasional Decisionism of Carl Schmitt," p. 146.

97. Ibid.

98. Michel Foucault, "What is Enlightenment?" in *The Foucault Reader*, ed. Paul Rabinow (New York: Pantheon Books, 1984), p. 39. Baudelaire for his own part is not always so unequivocal in subordinating the eternal to the present instant. Sometimes he appears to treat the present moment simply as our means of access to the eternal. He writes, for example, that "beauty always, inevitably, has a double composition. . . . Beauty made of an eternal element . . . and a relative, circumstantial element . . . . Without this second element . . . the first element could not be digested and appreciated, it would not be adapted and appropriate to the human condition." Charles Baudelaire, "Le peintre de la vie moderne," in *Oeuvres complètes*, vol. 2 (Paris: Gallimard/Pléiade, 1976), p. 685.

99. Foucault, "What is Enlightenment?" p. 41f.

100. Ibid., pp. 43, 45f.

101. Immanuel Kant, "An Answer to the Question: What Is Enlightenment?" in *Political Writings*, ed. H. S. Reiss (New York: Cambridge University Press, 2001), p. 57.

102. Foucault, "What is Enlightenment?" p. 48.

103. Michel Foucault, "Nietzsche, Genealogy, History," in *The Foucault Reader*, p. 76.

104. See Jürgen Habermas, "The Entry into Postmodernity: Nietzsche as a Turning Point," in *The Philosophical Discourse of Modernity: Twelve Lectures*, trans. Frederick G. Lawrence (Cambridge: M.I.T. Press, 1990), p. 93.

105. Foucault, "Nietzsche, Genealogy, History," pp. 77, 78f.

106. Nietzsche, "On Truth and Lies in a Nonmoral Sense," in *Philosophy and Truth*, p. 84.

107. Foucault, "Nietzsche, Genealogy, History," pp. 81, 83, 82, 86.

108. Ibid., p. 87.

109. Vincent Descombes, *Modern French Philosophy*, trans. L. Scott-Fox and J. M. Harding (Cambridge: Cambridge University Press, 1998), pp. 14, 32, 34.

110. Aristotle, *De anima* 3.5 at 430a20–25; Sigmund Freud, *The Future of an Illusion*, trans. James Strachey (New York: Norton, 1989), part 10.

2. POSTMODERNISM AND JUSTICE

1. Wolfe, *Animal Rites*, p. 69.

2. David Wood, *The Step Back: Ethics and Politics After Deconstruction* (Albany: State University of New York Press, 2005), p. 136f.

3. Peter Singer, *Animal Liberation*, updated ed. (New York: Harper Perennial, 2009), p. 229f.

4. Gary L. Francione, *Introduction to Animal Rights: Your Child or the Dog?* (Philadelphia: Temple University Press, 2000), pp. 6, 17.

5. Ibid., p. xxiv.

6. Francione states that there is an irreducible element of arbitrariness in such a choice; I might well choose to save the child "simply because I better understand what is at stake for the human than I do for the dog." Ibid., p. 159.

7. Tom Regan, *The Case for Animal Rights* (Berkeley: University of California Press, 1983), p. 351.

8. Francione, *Introduction to Animal Rights*, p. 178.

9. I say "so-called" because the designation "free range" has very little if any practical value. See my "Animal, Vegetable, Miserable," Week in Review, *New York Times*, November 22, 2009, p. 12.

10. Jacques Derrida, "The Animal That Therefore I Am (More to Follow)," in *The Animal That Therefore I Am*, ed. Marie-Louise Mallet, trans. David Wills (New York: Fordham University Press, 2008), p. 22.

11. Martin Heidegger, *Die Grundbegriffe der Metaphysik: Welt-Endlichkeit-Einsamkeit*, Gesamtausgabe vol. 29/30 (Frankfurt: Klostermann, 1983), pp. 261ff. I discuss this text along with Heidegger's other remarks about animals in *Anthropocentrism and Its Discontents*, pp. 204–14.

12. Derrida, "The Animal That Therefore I Am," p. 18.

13. Jacques Derrida, "'Eating Well', or the Calculation of the Subject: An Interview with Jacques Derrida," in *Who Comes After the Subject?* ed. Eduardo Cadava, Peter Connor, and Jean-Luc Nancy (New York: Routledge, 1991), p. 112.

14. Stephen K. White, *Political Theory and Postmodernism* (Cambridge: Cambridge University Press, 2009), pp. x, 119, 20, 61.

15. Ibid., p. 149.

16. Descartes, preface to the French edition of the *Principles of Philosophy*, in *The Philosophical Writings of Descartes*, 1:186.

17. Richard J. Bernstein, "Serious Play: The Ethical-Political Horizon of Derrida," in *The New Constellation*, p. 187f.

18. Drucilla Cornell, "Post-Structuralism, the Ethical Relation and the Law," in *Deconstruction: A Reader*, ed. Martin McQuillan (New York: Routledge, 2001), p. 443.

19. Jacques Derrida, "Hospitality, Justice and Responsibility: A Dialogue with Jacques Derrida," in *Questioning Ethics: Contemporary Debates in Philosophy*,

ed. Richard Kearney and Mark Dooley (London/New York: Routledge, 1999), pp. 77, 67.

20. Soren Kierkegaard, *Fear and Trembling*, in *Fear and Trembling/Repetition*, ed. Howard V. Hong and Edna H. Hong (Princeton: Princeton University Press, 1983).

21. Bernstein, "Appendix: Pragmatism, Pluralism, and the Healing of Wounds," in *The New Constellation*, p. 336.

22. John Locke, *Second Treatise of Government*, ed. Richard Cox (Arlington Heights, Ill.: Harlan Davidson, 1982), p. 13.

23. Cornell, "Post-Structuralism, the Ethical Relation and the Law," p. 445.

24. Jacques Derrida, *Positions*, trans. Alan Bass (Chicago: University of Chicago Press, 1982), p. 93.

25. Jean-François Lyotard, *The Postmodern Condition: A Report on Knowledge*, trans. Geoff Bennington and Brian Massumi (Minneapolis: University of Minnesota Press, 1985), p. xxiiif.

26. Ibid.; Jacques Derrida, "Mochlos, ou le conflit des facultés," *Philosophie* 2 (April 1984): 37, 40 ("C'est la loi du texte en général . . . une loi que je ne peux pas démontrer ici mais que je dois supposer").

27. Jacques Derrida, *Of Grammatology*, trans. Gayatri Chakravorty Spivak (Baltimore: Johns Hopkins University Press, 1976), p. 158.

28. Derrida, "Hospitality, Justice and Responsibility," p. 79.

29. Ibid.; Derrida, "Mochlos, ou le conflit des facultés," p. 37.

30. René Descartes, Second Meditation, in *The Philosophical Writings of Descartes*, 2:20.

31. Descartes, Second Set of Replies, in ibid., p. 113.

32. Friedrich Kluge, *Etymologisches Wörterbuch der deutschen Sprache*, 20th ed. (Berlin: Walter de Gruyter, 1967), p. 854.

33. Martin Heidegger, "The Question Concerning Technology," in *The Question Concerning Technology and Other Essays*, trans. William Lovitt (New York: Harper Torchbooks, 1977), p. 30.

34. Martin Heidegger, *An Introduction to Metaphysics*, trans. Ralph Manheim (New Haven: Yale University Press, 1980), pp. 62, 63, 181f.

35. Heidegger, "Science and Reflection," in *The Question Concerning Technology and Other Essays*, p. 161.

36. Martin Heidegger, "Letter on 'Humanism'," in *Pathmarks*, ed. William McNeill (Cambridge: Cambridge University Press, 1998), pp. 257, 261.

37. Heidegger, "The Question Concerning Technology," p. 35 (translation altered).

38. Heidegger, "Letter on 'Humanism'," p. 271f.

39. Heidegger, *Introduction to Metaphysics*, p. 62.

40. Jacques Derrida, "Limited Inc a b c . . . ," in *Limited Inc* (Evanston: Northwestern University Press, 1997), p. 93.

41. Derrida, *Positions*, p. 33.

42. Kant, *Critique of Pure Reason*, at A313/B370.

43. Ibid., at A369f.

44. Ibid., at Axv.

45. Derrida, *Positions*, p. 33.

46. Ferdinand de Saussure, *Course in General Linguistics*, ed. Charles Bally and Albert Sechehaye (New York: Philosophical Library, 1959), pp. 67, 69, 71, 100, 120f.

47. Jacques Derrida, "Structure, Sign and Play in the Discourse of the Human Sciences," in *Writing and Difference*, trans. Alan Bass (Chicago: University of Chicago Press, 1978), pp. 278, 280.

48. Derrida, *Positions*, p. 29.

49. Derrida, "Structure, Sign and Play in the Discourse of the Human Sciences," p. 280

50. Friedrich Nietzsche, "On Truth and Lies in a Nonmoral Sense," in *Philosophy and Truth*, p. 84

51. Friedrich Nietzsche, "On the Prejudices of Philosophers," in *Beyond Good and Evil*, sec. 19, p. 217

52. Here Derrida has altered the meaning of the Saussurean signifier. As noted above, for Saussure the signifier is a sound-image. For Derrida, it is something like what Saussure called a sign.

53. Derrida, "Structure, Sign and Play in the Discourse of the Human Sciences," p. 281.

54. Manfred Frank, *What Is Neostructuralism?* trans. Sabine Wilke and Richard Gray (Minneapolis: University of Minnesota Press, 1989), p. 25.

55. Jacques Derrida, "Force and Signification," in *Writing and Difference*, p. 25.

56. Derrida, "Structure, Sign and Play in the Discourse of the Human Sciences," p. 289.

57. Jacques Derrida, "Différance," in *Margins of Philosophy*, trans. Alan Bass (Chicago: University of Chicago Press, 1982), pp. 6, 11.

58. Hume, *A Treatise of Human Nature*, pp. 658, 204, 207.

59. Derrida, *Of Grammatology*, p. 47.

60. Derrida, *Positions*, p. 26.

61. Derrida, *Of Grammatology*, pp. 61, 93.

62. Derrida, "Hospitality, Justice and Responsibility," p. 79.

63. Derrida, "Signature Event Context," in *Writing and Difference*, p. 326.

64. On the difference between a "total" and an "immanent" critique of reason, see my "The Perils of a Total Critique of Reason: Rethinking Heidegger's Influence," *Philosophy Today* 47 (2003): 94f.

65. Derrida, *Positions*, p. 41.

66. Jacques Derrida, "Racism's Last Word," *Critical Inquiry* 12 (1995): 292f.

67. Ibid., p. 299.

68. Kierkegaard, *Fear and Trembling*, pp. 87f., 92, 111f.

69. Derrida, "Racism's Last Word," pp. 294, 297.

70. Ibid., p. 298.

71. Martin Heidegger, "On the Essence of Truth," in *Pathmarks*, pp. 152, 144.

72. Martin Heidegger, *Was ist das—die Philosophie?* (Tübingen: Neske, 1984), p. 20.

73. Martin Heidegger, "Conversation on a Country Path" (originally entitled *Zur Erörterung der Gelassenheit*), in *Discourse on Thinking*, trans. John M. Anderson and E. Hans Freund (New York: Harper Torchbooks, 1969), p. 68.

74. Derrida, "Hospitality, Justice and Responsibility," p. 66.

75. Coetzee's Elizabeth Costello draws this analogy between our treatment of animals and the Holocaust, with predictable results. J. M. Coetzee, *The Lives of Animals*, ed. Amy Gutman (Princeton: Princeton University Press, 1999), pp. 19–21.

76. Derrida, "Hospitality, Justice and Responsibility," p. 66f.

77. Derrida, "The Politics of Friendship," *Journal of Philosophy* 85 (1988): 640n7.

78. Ibid., pp. 633, 637.

79. Derrida, "Racism's Last Word," p. 296.

80. Derrida, "The Politics of Friendship," p. 640.

81. Derrida, "Hospitality, Justice and Responsibility," p. 77.

82. Derrida, "Violence and Metaphysics," in *Writing and Difference*, p. 138.

83. Ibid.

84. Derrida, "Racism's Last Word," p. 298.

85. Derrida, "Violence and Metaphysics," p. 141.

86. Ibid., p. 146.

87. Derrida, "The Politics of Friendship," p. 633f.

88. Jacques Derrida, "Force of Law: The 'Mystical Foundation of Authority'," *Cardozo Law Review* 11 (1989–90): 943.

89. Ibid., p. 939. Here Derrida's passing reference to Kafka's "Before the Law" helps to shed light on the sense in which Derrida considers the source of law and authority to lie beyond the grasp of reason and language.

90. Ibid., pp. 957, 955.

91. Derrida, "Politics of Friendship," p. 640f.

92. Derrida, "Force of Law," p. 955.

93. Derrida, "Politics of Friendship," p. 641f.

94. Ibid., pp. 643, 644, 644n13.

95. John Caputo, *Against Ethics: Contributions to a Poetics of Obligation with Constant Reference to Deconstruction* (Bloomington: Indiana University Press, 1993), p. 37. Another commentator has offered a different interpretation: that for Derrida justice must be conceived as "an infinitely open-ended possibility," and that the idea of justice or law as something universal constitutes a "viciously impossible regulative ideal." Catherine Kellogg, *Law's Trace: from Hegel to Derrida* (New York: Routledge, 2010), p. 131. On either interpretation, justice or law conceived as universally binding remains an unfulfillable and pernicious ideal.

96. Jean-Paul Sartre, *Being and Nothingness*, trans. Hazel Barnes (New York: Pocket Books, 1978), p. 346.

97. Kierkegaard, *Fear and Trembling*, pp. 54, 92.

98. Ibid., pp. 57, 82, 92, 78: "The knight of faith has simply and solely himself, and therein lies the dreadfulness."

99. Ibid., p. 7f.

100. The ethical is "social morality," whereas Abraham's faith "is a synthesis of its being for the sake of God and for his own sake." Ibid., pp. 55, 71.

101. White, *Political Theory and Postmodernism*, p. 27.

102. Jürgen Habermas, "Excursus on Leveling the Genre Distinction between Philosophy and Literature," in *The Philosophical Discourse of Modernity*, p. 210.

103. Bernstein, "The Rage Against Reason," in *The New Constellation*, p. 52.

104. Ibid., p. 53.

105. In *Descartes as a Moral Thinker: Christianity, Technology, Nihilism* (Amherst, NY: Prometheus/Humanity Books, 2004), I argue that even Descartes, almost universally received as the poster child for the claims of reason, implicitly accepts the proposition that reason is not the origin of moral commitments. It is misleading to characterize as specifically "Nietzschean (and Emersonian) [the] refusal to ground ethics in reason alone,

asserting that if there is not already an attachment to existence flowing from the self and overflowing into care for other lives, no rational ground of ethics will ever generate ethical conduct." William E. Connolly, *Identity\ Difference: Democratic Negotiations of Political Paradox* (Ithaca: Cornell University Press, 1991), p. 76. Nietzsche and Emerson are relative latecomers to this insight.

106. Werner Marx, *Gibt es auf Erden ein Maß? Grundbestimmungen einer nicht-metaphysischen Ethik* (Hamburg: Felix Meiner Verlag, 1983).

107. Bernstein, "Serious Play: The Ethical-Political Horizon of Derrida," in *The New Constellation*, p. 191; see also "An Allegory of Modernity/Postmodernity: Habermas and Derrida," in *The New Constellation*, p. 222.

108. Jacques Derrida, *The Beast and the Sovereign*, vol. 1, trans. Geoffrey Bennington (Chicago: University of Chicago Press, 2009), p. 301.

109. Jacques Derrida, *Rogues: Two Essays on Reason*, trans. Pascale-Anne Brault and Michael Naas (Stanford: Stanford University Press, 2005).

110. Nietzsche, "On the Prejudices of Philosophers," *Beyond Good and Evil*, p. 215.

111. Appealing to Antigone rather than Abraham does not solve the problem. Antigone's choice falls squarely within the ethical, at least as Kierkegaard characterizes it, even though Antigone is unable to express her anguish to others. Soren Kierkegaard, *Either/Or*, vol. 1, trans. David F. Swenson and Lillian Marvin Swenson (Princeton: Princeton University Press, 1971), pp. 153ff. One ought not imagine Agamemnon having sacrificed his daughter in such a manner that he could have communicated his pain to anyone. But that does not mean that the specifically ethical grounds for his (or Antigone's) choice are unintelligible.

112. Bouveresse, *Le Philosophe chez les autophages*, p. 73.

113. Nietzsche, *The Gay Science*, Book Four, sec. 290, p. 232.

114. Löwith, *Meaning in History*, p. 25.

115. Hans-Georg Gadamer, *Philosophical Apprenticeships*, trans. Robert R. Sullivan (Cambridge: M.I.T. Press, 1985), p. 169.

116. Karl Löwith, "Welt und Menschenwelt," in *Welt und Menschenwelt: Beiträge zur Anthropologie*, Sämtliche Schriften, vol. 1 (Stuttgart: Metzler, 1981), p. 303.

117. See Steiner, *Anthropocentrism and Its Discontents*, pp. 87ff., 169f.; Steiner, *Animals and the Moral Community*, chaps. 5 and 6; and chapter 5 below.

118. Heidegger, "Letter on 'Humanism,'" p. 271.

1. Derrida, "Racism's Last Word," p. 298; Derrida, "Hospitality, Justice and Responsibility," p. 66.

2. Heidegger, "Letter on 'Humanism,'" p. 261.

3. Martin Heidegger, "Postscript to 'What Is Metaphysics?'" in *Pathmarks*, p. 237.

4. Ibid. (translation altered: "Weil jedoch das Gleiche nur gleich ist als das Verschiedene . . .").

5. Heidegger, *Was ist das—die Philosophie?* p. 22.

6. Martin Heidegger, "What Are Poets For?" in *Poetry, Language, Thought*, trans. Albert Hofstadter (New York: Perennial Classics/HarperCollins, 2001), p. 130; "The Thing," in *Poetry, Language, Thought*, p. 182.

7. Heidegger, "The Question Concerning Technology," p. 35 (translation altered).

8. Heidegger, "Letter on 'Humanism,'" pp. 249, 275, 271.

9. Martin Heidegger, "The Origin of the Work of Art," in *Poetry, Language, Thought*, p. 60.

10. Ibid., p. 61; cf. "Postscript to 'What Is Metaphysics?'" p. 237: "The thinker says being. The poet names the holy."

11. Heidegger, "Letter on 'Humanism,'" p. 257; Novalis, "The Universal Brouillon: Materials for an Encyclopedia," sec. 857, in *The Early Political Writings of the German Romantics*, ed. Frederick C. Beiser (Cambridge: Cambridge University Press, 1996), p. 90 ("Philosophy is really homesickness, *the urge to be home everywhere in the world*").

12. Derrida, "Hospitality, Justice and Responsibility," p. 78.

13. Judith Butler, "For a Careful Reading," in *Feminist Contentions: A Philosophical Exchange*, ed. Seyla Benhabib et. al. (New York: Routledge, 1995), p. 130. Cf. p. 133: The aim here is "recasting agency within matrices of power."

14. Jacques Derrida, *On Cosmopolitanism and Forgiveness*, trans. Mark Dooley and Michael Hughes (London: Routledge, 2001), p. 44.

15. In their preface to *On Cosmopolitanism and Forgiveness*, p. xi, Simon Critchley and Richard Kearney explain Derrida's invocation and critique of universality in the following way. For Derrida, "universality . . . exceeds the pragmatic demands of the specific context" but "must not . . . be permitted to programme political action, where decisions would be algorithmically deduced from incontestable ethical precepts."

16. Ibid., p. 56.

17. See Wolfe, *Animal Rites*, p. 88.

18. I examine this history from Hesiod and Homer to Heidegger, Levinas, and Derrida in *Anthropocentrism and Its Discontents*. Readers are referred to this text for further details and the textual sources of the historical views I present in this section.

19. See ibid., chap. 9.

20. Derrida, "The Animal That Therefore I Am," p. 27.

21. Jeremy Bentham, *Introduction to the Principles of Morals and Legislation* (New York: Hafner/Macmillan, 1948), pp. 310–11n.

22. Singer, *Animal Liberation*, pp. 228–30.

23. Regan, *The Case for Animal Rights*, p. 245f.

24. Ibid., p. 351: "Indeed, numbers make no difference. A million dogs ought to be cast overboard if that is necessary to save the four normal humans."

25. Emmanuel Levinas, "The Name of a Dog, or Natural Rights," in *Difficult Freedom: Essays in Judaism*, trans. Seán Hand (Baltimore: Johns Hopkins University Press, 1990), pp. 151–53.

26. Ibid., p. 151f.; Tamra Wright, Peter Hughes, and Alison Ainsley, "The Paradox of Morality: An Interview with Emmanuel Levinas," in *The Provocation of Levinas: Rethinking the Other*, ed. Robert Bernasconi and David Wood (London: Routledge, 1988), p. 170.

27. Wright, Hughes, and Ainsley, "The Paradox of Morality," p. 172.

28. Matthew Calarco, *Zoographies: The Question of the Animal from Heidegger to Derrida* (New York: Columbia University Press, 2008), pp. 59, 71. See also p. 55: "Levinas's ethical philosophy is, or at least should be, committed to a notion of *universal ethical consideration*, that is, an agnostic form of ethical consideration that has no a priori constraints or boundaries."

29. Jacques Derrida, "And Say the Animal Responded?" in *The Animal That Therefore I Am*, p. 119.

30. Jacques Derrida, *The Beast and the Sovereign*, 1:237, 15f., 108.

31. Derrida, "The Politics of Friendship," p. 633f.; Derrida, "Racism's Last Word," p. 298.

32. Derrida, *The Beast and the Sovereign*, 1:109, 110, 109.

33. Ibid. (italics added).

34. Derrida, "The Animal That Therefore I Am," p. 29.

35. Jacques Derrida, "But as for me, who am I (following)?" in *The Animal That Therefore I Am*, p. 113.

36. Jacques Derrida, *Séminaire: La bête et le souverain*, vol. 2 (Paris: Galilée, 2010), p. 363.

37. Ibid., p. 208. Here Derrida is discussing a passage from *Robinson Crusoe* in which Crusoe considers different ways in which he might be killed and concludes that being killed by cannibals would be the worst kind of death.

38. Ibid., p. 226.

39. Derrida, "The Animal That Therefore I Am," p. 14.

40. Wolfe, *Animal Rites*, p. 217n26. See also Cary Wolfe, "Introduction: Exposures," in *Philosophy and Animal Life*, by Stanley Cavell, Cora Diamond, John McDowell, Ian Hacking, and Cary Wolfe (New York: Columbia University Press, 2008), p. 13.

41. Jacques Lacan, "The Subversion of the Subject and the Dialectic of Desire in the Freudian Unconscious," in *Écrits: A Selection*, trans. Alan Sheridan (New York: Norton, 1977), pp. 305, 86.

42. See Steiner, *Anthropocentrism and Its Discontents*, p. 70f.

43. Seneca, for example, tells us that a horse can remember a familiar road when it actually sees the road, but it cannot recall the road when it is standing in its stall. See ibid., p. 79.

44. Lacan, "Function and Field of Speech and Language in Psychoanalysis," p. 84f.

45. Derrida, "And Say the Animal Responded?" p. 119f.

46. Ibid., p. 125.

47. Derrida, *The Beast and the Sovereign*, 1:104, 102, 107, 108.

48. Calarco, *Zoographies*, pp. 110, 90.

49. Giorgio Agamben, *The Open: Man and Animal*, trans. Kevin Attell (Stanford: Stanford University Press, 2004), p. 37f., 16.

50. See Steiner, *Anthropocentrism and Its Discontents*, pp. 72ff.

51. See Porphyry, *On Abstinence from Killing Animals*, trans. Gillian Clark (Ithaca: Cornell University Press, 2000), passim; and Steiner, *Anthropocentrism and Its Discontents*, pp. 103ff.

52. Porphyry, *On Abstinence from Killing Animals* 3.22.6, p. 94.

53. Peter Carruthers, *The Animals Issue: Moral Theory in Practice* (Cambridge: Cambridge University Press, 1992), pp. 137ff., 180–89, 159.

54. Ibid., pp. 134f., 137.

55. René Descartes, Letter to Plempius for Fromondus, October 3, 1637, in *The Philosophical Writings of Descartes*, 3:61f. For a more complete description of Descartes's account of animal experience, see Steiner, *Anthropocentrism and Its Discontents*, pp. 138ff.

56. Thomas Nagel, "What Is It Like to Be a Bat?" in *Mortal Questions* (Cambridge: Cambridge University Press, 1979), pp. 165–80.

57. Carolyn A. Ristau, "Aspects of the Cognitive Ethology of an Injury-Feigning Bird," in *Readings in Cognitive Ethology*, ed. Marc Bekoff and Dale Jamieson (Cambridge: M.I.T. Press, 1996), p. 234.

58. See Marc Bekoff and Jessica Pierce, *Wild Justice: The Moral Lives of Animals* (Chicago: University of Chicago Press, 2009).

59. Marc Bekoff, *Minding Animals: Awareness, Emotions, and Heart* (Oxford: Oxford University Press, 2002), pp. 120ff.

60. Bernd Heinrich, "Raven Consciousness," in *The Cognitive Animal: Empirical and Theoretical Perspectives on Animal Cognition*, ed. Marc Bekoff, Colin Allen, and Gordon M. Burghardt (Cambridge: M.I.T. Press, 2002), p. 48f.

61. Gavin R. Hunt and Russell D. Gray, "Diversification and Cumulative Evolution in New Caledonian Crow Tool Manufacture," in *Proceedings of the Royal Society of* London B vol. 270 (2003), pp. 867–74. For a more extensive discussion of the subjective nature of animal experience and the ways in which life can matter to a nonlinguistic being, see Gary Steiner, *Animals and the Moral Community*, chaps. 1–3.

62. Frans de Waal, "Morally Evolved: Primate Social Instincts, Human Morality, and the Rise and Fall of Veneer Theory," in *Primates and Philosophers: How Morality Evolved*, by Frans de Waal, Robert Wright, Christine M. Korsgaard, Philip Kitcher, and Peter Singer (Princeton: Princeton University Press, 2006), pp. 49, 54.

63. De Waal, "Appendix C: Animal Rights," in ibid., pp. 75, 77.

64. Ibid., p. 78.

65. See Francione, *Introduction to Animal Rights*, chap. 1.

66. Wolfe, "Introduction: Exposures," in *Philosophy and Animal Life*, p. 26.

67. Wolfe, *Animal Rites*, p. 23.

68. Kelly Oliver, *Animal Lessons: How They Teach Us to Be Human* (New York: Columbia University Press, 2009), p. 30f. Cf. Karl Marx, *The German Ideology*, in *The Marx-Engels Reader*, 2d ed., ed. Robert C. Tucker (New York: Norton, 1972), pp. 172–74: "The ideas of the ruling class are in every epoch the ruling ideas: i.e., the class which is the ruling *material* force of society, is at the same time its ruling *intellectual* force. . . . The ruling ideas are nothing more than an expression of the dominant material relationships . . . each new class which puts itself in the place of one ruling before it, is compelled, merely in order to carry through its aim, to represent its interest as the common interest of all the members of society, that is, expressed in ideal form: it has to give its ideas

the form of universality, and represent them as the only rational, universally valid ones."

69. Calarco, *Zoographies*, p. 6f.

70. Derrida, *The Beast and the Sovereign*, 1:108.

71. Wolfe, *Animal Rites*, p. 69.

72. Derrida, *The Beast and the Sovereign*, 1:109.

73. John Locke, *An Essay Concerning Human Understanding*, ed. Peter H. Nidditch (Oxford: Oxford University Press, 1990), chap. 27, pp. 333–35.

74. See Descartes, *Discourse on Method*, in *The Philosophical Writings of Descartes*, vol. 1, Part 5, p. 140: "We see that magpies and parrots can utter words as we do, and yet they cannot speak as we do; they cannot show [*temoigner*] that they are thinking what they are saying."

75. Aristotle, *Parts of Animals*, 2.17 at 660a35–660b2.

76. Derrida, "The Animal That Therefore I Am," p. 50 (italics in English translation but not in French).

77. Readers would do best to consider the present discussion against the background of Steiner, *Anthropocentrism and Its Discontents*, chap. 9.

78. Ibid., p. 220f.

79. Karl Löwith, "Der Weltbegriff der neuzeitlichen Philosophie," *Sitzungsberichte der Heidelberger Akademie der Wissenschaften, Philosophisch-historischer Klasse* 44 (1960): 7; see also 19.

80. Heidegger, "Letter on 'Humanism,'" p. 247.

81. Martin Heidegger, *The Basic Problems of Phenomenology*, trans. Albert Hofstadter (Bloomington: Indiana University Press, 1982), p. 267 (translation altered).

82. Martin Heidegger, *Being and Time*, trans. John MacQuarrie and Edward Robinson (New York: Harper and Row, 1962), pp. 378, 387.

83. Ibid., pp. 288, 295.

84. Rainer Maria Rilke, "Die Achte Elegie," in *Duineser Elegien, Die Gedichte* (Frankfurt am Main: Insel, 2006), p. 709f. All references to the Eighth Duino Elegy are to this edition.

85. Martin Heidegger, "What Are Poets For?" in *Poetry, Language, Thought*, p. 104.

86. Ibid. See also Martin Heidegger, *Parmenides*, Gesamtausgabe, vol. 54 (Frankfurt: Klostermann, 1982), pp. 227ff.

87. Heidegger, "What Are Poets For?" p. 108.

88. Friedrich Nietzsche, "On the Uses and Disadvantages of History for Life," in *Untimely Meditations*, p. 61.

89. Heidegger, *Being and Time*, pp. 307, 318.

90. Heidegger, "What Is Metaphysics?" p. 87 (translation altered).

91. Ibid., pp. 95, 96.

92. Martin Heidegger, *Die Grundbegriffe der Metaphysik. Welt-Endlichkeit-Einsamkeit*, Gesamtausgabe, vol. 29/30 (Frankfurt-am-Main: Klostermann, 1983), pp. 360, 361, p. 285.

93. Heidegger, *Being and Time*, p. 199.

94. See ibid., pp. 51, 56.

95. Heidegger, *Die Grundbegriffe der Metaphysik*, p. 457.

96. Martin Heidegger, *Logik: Die Frage nach der Wahrheit*, Gesamtausgabe, vol. 21 (Frankfurt-am-Main: Klostermann, 1976), p. 159.

97. Heidegger, *Die Grundbegriffe der Metaphysik*, p. 462.

98. Heidegger, *Being and Time*, p. 201.

99. Kant, *Critique of Judgment*, sec. 90.

100. Heidegger, *Die Grundbegriffe der Metaphysik*, p. 284.

101. Heidegger, *Being and Time*, p. 233; "Postscript to 'What Is Metaphysics?' " in *Pathmarks*, p. 234.

102. Heidegger, "Introduction to 'What Is Metaphysics?' " in *Pathmarks*, p. 284. Here Heidegger states that even God and angels do not "exist," i.e., they do not relate to the future as open possibility but instead have an eternity's-eye standpoint on time.

103. Heidegger, "Letter on 'Humanism,' " p. 248.

104. Ibid.; Heidegger, *Being and Time*, p. 290.

105. Heidegger, *Die Grundbegriffe der Metaphysik*, p. 337.

106. Heidegger, "Letter on 'Humanism,' " p. 248.

107. Martin Heidegger, *Schellings Abhandlung über das Wesen der menschlichen Freiheit (1809)*, ed. Hildegard Feick (Tübingen: Niemeyer, 1971), p. 173f.

108. Heidegger, "Letter on 'Humanism,' " p. 247.

109. Martin Heidegger, *Was heißt Denken?* 4th ed. (Tübingen: Niemeyer, 1984), p. 51.

110. For an examination of this idea in thinkers from Aristotle through the Dutch Baroque, see William Schupbach, *The Paradox of Rembrandt's 'Anatomy Lesson of Dr. Tulp'*, *Medical History*, Supplement No. 2 (London: Wellcome Institute for the History of Medicine, 1982), pp. 57ff.

111. Heidegger, "Letter on 'Humanism,' " p. 248.

112. Ibid., p. 252; Heidegger, *Was ist das—die Philosophie?* p. 22.

113. Derrida, *Séminaire*, 2:184, 360, 310, 343, 279.

114. Heidegger, *Die Grundbegriffe der Metaphysik*, pp. 443, 486.

115. Derrida, "And Say the Animal Responded?" in *The Animal That Therefore I Am*, p. 125.

116. Saint Thomas Aquinas, *Quaestiones disputatae de veritate* q. 22, art. 4, resp.

117. Derrida, "And Say the Animal Responded?" p. 126.

118. Derrida, *The Beast and the Sovereign*, 1:33, 75.

119. Derrida, "And Say the Animal Responded?" p. 126.

120. Calarco, *Zoographies*, p. 142.

121. Derrida, *The Beast and the Sovereign*, 1:183; "But as for me, who am I?"; Derrida, *The Animal That Therefore I Am*, p. 94.

122. Calarco, *Zoographies*, p. 145.

123. Cary Wolfe, "On a Certain Blindness in Human Beings," in *The Death of the Animal: A Dialogue*, by Paola Cavalieri (New York: Columbia University Press, 2009), p. 126f.

124. Derrida, "The Animal That Therefore I Am," p. 166n36.

125. Jacques Derrida, "Geschlecht II: Heidegger's Hand," in *Deconstruction and Philosophy: The Texts of Derrida*, ed. John Sallis (Chicago: University of Chicago Press, 1987), p. 173.

126. Derrida, *La bête et le souverain*, 2:130.

127. See Heidegger, *Die Grundbegriffe der Metaphysik*, pp. 324–36.

128. Martin Heidegger, "Language," in *Poetry, Language, Thought*, p. 206.

129. Heidegger, *Being and Time*, p. 290.

130. Derrida, *La bête et le souverain*, 2:193.

131. Derrida, *The Beast and the Sovereign*, 1:137.

132. Ibid., p. 308.

133. Derrida, *La bête et le souverain*, 2:228, 175, 368.

134. Heidegger, *Being and Time*, p. 292: death in the existential sense "does not imply any ontical decision whether 'after death' still another Being is possible, either higher or lower, or whether Dasein 'lives on' or even 'outlasts' itself and is 'immortal'."

135. Derrida, *La bête et le souverain*, 2:184, 186, 281, 381, 310.

136. See, for example, "And Say the Animal Responded?" p. 173n9.

137. Derrida, *La bête et le souverain*, 2:59.

138. Ibid., pp. 159, 252f. The line comes from Celan's poem *Grosse, glühende Wölbung*.

139. This sense of desolation or solitude informs the entirety of Derrida's *La bête et le souverain*, vol. 2, in which Derrida undertakes a sustained

examination of Defoe's *Robinson Crusoe* and the 1929–30 lecture course in which Heidegger discusses both the human-animal boundary and the phenomenon of solitude.

140. Derrida, *La bête et le souverain*, 2:283.

141. Derrida suggests that "what is proper to man, his subjugating superiority over the animal, his very becoming-subject, his historicity, his emergence out of nature, his sociality, his access to knowledge and technics" all "derive from [an] originary fault" asserted between humans and animals. "The Animal That Therefore I Am," p. 45.

142. Steiner, *Animals and the Moral Community*, p. x.

143. I have argued for this conclusion at length in *Anthropocentrism and Its Discontents*, especially chaps. 1 and 10, and in *Animals and the Moral Community*.

144. Derrida, "The Animal That Therefore I Am," p. 27f.

145. Ibid.

146. Ibid., p. 41.

147. Derrida, *La bête et le souverain*, 2:182.

148. Derrida, "The Animal That Therefore I Am," p. 48.

149. Ibid., p. 29.

150. Ibid., p. 30.

151. Jacques Derrida and Elizabeth Roudinesco, "Violence Against Animals," in *For What Tomorrow . . . A Dialogue*, trans. Jeff Fort (Stanford: Stanford University Press, 2004), p. 66.

152. Wolfe, "On a Certain Blindness in Human Beings," p. 126f.

153. See Steiner, *Anthropocentrism and Its Discontents*, chap. 3; and *Animals and the Moral Community*, chaps. 1 and 2.

154. See Plutarch, *De sollertia animalium*; Porphyry, *On Abstinence from Killing Animals*; and Steiner, *Anthropocentrism and Its Discontents*, chap. 4.

155. Derrida, "Violence Against Animals," p. 73.

156. Derrida, " 'Eating Well', or the Calculation of the Subject," p. 100.

157. Derrida, "Force of Law," p. 953.

158. Derrida, " 'Eating Well', or the Calculation of the Subject," pp. 117, 112.

159. Derrida and Roudinesco, "Violence Against Animals," pp. 67, 69.

160. Derrida, "But as for Me, Who Am I?" in *The Animal That Therefore I Am*, pp. 89, 101.

161. Derrida, "'Eating Well', or the Calculation of the Subject," p. 111.

162. Wood, *Comment ne pas manger*—Deconstruction and Humanism," p. 27.

163. Calarco, *Zoographies*, pp. 137, 161n44.

164. Steiner, *Anthropocentrism and Its Discontents*, p. 220f.

165. Cavalieri, "Pushing Things Forward," in *The Death of the Animal*, p. 98.

166. Wood, "*Comment ne pas manger*—Deconstruction and Humanism," p. 32.

167. Of course animals are intelligent and can engage us in many ways not acknowledged by the anthropocentric tradition. But they cannot respond in ways that would make them capable of taking on responsibilities or defending themselves against injustice. To suppose otherwise is to misunderstand the notion of response, as I believe Oliver does when she suggests that "certainly, both human beings and animal beings respond. Even plants respond to their environment and perhaps even to human voices or touch. Living beings are responsive beings." Oliver, *Animal Lessons*, p. 77. Conflating reaction and response in this way fails to do justice to the crucial differences between human beings and other sorts of living being and, for that matter, between animals and plants.

168. Kathryn Paxton George, "A Feminist Critique of Ethical Vegetarianism," in *The Animal Ethics Reader*, ed. Susan J. Armstrong and Richard G. Botzler (London: Routledge, 2003), p. 219.

169. Gary Steiner, "Animal, Vegetable, Miserable," Week in Review, *New York Times*, November 22, 2009, p. 12.

170. Löwith, *Meaning in History*, pp. 21, 25.

171. Karl Löwith, "Welt und Menschenwelt," in *Welt und Menschenwelt*, 1:303. I discuss the ideal of a nonanthropocentric cosmopolitanism in chapter 5.

172. Leonard Lawlor, *This Is Not Sufficient: An Essay on Animality and Human Nature in Derrida* (New York: Columbia University Press, 2007), pp. 100, 144n49, 105, 146n57, 101, 110, 145n54.

173. Ibid., p. 105.

174. "The poverty of Derrida's response to vegetarianism suggests that the resources of deconstruction are not being fully deployed here." Wood, "*Comment ne pas manger*—Deconstruction and Humanism," p. 33.

4. ANIMAL RIGHTS AND THE EVASIONS OF POSTMODERNISM

1. See Matthew Calarco, "Toward an Agnostic Animal Ethics," in Cavalieri, *The Death of the Animal*, p. 76.

2. Richard A. Posner, "Animal Rights: Legal, Philosophical, and Pragmatic Perspectives," in *Animal Rights: Current Debates and New Directions*, ed. Cass R.

Sunstein and Martha C. Nussbaum (Oxford: Oxford University Press, 2004), pp. 63, 65, 56, 64.

3. Ibid., p. 70. Here Posner warns against valuing animals too highly by recalling "Hitler's zoophilia." That is, if you value nonhuman living beings, particularly animals, too highly, you might be just a little too much like a Nazi. Luc Ferry offers the same analogy in *The New Ecological Order*. I discuss the problems with this argument in *Anthropocentrism and Its Discontents*, pp. 226ff.

4. Posner, "Animal Rights," pp. 57f., 70. Here Posner explicitly calls his approach "humancentric."

5. Ibid., pp. 66, 73. Cf. p. 64: Posner doubts that even Peter Singer, "in his heart of hearts," believes that it would be wrong to inflict severe harm on a dog to prevent it from inflicting a slight harm on a human infant. This is one of the places where Posner appeals to his "any normal person" standard, and he states here that he "feel[s] no obligation to defend this reaction."

6. Richard A. Epstein, "Animals as Objects, or Subjects, of Rights," in Sunstein and Nussbaum, *Animal Rights: Current Debates and New Directions*, pp. 148, 151, 150, 152. In a similar vein, Posner intimates that we have overcome racism and sexism but must not abandon speciesism. "Animal Rights," p. 65.

7. Epstein, "Animals as Objects, or Subjects, of Rights," p. 154.

8. Posner, "Animal Rights," p. 67.

9. G. S. Kirk and J. E. Raven, *The Presocratic Philosophers: A Critical History with a Selection of Texts* (Cambridge: Cambridge University Press, 1979), frag. 15, p. 169.

10. Posner, "Animal Rights," pp. 51, 67, 66f, 65.

11. Ibid., p. 64.

12. See Epstein, "Animals as Objects, or Subjects, of Rights," p. 143.

13. Posner, "Animal Rights," p. 69. Implicit in such soft utilitarianism is the idea that we ought not to be indifferent to the sufferings of animals, but that we should not count these sufferings equally with our own in our utilitarian calculations.

14. Ibid., p. 64. Cf. Richard A. Watson, "Self-Consciousness and the Rights of Nonhuman Animals and Nature," in *The Animal Rights/Environmental Ethics Debate: The Environmental Perspective*, ed. Eugene C. Hargrove (Albany: SUNY Press, 1992), p. 23: "There is no argument that supports the view that causing merely sentient beings unnecessary suffering is bad because it deprives them of their rights, for there is no argument establishing that they have any rights."

15. See Steiner, *Anthropocentrism and Its Discontents*, pp. 62ff.

16. See Steiner, *Animals and the Moral Community*, chaps. 1–3.

17. Posner, "Animal Rights," p. 72.

18. Richard Rorty, *Philosophy and the Mirror of Nature* (Princeton: Princeton University Press, 1979), p. 190f.

19. Posner, "Animal Rights," pp. 57, 55.

20. Epstein, "Animals as Objects, or Subjects, of Rights," p. 156.

21. See Paul W. Taylor, *Respect for Nature: A Theory of Environmental Ethics* (Princeton: Princeton University Press, 1986), pp. 99f., 276, 282–87, 312.

22. Clare Palmer, *Animal Ethics in Context* (New York: Columbia University Press, 2010), p. 166.

23. Peter Singer, *Practical Ethics*, 2d ed. (Cambridge: Cambridge University Press, 2010), p. 287.

24. Singer, *Animal Liberation*, p. 165; John Lawrence Hill, *The Case for Vegetarianism: Philosophy for a Small Planet* (Lanham, Mass.: Rowman and Littlefield, 1996), p. 111.

25. Michael Allen Fox, *Deep Vegetarianism* (Philadelphia: Temple University Press, 1999), pp. 90–95.

26. This claim is advanced by J. Baird Callicott, who suggests not only that universal vegetarianism would be "probably ecologically catastrophic," but also that the idea of equal rights for animals is so "ludicrous" as to be a better subject of "satire" than "philosophical discussion." J. Baird Callicott, "Animal Liberation: A Triangular Affair," in Hargrove, *The Animal Rights/Environmental Ethics Debate*, pp. 57, 60; see also Mary Anne Warren, "The Rights of the Nonhuman World," in ibid., p. 200. Both Callicott and Warren base their predictions of environmental catastrophe on the assumption that the shift to a vegetarian diet would bring with it an increase in the world's population. What conclusion are we to draw from this—that we should refrain from making proper nutrition available to more of the world's population? The problem of overpopulation is one that will continue to confront us regardless of the kind of diet people follow; moreover, it is far from clear that any increase in population resulting from a shift to vegetarianism or veganism would come anywhere near outweighing the extensive ecological improvements that would result from a cessation of meat production.

27. It will ultimately be a matter of individuals *voluntarily* committing themselves to veganism as an ethical imperative, rather than the imposition of veganism by force; see Steiner, *Animals and the Moral Community*, chap. 6. Moreover, there is no reason to believe that a shift to universal vegetarianism

or veganism would take place suddenly and that this suddenness would give rise to all sorts of practical difficulties; see Fox, *Deep Vegetarianism*, p. 143. While nobody today can be certain exactly what the environmental consequences of a worldwide shift to veganism would be, it strikes me that warnings of ecological catastrophe and environmental fascism are motivated more by an interest in evasion than by anything else.

28. Epstein, "Animals as Objects, or Subjects, of Rights," p. 154.

29. Posner, "Animal Rights," p. 59; Epstein, "Animals as Objects, or Subjects, of Rights," p. 148.

30. See Bekoff and Pierce, *Wild Justice*; Gary L. Francione, *Animals, Property, and the Law* (Philadelphia: Temple University Press, 1995).

31. Gary L. Francione, *Rain Without Thunder: The Ideology of the Animal Rights Movement* (Philadelphia: Temple University Press, 1996); Gary L. Francione and Robert Garner, *The Animal Rights Debate: Abolition or Regulation?* (New York: Columbia University Press, 2010).

32. Michael Pollan, *The Omnivore's Dilemma: A Natural History of Four Meals* (New York: Penguin, 2006); Jonathan Safran Foer, *Eating Animals* (New York: Little, Brown, 2008).

33. On the distinction between a total and an immanent critique of reason, see Steiner, "The Perils of a Total Critique of Reason."

34. Friedrich Nietzsche, *On the Genealogy of Morals*, Second Essay, sec. 11, in *Basic Writings of Nietzsche*, p. 510f.

35. Richard Wolin, *The Terms of Cultural Criticism: The Frankfurt School, Existentialism, Poststructuralism* (New York: Columbia University Press, 1992), p. 156; Wolin, "Deconstruction at Auschwitz: Heidegger, de Man, and the New Revisionism," in *Labyrinths: Explorations in the Critical History of Ideas* (Amherst: University of Massachusetts Press, 1995), pp. 210, 228f.

36. Lawlor, *This Is Not Sufficient*, pp. 9, 141n34, 144n49, 104f.

37. See, for example, Gary L. Francione, "Taking Sentience Seriously," in *Animals as Persons: Essays on the Abolition of Animal Exploitation* (New York: Columbia University Press, 2008), pp. 129–47.

38. Judith Butler uses the expression "precarious life" to characterize the web of interrelationships that bind us not only to animals but to our environment. I have no idea whether Butler is a vegetarian or a vegan; I know only that her pronouncements about precarious life remain vague and undeveloped, so their specific implications for animal ethics are completely unclear. The most she does is "propose 'precarious life' as a non-anthropocentric

framework for considering what makes life valuable." "Antigone's Claim: A Conversation with Judith Butler," *Theory and Event* 12.1 (2009) (http://muse .jhu.edu/journals/theory_and_event/ v012/12.1.antonello.html). On the question whether veganism is easy or difficult, see my "Animal, Vegetable, Miserable," p. 12.

39. Derrida and Roudinesco, "Violence Against Animals," p. 65.

40. Ibid.

41. Immanuel Kant, "An Answer to the Question: 'What Is Enlightenment?' " in *Political Writings*, p. 57.

42. Derrida and Roudinesco, "Violence Against Animals," pp. 65 (italics added), 74.

43. Ibid., 64: "I will also not use the word 'rights,' but that is where the question becomes complicated."

44. Wolfe, *Animal Rites*, p. 191f.

45. Derrida and Roudinesco, "Violence Against Animals," p. 76.

46. Lawlor, *This Is Not Sufficient*, p. 105.

47. Derrida, *La bête et le souverain*, 2:360.

48. On the prospect of offering animals our hospitality, see ibid., p. 343.

49. Derrida, "Force of Law," p. 955. Cf. Lawlor, *This Is Not Sufficient*, p. 111: "Unconditional hospitality takes up the Kantian insight that the law must have the form of universality; it must be applied equally or univocally to everyone no matter who or what. And here we must not overlook the fact that what Derrida has called deconstruction maintains a deep alliance with the Western idea of enlightenment."

50. Derrida, *The Beast and the Sovereign*, 1:208, 296.

51. Ibid., pp. 111, 110, 213. Cf. Derrida, *La bête et le souverain*, 2:360f., where Derrida characterizes *logos apophantikos* (rational assertion) as violent appropriation.

52. Jacques Derrida, "But as for me, who am I?" p. 87f.

53. Dominic LaCapra, *History and Its Limits: Human, Animal, Violence* (Ithaca: Cornell University Press, 2009), p. 152, 189, 180f.

54. LaCapra for his own part refrains from taking a stand on the question "whether or not . . . humans have the right to kill other animals for food" and goes no further than observing that "how other animals live before they die . . . is an important ethicopolitical issue." Ibid., p. 178.

55. Derrida, "Violence Against Animals," p. 73.

56. Derrida, *The Beast and the Sovereign*, 1:176.

57. Derrida and Roudinesco, "Violence Against Animals," p. 76.

58. Derrida, *The Beast and the Sovereign*, 1:75. Similarly, Elisabeth de Fontenay calls for a "decisionistic humanism" that could ground ethical norms "but not in the spirit of Carl Schmitt." "Pourquoi les animaux n'auraient-ils pas droit à un droit des animaux?" *Le Debat* 109 (2000): 151.

59. LaCapra, *History and Its Limits*, p. 189.

60. See my remarks on Hayek in *Animals and the Moral Community*, pp. 150ff.

61. See F. A. Hayek, *The Road to Serfdom: Text and Documents*, ed. Bruce Caldwell (Chicago: University of Chicago Press, 2007), p. 104; Schmitt, *Political Theology*, p. 6.

62. Schmitt, *Political Theology*, p. 31.

63. Schmitt, *The Concept of the Political*, pp. 27, 46.

64. Hayek, *The Road to Serfdom*, p. 107n5; see also p. 111.

65. Ibid., pp. 112n2, 112f., 117, 119n7, 120. Joseph Raz makes an important observation about Hayek's conception of the rule of law: that Hayek errs in assuming that the rule of law guarantees justice and equality. Raz notes that in fact the rule of law is compatible with many forms of arbitrary power, and that the rule of law is a necessary but not a sufficient condition for a just society. Joseph Raz, *The Authority of Law*, 2d ed. (Oxford: Oxford University Press, 2009), pp. 219, 225f. Nonetheless the point remains that "deliberate disregard for the rule of law violates human dignity" (p. 221).

66. Ronald Dworkin, "The Court's Embarrassingly Bad Decisions," *New York Review of Books*, vol. 58, no. 9 (May 26, 2011): 40.

67. Raz, *The Authority of Law*, p. 214.

68. See Steiner, *Animals and the Moral Community*, pp. 156ff., where I develop this idea in terms of Hegel's dialectic.

69. Lawlor, *This Is Not Sufficient*, p. 145n54.

70. Ibid., p. 104.

71. Porphyry, *On Abstinence from Killing Animals*, 1.31.3, p. 43. See also Steiner, *Anthropocentrism and Its Discontents*, pp. 103ff.

72. Calarco, "Toward an Agonistic Animal Ethics," p. 76.

73. Ibid., p. 81.

74. Cary Wolfe, "On a Certain Blindness in Human Beings," in Cavalieri, *The Death of the Animal*, p. 125.

75. Ibid., p. 128.

76. Edmund Husserl, *The Crisis of the European Sciences and Transcendental Phenomenology: An Introduction to Phenomenological Philosophy*, trans. David Carr (Evanston: Northwestern University Press, 1970), p. 16.

77. Richard J. Bernstein, "An Allegory of Modernity/Postmodernity: Habermas and Derrida," in *The New Constellation*, p. 221.

78. Bernstein, "Serious Play: The Ethical-Political Horizon of Derrida," in *The New Constellation*, p. 191.

79. Derrida, *La bête et le souverain*, 2:69 (Heidegger's "obsession with orientation"), 78 (to pick a direction for investigation is to settle on a "dominant figure or trope"), 101 (Heidegger's choice to start with what lies closest to us is "forceful" and "arbitrary"), 137 (dislocation has priority in all textual events).

80. Paola Cavalieri, "Pushing Things Forward," in *The Death of the Animal*, p. 101.

81. See Derrida, *La bête et le souverain*, 2:101.

82. John M. Coetzee, "On Appetite, the Right to Life, and Rational Ethics," in Cavalieri, *The Death of the Animal: A Dialogue*, p. 121.

83. Cora Diamond, "Injustice and Animals," in *Slow Cures and Bad Philosophers: Essays on Wittgenstein, Medicine, and Bioethics*, ed. Carl Elliott (Durham: Duke University Press, 2001), pp. 120, 124. In this essay Diamond draws heavily on Weil's essay "Human Personality," in *Simone Weil: An Anthology*, ed. Siân Miles (New York: Weidenfeld & Nicolson, 1986), pp. 49–78.

84. Diamond, "Injustice and Animals," p. 120.

85. Cora Diamond, "The Difficulty of Reality and the Difficulty of Philosophy," in *Philosophy and Animal Life*, ed. Stanley Cavell et. al. (New York: Columbia University Press, 2008), pp. 74, 45f., 46f.

86. Ibid., 53.

87. Schopenhauer, *The World as Will and Representation*, vol. 1, Third Book, sec. 49, p. 235; sec. 51, p. 252f.

88. Ibid., sec. 52, p. 264.

89. Arthur Schopenhauer, *On the Basis of Morality*, trans. E. F. J. Payne (Providence: Berghahn Books, 1995), sec. 17, p. 152; *The World as Will and Representation*, vol. 1, Fourth Book, sec. 63, 64, pp. 350, 357. This call for eternal justice does not prevent Schopenhauer from succumbing to anthropocentric prejudice; see Steiner, *Anthropocentrism and Its Discontents*, p. 188f.

90. Wolfe, "On a Certain Blindness in Human Beings," p. 127.

91. Diamond, "Injustice and Animals," p. 123.

92. Weil, "Human Personality," pp. 73, 52, 66, 61. Cf. p. 63: "If someone tries to browbeat a farmer to sell his eggs at a moderate price, the farmer can say: 'I have the right to keep my eggs if I don't get a good enough price.' But if a young girl is being forced into a brothel she will not talk about her rights." Will *no one* talk about her rights?

93. Diamond, "Injustice and Animals," p. 120.

94. Weil, "Human Personality," pp. 64, 61.

95. Yan Thomas, "Le sujet de droit, la personne et la nature," *Le Débat* 100 (May–August, 1998): 98, 103.

96. Diamond, "Injustice and Animals," p. 139.

97. Ibid.

98. Watson, "Self-Consciousness and the Rights of Nonhuman Animals and Nature," p. 9.

99. Arthur Schopenhauer, "On Religion," in *Parerga and Paralipomena*, 2:375.

100. Diamond, "Injustice and Animals," p. 139.

101. Schopenhauer, *The World as Will and Representation*, vol. 1, Third Book, sec. 52, pp. 256–64; vol. 2, "On the Metaphysics of Music," p. 450.

102. Cora Diamond, "Eating Meat and Eating People," in *Animal Rights*, p. 105.

103. Ibid., pp. 106, 105.

104. Diamond, "The Difficulty of Reality and the Difficulty of Philosophy," p. 57.

105. Ibid., p. 55.

106. Coetzee, *The Lives of Animals*, p. 65.

107. Diamond, "The Difficulty of Reality and the Difficulty of Philosophy," p. 55.

108. Fontenay, "Pourquoi les animaux n'auraient-ils pas droit à un droit des animaux?" p. 153.

109. Diamond, "Eating Meat and Eating People," p. 102.

110. Heidegger, "On the Essence of Truth," in *Pathmarks*, p. 144. See also Steiner, *Animals and the Moral Community*, pp. 141, 163.

111. Werner Marx develops a "non-metaphysical ethics of proximity [*Nächstenethik*]" in *Is There a Measure on Earth? Foundations of a Nonmetaphysical Ethics*, trans. Thomas J. Nenon and Reginald Lilly (Chicago: University of Chicago Press, 1987). Marx's focus is the shared mortality of human beings. All that would be needed to expand the scope of ethical concern so as to include animals would be a recognition of the fact that animals, like us, are mortal.

5. TOWARD A NONANTHROPOCENTRIC COSMOPOLITANISM

1. See Hesiod, *Works and Days* 105–201. On the recurrence of this golden age myth in Western thought, see Steiner, *Anthropocentrism and Its Discontents*, pp. 39, 44f.. 50f., 95, 106–113, 137.

2. Hesiod, *Works and Days* 213, 275.

3. Ovid, *Metamorphoses* I, 90–162.

4. John Rawls, *A Theory of Justice*, rev. ed. (Cambridge: Belknap/Harvard University Press, 1999), p. 448.

5. See Cicero, *De natura deorum* 2.37–39, in A. A. Long and D. N. Sedley, ed. and trans., *The Hellenistic Philosophers*, 2 vols. (Cambridge: Cambridge University Press, 1990), 54H. See also Epictetus, *Discourses* 1.6.18, 1.16.1–5, 2.8.6–8 and Steiner, *Anthropocentrism and Its Discontents*, p. 85.

6. In the twentieth century the most illuminating account of the concept of human willing as a secularized version of the divine will is Carl Schmitt's. See Schmitt, *Political Theology*.

7. Aristotle, Politics 1.8 at 1256b15–21, in *Complete Works of Aristotle*, 2 vols., rev. Oxford translation, ed. Jonathan Barnes (Princeton: Bollingen/Princeton University Press, 1995), 2.1993–94.

8. Heidegger, "Letter on 'Humanism,'" p. 269f.

9. Aristotle, *Nichomachean Ethics* 10.8 at 1178b22–29.

10. Aristotle, *Eudemian Ethics* 1.7 at 1217a24–25, in *Complete Works of Aristotle* 2.1926.

11. Seneca, *Ad lucilium epistulae morales*, vol. 3, Latin-English, trans. Richard M. Gummere (London: William Heinemann/New York: G. P. Putnam's Sons, 1925), 124.8, 124.14, pp. 441, 445.

12. Epictetus, *Discourses* 1.6.14–17, in *The Discourses as Reported by Arrian, Books I–II*, Greek-English, trans. W. A. Oldfather (Cambridge: Harvard University Press, 2000), p. 43.

13. Cicero, *De finibus bonorum et malorum*, Latin-English, trans. H. Rackham (Cambridge: Harvard University Press, 1999), 3.21, p. 240f.

14. See Cicero, *De natura deorum* 2.37–39; see also 2.133 and Diogenes Laertius 7.138.

15. See Epictetus, *Discourses* 1.16.1–5 and 2.10.3, p. 268f.

16. See Saint Augustine, *Confessions* 7.17.

17. Saint Augustine, *On Free Choice of the Will*, trans. Thomas Williams (Indianapolis: Hackett, 1993), 1.9, p. 15; see also *Confessions* 10.31.

18. Saint Augustine, *The Catholic and Manichaean Ways of Life*, trans. Donald A. Gallagher and Idella J. Gallagher, Fathers of the Church, vol. 56 (Washington, D.C.: Catholic University of America Press, 1966), 2.17.59, 2.17.54, pp. 105, 102.

19. Saint Thomas Aquinas, *Quaestiones disputatae de veritate*, q. 5, art. 8, resp., *Summa Contra Gentiles* 3.97; q. 24, art. 1, resp.

20. Saint Thomas Aquinas, *Summa Theologica* 1–2, q. 96, art. 1, resp., *Basic Writings of St. Thomas Aquinas*, 2 vols., ed. Anton C. Pegis (Indianapolis: Hackett, 1997), 1.692.

21. Saint Thomas Aquinas, *Summa Contra Gentiles* 3.92, and *Summa Theologica* 1–2, q. 102, art. 6.

22. Saint Thomas Aquinas, *Summa Contra Gentiles* 3.92, in *Basic Writings of St. Thomas Aquinas* 2.222.

23. Immanuel Kant, *The Metaphysics of Morals*, ed. Mary Gregor (Cambridge: Cambridge University Press, 1996), p. 186. For a more detailed discussion of Kant, see Steiner, *Anthropocentrism and Its Discontents*, pp. 166–71.

24. Kant, *The Metaphysics of Morals*, p. 186. On the person-thing distinction, see Immanuel Kant, *Lectures on Ethics*, ed. Peter Heath and J. B. Schneewind, trans. Peter Heath (Cambridge: Cambridge University Press, 1997), p. 147; and *Grounding for the Metaphysics of Morals*, trans. James W. Ellington (Indianapolis: Hackett, 1981), pp. 35–37.

25. Immanuel Kant, *Critique of Judgment*, trans. Werner S. Pluhar (Indianapolis: Hackett, 1987), sec. 83, p. 318 (Ak. 431).

26. Immanuel Kant, "Idea for a Universal History with a Cosmopolitan Purpose," in *Political Writings*, pp. 41, 51 (translation altered).

27. Immanuel Kant, "The Contest of Faculties," in *Political Writings*, p. 188.

28. Kant, *The Metaphysics of Morals*, pp. 192, 215.

29. Immanuel Kant, *Lectures on Ethics*, p. 213. Here Kant goes on to say that animal cruelty "is never [acceptable] in sport."

30. Kant, *The Metaphysics of Morals*, p. 232.

31. Immanuel Kant, *Critique of Practical Reason*, 3d ed., trans. Lewis White Beck (Upper Saddle River, N.J.: Library of Liberal Arts/Prentice Hall, 1993), p. 134n.

32. Rawls, *A Theory of Justice*, p. 448.

33. Löwith, *Welt und Menschenwelt*, 1:303, 295, 307.

34. Heidegger, "On the Essence of Truth," p. 144; "Letter on 'Humanism,'" p. 271.

35. Heidegger, "Letter on 'Humanism,'" pp. 243, 252.

36. Heidegger, "The Question Concerning Technology," p. 35 (translation altered).

37. Derrida, "'Eating Well', or the Calculation of the Subject," p. 112f.

38. Jacques Derrida, from the Cerisy Conference, 1993, cited in Wood, "*Comment ne pas manger*—Deconstruction and Humanism," p. 20.

39. Derrida, "Force of Law," p. 953; "Eating Well," p. 112.

40. See Steiner, *Anthropocentrism and Its Discontents*, pp. 217–22.

41. Heidegger, *Die Grundbegriffe der Metaphysik*, p. 368. On ek-sistence, see Heidegger, "Letter on 'Humanism,'" pp. 246–51.

42. See Steiner, *Anthropocentrism and Its Discontents*, pp. 182, 185, 189.

43. Heidegger, *Die Grundbegriffe der Metaphysik*, p. 361; see also Heidegger, "What Are Poets For?" in *Poetry, Language, Thought*, p. 106.

44. Heidegger, *Die Grundbegriffe der Metaphysik*, pp. 361, 368.

45. Heidegger, "Letter on 'Humanism,'" p. 247f.; Heidegger, *On the Way to Language*, trans. Peter D. Hertz (San Francisco: Harper and Row, 1971), p. 107.

46. Martin Heidegger, *Schellings Abhandlung über das Wesen der menschlichen Freiheit*, p. 173f.

47. Heidegger, *Die Grundbegriffe der Metaphysik*, p. 286f.

48. Heidegger, "Letter on 'Humanism,'" p. 248; Heidegger, "Building, Dwelling, Thinking," in *Poetry, Language, Thought*, p. 147.

49. Heidegger, "Building, Dwelling, Thinking," p. 147 (translation altered).

50. Porphyry, *On Abstinence from Killing Animals* 1.31.3, p. 43; 3.26.9, p. 98; 3.2.4; 3.3.3; 3.19.2; 3.1.4; 3.2.4; Pierre Gassendi, Fifth Set of Objections to the Meditations, in *The Philosophical Writings of Descartes*, 2:189.

51. Aristotle, *Nichomachean Ethics* 8.11 at 1161b1–3; Kant, *The Metaphysics of Morals*, p. 215.

52. Porphyry, *On Abstinence from Killing Animals* 2.22.1, p. 63; 4.9; 3.26.6, p. 97.

53. Ibid. 2.22.1–2.

54. Ibid. 3.18.4, p. 90; 1.27.1, p. 40; 1.31.3, p. 43.

55. Cicero, *On Ends* 3.16, *De finibus bonorum et malorum*, p. 232f., 3.62, 3.63.

56. Hierocles (Stobaeus 4.671, 7–4.673.11), *The Hellenistic Philosophers* 57G.

57. Cicero, *On Duties* 1.107, *The Hellenistic Philosophers* 66E.

58. Martha C. Nussbaum, "Patriotism and Cosmopolitanism," in *For Love of Country: Defining the Limits of Patriotism*, ed. Joshua Cohen (Boston: Beacon Press, 1996), pp. 9, 4, 15, 8.

59. Martha C. Nussbaum, *Cultivating Humanity: A Classical Defense of Reform in Liberal Education* (Cambridge: Harvard University Press, 1997), pp. 67, 69, 83.

60. Martha C. Nussbaum, *Frontiers of Justice: Disability, Nationality, Species Membership* (Cambridge: Belknap/Harvard University Press, 2006), pp. 383, 389, 381f., 383.

61. Ibid., pp. 387, 386; cf. p. 187f., where Nussbaum draws the line at anencephalic children and humans in persistent vegetative states, arguing that "only sentiment leads us to call [such persons] human"; to count as human,

people must possess "the ability to love and relate to others, perception, delight in movement and play," i.e., the capacity to live one's life "bound up in a network of human relations."

62. Ibid., p. 383f.

63. See Steiner, *Animals and the Moral Community*, p. 149.

64. Nussbaum, *Frontiers of Justice*, p. 393. But cf. p. 377, where Nussbaum justifies training horses to race and engage in dressage, dismissing criticisms of such practices as flights of "romantic fantasy." On the inadequacy of Nussbaum's view regarding such practices, see Steiner, *Animals and the Moral Community*, pp. 107–9.

65. Nussbaum, *Frontiers of Justice*, pp. 405f., 402f.

66. Kwame Anthony Appiah, *Cosmopolitanism: Ethics in a World of Strangers* (New York: Norton, 2006), pp. 63, 71, 84f., 97, 113, 153, 165.

67. Ibid., p. 59f.

68. Seyla Benhabib, *Another Cosmopolitanism* (Oxford: Oxford University Press, 2006), pp. 18, 19f., 32.

69. Ibid., p. 35.

70. Seyla Benhabib, *The Rights of Others: Aliens, Residents, and Citizens* (Cambridge: Cambridge University Press, 2004), pp. 179, 209; see also *Another Cosmopolitanism*, pp. 48, 67, 70.

71. Benhabib, *Another Cosmopolitanism*, p. 162.

72. See Seyla Benhabib, *Situating the Self: Gender, Community, and Postmodernism in Contemporary Ethics* (New York: Routledge, 1992).

73. Benhabib, *Another Cosmopolitanism*, p. 19f.; Benhabib, *The Rights of Others*, p. 13.

74. Benhabib, *The Rights of Others*, p. 13f.

75. Benhabib, *Another Cosmopolitanism*, p. 43n36.

76. See R. Radhakrishnan, "Minority Theory, Re-Visited," *CR: The New Centennial Review*, vol. 6, no. 2 (2006): 48f.; Foucault, "Nietzsche, Genealogy, History," in *The Foucault Reader*, pp. 86, 88.

77. Radhakrishnan, "Minority Theory, Re-Visited," pp. 50, 52.

78. Paul Rabinow, "Representations are Social Facts: Modernity and Post-Modernity in Anthropology," in *Writing Culture: The Poetics and Politics of Ethnography*, ed. James Clifford and George E. Marcus (Berkeley: University of California Press, 1986), p. 258.

79. Pheng Cheah, "Introduction," in *Cosmopolitics: Thinking and Feeling Beyond the Nation*, ed. Pheng Cheah and Bruce Robbins (Minneapolis: University of Minnesota Press, 1998), p. 36.

80. Simon Critchley, "Preface," in Derrida, *On Cosmopolitanism and Forgiveness*, p. xi.

81. Butler, "For a Careful Reading," p. 130. Cf. p. 133: the aim here is "recasting agency within matrices of power."

82. Amanda Anderson, "Cosmopolitanism, Universalism, and the Divided Legacies of Modernity," in Cheah and Robbins, *Cosmopolitics: Thinking and Feeling Beyond the Nation*, p. 274. Situated cosmopolitanism also has its humanist proponents; see for example Lorenzo C. Simpson, *The Unfinished Project: Toward a Postmetaphysical Humanism* (New York: Routledge, 2001).

83. David Harvey, *Cosmopolitanism and the Geographies of Freedom* (New York: Columbia University Press, 2009), pp. 37, 39f.

84. Ibid., p. 50 (following an idea proposed by Chandra Mohanty). Cf. p. 162: What is needed is a conception of space and time as "dialectical and alive" rather than "dead and fixed," as "relational" rather than as "absolute." Cf. also pp. 180 and 185, where Harvey criticizes Heidegger's conception of place as "essentialist" and as "notoriously abstract and vague."

85. Boaventura de Sousa Santos and César A. Rodríguez-Garavito, "Law, Politics, and the Subaltern in Counter-Hegemonic Globalization," in *Law and Globalization from Below: Towards a Cosmopolitan Legality* (Cambridge: Cambridge University Press, 2005), pp. 15, 13.

86. Harvey, *Cosmopolitanism and the Geographies of Freedom*, p. 283.

87. Butler, "For a Careful Reading," p. 130.

88. Benedict Anderson, "Nationalism, Identity, and the World-in-Motion: On the Logics of Seriality," in Cheah and Robbins, *Cosmopolitics: Thinking and Feeling Beyond the Nation*, pp. 121, 130.

89. Anderson, "Cosmopolitanism, Universalism, and the Divided Legacies of Modernity," p. 275.

90. See, for example, Harvey, *Cosmopolitanism and the Geographies of Freedom*, p. 259f.

91. Cheah, "Introduction," p. 33; Iris Marion Young, *Justice and the Politics of Difference* (Princeton: Princeton University Press, 1990), p. 14.

92. Young, *Justice and the Politics of Difference*, p. 4.

93. See Steiner, *Animals and the Moral Community*, chaps. 5 and 6.

6. Cosmopolitanism and Veganism

1. On the ideal of cosmic holism and the notion of cosmic justice, see Steiner, *Animals and the Moral Community*, chaps. 5 and 6.

2. Aristotle argues that women are excluded in principle from citizenship, on the grounds their rational ability is inherently limited and inferior to that of free men; he states that women possess rational capacity but that it "lacks authority." He excludes slaves from citizenship on the grounds that "the slave has no deliberative faculty at all." Aristotle, *Politics* I.13 at 1260a13–14, 2.1999. Cf. *Politics* 1.5 at 1254b13ff., 2.1990: "Again, the male is by nature superior, and the female inferior; and the one rules, and the other is ruled. This principle, of necessity, extends to all mankind. Where then there is such a difference as that between soul and body, or between men and animals . . . the lower sort are by nature slaves, and it is better for them as for all inferiors that they should be under the rule of a master."

3. Diogenes Laertius, *Lives of the Eminent Philosophers*, vol. 2, trans. R. D. Hicks (Cambridge: Loeb/Harvard University Press, 2000), 6.63, 65.

4. Richard Wolin, "Antihumanism and the Discovery of French Postwar Theory," in *Labyrinths*, p. 194.

5. Francione, *Introduction to Animal Rights*, chap. 1.

6. Rawls, *A Theory of Justice*, p. 448.

7. See Steiner, *Anthropocentrism and Its Discontents*, pp. 57–76.

8. See ibid., pp. 77–92.

9. Steiner, *Animals and the Moral Community*, pp. 137, 163.

10. Warren, "The Rights of the Nonhuman World," p. 192.

11. Hesiod, *Works and Days* 213, 275.

12. See Epicurus, *Key Doctrines* 31–7, in *The Hellenistic Philosophers*, 22A–B.

13. Sorabji, following an argument made by Victor Goldschmidt, suggests that Epicurus "leaves it open whether there might be any non-human animals which did make such agreements." Richard J. Sorabji, *Animal Minds and Human Morals: The Origins of the Western Debate* (Ithaca: Cornell University Press, 1993), p. 162. In a similar vein, Jo-Ann Shelton attributes to Lucretius the belief that human beings and some animals made "contracts" that took the form of "tacit agreements to swap goods and services: food and protection from predators in exchange for meat, milk, wool, and labor, *tutela* for *utilitas*." Jo-Ann Shelton, "Lucretius on the Use and Abuse of Animals," *Eranos* 94 (1996): 52. The evidence in Lucretius on this point shows Shelton's claim that there were *contracts* between human beings and animals to

be questionable; Lucretius states simply that certain animals such as dogs and sheep "have been entrusted to the protection of humankind. For they fled eagerly from wild beasts, and came in pursuit of peace and the plentiful fodder, obtained without any effort on their part, which we give them as a reward in return for their usefulness." Lucretius, *De Rerum Natura V*, ed. and trans. Monica R. Gale (Oxford: Oxbow Books, 2009), ll. 868–70, p. 71.

14. Steiner, *Animals and the Moral Community*, p. 163.

15. Posner, "Animal Rights," pp. 58, 63.

16. Francione, *Introduction to Animal Rights*, p. xxxiv.

17. I say "purported" because Schweitzer's view turns out to be pointedly anthropocentric. See Steiner, *Anthropocentrism and Its Discontents*, pp. 197–201.

18. As I have noted before, one rare and conspicuous exception is Gary Francione. See Steiner, *Animals and the Moral Community*, p. 120.

19. I received these criticisms via e-mail in the several weeks following the publication of "Animal, Vegetable, Miserable."

20. Isaac Bashevis Singer, "The Letter Writer," in *The Collected Stories of Isaac Bashevis Singer* (New York: Farrar, Straus, and Giroux, 1982), p. 264; see also p. 271: for animals, "all people are Nazis; for the animals it is an eternal Treblinka."

21. Judith Butler, *Precarious Life: The Powers of Mourning and Violence* (London: Verso, 2006), p. 134; see also pp. 46, 49.

22. Ibid., p. 78. Butler appears to have in mind views such as Aristotle's, according to which human beings can control their passions and desires with reason, whereas animals are strictly determined by their desires and cannot step back from them and evaluate them. See Steiner, *Anthropocentrism and Its Discontents*, p. 61f.

23. Butler, *Precarious Life*, p. 150f.

24. Oliver, *Animal Lessons*, pp. 14, 11.

25. See Francione, *Introduction to Animal Rights*, p. 101.

26. I discuss this question at greater length in *Animals and the Moral Community*, pp. 106ff.

27. See Jean-Jacques Rousseau, *On Social Contract or Principles of Political Right*, in *Rousseau's Political Writings*, ed. Alan Ritter and Julia Conway Bondanella (New York: Norton, 1988), p. 87.

28. See, for example, Bekoff and Pierce, *Wild Justice*.

29. Descartes, *Discourse on Method*, Part 2, in *The Philosophical Writings of Descartes*, I:120.

30. Derrida, *La bête et le souverain*, 2:206, 209.

31. Ovid, *Metamorphoses*, Book 15, ll. 453ff., 2.397f.

32. This example is adapted from Kant, *Grounding for the Metaphysics of Morals*, p. 10 (Ak. 397).

33. "The Ethical Choices in What We Eat," *New York Times*, November 23, 2009, http://www.nytimes.com/2009/11/24/opinion/l24vegan.html?ref=opinion.

34. http://kazez.blogspot.com/search?updated-min=2009–01–01T00%3A00%3A00–06%3A00&updated-max=2010–01–01T00%3A00%3A00–06%3A00&max-results=50 (entry for December 1, 2009). See also Jean Kazez, *Animalkind: What We Owe to Animals* (Chichester: Wiley-Blackwell, 2010). Kazez insists that her reasoning is not utilitarian, but even a little reflection on her arguments suggests otherwise.

35. See Francione, *Rain Without Thunder*; and Francione and Garner, *The Animal Rights Debate*.

36. Aldo Leopold, *A Sand County Almanac and Sketches Here and There* (New York: Oxford University Press, 1949), pp. 224f., 178, 165, 169. See also p. 181: "I do not pretend to know what is moderation, or where the line is between legitimate and illegitimate gadgets. . . . I use many factory-made gadgets myself. Yet there must be some limit beyond which money-bought aids to sport destroy the cultural value of sport."

37. Ibid., p. 110.

38. James Hatley, "The Uncanny Goodness of Being Edible to Bears," in *Rethinking Nature: Essays in Environmental Philosophy*, ed. Bruce V. Foltz and Robert Frodeman (Bloomington: Indiana University Press, 2004), pp. 19, 13, 14f.

39. Ibid., pp. 19, 27, 15, 20, 26f.

40. Ibid., pp. 19, 30n15.

41. Dominique Lestel, *Apologie du carnivore* (Paris: Fayard, 2011), pp. 104, 110, 105f., 67, 107f. Here I can offer only an adumbrated discussion and critique of Lestel's arguments. The reader is encouraged to read Lestel's thought-provoking book in its entirety.

42. See ibid., p. 16: "In the face of a defective memory," what is needed is a "recollection of man's animality."

43. Ibid., pp. 84, 15, 124. Lestel presents a sustained argument against laboratory experimentation on animals in Dominique Lestel, *L'animal est l'avenir de l'homme: Munitions pour ceux qui veulent (toujours) défendre les animaux* (Paris: Fayard, 2010), pp. 143ff.

44. Lestel, *Apologie du carnivore*, p. 94f.; see also Lestel, *L'animal est l'avenir de l'homme*, pp. 111, 134.

45. Lestel, *Apologie du carnivore*, pp. 125, 122, 85.

46. Ibid., pp. 112, 16; see also p. 70. Lestel stresses this "metabolic" identity or continuity of all life throughout *Apologie du carnivore*.

47. Ibid., pp. 121, 129f., 43, 63, 60. See p. 57: in this respect, "it is thus the vegetarian who is speciesist, not the carnivore."

48. Ibid., pp. 46, 80, 77.

49. Ibid., pp. 56f., 70, 132.

50. Ibid., pp. 48, 49, 51, 52 (citing the botanist Anthony Trewawas and the anthropologist Jeremy Narby).

51. See Lestel, *L'animal est l'avenir de l'homme*, ch. 1.

52. Oliver, *Animal Lessons*, p. 77.

53. Aristotle, *History of Animals* at 588a7ff.

54. John R. Searle, "The Explanation of Cognition," in *Thought and Language*, Royal Institute of Philosophy Supplement 42, ed. John Preston (Cambridge: Cambridge University Press, 1997), p. 123f.

55. Natalie Angier, "Sorry, Vegans: Brussels Sprouts Like to Live, Too," *New York Times*, December 21, 2009, http://www.nytimes.com/2009/12/22/science/22angi.html?ref=science.

56. Lestel, *Apologie du carnivore*, p. 120.

57. See ibid., pp. 104, 126; *L'animal est l'avenir de l'homme*, p. 136.

58. See chapter 3.

59. Aristotle, *Politics*, Book 1, chap. 8 at 1255b39.

60. Noëlle Châtelet, *Le corps à corps culinaire* (Paris: Éditions du Seuil, 1998), pp. 10, 16.

61. Pascal Ory, "La Gastronomie," in *Les Lieux de Mémoire: Les Frances*, vol. 3, ed. Pierre Nora (Paris: Gallimard, 1992), p. 828f.

62. Châtelet, *Le corps à corps culinaire*, p. 31.

63. Michel de Montaigne, "De la Vanité des paroles," *Essais, Tome I* (Paris: Éditions Garnier Frères, 1962), p. 339; Dick Humelbergius Secundus, *Apician Morsels, Gusto: Essential Writings in Nineteenth Century Gastronomy*, ed. Denise Gigante (New York: Routledge, 2005), p. 180.

64. Aristotle, *Nicomachean Ethics*, Book 10, chap. 5 at 1175a28ff., 1176a1ff., 2.1858; chap. 8 at 1178b23ff.

65. John Stuart Mill, *Utilitarianism, On Liberty and Other Essays*, ed. John Gray (Oxford: Oxford University Press, 1998), p. 138. See also Steiner, *Anthropocentrism and Its Discontents*, pp. 164–66.

66. Mill, *Utilitarianism, On Liberty and Other Essays*, p. 140.

67. Jean Anthèlme Brillat-Savarin, *Physiologie du goût: Méditations de gastronomie transcendentale* (Paris: Elibron Classics, 2005), p. 9.

68. Pascal Ory, *Le Discours gastronomique français des origines à nos jours* (Paris: Gallimard, 1998), p. 34.

69. Jean-Robert Pitte, *French Gastronomy: The History and Geography of a Passion*, trans. Jody Gladding (New York: Columbia University Press, 2002), p. 7, 9.

70. Brillat-Savarin, *Physiologie du goût*, pp. 47f., 160.

71. Ibid., pp. 147, 308, 259.

72. Pitte, *French Gastronomy*, p. 147.

73. Alexandre Balthazar Laurent Grimod de la Renyière, *Écrits gastronomiques*, ed. Jean-Claude Bonnet (Paris: Union Générale d'Éditions/Bibliotheque 10/18, 1978), p. 125f.

74. Porphyry, *On Abstinence* 3.20.3, *The Hellenistic Philosophers*, 54P.

75. Grimod de la Renyière, *Écrits gastronomiques*, p. 158f.

76. Pitte, *French Gastronomy*, p. 55.

77. Ory uses this term, although not with specific reference to Barthes. Pascal Ory, *La raison gourmande: Philosophie du goût* (Paris: Grasset, 1995), p. 158.

78. Roland Barthes, *Mythologies*, trans. Annette Lavers (New York: Hill and Wang, 1972), p. 62f, 78. Cf. p. 59: wine provides "a foundation for a collective morality, within which everything is redeemed."

79. Ibid., p. 79.

80. Roland Barthes, *Empire of Signs*, trans. Richard Howard (New York: Hill and Wang, 1982), pp. 18, 15f., 18.

81. Marcela Iacub, *Confessions d'une mangeuse de viande: Pourquoi je ne suis plus carnivore* (Paris: Fayard, 2011), pp. 99ff., 135.

BIBLIOGRAPHY

Agamben, Giorgio. *The Open: Man and Animal*. Trans. Kevin Attell. Stanford: Stanford University Press, 2004.

Angier, Natalie. "Sorry, Vegans: Brussels Sprouts Like to Live, Too." *New York Times*, December 21, 2009. http://www.nytimes.com/2009/12/22/science/22angi.html?ref=science.

Appiah, Kwame Anthony. *Cosmopolitanism: Ethics in a World of Strangers*. New York: Norton, 2006.

Aquinas, Saint Thomas. *Basic Writings of St. Thomas Aquinas*. 2 vols. Ed. Anton C. Pegis. Indianapolis: Hackett, 1997.

Aristotle. *The Complete Works of Aristotle*. 2 vols. Revised Oxford translation. Ed. Jonathan Barnes. Princeton: Bollingen/Princeton University Press, 1995.

Augustine, Saint. *The Catholic and Manichaean Ways of Life*. Trans. Donald A. Gallagher and Idella J. Gallagher. Fathers of the Church, vol. 56. Washington, D.C.: Catholic University of America Press, 1966.

———. *On Free Choice of the Will*. Trans. Thomas Williams. Indianapolis: Hackett, 1993.

Bacon, Francis. *The New Organon*. Ed. Lisa Jardine and Michael Silverthorne. Cambridge: Cambridge University Press, 2000.

Barthes, Roland. *Empire of Signs*. Trans. Richard Howard. New York: Hill and Wang, 1982.

———. *Mythologies*. Trans. Annette Lavers. New York: Hill and Wang, 1972.

Baudelaire, Charles. *Oeuvres complètes*, volume 2. Paris: Gallimard/Pléiade, 1976.

Beiser, Frederick C., ed. *The Early Political Writings of the German Romantics*. Cambridge: Cambridge University Press, 1996.

Bekoff, Marc. *Minding Animals: Awareness, Emotions, and Heart*. Oxford: Oxford University Press, 2002.

Bekoff, Marc, and Jessica Pierce. *Wild Justice: The Moral Lives of Animals*. Chicago: University of Chicago Press, 2009.

Benhabib, Seyla. *Another Cosmopolitanism*. Oxford: Oxford University Press, 2006.

——. *The Rights of Others: Aliens, Residents, and Citizens*. Cambridge: Cambridge University Press, 2004.

——. *Situating the Self: Gender, Community, and Postmodernism in Contemporary Ethics*. New York: Routledge, 1992.

Benjamin, Walter. *Illuminations*. Ed. Hannah Arendt. New York: Schocken Books, 1968.

Bentham, Jeremy. *Introduction to the Principles of Morals and Legislation*. New York: Hafner/Macmillan, 1948.

Bernstein, Richard J. *The New Constellation: The Ethical-Political Horizons of Modernity/Postmodernity*. Cambridge: M.I.T. Press, 1991.

Bouveresse, Jacques. *Le philosophe chez les autophages*. Paris: Les Éditions de Minuit, 1984.

Brillat-Savarin, Jean Anthèlme. *Physiologie du goût. Méditations de gastronomie transcendentale*. Paris: Elibron Classics, 2005.

Butler, Judith. "Antigone's Claim: A Conversation with Judith Butler." *Theory and Event* 12.1 (2009). http://muse.jhu.edu/journals/theory_and_event/vo12/12.1.antonello.html.

——. "For a Careful Reading." In *Feminist Contentions: A Philosophical Exchange*. Ed. Seyla Benhabib et. al., 127–43. New York: Routledge, 1995.

——. *Precarious Life: The Powers of Mourning and Violence*. London: Verso, 2006.

Calarco, Matthew. *Zoographies: The Question of the Animal from Heidegger to Derrida*. New York: Columbia University Press, 2008.

Callicott, J. Baird. "Animal Liberation: A Triangular Affair." In *The Animal Rights/Environmental Ethics Debate: The Environmental Perspective*. Ed. Eugene C. Hargrove, 37–69. Albany: SUNY Press, 1992.

Caputo, John. *Against Ethics: Contributions to a Poetics of Obligation with Constant Reference to Deconstruction*. Bloomington: Indiana University Press, 1993.

Carruthers, Peter. *The Animals Issue: Moral Theory in Practice*. Cambridge: Cambridge University Press, 1992.

Cavalieri, Paola. *The Death of the Animal: A Dialogue*. New York: Columbia University Press, 2009.

Cavell, Stanley, Cora Diamond, John McDowell, Ian Hacking, and Cary Wolfe. *Philosophy and Animal Life*. New York: Columbia University Press, 2008.

Châtelet, Noëlle. *Le corps à corps culinaire*. Paris: Éditions du Seuil, 1998.

Cheah, Pheng, and Bruce Robbins, eds. *Cosmopolitics: Thinking and Feeling Beyond the Nation*. Minneapolis: University of Minnesota Press, 1998.

Cicero. *De finibus bonorum et malorum*. Latin-English. Trans. H. Rackham. Cambridge: Harvard University Press, 1999.

Coetzee, J. M. *The Lives of Animals*. Ed. Amy Gutman. Princeton: Princeton University Press, 1999.

Connolly, William E. *Identity\Difference: Democratic Negotiations of Political Paradox*. Ithaca: Cornell University Press, 1991.

Cornell, Drucilla. "Post-Structuralism, the Ethical Relation and the Law." In *Deconstruction: A Reader*. Ed. Martin McQuillan, 443–49. New York: Routledge, 2001.

Derrida, Jacques. *The Animal That Therefore I Am*. Ed. Marie-Louise Mallet. Trans. David Wills. New York: Fordham University Press, 2008.

——. *The Beast and the Sovereign*. Volume I. Ed. Michel Lisse, Marie-Louise Mallet, and Ginette Michaud. Trans. Geoffrey Bennington. Chicago: University of Chicago Press, 2009.

——. "'Eating Well', or the Calculation of the Subject: An Interview with Jacques Derrida." In *Who Comes After the Subject?* Ed. Eduardo Cadava, Peter Connor, and Jean-Luc Nancy, 96–119. New York: Routledge, 1991..

——. "Force of Law: The 'Mystical Foundation of Authority'." *Cardozo Law Review* 11 (1989–90): 920–1045.

——. "Geschlecht II: Heidegger's Hand." In *Deconstruction and Philosophy: The Texts of Derrida*. Ed. John Sallis. Chicago: University of Chicago Press, 1987.

——. "Hospitality, Justice and Responsibility: A Dialogue with Jacques Derrida." In *Questioning Ethics: Contemporary Debates in Philosophy*. Ed. Richard Kearney and Mark Dooley, 65–83. London: Routledge, 1999.

——. *Limited Inc*. Evanston: Northwestern University Press, 1997.

——. *Margins of Philosophy*. Trans. Alan Bass. Chicago: University of Chicago Press, 1982.

——. "Mochlos, ou le conflit des facultés." *Philosophie* 2 (April 1984): 21–53.

——. *Of Grammatology*. Trans. Gayatri Chakravorty Spivak. Baltimore: Johns Hopkins University Press, 1976.

——. *On Cosmopolitanism and Forgiveness*. Trans. Mark Dooley and Michael Hughes. London: Routledge, 2001.

———. "The Politics of Friendship." *Journal of Philosophy* 85 (1988): 632–44.

———. *Positions*. Trans. Alan Bass. Chicago: University of Chicago Press, 1982.

———. "Racism's Last Word." *Critical Inquiry* 12 (1995): 290–99.

———. *Rogues: Two Essays on Reason*. Trans. Pascale-Anne Brault and Michael Naas. Stanford: Stanford University Press, 2005.

———. *Seminaire. La bête et le souverain*. Volume 2. Paris: Galilée, 2010.

———. *Writing and Difference*. Trans. Alan Bass. Chicago: University of Chicago Press, 1978.

Derrida, Jacques, and Elizabeth Roudinescu. "Violence Against Animals." In *For What Tomorrow . . . A Dialogue*. Trans. Jeff Fort, 62–76. Stanford: Stanford University Press, 2004.

Descartes, René. *The Philosophical Writings of Descartes*. Volumes 1–3. Trans. John Cottingham et. al. Cambridge: Cambridge University Press, 1984, 1985, 1991.

Descombes, Vincent. *Modern French Philosophy*. Trans. L. Scott-Fox and J. M. Harding. Cambridge: Cambridge University Press, 1998.

Diamond, Cora. "The Difficulty of Reality and the Difficulty of Philosophy." In *Philosophy and Animal Life*. Ed. Stanley Cavell et. al., 43–89 New York: Columbia University Press, 2008.

———. "Eating Meat and Eating People." In *Animal Rights: Current Debates and New Directions*. Ed. Cass R. Sunstein and Martha C. Nussbaum. Oxford: Oxford University Press, 2004. Pp. 93–107.

———. "Injustice and Animals." In *Slow Cures and Bad Philosophers: Essays on Wittgenstein, Medicine, and Bioethics*. Ed. Carl Elliott, 118–48. Durham: Duke University Press, 2001.

Diogenes Laertius. *Lives of the Eminent Philosophers*. Volume 2. Trans. R. D. Hicks. Cambridge: Loeb/Harvard University Press, 2000.

Dosse, François. *History of Structuralism*. Volume 1: *The Rising Sign, 1945–66*. Trans. Deborah Glassman. Minneapolis: University of Minnesota Press, 1998.

Dworkin, Ronald. "The Court's Embarrassingly Bad Decisions." *New York Review of Books* vol. 58, no. 9 (May 26, 2011): 40–41.

Epictetus. *The Discourses as Reported by Arrian, Books I-II*. Greek-English. Trans. W. A. Oldfather. Cambridge: Harvard University Press, 2000.

Epstein, Richard A. "Animals as Objects, or Subjects, of Rights." In *Animal Rights: Current Debates and New Directions*. Ed. Cass R. Sunstein and Martha C. Nussbaum, 143–61. Oxford: Oxford University Press, 2004.

Ferry, Luc, and Alain Renaut. *Why We Are Not Nietzscheans*. Trans. Robert de Loaiza. Chicago: University of Chicago Press, 1997.

Foer, Jonathan Safran. *Eating Animals*. New York: Little, Brown, 2008.

Fontenay, Elisabeth de. "Pourquoi les animaux n'auraient-ils pas droit à un droit des animaux?" *Le Debat* 109 (2000): 138–55.

Foucault, Michel. *The Foucault Reader*. Ed. Paul Rabinow. New York: Pantheon Books, 1984.

———. *The History of Sexuality*. Volume 1: *An Introduction*. Trans. Robert Hurley. New York: Vintage Books, 1980.

———. *The Order of Things: An Archaeology of the Human Sciences*. New York: Vintage Books, 1973.

Fox, Michael Allen. *Deep Vegetarianism*. Philadelphia: Temple University Press, 1999.

Francione, Gary L. *Animals as Persons: Essays on the Abolition of Animal Exploitation*. New York: Columbia University Press, 2008.

———. *Animals, Property, and the Law*. Philadelphia: Temple University Press, 1995.

———. *Introduction to Animal Rights: Your Child or the Dog?* Philadelphia: Temple University Press, 2005.

———. *Rain Without Thunder: The Ideology of the Animal Rights Movement*. Philadelphia: Temple University Press, 1996.

Francione, Gary L., and Robert Garner. *The Animal Rights Debate: Abolition or Regulation?* New York: Columbia University Press, 2010.

Frank, Manfred. *What Is Neostructuralism?* Trans. Sabine Wilke and Richard Gray. Minneapolis: University of Minnesota Press, 1989.

Gadamer, Hans-Georg. *Philosophical Apprenticeships*. Trans. Robert R. Sullivan. Cambridge: M.I.T. Press, 1985.

George, Kathryn Paxton. "A Feminist Critique of Ethical Vegetarianism." In *The Animal Ethics Reader*. Ed. Susan J. Armstrong and Richard G. Botzler, 216–21. London: Routledge, 2003.

Gigante, Denise, ed. *Gusto: Essential Writings in Nineteenth Century Gastronomy*. New York/London: Routledge, 2005.

Grimod de la Renyière, Alexandre Balthazar Laurent. *Écrits gastronomiques*. Ed. Jean-Claude Bonnet. Paris: Union générale d'éditions/Bibliotheque 10/18, 1978.

Habermas, Jürgen. *The Philosophical Discourse of Modernity: Twelve Lectures*. Trans. Frederick G. Lawrence. Cambridge: M.I.T. Press, 1990.

Harvey, David. *Cosmopolitanism and the Geographies of Freedom*. New York: Columbia University Press, 2009.

Hatley, James. "The Uncanny Goodness of Being Edible to Bears." In *Rethinking Nature: Essays in Environmental Philosophy*. Ed. Bruce V. Foltz and Robert Frodeman, 13–31. Bloomington: Indiana University Press, 2004.

Hayek, F. A. *The Road to Serfdom: Text and Documents*. Ed. Bruce Caldwell. Chicago: University of Chicago Press, 2007.

Hegel, Georg Wilhelm Friedrich. *Introductory Lectures on Aesthetics*. Trans. Bernard Bosanquet. London: Penguin, 1993.

Heidegger, Martin. *The Basic Problems of Phenomenology*. Trans. Albert Hofstadter. Bloomington: Indiana University Press, 1982.

——. *Being and Time*. Trans. John MacQuarrie and Edward Robinson. New York: Harper and Row, 1962.

——. *Discourse on Thinking*. Trans. John M. Anderson and E. Hans Freund. New York: Harper Torchbooks, 1969.

——. *Die Grundbegriffe der Metaphysik: Welt-Endlichkeit-Einsamkeit*. Gesamtausgabe. Volume 29/30. Frankfurt: Klostermann, 1983.

——. *An Introduction to Metaphysics*. Trans. Ralph Manheim. New Haven: Yale University Press, 1980.

——. *Logik: Die Frage nach der Wahrheit*. Gesamtausgabe. Volume 21. Frankfurt-am-Main: Klostermann, 1976.

——. *On the Way to Language*. Trans. Peter D. Hertz. San Francisco: Harper and Row, 1971.

——. *Pathmarks*. Ed. William McNeill. Cambridge: Cambridge University Press, 1998.

——. *Parmenides*. Gesamtausgabe. Volume 54. Frankfurt: Klostermann, 1982.

——. *Poetry, Language, Thought*. Trans. Albert Hofstadter. New York: Perennial Classics/HarperCollins, 2001.

——. *The Question Concerning Technology and Other Essays*. Trans. William Lovitt. New York: Harper Torchbooks, 1977.

——. *Schellings Abhandlung über das Wesen der menschlichen Freiheit (1809)*. Ed. Hildegard Feick. Tübingen: Niemeyer, 1971.

——. *Was heißt Denken?* 4th ed. Tübingen: Niemeyer, 1984.

——. *Was ist das—die Philosophie?* Tübingen: Neske, 1984.

Heinrich, Bernd. "Raven Consciousness." In *The Cognitive Animal: Empirical and Theoretical Perspectives on Animal Cognition*. Ed. Marc Bekoff, Colin Allen, and Gordon M. Burghardt, 47–57. Cambridge: M.I.T. Press, 2002.

Hill, John Lawrence. *The Case for Vegetarianism: Philosophy for a Small Planet.* Lanham, Mass.: Rowman and Littlefield, 1996.

Hume, David. *A Treatise of Human Nature.* 2d ed. Ed. L. A. Selby-Bigge. Oxford: Clarendon Press, 1981.

Hunt, Gavin R., and Russell D. Gray. "Diversification and Cumulative Evolution in New Caledonian Crow Tool Manufacture." In *Proceedings of the Royal Society of London B.* Volume 270 (2003), pp. 867–74.

Husserl, Edmund. *The Crisis of the European Sciences and Transcendental Phenomenology: An Introduction to Phenomenological Philosophy.* Trans. David Carr. Evanston: Northwestern University Press, 1970.

Iacub, Marcela. *Confessions d'une mangeuse de viande: Pourquoi je ne suis plus carnivore.* Paris: Fayard, 2011.

Kant, Immanuel. *Critique of Judgment.* Trans. Werner S. Pluhar. Indianapolis: Hackett, 1987.

——. *Critique of Practical Reason.* 3d ed. Trans. Lewis White Beck. Upper Saddle River, N.J.: Library of Liberal Arts/Prentice Hall, 1993.

——. *Critique of Pure Reason.* Trans. Norman Kemp Smith. New York: Humanities Press, 1950.

——. *Grounding for the Metaphysics of Morals.* Trans. James W. Ellington. Indianapolis: Hackett, 1981.

——. *Lectures on Ethics.* Ed. Peter Heath and J. B. Schneewind. Trans. Peter Heath. Cambridge: Cambridge University Press, 1997.

——. *The Metaphysics of Morals.* Ed. Mary Gregor. Cambridge: Cambridge University Press, 1996.

——. *Political Writings.* Ed. H. S. Reiss. New York: Cambridge, 2001.

Kazez, Jean. *Animalkind: What We Owe to Animals.* Chichester: Wiley-Blackwell, 2010.

——. Blog entry dated December 1, 2009. http://kazez.blogspot.com/search?updated-min=2009–01–01T00%3A00%3A00–06%3A00&updated-max=2010–01–01T00%3A00%3A00–06%3A00&max-results=50.

Kazez, Jean, et. al. "The Ethical Choices in What We Eat." *New York Times,* November 23, 2009. http://www.nytimes.com/2009/11/24/opinion/l24vegan.html?ref=opinion.

Kellogg, Catherine. *Law's Trace: from Hegel to Derrida.* New York: Routledge, 2010.

Kierkegaard, Soren. *Either/Or.* Volume 1. Trans. David F. Swenson and Lillian Marvin Swenson. Princeton: Princeton University Press, 1971.

———. *Fear and Trembling/Repetition.* Ed. Howard V. Hong and Edna H. Hong. Princeton: Princeton University Press, 1983.

Kirk, G. S., and J. E. Raven. *The Presocratic Philosophers: A Critical History with a Selection of Texts.* Cambridge: Cambridge University Press, 1979.

Kluge, Friedrich. *Etymologisches Wörterbuch der deutschen Sprache.* 20th ed. Berlin: Walter de Gruyter, 1967.

Lacan, Jacques. *Écrits: A Selection.* Trans. Alan Sheridan. New York: Norton, 1977.

LaCapra, Dominic. *History and Its Limits: Human, Animal, Violence.* Ithaca: Cornell University Press, 2009.

Lawlor, Leonard. *This Is Not Sufficient: An Essay on Animality and Human Nature in Derrida.* New York: Columbia University Press, 2007.

Leopold, Aldo. *A Sand County Almanac and Sketches Here and There.* New York: Oxford University Press, 1949.

Lestel, Dominique. *L'animal est l'avenir de l'homme: Munitions pour ceux qui veulent (toujours) défendre les animaux.* Paris: Fayard, 2010.

———. *Apologie du carnivore.* Paris: Fayard, 2011.

Levinas, Emmanuel. "The Name of a Dog, or Natural Rights." In *Difficult Freedom: Essays in Judaism,* 151–53. Trans. Seán Hand. Baltimore: Johns Hopkins University Press, 1990.

Locke, John. *An Essay Concerning Human Understanding.* Ed. Peter H. Nidditch. Oxford: Oxford University Press, 1990.

———. *Second Treatise of Government.* Ed. Richard Cox. Arlington Heights, Ill.: Harlan Davidson, 1982.

Long, A. A., and D. N. Sedley, ed. and trans. *The Hellenistic Philosophers.* 2 vols. Cambridge: Cambridge University Press, 1990.

Löwith, Karl. *Martin Heidegger and European Nihilism.* Trans. Gary Steiner. New York: Columbia University Press, 1995.

———. *Meaning in History.* Chicago: Phoenix Books/University of Chicago Press, 1962.

———. *Welt und Menschenwelt: Beiträge zur Anthropologie. Sämtliche Schriften.* Volume 1. Stuttgart: Metzler, 1981.

———. "Der Weltbegriff der neuzeitlichen Philosophie." *Sitzungsberichte der Heidelberger Akademie der Wissenschaften, Philosophisch-historischer Klasse* 44 (1960): 7–23.

Lucretius. *De Rerum Natura V.* Ed. and trans. Monica R. Gale. Oxford: Oxbow Books, 2009.

Lyotard, Jean-François. *The Postmodern Condition: A Report on Knowledge*. Trans. Geoff Bennington and Brian Massumi. Minneapolis: University of Minnesota Press, 1985.

Marx, Karl. *The German Ideology*. In *The Marx-Engels Reader*, 2d ed., ed. Robert C. Tucker. New York: Norton, 1972.

Marx, Werner. *Gibt es auf Erden ein Maß? Grundbestimmungen einer nichtmetaphysischen Ethik*. Hamburg: Felix Meiner Verlag, 1983.

———. *Is There a Measure on Earth? Foundations of a Nonmetaphysical Ethics*. Trans. Thomas J. Nenon and Reginald Lilly. Chicago: University of Chicago Press, 1987.

Mill, John Stuart. *On Liberty and Other Essays*. Ed. John Gray. Oxford/New York: Oxford University Press, 1998.

Montaigne, Michel de. *Essais, Tome I*. Paris: Éditions Garnier Frères, 1962.

Nagel, Thomas. "What Is It Like to Be a Bat?" In *Mortal Questions*. Cambridge: Cambridge University Press, 1979.

Nietzsche, Friedrich. *Basic Writings of Nietzsche*. Trans. Walter Kaufmann. New York: Modern Library, 1992.

———. *Daybreak: Thoughts on the Prejudices of Morality*. Trans. R. J. Hollingdale. Cambridge: Cambridge University Press, 1982.

———. *The Gay Science*. Trans. Walter Kaufmann. New York: Vintage, 1974.

———. *Human, All Too Human: A Book for Free Spirits*. Trans. R. J. Hollingdale. Cambridge: Cambridge University Press, 1987.

———. *Philosophy and Truth: Selections from Nietzsche's Notebooks of the Early 1870's*. Ed. and trans. Daniel Breazeale. Atlantic Highlands, N.J.: Humanities Press International, 1992.

———. *The Portable Nietzsche*. Ed. and trans. Walter Kaufmann. New York: Penguin, 1982.

———. *Thus Spoke Zarathustra: A Book for All and None*. Trans. Walter Kaufmann. New York: Viking Press, 1972.

———. *Untimely Meditations*. Trans. R. J. Hollingdale. Cambridge: Cambridge University Press, 1987.

———. *The Will to Power*. Trans. Walter Kaufmann and R. J. Hollingdale. New York: Vintage, 1968.

Nussbaum, Martha C. *Cultivating Humanity: A Classical Defense of Reform in Liberal Education*. Cambridge: Harvard University Press, 1997.

———. *Frontiers of Justice: Disability, Nationality, Species Membership*. Cambridge: Belknap/Harvard University Press, 2006.

———. "Patriotism and Cosmopolitanism." In *For Love of Country: Defining the Limits of Patriotism*. Ed. Joshua Cohen, 2–17. Boston: Beacon Press, 1996.

Oliver, Kelly. *Animal Lessons: How They Teach Us to Be Human*. New York: Columbia University Press, 2009.

Ory, Pascal. *Le Discours gastronomique français des origines à nos jours*. Paris: Gallimard, 1998.

———. "La Gastronomie." In *Les Lieux de Mémoire: Les Frances*. Volume 3. Ed. Pierre Nora, 822–53. Paris: Gallimard, 1992.

———. *La raison gourmande: Philosophie du goût*. Paris: Grasset, 1995.

Ovid. *Metamorphoses*. 2 vols. Latin-English. Trans. Frank Justus Miller. Cambridge: Harvard University Press, 1977.

Palmer, Clare. *Animal Ethics in Context*. New York: Columbia University Press, 2010.

Pitte, Jean-Robert. *French Gastronomy: The History and Geography of a Passion*. Trans. Jody Gladding. New York: Columbia University Press, 2002.

Pollan, Michael. *The Omnivore's Dilemma: A Natural History of Four Meals*. New York: Penguin, 2006.

Porphyry. *On Abstinence from Killing Animals*. Trans. Gillian Clark. Ithaca: Cornell University Press, 2000.

Posner, Richard A. "Animal Rights: Legal, Philosophical, and Pragmatic Perspectives." In *Animal Rights: Current Debates and New Directions*. Ed. Cass R. Sunstein and Martha C. Nussbaum, 51–77. Oxford: Oxford University Press, 2004.

Rabinow, Paul. "Representations are Social Facts: Modernity and Post-Modernity in Anthropology." In *Writing Culture: The Poetics and Politics of Ethnography*. Ed. James Clifford and George E. Marcus, 234–61. Berkeley: University of California Press, 1986.

Radhakrishnan, R. "Minority Theory, Re-Visited." *CR: The New Centennial Review*, vol. 6, no. 2 (2006): 39–55.

Rawls, John. *A Theory of Justice*. Revised ed. Cambridge: Belknap/Harvard University Press, 1999.

Raz, Joseph. *The Authority of Law*. 2d ed. Oxford: Oxford University Press, 2009.

Regan, Tom. *The Case for Animal Rights*. Berkeley: University of California Press, 1983.

Rilke, Rainer Maria. *Duineser Elegien, Die Gedichte*. Frankfurt am Main: Insel, 2006.

Ristau, Carolyn A. "Aspects of the Cognitive Ethology of an Injury-Feigning Bird." In *Readings in Cognitive Ethology*. Ed. Marc Bekoff and Dale Jamieson, 79–89. Cambridge: M.I.T. Press, 1996.

Rorty, Richard. *Philosophy and the Mirror of Nature*. Princeton: Princeton University Press, 1979.

Rousseau, Jean-Jacques. *Rousseau's Political Writings*. Ed. Alan Ritter and Julia Conway Bondanella. New York: Norton, 1988.

Sartre, Jean-Paul. *Being and Nothingness*. Trans. Hazel Barnes. New York: Pocket Books, 1978.

Saussure, Ferdinand de. *Course in General Linguistics*. Ed. Charles Bally and Albert Sechehaye. New York: Philosophical Library, 1959.

Schmitt, Carl. *The Concept of the Political*. Trans. George Schwab. Chicago: University of Chicago Press, 1996.

——. *Political Theology: Four Chapters on the Concept of Sovereignty*. Trans. George Schwab. Chicago: University of Chicago Press, 2005.

Schopenhauer, Arthur. *On the Basis of Morality*. Trans. E. F. J. Payne. Providence: Berghahn Books, 1995.

——. *Parerga and Paralipomena*. Volume 2. Trans. E. F. J. Payne. Oxford: Clarendon Press, 2000.

——. *The World as Will and Representation*. Volume 1. Trans. E. F. J. Payne. Indian Hills, Colo.: Falcon's Wing Press, 1958.

——. *The World as Will and Representation*. Volume 2. Trans. E. F. J. Payne. New York: Dover, 1958.

Schupbach, William. *The Paradox of Rembrandt's 'Anatomy Lesson of Dr. Tulp'*. Medical History, Supplement No. 2. London: Wellcome Institute for the History of Medicine, 1982.

Searle, John R. "The Explanation of Cognition." In *Thought and Language*. Royal Institute of Philosophy Supplement 42. Ed. John Preston, 103–26. Cambridge: Cambridge University Press, 1997.

Seneca. *Ad lucilium epistulae morales.*, Volume 3. Latin-English. Trans. Richard M. Gummere. London: William Heinemann/New York: G. P. Putnam's Sons, 1925.

Shelton, Jo-Ann. "Lucretius on the Use and Abuse of Animals." *Eranos* 94 (1996): 48–64.

Simpson, Lorenzo C. *The Unfinished Project: Toward a Postmetaphysical Humanism*. New York: Routledge, 2001.

Singer, Isaac Bashevis. *The Collected Stories of Isaac Bashevis Singer*. New York: Farrar, Straus, and Giroux, 1982.

Singer, Peter. *Animal Liberation*. Updated ed. New York: Harper Perennial, 2009.

——. *Practical Ethics*. 2d ed. Cambridge: Cambridge University Press, 2010.

Sorabji, Richard J. *Animal Minds and Human Morals: The Origins of the Western Debate*. Ithaca: Cornell University Press, 1993.

Sousa Santos, Boaventura de, and César A. Rodríguez-Garavito, eds. *Law and Globalization from Below: Towards a Cosmopolitan Legality*. Cambridge: Cambridge University Press, 2005.

Steiner, Gary. "Animal, Vegetable, Miserable." Week in Review, *New York Times*, November 22, 2009, p. 12.

——. *Animals and the Moral Community: Mental Life, Moral Status, and Kinship*. New York: Columbia University Press, 2008.

——. *Anthropocentrism and Its Discontents: The Moral Status of Animals in the History of Western Philosophy*. Pittsburgh: University of Pittsburgh Press, 2005.

——. *Descartes as a Moral Thinker: Christianity, Technology, Nihilism*. Amherst, N.Y.: Prometheus/Humanity Books, 2004.

——. "The Perils of a Total Critique of Reason: Rethinking Heidegger's Influence." *Philosophy Today* 47 (2003): 93–111.

Taylor, Paul W. *Respect for Nature: A Theory of Environmental Ethics*. Princeton: Princeton University Press, 1986.

Thomas, Yan. "Le sujet de droit, la personne et la nature." *Le Débat* 100 (May–August, 1998):85–107.

Tucker, Robert C., ed. *The Marx-Engels Reader*. 2d ed. New York/London: Norton, 1972.

Waal, Frans de, Robert Wright, Christine M. Korsgaard, Philip Kitcher, and Peter Singer. *Primates and Philosophers: How Morality Evolved*. Princeton: Princeton University Press, 2006.

Warren, Mary Anne. "The Rights of the Nonhuman World." In *The Animal Rights/Environmental Ethics Debate: The Environmental Perspective*. Ed. Eugene C. Hargrove, 185–210. Albany: SUNY Press, 1992.

Watson, Richard A. "Self-Consciousness and the Rights of Nonhuman Animals and Nature." In *The Animal Rights/Environmental Ethics Debate: The Environmental Perspective*. Ed. Eugene C. Hargrove, 1–35. Albany: SUNY Press, 1992.

Weil, Simone. "Human Personality." In *Simone Weil: An Anthology*. Ed. Siân Miles, 49–78. New York: Weidenfeld & Nicolson, 1986.

White, Stephen K. *Political Theory and Postmodernism*. Cambridge: Cambridge University Press, 2009.

Wolfe, Cary. *Animal Rites: American Culture, the Discourse of Species, and Posthumanist Theory.* Chicago: University of Chicago Press, 2003.

Wolin, Richard. *Labyrinths: Explorations in the Critical History of Ideas.* Amherst: University of Massachusetts Press, 1995.

———. *The Seduction of Unreason: The Intellectual Romance with Fascism from Nietzsche to Postmodernism.* Princeton: Princeton University Press, 2004.

———. *The Terms of Cultural Criticism: The Frankfurt School, Existentialism, Poststructuralism.* New York: Columbia University Press, 1992.

Wood, David. "*Comment ne pas manger*—Deconstruction and Humanism." In *Animal Others: On Ethics, Ontology, and Animal Life.* Ed. H. Peter Steeves, 15–35. Albany: SUNY Press, 1999.

———. *The Step Back: Ethics and Politics After Deconstruction.* Albany: State University of New York Press, 2005.

Wright, Tamra, Peter Hughes, and Alison Ainsley. "The Paradox of Morality: An Interview with Emmanuel Levinas." In *The Provocation of Levinas: Rethinking the Other.* Ed. Robert Bernasconi and David Wood, 168–81. London: Routledge, 1988.

Young, Iris Marion. *Justice and the Politics of Difference.* Princeton: Princeton University Press, 1990.

INDEX

Abraham, 49, 50, 63f., 70f., 74, 122
Agamben, Giorgio, 90f.
agency: Aristotle on the question of in
    animals, 91; Butler on, 247n13; Der-
    rida on, 89, 114, 125f.; as a grammatical
    notion, 23; Heidegger on lack of in
    animals, 103; lack of in plants, 222;
    Levinas on the question of in animals,
    84; Nietzsche's critique of, 23, 26, 38,
    40f.; traditional conception of, 2, 4, 22,
    112, 133f., 147, 156f., 177, 222
Aristotle: on cognitive abilities of ani-
    mals, 82, 89, 91, 99, 103, 110, 139, 197,
    228; on language, 16, 18, 108; on moral
    status of animals, 82, 91, 169f., 197, 228
as such: Derrida's critique of, 89, 113,
    117f., 120, 122; Heidegger on the
    exclusively human possession of,
    102–112, 178f.

Barthes, Roland, 227, 230f.
Bekoff, Marc, 94, 145, 207
Benhabib, Seyla, 187–190
Bentham, Jeremy: anthropocentrism in,
    83f., 198f., 207; on suffering as the
    basis for moral status, 82, 120
Bernstein, Richard: on the ethical moti-
    vations underlying deconstruction 48,
    157; on the limits of Derrida's thought,

72f.; on the need to warrant ethical
    decisions, 50, 157
Bouveresse, Jacques, 11
Brillat-Savarin, 227–229
Butler, Judith, 80, 205

Calarco, Matthew, 85f., 90, 97f., 115, 120,
    127
Carruthers, Peter, 92f.
Christianity: eschatology in, 13, 35, 37;
    idea of soul in, 23–25; moral status of
    animals in, 171f.
compassion: Derrida on, 83, 120f., 124,
    127, 130; Diamond on, 159, 162f.;
    evidence of in animals, 94f.; Kant on,
    173; Lawlor on, 148, 155; Lestel on, 219;
    Nietzsche's critique of, 30; role of in
    establishing moral obligations toward
    animals, 87, 120f., 127, 129, 201; Scho-
    penhauer on, 17
contractualism: in Carruthers, 92; central
    tenets of, 199 ; critique of, 201; in
    Rawls, 43. *See also* justice
cosmopolitanism: Appiah on, 186f.;
    Benhabib on, 187–190; Derrida
    on, 80; Diogenes Laertius on, 196;
    Harvey on, 192; Held on, 189, Kant's
    conception of, 37, 75, 172–175;
    Löwith's conception of, 75, 129, 176f.;

cosmopolitanism (*continued*)
nonanthropocentric, 196; Nussbaum
on, 183–186; Rabinow on, 191; Rawls
on, 169; Schmitt's critique of, 34; Stoic
conception of, 75, 168–171.
Costello, Elizabeth, 147, 159, 165, 244n75
critique of reason, immanent versus
total, 61, 147, 152f., 156f., 204, 244n64

death: Agamben on, 90; Derrida on in
animals, 88f., 114, 116, 118, 178; Heidegger on deprivation of in animals,
116f., 122; Heidegger's existential
conception of, 102f., 105f., 110, 116,
178f.; inevitability of as justification
for killing animals, 83, 146, 207f.;
reality of in animals, 165, 198, 206f.;
Rilke on the animal's freedom from,
104; traditional view that death is less
grave in animals than in humans, 185,
207f., 230
decisionism: Fontenay on, 260n58;
Hayek's critique of, 154; Schmitt on,
153; problem of in postmodernism,
34f., 41, 60f., 114, 118. *See also* exception,
politics of
différance. See Derrida
Derrida, Jacques: ambivalence about
rights, 149f., 152; on animot, 122f.; on
apartheid, 61f., 72; on *différance*, 49, 55,
59, 64; critique of Lacan, 89f.; critique
of traditional metaphysics, 54; critique
of the traditional conception of
language, 9, 56; critique of traditional
conception of universals, 62, 67, 151;
deconstruction of traditional binary
oppositions, 85, 114–116, 121, 125f.,
140; desire to distance himself from
Schmitt, 114, 153; evasion of vegetarianism and veganism, 3, 47, 126–128,
151, 178f., 210; on groundlessness

of sovereignty, 73; on Kierkegaard's
Abraham, 49; on limitrophy, 88, 123;
on responsibility, 65; on the trace, 68,
210; on the undecidability of meaning,
46, 51f., 60, 64, 81
Descartes, René: on animals, 93, 99, 109,
111, 126, 180; conception of language,
16, 56; conception of mind or soul in,
24f., 55, 59, 101; on the extra-rational
origin of ethical commitments,
245n105; ideal of clarity and distinctness, 4, 38, 40, 51; on method, 209;
provisional morality, 48
Descombes, Vincent, 8, 33, 39
Diamond, Cora, 158–166
duties: direct versus indirect, 172f., 174;
Porphyry on, 181f.; Schopenhauer on,
43; toward animals, 14f., 43, 142f., 160,
177, 195, 208, 226

Epstein, Richard, 135f., 141f., 144f.
eschatology, 10, 13, 35f., 37
ethics, feel-good, 3, 146, 211f.
exception, politics of: in Carl Schmitt,
34f., 37, 74, 153; in Derrida, 114, 153;
Dworkin's critique of, 154; Hayek's critique of, 153; in Kierkegaard, 70f., 74;
Löwith's critique of, 34; in Nietzsche,
37f., 74; in postmodernism, 34. *See also*
decisionism; singularity
exceptionalism, human: Carruthers's
defense of, 92; Heidegger's defense of,
112, 117; Lestel's critique of, 219f., 224;
postmodern critique of traditional
claim of, 1, 118, 224, 231; terms of traditional claim of, 92, 124, 224, 228

Fontenay, Elisabeth de 166, 260n58
Foucault, Michel: on Baudelaire, 36, 39,
240n98; decisionistic implications
of, 38; on genealogical method, 38;

on *Herkunft* versus *Ursprung*, 39; on the
fundamentally polemical character of
discourse, 40, 50, 72, 165, 190; and
poststructuralism, 233n7; on the prospects for liberation, 4, 235n9
Francione, Gary: critique of welfarism,
145, 214f.; on equal consideration of
interests, 45f., 206; on the impossibility of mathematical certainty in moral
judgment, 201; on moral schizophrenia,
96, 141, 196; on the need to abolish
the property status of animals, 45, 145;
rejection of similar-minds theory, 148
friendship: Aristotle on, 181; Derrida on,
67f.; Kant on, 173, 181; Lawlor on, 148,
155; Porphyry on, 181

golden age story, 11, 168, 181, 199
grammar: as the determining basis of justice, 158, 161; subjectivity as a matter
of, 23f.; of representation, 193; virtue
as a matter of, 237n49
Grimod de la Renière, Alexandre Balthazar Laurent, 227, 229f.

Hatley, James, 216f.
Hayek, Friedrich, 27, 153f.
Heidegger, Martin: on the 'as' structure
of understanding, 107f., 112, 117f.; on
contemplative versus calculative thinking, 53f., 60, 62f., 78, 170; critique of
the traditional notion of essence, 52f.,
66; on ethics, 31f., 75, 78, 177; existential conception of death, 103–106, 110,
116f., 178; on human ek-sistence, 101f.;
on letting beings be, 62f., 65, 166, 179;
on the open, 103–105, on *physis*, 53; on
the world-poverty of animals, 46, 69,
107, 109–112, 179
Hesiod, 11f., 15, 29, 32, 43, 138, 168, 199,
226

holism, cosmic, 194f., 200, 213, 215f., 224,
226. *See also* kinship
Holocaust: analogy between animal
exploitation and, 63, 127, 159, 204;
Elizabeth Costello on 159, 244n75
humanism, postmodern critique of, 1–5,
11, 62, 96f., 113, 151f., 155f., 167, 219,
224

Iacub, Marcela, 231
imperative, vegan. *See* veganism

justice: contractualist conception of,
11, 199f.; cosmic, 2, 14f., 17, 43, 160,
177, 180, 183, 194f., 197, 201, 203;
Derrida on, 8, 61, 66f., 80, 86, 97,
151; Diamond on, 158, 162; duties of,
toward animals, 194; Epicurus on, 43;
golden age story and the advent of,
11f., 15, 225; Nietzsche on, 11, 30, 33,
147; Nussbaum on, 184f.; Porphyry
on, 1, 180f.; postmodern *aporia* of, 4.
7f., 32, 44, 49, 72, 82; Rawls on, 43,
168f., 184; Schopenhauer on 14f., 43,
160; Stoic conception of, 15, 168, 171;
de Waal on, 95f.; Weil on, 158, 161;
Young on, 194. *See also* contractualism;
cosmopolitanism

Kant, Immanuel: on cosmopolitanism,
37, 51, 75, 80, 167, 172–175, 184; on
enlightenment, 35, 37, 149, 172; on
friendship, 173, 181; on indirect duties,
173; on justice, 167; on morality, 31,
64f., 174f., 177; on the moral status
of animals, 172f.; on representation
in animals, 109; on things versus
persons, 126; on what can be known,
16, 40, 55f.
Kierkegaard, Soren, 49f., 62, 70f., 106,
125, 246n111

kinship: as basis for moral obligations toward animals, 5, 75, 129, 138, 149, 154f., 166, 181, 195, 206, 209f., 213, 215, 223; Brillat-Savarin's anthropocentric conception of, 229; Derrida on, 120; Heidegger's denial of between human beings and nonhuman animals, 112; Lestel on, 219; Porphyry on, 181, 183; rooted in affect rather than reason, 138; Schopenhauer on, 160; Stoic denial of between humans and animals, 195, 197. *See also* holism; cosmic

Kojève, Alexandre, 39

Lacan, Jacques: Derrida's critique of, 89f.; on the distinction between reaction and response, 113; on *logos* as basis for moral status, 4

LaCapra, Dominic, 152f.

language: Aristotle on, 16, 18, 82, 108, 110; as a criterion for moral status, 1, 98, 166, 176f., 195, 197, 224; Derrida's critique of the traditional conception of, 9, 52, 55f., 58f., 79, 113, 122–125, 245n89; Diamond's critique of, 162f.; Descartes on, 16f., 99; Heidegger on, 108, 111, 115; Kant on, 55f.; Lacan on, 89f.; limits of in moral reflection, 206; Nietzsche's critique of the correspondence theory of, 16–18, 23; polemical conception of, 8; role of in the endeavor to know reality, 8; Saussure's conception of, 9, 56f. See also *logos*

Lawlor, Leonard, 130f., 147f., 150, 155

Leopold, Aldo, 216

Lestel, Dominque, 218–225

Levinas, Emmanuel: on alterity, 81; on Bobby the dog, 84f.; Butler's invocation of, 205; Calarco's critique of, 85; Derrida's critique of, 85f.; on the question of a face in animals, 84

liberalism: evasion of animal rights in, 140f., 145f., 151, 196, 203, 212; immanent critique of reason in, 147, 203f.; postmodern critique of, 11, 96f., 156, 190, 192–194, 204; tenets of, 81f., 133f., 147, 156, 167, 183, 185f., 188, 193

Locke, John, 14, 27, 50, 70, 99

logos: Aristotle on, 82, 91, 99, 108, 124, 139; Derrida on, 82f., 124; Heidegger on, 107–109, 112f.; Kant on, 175f.; Lacan on, 89; Locke on, 14; Nietzsche on, 21; Porphyry on, 92, 124, 180f.; Stoics on, 195, 197; as the structure of reality, 18, 180. *See also* language

Löwith, Karl: on cosmo-politics, 75, 129, 176f.; critique of decisionism, 34; on the inevitability of suffering, 75, 129, 160

Montaigne, Michel de: on the natural freedom of animals, 139f.; on gastronomy, 227; on law, 66; pathocentrism of, 166; *science de la gueule*, 227

mortality: as basis for moral status, 69, 72f., 76, 83f., 89, 91, 98–100, 120–122, 131, 138, 157, 161, 164, 166, 195, 198, 201; denial of in animals, 116–118, 180

Nagel, Thomas 94

Nietzsche, Friedrich: on Apollo and Dionysus, 21; critique of traditional metaphysics, 20, 22, 23, 25f., 59, 156; critique of traditional ideals, 11, 22, 24, 28–31, 33–35, 37; critique of Schopenhauer, 21, 25f.; on higher and lower types, 27–31, 34f., 37, 147; on metaphor, 16–18, 23, 37; on the *nomos-physis* distinction, 12, 28f.; perspectivism in, 3, 33, 153; on the primacy of embodiment, 25f., 31, 57; on suffering, 15–17; on the will to power, 28, 37, 48, 55, 73f., 147

Novalis 79, 119

oikeiosis, 181–183, 195, 198

Oliver, Kelly, 97, 205, 221, 225n167

open, the, 103–105, 107, 110, 179

Ovid, 11, 168, 199, 210, 226

perspectivism, 3, 7–9, 16, 32f., 35, 39, 55, 74, 85, 142, 148, 153, 158, 165. *See also* Nietzsche, Friedrich

physis, 11–13, 21, 28f., 32, 53–55, 85f., 88. *See also* Nietzsche, Friedrich

poetry: Nietzsche on, 29; potential of, in comparison with music, 14, 236n22; role of, in establishing a sense of the moral status of animals, 159f., 163f.

Porphyry, 1, 92, 95, 118, 124, 139, 155, 166, 180–183

Posner, Richard, 134–147, 157f., 201

posthumanism, 4, 155

postmodernism: dilemma of quietism and decisionism, 41, 60, 156; guiding tenets of, 1–7, 9f., 16, 32–35, 39–41, chap. 2 *passim*; Lyotard's definition of, 51; relationship of poststructuralism to, 4, 72, 82, 118, 147, 190f., 233n7. *See also* decisionism; exception, politics of

poststructuralism. *See* postmodernism

principles: Kant on the application of, 149f.; need for in political theory, 10, 43, 74f., 129, 130f., 149, 153f., 189, 204, 208, 234; only human beings are capable of, 179; postmodern rejection of, 2–5, 7, 10, 32–35, 44, 46–48, 64–69, 71, 74, 77, 96f., 106, 126, 130f., 146, 190, 210, 234; positive role of in animal rights, 70, 74f., 130f., 155, 157,

164, 183, 187f., 206; veganism, 206, 208, 225

Putnam, Hilary, 4

quietism, 41, 48, 60, 78. *See also* decisionism

Rawls, John, 11, 27, 32, 43, 168f., 176, 184–187, 193, 197, 200, 202

reaction: 5, 89, 90, 92, 113–115, 125f., 203, 205, 221f. *See also* response

Regan, Tom, 45f., 82, 84, 144

response: Derrida's critique of the reaction-response distinction, 90, 113–115, 125f.; Diamond on the fellow-creature response, 164; distinguished from reaction, 91; Heidegger on responsiveness, 110, 116; inadequacy of postmodern conception of, 131, 221–223; incapacity for in animals, 92, 255n167; Lacan on, 89; Lestel on the possibility of in animals, 220f.; Oliver on the reality of in plants, 221, 255n67. *See also* reaction

rights: Derrida's ambivalence regarding, 150, 152; Diamond's critique of, 162f.; in humanism, 1, 72, 87, 92f., 96, 121, 196, 201, chap. 4 and 5 *passim*; postmodern rejection of, 97f., 121, 125f., 133, 141, 156, 187, chap. 4 and 5 *passim*

Rilke, Rainer Maria, 103–105, 107

Rorty, Richard, 140f., 148, 150, 156

rule of law: Dworkin on, 154; Hayek on, 153f.; Raz on, 260n65

Saussure, Ferdinand de. *See* language

Schmitt, Carl, 34f., 37f., 74, 114, 153

Schopenhauer, Arthur: anthropocentrism in, 198; on the arts, 14, 159, 163; on compassion as the basis of morality,

Schopenhauer, Arthur (*continued*)
13–15, 163, 166; on duties of justice
toward animals, 14f., 160; on freedom
in animals, 139f.; on the inherent
meaninglessness of existence, 12, 19;
on kinship with animals, 179, 209
silence: Abraham's need for 50, 64, 70,
74; Derrida on, 61f.; Heidegger on, 62,
78f., 106, 206; Rilke on, 105
Singer, Peter. *See* utilitarianism
singularity: critique of as basis for decision, 34, 44, 49f., 70, 74, 81, 114, 130f.,
150–152; Derrida on, 51, 62, 65–68,
79, 81, 88, 114, 121–123, 125, 149;
Kierkegaard on, 70f.; Nietzsche on, 37;
Schmitt on, 74, 114. *See also* decisionism; exception, politics of
suffering: Bentham on, 82f., 120, 207;
as a criterion for moral status, 120,
129–131, 148, 157f., 161f., 164f., 185,
195, 203, 223, 225; Lestel on, 219–221,
Löwith on, 75, 160; Nietzsche on,
15, 17, 19–21; postmodern focus on,
44, 46, 49, 83f., 88, 98f., 116, 120f.,
123–125, 127; Schopenhauer on, 12–15,
160, 209, 225; Singer on, 82, 139

trace. *See* Derrida, Jacques

universals: Benhabib on, 187; Hume's
critique of, 22–24, 59; Nietzsche's
critique of, 22–24; Oliver's critique of,
97; role of in cosmopolitanism, 187;
Wolfe's critique of, 96

veganism: Derrida's evasion of, 128, 210;
discussion of in "Animal, Vegetable,
Miserable," 129; distinguished from
vegetarianism, 127, 212; ecological
implications of, 143f.; critique of free
range designation, 44, 46, 141, 212,
241n9; as a regulative ideal, 128, 209,
226; as a strict moral imperative, 5,
143, 198, 203, 206–209, 211–213, 215,
225–227, 257n27. *See also* vegetarianism
vegetarianism: Derrida's evasion of, 127,
210; distinguished from veganism, 3,
76, 127f., 211–215; Lestel's critique of,
219–224; Porphyry on, 181
violence: against animals, 213f.; Derrida
on the inevitability of, 61, 66, 126,
149f.; inability of postmodernism
to argue coherently against, 74, 76,
131, 226; Lestel on the inevitability
of, 220; need to overcome, 127f., 151,
168, 200f., 203f., 206, 208f., 211, 213,
225–227; Nietzsche's glorification of,
16, 29f., 35, 151

Waal, Frans de, 95f., 112, 225
Weil, Simone, 158, 161f., 166
White, Stephen, 47f., 67
welfarism, 141, 145, 214f.
Wolfe, Cary, 7f., 89, 96f., 115, 123, 150,
156, 160f.
Wolin, Richard, 9f., 147, 196, 234n7
Wood, David, 127, 129, 131
world-poverty of animals, 46, 69, 107,
109, 111, 118f., 179